The Formation of the Modern Self

Also Available from Bloomsbury

Apperception and Self-Consciousness in Kant and German Idealism, Dennis Schulting
The Invention of the Self: Personal Identity in the Age of Art, Andrew Spira
Simulated Selves: The Undoing of Personal Identity in the Modern World, Andrew Spira
French and Italian Stoicisms: From Sartre to Agamben, edited by Kurt Lampe and Janae Sholtz
German Stoicisms: From Hegel to Sloterdijk, edited by Kurt Lampe and Andrew Benjamin

The Formation of the Modern Self

Reason, Happiness and the Passions from Montaigne to Kant

Felix Ó Murchadha

BLOOMSBURY ACADEMIC
LONDON • NEW YORK • OXFORD • NEW DELHI • SYDNEY

BLOOMSBURY ACADEMIC
Bloomsbury Publishing Plc
50 Bedford Square, London, WC1B 3DP, UK
1385 Broadway, New York, NY 10018, USA
29 Earlsfort Terrace, Dublin 2, Ireland

BLOOMSBURY, BLOOMSBURY ACADEMIC and the Diana logo are
trademarks of Bloomsbury Publishing Plc

First published in Great Britain 2022
This paperback edition published 2023

Copyright © Felix Ó Murchadha, 2022

Felix Ó Murchadha has asserted his right under the Copyright, Designs and
Patents Act, 1988, to be identified as Author of this work.

For legal purposes the Acknowledgements on pp. ix–x constitute an
extension of this copyright page.

Cover image: Ad Parnassum, Paul Klee (1932)
(© Artefact / Alamy Stock Photo)

All rights reserved. No part of this publication may be reproduced or transmitted in
any form or by any means, electronic or mechanical, including photocopying,
recording, or any information storage or retrieval system, without prior
permission in writing from the publishers.

Bloomsbury Publishing Plc does not have any control over, or responsibility for, any
third-party websites referred to or in this book. All internet addresses given in this
book were correct at the time of going to press. The author and publisher regret any
inconvenience caused if addresses have changed or sites have ceased to exist, but
can accept no responsibility for any such changes.

A catalogue record for this book is available from the British Library.

Library of Congress Cataloging-in-Publication Data
Names: Ó Murchadha, Felix, author.
Title: The formation of the modern self: reason, happiness and the
passions from Montaigne to Kant / Felix Ó Murchadha.
Description: London, UK; New York, NY, USA: Bloomsbury Academic, 2022. |
Includes bibliographical references and index.
Identifiers: LCCN 2021030355 (print) | LCCN 2021030356 (ebook) |
ISBN 9781350245457 (hb) | ISBN 9781350245471 (epdf) | ISBN 9781350245488 (ebook)
Subjects: LCSH: Self (Philosophy)–History. | Philosophy, Modern–History.
Classification: LCC BD438.5.O24 2022 (print) | LCC BD438.5 (ebook) | DDC 126–dc23
LC record available at https://lccn.loc.gov/2021030355
LC ebook record available at https://lccn.loc.gov/2021030356

ISBN: HB: 978-1-3502-4545-7
PB: 978-1-3502-4546-4
ePDF: 978-1-3502-4547-1
eBook: 978-1-3502-4548-8

Typeset by Newgen KnowledgeWorks Pvt. Ltd., Chennai, India

To find out more about our authors and books visit www.bloomsbury.com
and sign up for our newsletters.

To Markus Wörner, as a token of gratitude, friendship and respect

Contents

Acknowledgements   ix

Introduction   1
1   Four faces of the self in the emergence of modernity   7
    1.1   Grace and responsibility   8
    1.2   Freedom and tranquillity: Stoicism and Scepticism   17
    1.3   World, God and origins: Modern transformations   22
    1.4   The self and crisis   30
2   Montaigne: Sceptical alterity   41
    2.1   Openness to the strange   43
    2.2   Experience   50
    2.3   Language and self   53
    2.4   Contingency and constancy   56
    2.5   Faith and reason   64
3   Descartes, Pascal and the ambiguity of the self   69
    3.1   Cartesian will / Pascalian heart   72
    3.2   The sceptical moment   80
    3.3   The beginnings and ends of philosophy   88
    3.4   God: Creation and salvation   97
    3.5   Evil, ethics and the passions   101
4   Spinoza and Hume on the good life   113
    4.1   The aims of philosophy   114
    4.2   Genesis and nature of ideas   121
    4.3   Substance and cause   128
    4.4   The passions and tranquillity   134
    4.5   God and the state   142
5   Desire, *aporia* and reason in Kant   151
    5.1   The desire of reason   154
    5.2   Antinomic reason and *Schwärmerei*   158
    5.3   Nature and freedom   165

6	Kant on the heart, evil and grace (starting from Rousseau)	171
	6.1 The will and the heart	171
	6.2 Radical evil, grace and the Kingdom of God	176
Conclusion		189
Notes		193
Bibliography		231
Index		243

Acknowledgements

A book such as this one, which has gone through a long germination, owes more than can be adequately said to many people.

The first to introduce me to Modern Philosophy was Edwin Rabbitte in University College Galway (known today as the National University of Ireland, Galway (NUIG)) many years ago. In his quiet but compelling way, he first initiated me into philosophy as 'radical thinking' – getting to the roots of things – and this inspiration has never lessened.

Klaus Held and Heinrich Hüni of Bergische Universität Wuppertal taught me how to read historical texts phenomenologically. I owe them both a debt of gratitude.

I was extremely fortunate to receive a Fulbright grant to spend a year in New York at Fordham University. I am most grateful to the Fulbright Commission for this funding. Colleen Dube and Sonya McGuinness in the Dublin Fulbright office were wonderfully supportive. John Drummond and Merold Westphal were gracious hosts at Fordham, as was the departmental administrator Margaret Donavon, who looked out for a fellow Irish person!

In New York, I experienced the true splendour of American libraries. The New York Public Library (NYPL) was my refuge for weeks on end. Special thanks are due to Jay Barksdale at the NYPL for facilitating my use of the Wertheim Study Room in the library. The magnificent William D. Walsh Library at Fordham was also a wonderful resource.

Crucial to a good sabbatical is that it works for all involved. For my son, Felix Alexander, the welcome he received at St. Ignatius Loyola School in the Upper East Side was warm and reassuring. The teachers and fellow parents of the school helped make our stay in New York so much richer.

My thinking on the themes of this book have been inspired by many conversations with colleagues, friends and doctoral students over the years. In this respect, particular thanks should go to Babette Babich, Dominic Balestra, Rebecca Barr, David Beirne, Dan Bradley, Aengus Daly, William Desmond, Tsarina Doyle, John Drummond, Ricca Edmondson, Rolf Elberfeld, Marty Fairbairn, Ane Faugstad-Aarø, Jennifer Gosetti-Ferencei, Erin Flynn, Niall Keane, Róisin Lally, Sebastian Luft, Charlotte McIvor, Anne O'Byrne, Veronica O'Neill, Gino Querini, Andrea Rehberg, Trine Riel, John Roe, Inga Römer, Rod Stoneman, Lazlo Tengelyi, Merold Westphal and Markus Wörner (to whom this book is dedicated).

The reflections which led to this book arose as a direct result of teaching undergraduate classes in Modern Philosophy at NUI Galway. I am grateful to the students who attended those classes for their questions and their patience. Barbara Preston and Jonathan O'Rourke helped immensely as undergraduate research assistants in researching the book.

Many colleagues at NUI Galway have helped in various ways to make this research possible. I am grateful to have been granted generous research leave and would particularly like to acknowledge the then dean of arts, Cathal O'Donoghue, for his support. Lionel Pilkington, Steve Ellis and Enrico Dal Lago have all been collegial heads of school during the time in which this book was in preparation, and my colleague in philosophy, Heike Felzmann, has been unfailingly supportive.

Much of the research and writing of this book happened during the COVID-19 pandemic. This has brought its challenges, particularly with respect to sourcing books and articles. Grateful thanks are due to the staff of the Hardiman Library, NUI Galway, for their tireless efforts in maintaining library support in these difficult times.

Special thanks are due to the staff at Bloomsbury, especially Liza Thompson, for making the publishing experience very pleasant. I am also very grateful to the two anonymous reviewers whose advice helped strengthen this book.

Most of the material in this work is published here for the first time, but Chapter 3 is a reworked and greatly expanded version of 'Sceptical Wisdom: Descartes, Pascal and the Challenge of Pyrrhonism', in R. Edmondson and K-H. Hülser, *Practical Reasoning and Human Engagement: Language, Ethics and Action* (London: Rowman & Littlefield, 2012), 245–66, appearing here with the kind permission of Rowman & Littlefield. All rights reserved.

Most of the writing of this book happened in the midst of my family. They know the joys and the frustrations of such a project up close. My son, Felix Alexander, is a constant source of hope and inspiration; our conversation has lasted almost two decades and has never tired. Anne has read every word, been there every step of the way and remains, always, my reason, my happiness and my passion.

Introduction

'All the world's a stage / And all the men and women merely players'.[1] These lines from William Shakespeare, of Ancient lineage, spotlight the drama of human existence emphasizing the players and their roles. Not the director, not the audience, not the stage props, but the selves populating the world have moved to the centre. The nature of the play, whether comedy or tragedy, needs to be decided, but in Modernity the stage belongs to the players, acting together in collaboration or opposition, faced with endings but expressing what it is to be a self in all its passions and reasons. The very drama on stage can come to seem more like a devised performance, the improvisatory work by a performing ensemble, where director and playwright play little active role even when their hidden relevance is recognized. The centrality of the self and the concern with its perspectives, feelings and projects no longer surprise us. Rather, we have begun to question it, to even doubt the ontological sense of selfhood. Yet, there is a drama here that concerns Modernity and, as such, concerns us.

Somehow the Moderns brought us to where we are today. Looking back over the road travelled, we have the illusion that it was always heading in our direction, that any bends or dead ends we see looking down the valley of history are incidental: A road has been built and has led to our present situation. But, in fact, history is in large part the unintended product of actions, including thoughts, by people who are like wanderers in a morass, facing into a fog through which they can only dimly see possible futures. As they put one step before another, a path begins to form behind them, taking on an aspect of inevitability. The Modern self was formed by multiple wanderers along the peaks and valleys of some centuries, amongst them philosophers, who gradually began to see their lives not as inhabiting inherited locations but as destined to seek out a new, unheard of, place. The peculiarity of Modernity is to mistake the fog-bound future as illuminated and the past trailing off to the horizon as dark and obscure. Yet they came from somewhere and only guessed at the direction of their going.

A central philosophical question which troubled these brave, anxious travellers was that of the self and its capacity to be: the self as its own becoming of itself. This is not surprising, because these were not wise men of Ancient Greece or Arabia, nor scholars dedicated to God and learning, but rather laymen (and, although largely obscured in later telling, laywomen[2]) who, in taking on the task of thinking, needed at the same time to describe and defend an account of their own selves: the self they became in and through the task of thinking. Testing, experimenting, doubting and anxious, desperate, hopeful, this self is both the object and subject of their reflections. From Michel de Montaigne to Immanuel Kant, the project was set to form this self and eventually to form everything else in relation to it. But at the core of this self is a gaping wound, an abyss, an immemorial failing, which its whole being is striving to make good. The formation of the Modern self has at its core a tale, that of the Fall and its overcoming, or rather it is the conceptual articulation of what such a fallen self must be and what the world in which it struggles to find perfection must be like. To overcome the Fall is to build a new heaven and a new earth. Gradually, at first dimly, this project emerges more clearly in Kant, prior to G. W. F. Hegel and Marx.

Since Francis Bacon and René Descartes, philosophers have understood themselves to be thinking in respect of the future, thinking towards a world to come. With them, philosophy took its place in a new Sabbath, the first, not the final, day, where thinking is Sabbatarian by not so much reflecting on accomplished creation, giving thanks for the work of God, but rather recapitulating the world again in thought, as if beginning again, and through thought perfecting things. It is Christianity that changed the Sabbath from the seventh day of the week, reflecting God's day of rest (according to Gen. 2.1-3), to the first day, Sunday – under the influence of the day of the Resurrection. This first day can be understood both as the beginning of a new covenant and as repeating the first day of creation; in either case it opens up the possibility of renewal, of re-creation more than recreation. Modernity is the effective emergence of this, putting the self in an ambiguous place, as creature, but also as an agent of creation.

Philosophers from Montaigne onwards in responding to a collapse of the world of 'Christendom' helped bring about the Modern world, but in so doing had in their hands only inherited materials. In this context, the fixation on the problem of knowledge in our historiography of the period – the setting forth of an epistemological subject as the human self – belies the rich ethical and religious concerns of whole generations of thinkers up to and including Kant. It obscures the centrality of salvation in their thought as they encountered great convulsions of understanding from the religious to the geographical, from the anatomical to the astronomical, from the political to the psychological. While we often picture these thinkers – and they sometimes pictured themselves – as determined pioneers, impatient with the past, striving to build a more enlightened future, in reading them as they engaged with their own times what we find are philosophers who were attempting to achieve what past philosophers (they believed) had not achieved, namely, a path to truth, goodness and happiness. They lived in their respective 'spaces of experience' and within 'horizons of expectations', to use Reinhart Koselleck's terms.[3] These formal historical categories express well the situation of any philosopher, but specifically Modern philosophers, who live with the presence of the past and in the absence of the future. Koselleck states, 'It is the tension between experience and expectation which, in ever-changing patterns, brings about new resolutions and through this generates historical time.'[4] What happens in Modernity (*Neuzeit* – literally 'the time of the new' or 'new time') is 'that expectations have distanced themselves evermore from all previous experience'.[5]

While the distancing of expectation from experience only becomes fully explicit with Kant's philosophy of history, the tension which emerges here characterizes the manner in which the self transforms from a being directed towards salvation in an afterlife to a being seeking to create itself and in doing so achieve its own salvation. What is vital to see is that the precondition here is the concern with salvation, the question of human happiness and the issue of the capacity of the self to achieve it. This was a question of expectation, but that expectation could only be articulated out of the space of experience open to the philosophers of these times, no matter how much they tried to free themselves from, or indeed disparage, the edifice of experience bequeathed to them. The building blocks of that experience were both Christian and Hellenistic. In understanding the self and in thinking as selves, projecting what it was to be a self, these thinkers drew on both of these sources even in the midst of undoing the Medieval synthesis that Christian Aristotelianism represented. In encountering their times, these thinkers were responding to a series of crises through which the structure of the Medieval world gradually fell apart. In addressing salvation, human capacity, happiness and misfortune, Modern philosophers drew on four main strands of Ancient and Medieval philosophy, two pairs, one Christian and one Hellenistic: Augustinianism and Pelagianism, Scepticism and Stoicism. All this happened as the framework of Medieval thought became inoperative. In each of these strands, they found answers to fundamental questions of how to be a self, how to act as a self in the face of passions, what the capacities were of the self for truth and goodness and to what the self was destined or what destiny it could create. These functioned as models for the self, that is, as principles through which the self could live and could be understood.

The focus on the self needs to be understood in this context. It is crucially important to see the self not simply as a philosophical theme but also as the condition of philosophical reflection. What remains largely implicit in Antiquity and Medieval philosophy – namely the thematic of the self as conditional to philosophical thought – becomes explicitly theorized in Modernity. 'Existential' concerns of the good life and salvation do not disappear but rather are found in different guises as these thinkers engage philosophically in a context of deep uncertainty. The normative issues concerning the self can thereby become obscured in descriptive accounts, and one of the tasks of this book is to show how these descriptive accounts articulate normatively charged responses to the crises at the root of Modernity.

While the reception of the approaches and doctrines of the schools of Ancient Philosophy and Christian thought in early modernity will be discussed, this will be done in order to show how these diverse philosophical and religious accounts were transformed in Modernity. The primary and overriding concern of this book is genealogical: How did the Modern self become articulated as a philosophical project? There is no alternative to a close textual reading in exploring this question but a reading which strives to capture both the motivating horizon of the philosophers' thinking and how that motivation is based in a fundamental experience of the world. For this reason, textual reading will be carried out phenomenologically; a hermeneutical-phenomenological endeavour to return to the world of the philosopher concerned.[6] The attempt is to think these figures in terms of their fundamental experience. To do this we need to read their works as responses – both thematic and operative – to the world as they experienced it and expressed their expectations with respect to it. This is not to be confused with biography: The key question is not primarily *what* they experienced, but *how*. The two questions are indeed related: war, institutional transformation, social upheaval, religious convulsion, paradigm shifts in knowledge framed the times of the philosophers under consideration. The philosophical response to such events is to ask how the world in which such things happen can be understood, how to act well in such a world and how to think the origins and goals of such a world.

The self is not simply a theme of Modern philosophy; it is also *operative* in the work of these philosophers as they style the selves which are engaged in philosophical thought. Operatively, the most metaphysical concerns of Modern philosophy express the contested place of the self in relation to itself, with others, against nature and towards God. The distinction between operative and thematic was first formulated by Eugen Fink in a discussion of the work of Edmund Husserl and referred to the manner in which some concepts remain 'shadowy', employed, but not lit up by the light of thematic reflection, in the work of a philosopher.[7] In this case the concept of the self is thematic to the extent to which it is set down as a subject of discussion by each of the philosophers under consideration. However, throughout their philosophical endeavours – due to the centrality each gives to the manner that metaphysical and ethical accounts relate back to the self who thinks them and must justify itself in doing so – the philosophical process becomes entwined with the journey of the self from its pre-philosophical understanding of itself to the philosophical, whereby it is never clear whether the self can be exhaustively subsumed in the latter. In the case of the concept of the self, the intersection of thematic and operative is particularly important because the self functions as both a descriptive and a prescriptive concept and does so for a fundamental reason: If the act of philosophizing depends on the self, this requires that self to be capable of philosophy. However, experience seems to indicate that selves are not always – perhaps rarely – capable of such thinking. The question of the self then becomes how to cultivate a self which can think philosophically (including about the self). This question takes on a prescriptive aspect both thematically and operatively: What ought the self be like, and how ought I – this particular self – be, in order to engage philosophically with this question? In thinking this intersection of thematic and operative, descriptive and prescriptive, the question becomes, what is it to be a reasoning (and reasonable) self? It becomes a question of reason on the basis that philosophy is the act of reason, but reason practiced by a self.

Every book of philosophy – whether this is admitted or not – is written against something as much as for something. This book is no different. There are at least three theses that are generally, though certainly not universally, accepted, which it is part of the task of this book to show to be false or at least needing substantial qualification. These theses may together be said to form the 'standard view':

1. Modern philosophy is characterized by the priority of theoretical over practical philosophy.
2. Modern philosophy is driven by a repudiation of religious themes and particularly of such 'theological' concepts as original sin, grace and salvation.
3. In Modern philosophy a clear distinction can be drawn between the epistemological, neutral subject and the moral self.

These three theses stand up to engagement neither with the texts of these philosophers nor with an understanding of the world in which they found themselves. At best they can be defended through an arbitrary devaluing of certain texts (e.g. Descartes's *Passions*, Kant's third *Critique*), an equally arbitrary denial of the status of 'philosopher' to philosophical thinkers (Montaigne, Blaise Pascal) or the supposition of insincerity in some of the utterances of these philosophers. In contrast, I will address the totality of their works and will take each of the philosophers at their word. Montaigne and Kant both stated the same thing: They might not always say all they think, but they never claim to think what they do not.[8] To assume otherwise is to assume bad faith and to find oneself in hermeneutical quicksand.

The present book deals intensively with six philosophers: Montaigne, Descartes, Pascal, Baruch Spinoza, David Hume and Kant. My aim has not been to give a comprehensive account of the period, and a number of philosophers have necessarily been passed over. Of these, Locke and Leibniz are the most obvious omissions. However, within the terms of the discussions here, what could be gained by discussing those thinkers, particularly with respect to identity and to grace, has been adequately accounted for, I believe, in the book as a whole.[9]

1

Four faces of the self in the emergence of modernity

All four had a human face, and a lion's face to the right, and all four had a bull's face to the left, and all four had an eagle's face.[1]

Facing God and nature out of doubt and anxiety, but seeking truth and tranquillity, it is not immediately apparent which face to wear. This is not necessarily a matter of masquerade – although Descartes and Montaigne before him pondered the state of being masked – but rather of deciding how best to be in the face of things as they are and as they ought to be. To be a self is to be responsible for oneself in the face to face with another. This is to testify as a self regarding the origins, state of affairs and ends of one's own being. If this becomes a philosophical decision in Modernity or rather if such a decision is constitutive of how it is to be Modern, then this is so because Modernity emerges in and from a crisis of reason, a crisis of faith and a crisis of world.

This triple crisis cannot be simply marked chronologically but rather emerges in different ways through the history of the Modernity. The crisis of world is a crisis of the *metaphysica specialis*: God, nature and human – not simply a crisis of those three metaphysical domains but fundamentally a crisis of their interrelation. The crisis of faith is a crisis not only of the division of faith into faith*s* through the Reformation but also characterized by a sense of God as increasingly obscure and distant, removing faith in him of worldly support and correlates. The crisis of reason is a crisis concerning both the limits of reason and its possible limitlessness threatening the very conditions of its own exercise. From its beginnings and for us today, Modernity remains a fundamentally theological question: Is the secularization of reason possible? The question is not, in its origins, an atheistic one. On the contrary, to secularize reason can be understood as the correlate of a passionate faith in God. This is not simply an abstract metaphysical issue, nor is it only an epistemological one: To secularize reason is to disengage the world from God; it is to set faith afloat on a sea of uncertainty.[2] It is to place the self in a new and precarious position, where happiness and salvation are in play.

The four faces in the chapter title name the four visages of the self which we find in Modern philosophy, based on templates inherited from Graeco-Roman Philosophy and Judaeo-Christian thought: those of Augustinianism, Stoicism, Pelagianism and Scepticism. Each face bears a different countenance, of humility or autarky, of resolve or disinterest. But each is facing forward, seeking in hope or desperation, confidence or anxiety, a new world beyond the crisis of the world out of which the Modern self emerges. Like those faces appearing in Ezekiel's vision, they carry forward a promise, in this case that of philosophy and the Gospels, into a foreign land, a land in which the frameworks of Antiquity and Medieval Europe were being lost forever.[3] These are the faces that face off against each other in the drama of the self, a drama of the stage in Montaigne and of the courtroom in Kant. The self playing the role of itself and facing up to the ideal of what it ought to be.[4]

The aim of the present chapter is twofold: first, give an account of these four 'sources of the self'[5] as they developed and, second, explore some of the factors that transformed the reception of these sources in Modernity. To discuss the latter it will be necessary to engage in the debate as to the nature of the emergence of Modernity, whether it is rupture (as Hans Blumenberg[6] claimed) or secularization (as Karl Löwith[7] and, more recently, Charles Taylor[8], argued), the rootedness of the Modern in Voluntarism (which John Milbank[9] among others has stressed) and its theological origins (as Michael Gillespie has shown[10]).

This chapter is divided into four sections. The first discusses the origins and nature of the debate between Augustinian and Pelagian accounts of grace (1.1). The second then outlines the Stoic and Sceptical accounts (1.2). The third charts the relevant conceptual transformations at the origins of Modernity within the context of late Medieval debates (1.3). The final section develops the implications of these transformations for the account of the self (1.4).

1.1 Grace and responsibility

The question of grace, that is, the gratuitousness of human destiny in relation to its ultimate source and purpose, concerning origins and purpose, creation and salvation, is addressed again and again from Martin Luther to Kant. This concerns the economy of the human relation to a God who is not in our debt:[11] Given that human beings exist and have their final end in relation to God, what are the respective roles, obligations and responsibilities of each within the economy of that relation? This question concerns the nature of both God and human, the capacity of human reason and will to act well, and the question of the ultimate purpose of human life. All of this was understood against the backdrop of the Christian account of the Fall: the lapsing of human beings, their state of being somehow less than their original – God-given – destiny. In this context humility seems to be the only adequate response to the human condition, a humility scandalized by the presumption of adequacy, the presumption of being capable of reaching the goal of salvation, of being adequate to human fulfilment.[12] The question of grace centres on the issue of the extent to which such a claim to adequation is presumptuous and scandalous. It appears to be so not only in the light of the 'sinful' nature of the human being (I will return to this) but also because of the nature of God, as an absolute being to whom the human stands in absolute relation.[13] Because of the nature of this relation, mediation between the self and the divine is necessary for Augustine, through churches, sacraments and Scriptures. But the opposite conclusion is also possible, namely, that an absolute relation requires the minimum of mediation. In the early modern period this becomes a contested matter, bringing together questions of power, authority, legitimacy, reason and faith.

The Bible narrative purports to tell of the beginning (Genesis) and the end (Revelations) of the human journey, its turns and what gives it purpose. Those who hear the narrative are themselves contained within it: its claim is to give them a place, an origin and a destination. The narrative is revelatory to the extent to which that place, origin and destination cannot be read unaided (or at all) from human experience or the exercise of human reason. It is this that makes it a narrative of faith. As Augustine makes clear on a number of occasions, faith is only faith, if it breaks from the economy of reward.[14] This break is inherent in the delay between giving and receiving, in the uncertainty of the response reflected in the relief of every gesture of thanks. In faith there is only this delay, or rather the act of faith is a living in and with this delay, this (to speak with Derrida) diffe*r*ance.[15] As such, there is no faith without hope. Augustine thinks this under the figure of testing: Faith is forever being tested precisely because its reward is never either complete or certain.[16] The biblical narrative is one of origins before time, before the possibility of exchange and of the promise of an end, which, however, cannot be seen. Faith is aporetic in its trust in that which is believed but cannot be shown.[17] Such faith is not, however, provisional: The martyr dies giving witness to what she asserts to be without worldly reason. If her action had worldly justification, it would be without ultimate reason. As Augustine puts it, in responding to the question of why, if death was punishment for original sin, the baptized still suffered bodily death,

> they [the martyrs] certainly could not have won neither victory nor glory in their struggle ... if, after the fount of regeneration, saints could no longer suffer bodily death ... For if faith sought and received an immediate reward for its works, it would not be tested by means of an invisible prize and so it would not even be faith.[18]

Understood from grace, faith is praise and gratitude: the language of faith is neither the constative language of facts nor the performative language that depends on conventional contexts of meaning. Rather, the language of faith always opens up anew to a future without reward and a past without determination. The grace of creation and of the continual providence of God in the world requires constant affirmation and interpretation. Augustine does not so much speak about God as *to* God, or his speaking of God is a further expression of his speaking to God. As such, his works – the *Confessions* especially, but not just that work – have a prayerful quality to them. This is not accidental, nor is it simply a stylistic convention. Discourse about God begins at the very origins of sin and the Fall, namely, in the conversation of Eve with the serpent about the words of God.[19] Speaking about God is implicated in an attempt to capture God within constative sentences. But the grammar of Augustine's discourse is precisely not the grammar through which Friedrich Nietzsche feared God would also inscribe himself in our thinking:[20] It is not the language of subject and object but rather the vocative language of address, the language of love and desire. These words of address are themselves responses; they refer back to a prior experience. To address words of love and desire is to address someone, and that someone comes first. This does not mean for Augustine that knowledge precedes desire. This is impossible for two reasons: First, such knowledge would already amount to a form of possession of the divine, making desire and love derivative; and, second, the comprehension of God would mean that the divine being was contained in our understanding, whereas the nature of the desire he is describing is one of acute awareness of not already containing its object. Augustine's insight is that human beings find themselves in the opposite position: being drawn, enticed, attracted, first addressed, called.

Human existence is characterized by this tension of responding to a prior but constituting call. Augustine's account of natality and freedom, but also of sin, Fall, grace and election, all centre around this basic anthropological tension and ambiguity. The being with a rational soul (*animus*) responds not as those living beings without reason (with only *anima*) do, simply with instinct, but with judgement. Such judgement, however, is not sovereign but rather itself an expression of a nature that is both fallen and open to grace, both wretched and possibly gifted to transcend its own capacities and even the prelapsarian state of innocent humanity. It is, however, in a sense impossible to speak of 'humanity' or 'human' for Augustine. This is so not so much because of the difference between innocent and fallen humanity, but more so because of the invisible and imperceptible difference between saved and unsaved, between the elect and the non-elect. This difference is invisible because election is an inner turning, of which there can be no conclusive external sign. This has far-reaching consequences, because it in effect means that we cannot speak of a human nature as such, nor of human will or human freedom, but rather different distinct modes of being human, which are either free or enslaved. The contingency of the call is fundamental and decisive.

The first issue here is that of the turn within. Following Plotinus, Augustine develops an account of human origins and ends in terms of a dynamic of inner and outer, of unity and dispersal. Just as for Plotinus multiplicity arises from the outward turn of the soul towards bodily reality, while the inward turn of gaze shows the soul its identity with God, for Augustine the Fall is a turning outwards, and the path to God is an inward turning of the soul into itself. However, what the soul finds in this turning is not its identity to God but rather its utter dependence on God and on divine grace.[21] Crucial here is not just the Fall but indeed creation itself. There can be no identity with God for Augustine because of the gulf between Creator and Creature that replaces Plotinus's account of emanation. Nevertheless, this inward turn is one through which the human self recognizes its own natural yearning for God. He enters into the 'depth of his soul' and can do this because 'your [God's] aid befriended me (Psalms, 29:11])'.[22] The Platonic metaphorics of light prevail here: 'With the eye of my soul' he 'saw the Light that never changes'. This light is that of the Platonic sun, now understood as God. Augustine makes clear the relation of verticality here: 'It was above me because it was the Light that made me, and I was below because I was made by it.' But this vertical relation does not inhibit understanding. The grace which 'befriends him' is what heals or repairs the soul.[23] Only through such divine healing can the soul turn inwards from the external things to the inner domain, which is the place where divine healing can take place. In this sense, grace is not in conflict with reason for Augustine but rather is what which allows reason to be fulfilled, that is, to come to see God as the source of all intelligibility.[24]

The Platonic metaphorics of light go hand in hand with the more biblical aural metaphor of the call. To be called is to be attracted, to be enticed, to be led by beauty. To be is to desire, and to desire is to be touched by beauty. The difference is not in desire itself but rather in what entices desire, more specifically, the trajectory of that desire. The human being responds – it does not initiate. What she responds to is that which excites her desire and her love. Love is fundamentally a self-relation to itself, which remains always an originating and an ending presence. As such, the self-presence to itself is a presence to its own insufficiency. The mind is changeable; it is in a constant dynamic relation to the hope of its own happiness.[25] If, however, it responds to the call of worldly things, of carnal pleasures, of reputation, glory and wealth, it does so because it is loving, because it senses beauty in these things and seeks that sufficiency through which it will be sufficient to itself.[26] But following such a path leads the self away from itself, away from its own nature.

The love that does satisfy is the love that responds not to worldly beauty; rather, it responds to such beauty only in its relation to the source and origin of that beauty, namely, God. In doing so, it analogously responds to its own nature as a lover, coming to know itself as itself, not as a carnal being of the world. Hence, the path of the love of God is as much a path of the lover to itself. The beauty of the self is the reflected beauty of Christ, the loving relation to itself in its own remembering and understanding of itself. In that way the self-relation is an image of the Trinity and on a basic, ontological level reflects that Trinitarian being.[27] Crucially here, the relation of self to itself is a relation of the self to its own self in the origins of its being. That self-relation finds itself not over against God, because it finds a path to God within its own being. In this sense, human nature is found to be a complex thing, both fallen and called, both turned away from God and essentially directed towards God. Similarly, the love of others is a participation in divine beauty. For Augustine these three forms of love – towards self, others and God – belong together.[28]

Augustine is not an *auto*biographical writer, because he does not believe that the life of the self is in its own hands. What appears as autobiographical is rather a journey to an origin prior to the self, through which the self becomes itself.[29] Augustine does not express this groundlessness of the self directly but rather obliquely in the manner in which he addresses himself to God, who knows him better than he knows himself. He addresses himself to that which calls him, indicating his place as a listener, and the place of the listener (*auditor*) is its being called to obey (*ob – audire*). It is in relation to that call that the self is free – free, however, not in the sense of choosing between obedience and disobedience but rather free when he obeys. This, for Augustine, is created freedom – freedom for and in relation to a Creator who 'sees' from elsewhere, from beyond worldly horizons; freedom not in the free space of the world but in the private inner space of the self.[30] But inasmuch as the self is a being in the world, the freedom of that self is in relation to the world. For such a freedom, the world appears as deeply ambiguous: as that place in which the self finds itself as a created being, hence as one creature amongst others, and yet as that which gives itself to final arbitration in a forum which is 'before' the world. That inner forum, however, judges not so much the world as itself in its relation to the world. But that self cannot find the criteria for such a judgement in the world, because the relation to the world is precisely what is in question. However, such criteria are to be found in the self's own relation to a source, an origin, which is experienced as before and beyond the world. Free will as created freedom finds itself in this place, at the edges of the world, being at once within and without, prior and posterior, creature and yet in the image of the Creator.

Freedom as created freedom owes itself to that which it reflects and yet cannot return to, namely, a prior, originating and fundamental gift. As understood by many of the early Christian fathers, the myth of creation recounted in Genesis attempts to narrate that gift in a manner which can be understood sometimes literally, sometimes allegorically.[31] The myth of creation is a narrative which comes too late, beginning as it does with the created, reading back from there a creating act beginning before all beginning, prior to the world itself, hence prior to time as the relation to beginning.[32] The question – from whence came the world? – can receive no answer in terms of anything in experience. To say that God created the world is for orthodox Christianity (albeit not for many Gnostic accounts) an analytical truth: God just is the one who creates. But the further question concerns the nature of that creative act, more specifically the relation of God to the creative act and to the created itself. The account which was developed in the early Christian era was summed up in the phrase *creatio ex nihilo*, creation out of nothing. Out of nothing: out of no prior obligation or necessity, an act of unheard of freedom, a pure gift. The gift of creation is a gift which transcends any demiurgic act, because it is understood as a radically contingent act, an act which comes from nothing and goes towards nothing other than itself, as the ultimate 'recipient', the one who can know and give praise for this creation, comes into being only in and through the gift itself.[33]

The Augustinian and Pelagian accounts agree as to the gratuitousness of creation: nothing compelled God to create the world, nor to create the world as he did so. Creation is in that sense radically contingent, an act of grace. The world did not have to exist; that it exists is solely a matter of God's will. For Augustine that will is itself desirous, itself loving. The divine will creates from love, that love which emerges at the very essence of the divine, namely, in the delight which the Father has in the Son.[34] The Trinitarian context here is theologically crucial, but what characterizes Augustine's understanding of that context is a displacement of the intellect with respect to the heart, an ontology of beauty and a philosophy of love.[35] Crucially, for Augustine, will is tied to love; there is no indifference of the will either in God or in human beings.[36] The will is always a motivated will, and as loving, it is motivated by delight in its object. The account of freedom which emerges from this, as Blumenberg states, justifies creation, but not in the sense he seems to mean:[37] The point is not that the will sovereignly chooses evil but rather that the will as loving is from the beginning – that is, from the created nature of Adam – vulnerable to being enticed to love that which draws the self away not only from God but also from itself. Understood in this way, the human being is radically dependent; as a loving, desiring being it craves; for Augustine, to love is to 'crave something for its own sake'.[38] There is no moment of self-sufficient tranquillity (as we will see there is in Stoicism) in the deciding of the will: The present now does not abstract the self from the tides of its desiring movement but rather is itself constituted by that past memory and future anticipation which makes it a temporal being.[39]

The difference here between Augustine and Pelagius can best be seen in the place of prayer. For Pelagius, prayer is important in two main ways. First, the Christian prays to be forgiven of his sins. Forgiveness depends on God, and in praying to God the Christian is asking for the expiation of his sins. There is here an acknowledgment of the temporal condition of being human: What is past cannot be undone, so no action of the self can change the past; only through God can the present stain of that past be wiped clean.[40] Second, prayer allows the self to draw on its own inner possibilities, ultimately revealed to it by the example of Christ, in order to achieve holiness. In other words, prayer is an aid to discovering the self's inner capacity through reflection on the laws.[41] For Augustine, on the contrary, prayer is a response to the self's own weakness; it is a constant calling for help to give him the strength which – as a fallen human being – he does not of himself possess.[42] Against Pelagius he argues that the point of prayer is not only the expiation of sin but also the request for help not to sin. It is for him 'foolish to pray that you may do what you have in your own power to do'.[43] But there is a paradox here: In his prayer Augustine confesses himself, but he does so to a God who he believes knows him better than he knows himself. His prayer is not a communication of information, because 'you [God] heard nothing true from my lips which you have not first told me'.[44] Prayer is rather an act of humility, a placing of himself in his true relation of absolute dependence on God. The inner movement within himself finds not the self as authority over itself but rather the illumination from God as the author of his being.[45] It is in the context of the movement away from and towards God, to whom Augustine cries in prayer, that the Augustinian account of the will should be understood.

Augustine does not speak of the will as arbiter but rather of a conflict of wills, 'a morbid condition of the mind which, when it is lifted up by the truth, does not unreservedly rise to it but is weighed down by habit'.[46] Or, as he puts it a little later, 'the delight of the eternal draws us upwards and the pleasure of temporal goods holds us down'.[47] At issue here is a conflict which tears the mind apart. The will is divided when it is not wholehearted, and its wholeheartedness depends precisely on the heart: the true longing of the self for itself, which is to say its longing for itself as the image of God. The freedom of the will does not lie in those conflicts; they rather point to its enslavement. To state otherwise for Augustine is to identify freedom with sin rather than with created nature. Just as the Fall arose from disobedience, so too it marks the body with the disobedience to the will. Such conflicts – which Augustine most graphically illustrates with respect to sexual desire[48] – are not inherent in human nature but rather arise only as a result of fallen human nature. As such, the Fall is for him the fundamental and crucial event situating the human self with respect to God and nature.

The Fall, like creation, is not simply an event in the distant past in either an Augustinian or Pelagian account. The stories of the Creation and the Fall are relevant because they concern the present as created and fallen. The debates concerning that

Fall then concern the present; but at the same time they concern the relation of present to past.

The Fall is an account of the origins of evil, an account which 'saves' God and creation from implication in that origin. Or at least saves them to some extent. Pelagius sees himself as following Augustine in placing the origin of evil in human freedom. This answers the question, from whence comes evil? It is indeed the case that both understand the phenomena of morality, the giving of praise for good actions and condemnation for evil ones, as unintelligible without free will.[49] Only a free being can do evil for Augustine, but freedom is not indifferent to good and evil. On the contrary, the truth is from God and 'steals into our minds with a kind of eloquent silence … Our freedom is found in submission to this truth'.[50] A free being wills its own good and follows that good. The will is as such not evil, but rather evil arises out of a perversion of the will, a turning away: 'Evil consists in the will's turning away (*aversio*) from the changeless ground, in its turn towards (*conversio*) goods that are changeable.'[51] Hence, this movement of turning away is of itself a defect, and – given that all which *is* is good – this defect comes not from being but from nothing. Thus, the origin of evil does lie in creation but is inherent in createdness itself: A creature is separated from its Creator by nothing, that is, by the nothing out of which it comes qua creature. Creation is good because it is, but is imperfect – hence lacking in being – because it is created. But Augustine is quick to add that this defect is in the power of the creature – if the creature wills non-being, it exists in the form of evil.[52] The turning away from the changeless ground is itself an act of love, but a love which has misplaced its object. There is for Augustine a fundamental misperception and ignorance in this first sin arising out of the creaturely essence itself. A creature which comes out of nothing has the trace of that nothing in it and mistakes that non-being for itself. However, the non-being is not its true origin but rather what characterizes it as a creature. In choosing non-being, it is choosing that in it which is not from the being of God but rather marks the distance between it and God. As such, the origin of sin is a self-assertion, mistaking the self as what is other than God, while the self can find itself only in its relation to God.

For Pelagius, too, the origins of sin lie in disobedience. What is important is not the content of the sin but the fact of disobeying divine orders.[53] The source of that disobedience is the free choice of the will. That free choice is of the one who deliberates on what he should do. In making those choices he has available to him the examples of others, the teachings of the Scriptures (especially the Laws) and the warnings of the prophets. In that sense the sin of Adam is a lesser sin than those which came subsequently, as those who come after Adam have all those different aids: 'Adam, who was still ignorant and inexperienced and did not have the example of anyone who had previously sinned and died for his sins to deter him.'[54] For Pelagius, there is no difference in human nature prior to and subsequent to the Fall. In both cases a created freedom is at play; in both cases the grace of that creation is operative and there is no diminishing of that grace. While for Augustine the punishment of sin is a weakening of both will and intellect, such that while prelapsarian human nature has the power of its own being to obey the commandments, the postlapsarian self does not, for Pelagius, sin is an act and as such cannot weaken or change human nature; furthermore, neither in terms of that nature nor in terms of justice is it intelligible that something can be commanded of human beings that they do not have the power to accomplish. Indeed, for Pelagius the self has the capacity to sin or not to sin and the Christian should be without sin.[55] For Augustine the Fall is the result of an evil will, a will which gains the assent of reason; the Fall has efficacy not simply in external terms – suffering and death – but also internally, in the weakness of the will and intellect to know or obey God.[56] For Pelagius the effects of the Fall are different – Adam's sin acts as an example which is then imitated, and historically that imitation spreads. Pelagius emphasizes the role of habit here. Following the example of Adam, human beings fall into the habit of sinning, and the task of overcoming sin is one of breaking these bad habits: 'Nor is there any reason which it is made difficult for us to do good other than that long habit of doing wrong has infected us from childhood.'[57] What is pictured here is not so much an event as a historical process of corruption where an original capacity of reason to understand God's will is gradually forgotten due to the increased enslavement to sin. What this implies is that the original relation to God is an external one.[58] The prelapsarian human being had the free choice to turn away or towards God: Creation as an act of grace was a setting up of nature as other than God. That other nature is not radically changed by sin, because that free will which is essential to its being is indifferent to sin and holiness. The historical process of corruption then is not an infection of the will but rather a habituation to a willing sin rather than holiness. The fact of being able to do evil is an indication of freedom, hence the lapsarian human being shows more clearly his true being than the prelapsarian does.

The question of law here is vital. For Pelagius the relation to the law is an unambiguous one: The law commands what is right, and the human being through her own free will can follow the law and reach the sinless state. There is for Pelagius no significant gap between the inner will and the external action: In the good man they are one. For Augustine, however, the law is characterized by its externality and is written in stone. The point of Christ is to write the law in the heart. But there is no easy path – indeed without grace no path at all – between the stone and the heart. Basing himself on the famous passage on the law in the letter to the Romans (3.17-29), Augustine states, 'For whoever did even what the law commanded, without the assistance of the Spirit of grace, acted through fear of punishment, not from love of righteousness, and hence in the sight of God that was not in the will, which in the sight of men appeared in the work.'[59] In fact, far from helping the will, the law tends to work in the opposite direction: 'The very object that we covet becomes all the more pleasant when it is forbidden.'[60] The law functions differently for fallen humanity not because it is foreign to human nature but because that nature is turned away from itself. The postlapsarian self for Augustine is turned away from itself. The law is not an instruction to be followed but that which commands what is impossible for human beings to accomplish unaided. What Augustine affirms here, and Pelagius denies, is that God commands what is impossible.[61] But this command for Augustine is instructive in another sense: The impossibility to follow the command – to act well with a good will – shows the self its dependence on God's grace and in so doing shows it its true nature.

Both Augustine and Pelagius share a common rejection of Manichaeanism, but the emphasis of this rejection differ. While Pelagius denies the Manichaean understanding of creation as evil and emphasizes the human capacity for good as the pinnacle of created being,[62] Augustine rejects the materialism of Marcion, affirming with Plotinus the immaterial nature of the soul and of God.[63] Pelagius objects to the manner in which Manichaeanism makes the human into a plaything in a cosmic myth. There is, he affirms, a dignity in the human which raises it above the necessity of nature.[64] Augustine also emphasizes the goodness of creation,[65] but the driving force of his rejection of Manichaeanism is the way it understands God. The goodness of creation is tainted by the Fall, as is the history of humanity thereafter. For Pelagius the history of humanity subsequent to the Fall is one in which God intervenes through the law and the prophets and finally through Christ. In each case, through the *lex litterae* (the laws as recounted in Scripture), the laws of nature, which had been forgotten, could be relearned.[66] These were aids to reason, aids for a remembering of a nature that had been covered over and hidden. The law, the teaching of Christ and his example are nothing other than means of disclosing her own nature to the human. These were all acts of grace, but acts which were external, which acted as spurs to remembrance. The human being could by the power of her own nature alone avoid sin, and, indeed, Pelagius claims that we can find examples of this in the Hebrew Scriptures.[67] The significance and importance of Christ is crucial here: If Pelagius is right, Augustine argued, and human beings could on the basis of their natures alone earn salvation, then the saving sacrifice of Christ was unnecessary, superfluous. As Augustine puts it, 'we ought not … so to magnify the Creator as to be compelled to say, nay, convicted of saying, that the Saviour is superfluous'.[68]

In sum, the issues between Augustine and Pelagius are the following. First, just as for Pelagius the Fall as an event makes no fundamental change in the ontological constitution of the human being, neither does the Incarnation. To the pagan who is without the message of Christ the nature of beings created by God can be disclosed.[69] In this sense the grace of creation is that which can be understood naturalistically, in abstraction from the Scriptures and from Christ. The revelations of the *lex litterae* (culminating in Christ) release human beings to achieve the perfection of their own nature, rooted in their free will. This places them in a position in which they have the power not to sin or to sin.[70] For Augustine, human nature is transformed by Christ in that Christ's death wipes out original sin. Baptism is efficacious in bringing about that purification in each Christian. The event of Christ in that sense has ontological significance in reversing the effects of the first event, that of Adam's sin. It is this that grounds Augustine's discussions of grace and freedom. For Augustine there is no conflict of grace and freedom, nor is there ultimately any conflict between grace and human nature. Without grace there can be no freedom; nature without grace is incomplete.[71] The latter claim is the most revealing and the most difficult. At its core is a paradox, namely, that human nature (and perhaps non-human nature also) has an end, and a desire for that end, that is both natural to it and which it does not have sufficient capacity to bring about.[72]

Second, Christ can be understood on the basis of human nature for Pelagius. This is not to say that he denies the divinity of Christ but rather that the sinlessness of Christ is the actualization of an already present potentiality in human nature.[73] For Augustine, human beings can be understood only from Christ: The human being sees his fallen nature in the mirror of Christ and sees in Christ the efficacy of God, which works through each individual in achieving perfection.[74]

Third, for Pelagius, following the example of Christ means freedom from sin: 'No Christian is permitted to sin.'[75] Baptism is necessary to purify the effects of past sins, and a commitment to Christ means a permanent conversion, a commitment not to sin again. The grace of Christ lies in part in the forgiveness of sins. Such forgiveness concerns the past for Pelagius: It is a mark of discontinuity in which through the grace of Christ what cannot be undone is wiped clean, but following the conversion to God human beings have the natural capacity to remain sinless. This Augustine denies. Baptism wipes out the 'guilt' of original sin for Augustine, but concupiscence remains: 'In baptized adults ... whatever consent their mind gives to this concupiscence for the commission of sin is an act of their own will.'[76]

Fourth, knowledge is insufficient for salvation, according to Augustine: 'They who know from the law how man ought to live, are not made righteous by their knowledge.'[77] The claim to knowledge is rooted in pride, and Augustine accuses the Pelagians of pride. For Augustine, there is a split between the claim to know and the claim to intelligibility: Intelligibility lies in God, and the path of faith leads to understanding, but only through giving up the claim to knowledge and recognizing the dependence on grace.[78]

Despite Augustine's 'victory' in this debate,[79] Pelagianism remained operative in Christian thought as a mode in which Stoic presuppositions and doctrines moulded Christian practice. This can be seen particularly in the so-called Semi-Pelagians.[80] Despite himself drawing from the Stoics, Augustine refused what he saw as the self-assertion and pride at the heart of Stoicism, and he sees this too in Pelagius and the Pelagians.[81] But for Pelagius such a self-assertion is not pride; it is rather how a Christian follows the Gospels by obeying the divine law and living without sin. It views the sin of Adam as original only in a chronological sense. It does not mean an originary fault in the human being but rather arises from the autonomous freedom of the human self.[82]

1.2 Freedom and tranquillity: Stoicism and Scepticism

'Freedom is not achieved by satisfying desire, but by eliminating it.'[83] In this sentence Epictetus sums up his understanding of freedom, desire and the good life and in so doing points towards the Stoic ideal of the self: free through a liberation from passion (*apatheia*). This ideal is premised on setting up as ultimate an ontological difference between what is in the power of the self and that beyond the self's power: 'Of all things that are, God has put some under our control and others not. The best and most important thing is under our control and the basis of God's own well-being – the use of external impressions ... He did not put anything else under our control.'[84] The Pyrrhonian Sceptics were similarly convinced that this difference between what is and what is not in our control, corresponding to some form of a distinction between inner and outer, was central to the philosophical project and the happy life. While Augustine and Pelagius both agreed that the purpose of life was salvation and thus an overcoming of the present situation of the self, for the Stoics and the Sceptics the goal of philosophy was tranquillity, the acceptance of the self's present situatedness. The goal of philosophy was to achieve for human beings that calmness evident in the heavenly bodies: unperturbed, moving eternally with inner harmony.

This difference of self and other is experienced in the self through the temporal difference between impression and judgement. The ascetics of the self, which Stoicism practices, amounts to the cultivation of an inner temporality, a temporality of hesitation, reflection and assent (or dissent). The time of the world, the time of determinate events governed by Zeus, governed, that is, by the divine principle of the universe, is both determinate and good. The fundamental metaphysical claim of Stoicism is that everything is determined because everything is for the good. The idea of divine providence is central here – the world is guided by God, who wills all things for the good: 'It is easy to praise providence for everything that happens in the world provided you have the ability to see individual events in the context of the whole and a sense of gratitude.'[85] The idea of divine providence is both a metaphysical principle and one that requires a certain state of mind to grasp. The wise man is one who is capable both of the intellectual act of seeing all things in the context of the whole and the disposition of gratitude towards God as the one who directs all things. In this sense, Stoic ethics is grounded in their physics, or, to put it more correctly, the good of all things is foundational for the human good. The inner time of the thinker needs to maintain pace with the time of things, find harmony with them and not give itself over to hopes or fears towards what happens determinately and for good reason. In all of this, Epictetus reminds his readers to think of themselves as on a stage: 'Remember that you are an actor in a play, the nature of which is up to the director to decide.'[86] To be is to play a role, which Epictetus understands in terms of the place within the society of other people: poor, cripple, king, commoner. The self is as actor who should accept the role impartially. He ought not to be partial because the role he plays is not in his choosing; all he can choose is how to play the role for as long as it lasts. The play is under the sway of the director, God, Zeus, such that everything has a purpose and everything is directed towards the good. This is so even though this purpose may not be obvious to an individual, particularly one suffering from a misfortune. But as fortune is that which the self cannot control, it is not that on which it ought to focus its attention.

The time of the world is guided by divine providence, such that all that happens is for the greater good, even if the immediate effect is one of suffering. Furthermore, this time is governed by a certain economy in which all that is has been given and can be taken back.[87] This time regulates the mode by which the self is affected through impressions (*phantasia*). Such impressions will come when they do and the self cannot control them; sometimes they affect the self violently. In discussing anger, Seneca speaks of 'involuntary movements', such as 'cold water being sprinkled on us' or the 'way bad news makes our hair stand on end', to illustrate how impressions can affect us in a surprising and painful manner.[88] However, the emotion of anger involves the act of the mind that assents to a reaction of indignation (to the perceived wrong), condemnation (of the guilty party) and a desire of retribution. Similarly, Epictetus states that on hearing a frightening noise, 'the mind even of a wise man is inevitably shaken a little, blanches and recoils – not from any preconceived idea that something bad is about to happen, but because certain irrational reflexes forestall the action of the rational mind'.[89] While such violent impressions are determinate in the sense of being brought about by the immanent divinity of the world, they can provoke responses in the self which are not adequate to them, emotional responses of anger, fear and so forth. These responses involve the action of the mind that comes after the impression, action which is constitutive of any provocation.[90] This requires of the mind the capacity for hesitation, for inserting a rational response into the natural relations of cause and effect. Strictly speaking, the 'insertion' here is none at all: The time of cause and effect is unaffected by the mind's deliberations. But the mind withdraws from the world of affects through the power of the will which can give assent or dissent to every impression. This capacity is the ability to command. It is that which separates the human from the animal and amounts to 'a bit of God' within the self.[91] But that 'bit of God' is the capacity to live the impression again, to live it in reflecting on it, and the time of that reflection is a circling back on that which has been retained and applying to those 'preconceptions' written into the nature of each rational being.[92]

The Stoic claim is that this parallel time of judgement is that freedom necessary for rational beings. Indeed, it is characteristic of reason that it can analyse itself: The faculty of reason is 'the faculty that analyses itself as well as the others'.[93] While the arts (*techné*) are directed towards their own goals but cannot reflect on those goals, reason, in evaluating itself, evaluates all things. Reason allows the self to evaluate and utilize the impressions things make on it: 'the proper use of the impressions'.[94] It is will, not reason, that manifests human freedom, because it is the will which decides whether to follow reason or not. Indeed, it is the will that is the source of human happiness. As Hannah Arendt puts it, for Epictetus, 'life … was incapable of giving real happiness without a special effort of man's will'.[95] But as she points out, happiness is characterized as stillness after a storm, as tranquillity: happiness understood negatively as the absence of disturbance.[96] This is in line with his understanding of the will as unaffected by the things in the world. His will has been given to him outright by God; God has 'conferred on me the functions of the will, made them mine and made them proof against resistance of obstruction. But the body … he assigned it its place in the cosmic cycle.'[97] The will's divinity is shown in its indifference to any affective pull, its impassibility.

The issue here – and it is at this point that we need to introduce the Pyrrhonian Sceptics[98] – is that for any given impression the mind has three choices – to accept it as true, to reject it as false or to suspend judgement regarding it – and it is the task of the will to make the decision between them. The Stoic understanding of the wise man is the one who chooses what to accept on a rational basis, accepts what is as necessary and always wills on the basis of good reason. But it is precisely the possibility of such rational choice which Pyrrhonian Sceptics deny.

Sextus Empiricus's Sceptical strategy is twofold. He begins with arguments from different philosophers (often Stoics) which purport to be compelling regarding questions of truth and goodness, and shows that despite the claims to being evidential, these arguments can be opposed by counterarguments. This amounts to the claim that they are dogmatic claims: They give assent to claims as evidential which are not (or can be shown to be not) evidential. Second, he shows that we have no valid criteria for deciding between these two positions. There are seventeen different tropes, divided into ten ancient ones, five newer ones and two which Sextus claims as his own, for showing that all claims to have criteria to decide these matters are fallacious. The first ten tropes show that differences in those making judgements, in the modes of appearances of the objects of judgement or in both, are irreducible. In such a situation, in the absence of valid criteria for deciding between rival arguments, the rational course is to withhold belief and judgement – *epoché*. In such a state, the thinker finds himself in an *aporia*: literally one in which he cannot decide either for one or the other position. The *aporia* leads the thinker to a state of tranquillity – *ataraxia* – because he realizes that he is in the only justifiable position: Both alternatives being equal, he can with full confidence withhold assent – *epoché* – from both. This state is precisely not a state of doubt. The state of doubt is one in which the self finds itself divided and uncertain. Furthermore, the claim that everything is doubtful is that which Sextus says we find with the Academics, whereas the true Sceptic is the one who continues to search. The Sceptic is open to finding truth: it is precisely this openness which motivates his rigor in critiquing claims to truth. 'Sceptic' means seeker after truth.[99]

While since Plato's reflections on the structure of desire Greek philosophy is characterized by a drive towards completion, the Sceptical seeking after truth suggests an almost Modern sense of futuricity. The lack at the heart of Platonic desire is after all tied to directedness at recouping lost truth and goodness within the structure of *anamnesis*, and this is reflected in the Stoic doctrine of the conflagration such that everything that is repeats past worlds returned to fire. For the Sceptics, however, there is no such emphasis. On the contrary, the Sceptic in seeking truth ventures forward, is open to that which is other, strange, as possible sources of truth. The Sceptic does not expect to find truth within herself but rather seeks always to transcend the horizon of the current dogma. This transcending is motivated by a seeking which at the very least does not privilege past experience or indeed the immemorial but rather has more a sense close to the Modern idea of research.

Tranquillity is possible for the Sceptic because she understands wisdom in negative rather than positive terms: To be wise is not to accept anything as true, which cannot be shown evidentially to be true. This assumes two things: first, that there is a truth which can be discovered or at the very least that we have good reason to trust that there is such truth (otherwise we would not seek it) and, second, that to be in the truth is to assent only to that which one knows oneself justified in affirming. It could well be that certain doctrines held, say, by the Stoics are true, but holding those truths is not enough: The one asserting them must know them to be true. There are therefore implicit ontological, epistemological and anthropological theses in the setting forth of the aporetic as the state of the wise man.

For Sextus, the Sceptic lives his life without beliefs, because to believe is to assent to the non-evidential, which is precisely what is not open to the Sceptic.[100] To live without beliefs is to refuse to make the move from the evident claim of how something appears to me to the non-evident claim that this is how that thing is. The difference here is between appearance and reality, between a thing appearing to me and that thing in itself.[101] Assuming a distinction between the thing as it really is and the thing as it appears, Sextus claims that the real is hidden within appearance. This is not to say that there is nothing real: that would be a dogmatic statement.[102] On the contrary, the real is assumed, but the access to it through appearance is questioned. Again, this is not to say that appearances are illusory but rather that what appears can only be accepted as real if it is evidential. To live without beliefs is to only accept that which was evidential to reason as true. Implicit here is a thoroughgoing rationalism and perspectivism: The intelligibility of appearance lies in the mode in which it appears to me (the one perceiving). That appearance is never fully complete; it indicates beyond itself that which is true not only for me but also of the thing itself. The coherency of any claim to know that which is indicated in the appearance depends on my capacity to give compelling reasons for the truth of my claims. If, however, my claims are always confined to the mode of appearance, and if I lack the criteria for deciding definitively what is true on the basis of that finite experience, then reason tells me that I am in an *aporia*. To choose one side or the other, to take the path to assent or negation despite everything, is to go beyond reason. Tranquillity comes from refusing to take that step. It is a rational tranquillity.[103]

The tranquillity of the Sceptic is made possible by his refusal to accept the non-evidential as true, while assuming that there is no principled division between the evidential and the non-evidential. In other words, the distinction between the evidential and the non-evidential is a reflective one, a distinction having to do with the perceiver's capacity to justify his beliefs. The understanding of the limits of capacity is not based in any ontology of incapacity but rather in a reflective and revisable recognition of limits. It is for this reason that the Sceptic can truly claim to be a searcher after knowledge and truth. Only because truth is in principle open to reason does Sceptical reflection rigorously delimit the claims to know. The search for knowledge is, however, not satisfied by the accumulation of knowledge (quantity), but rather by the certainty of knowledge (quality). In the end, then, the goal of the Sceptic is self-knowledge, but self-knowledge is that of a self in a world of appearances.

The Pyrrhonian Sceptic responds to this situation by not asserting (*aphasia*) in the form of assenting or denying, by a suspension of judgement and belief (*epoché*).[104] But the Sceptic speaks, makes choices and acts in terms that imply belief. The objection to the Sceptic as old as Scepticism itself is that the Sceptic is constantly contradicting himself. But the Sceptic raises questions not about appearances but about that which is *said* about appearances (*legetai tou phaino*).[105] To assent, to judge, to believe in the realm of appearances, is to state how things appear to be. How things appear to be is how things are for the perceiving self. The question is how do we talk about appearances with respect to those assertions, beliefs and judgements? It is on this self-reflective level, this level of meta-discourse, that the Sceptical considerations arise. In this sense, it is quite consistent for Sextus to say, on the one hand, that he 'gives trust (*pistin*) to the apparent thing', while denying that he is believing that the thing is the way it appears.[106] What this means is that the Sceptical is ultimately an exercise in self-discipline, in disciplining the self regarding the limits of the range of its own cognitions. But this self-discipline requires both a sense of being at home in the world and a belief in the self as capable of justifying itself.

The appearance of things is for him those things as they appear. They appear always differently relative to the circumstances of the one to whom they appear.[107]

Furthermore, the experience of an appearance is adverbial rather than adjectival: the self perceives sweetly, or whitely, but this does not allow her to state that the thing itself (*hyperkeimenon*) *is* white or sweet.[108] The thing is perceived in the action and motion of perceiving; the qualities perceived cannot be abstracted from this motion and action and as such can only be expressed in terms of that action. He goes on to employ Stoic arguments against the Stoics themselves: If the appearance is an effect of the thing itself, then what we experience is the effect, not the cause.[109] The very distinction Sextus draws implies the existence of the thing in itself, as that which is experienced in its effects or in the motion of the interaction with it. Neither the existence nor the rational order of this thing in itself is called into doubt; indeed the rationality of the Sceptic depends on the assumption that she is living in a rational world: To accept only what can be rationally grounded is a viable and tranquillity-inducing way of life on the condition that the world as it is (the things in themselves) is rationally grounded.

In Stoicism and Scepticism we find two modes of reaching the same goal of tranquillity. The happiness of the self is understood in terms of being tranquil. To achieve this, the passions need to be quieted, and this involves the lessening of affective dependence on external factors. In an important respect the Sceptical way is the more radical: It excludes also the possession of truth as a condition of happiness. The pursuit of truth in and of itself gives happiness, while the persuasion that something doubtful is true leads only to anxiety. For the Stoic, on the contrary, reason gives positive results. But the assumption of a rational universe, guided by providence, explicitly held by Stoicism, is also implicit in Scepticism: The tranquillity of not knowing is based on the assumption that there is an order, even if not yet seen.

1.3 World, God and origins: Modern transformations

A crisis of sense – the crises of faith, world and reason referred to above – led to a revitalization of Augustinian, Pelagian, Stoic and Sceptical concerns and motifs, while at the same time provoking a transformation of meaning in these respective ways of thinking of and being a self, which they proclaimed, implied or embodied. A crisis of sense, manifest in transformations of the relations of reason to faith and faith to reason, it destabilized and put up for decision the meaning of 'world'. 'World' is not a neutral term towards which 'worldviews' can be taken. As Blumenberg states, 'world is not a constant whose reliability guarantees that in the historical process and original constitutive substance must come back to life undisguised as soon as the superimposed elements of theological derivation and specificity are cleaned away'.[110] Rather, 'world' is that order of relation in which sense is first possible, and the crisis of world is the calling into question of that order and such sense. The crisis of world that we find in late Medieval and early modern thought and practice revolves around three relata which, with variations great and small, were constitutive of the Medieval and Ancient worlds: God(s), human and (physical) nature.[111] In the inner relations of these domains, within their respective *metaphysica specialis*, world could be understood as the unity of relations of creatures with respect to the ground of worldly being in the Creator.

The 'worldly' in the Christian understanding is rooted in a transforming of the meaning of 'cosmos' that we find first in St. Paul. The ordered totality of all that is, Paul sets against the other-worldly, the divinity, who as Creator is beyond the world and who is the final end of human beings: not, as Aristotle's first mover, an immanent end, but a transcendent one. This account of world opens up the possibility of a radical dualism of world and God, which is manifest in different forms of Gnosticism. Once God is understood as transcendent, evil can be identified with the world and salvation becomes a saving *from* the world rather than *of* the world. For Blumenberg, this is in effect the logical consequence of Christianity, making any effort to sustain the world insupportable. Christianity is an ambiguous presence, replacing Greek philosophy, but doing so at the price of a fundamental inconsistency: The usurpation of the Stoic notion of divine providence is merely a veil covering over the disappointed expectation of the end of the world.[112] The coming to be of a Christian world while Christianity denied the worldly certainly held within itself fundamental tensions, if not contradictions. In the *City of God*, Augustine classically addresses this with the bifurcation of the two cities, divine and human. Gnosticism, in its various forms, pushed the implicit dichotomy to its extreme by demonizing the created world and portraying it as an alien place from which the human could only be saved by knowledge of unworldly rituals.[113] While Blumenberg sees Marcion as offering the only solution to the Christian state of disappointed expectation of the end and understands the preoccupation in the Patristic period with the story of creation as a doomed attempt to reconcile with the continued existence of the world,[114] he discounts the equally – indeed more intense – preoccupation with Christology and the manner in which the Christ figure allowed Christians to reimagine creation and the created world.[115] In this way orthodox Christianity proved very adept at living with the contradictions that the deferred world-ending posed for them. The synthesis of Christian experience and Greek thought was crucial to this process. The resulting account of world necessarily contained the secular within it: the *saeculum* referring to an age suspended between the moments of the Incarnation – which 'recapitulated' all history since creation[116] – and the Second Coming. Within this end time, eschatological expectations disclose the worldly as potentially an exclusively secular domain. What we find here is the opening up within Christianity itself of a secular domain. The transformations, which characterize the 'modern', disorientate the secular and the sacred with respect to each other. All of this produces a crisis of world understood in a formal sense as the manner in which domains of reality, which are different in kind, hang together and thereby form an intelligible sense. In that regard, the unworldly is necessarily tied to world: It is that which needs to be meaningfully articulated in a world that had not (yet) ended. Modernity, in this sense, is a project in articulating a new sense of the world, and it does so with an increased rather than diminished sense of the eschatological precisely because it is responding to an 'intensification' rather than a relaxing of the Christian experience and reflection upon that experience.[117]

As Kurt Flasch has shown, novelty, modernity, was a not a value of Medieval Europe: Imitation, not originality, characterized the self-understanding of much of that era.[118] But this shifts in the High Middle Ages above all through the shock of the encounter with Aristotle's works. What arises out of the reaction to the attempt to synthesize Aristotle and Christianity, particularly in the work of Aquinas, is a break between the Ancient way (*via antiqua*) and the Modern way (*via moderna*). The Modern, in the sense of that distinction between old and new which valorized the new over the old, is a theological and Medieval distinction.

In 1277 a commission set up by the Archbishop of Paris, Étienne Tempier, issued a condemnation of 219 propositions. This condemnation targeted the growing influence of Aristotelianism in the University of Paris, particularly among the 'Masters of Arts' who were effectively transforming themselves into a faculty of philosophy.[119] At the heart of these condemnations is a resistance against what was understood (by Tempier and the majority of the theologians of Paris) as a claim to a doubling of truth: a religious truth and a philosophical truth. The charge of double truth is directed against a claim to the independent operation of human reason, not subject to the 'truths' of faith. The 1277 Condemnation is a reaction against the very idea of philosophy as independent of theology. As Alain de Libera makes clear, it is only gradually in the thirteenth century that the self-understanding of practicing philosophy emerged. The 'philosopher' was an exotic being, either Arab or Ancient Greek. It is used as a word of condemnation by the theologians against the Masters of Arts of Paris.[120] However, rather than curbing the development of philosophy, the condemnations laid bare a division between faith and reason in a fundamental manner. This can be illustrated by two examples.

First, Condemnation 89 of the 1277 Condemnations states as condemnable the claim that 'it is impossible to refute the argument of the philosophers [in favour] of the eternity of the world [*Quod impossible est solvere rationes philosophi de eternitate mundi*]'. Condemnation 90 goes on to condemn the proposition that the 'faithful ... are able to deny the eternity of the world, because it relies on supernatural causes [*Fidelis autem potest negare mundi eternitatem, quia innititur causis supernaturalibus*]'.[121] What is crucial here is the distinction between natural and supernatural, affirmed by the Masters of Arts and denied by the theologians. For Aquinas, the supernatural is not a domain distinct from the natural but rather is the means for nature to attain its final end.[122] This is very much in line with Augustine's account of grace, where grace is not foreign to nature but rather that which fulfils nature: in Aquinas' terms, grace perfecting nature.[123] The 1277 Condemnations, however, point to the opening up of a distinction between natural and supernatural causal explanation, which we can find in Boethius of Dacia, the only person actually named and against whom a good number of the condemnations were probably directed. He sets out and defends a clear distinction between natural causes and causes of 'a higher cause than nature (*causam superiorem quam naturam*)'.[124] A corollary of this is that two distinct levels of explanation emerge for 'acts of the soul', natural and supernatural explanations. As such, a religious experience could be understood as a natural psychological occurrence, and a mystical experience could be given explained in natural terms.[125]

Second, thirteen propositions concerned God, claiming that their opponents believe God to be limited in knowledge and efficacy. With respect to knowledge, the condemned view is that God can only know himself due to his eternal nature and that he cannot apprehend singular realities and in consequence that specific human acts lie outside his providence. What is condemned here is a quasi-Stoic account of providence whereby there is an eternal rational order that is good and aims at the good, but which is indifferent towards the suffering of individual selves. These condemnations are also aimed at the realist account of universals, which are understood to limit divine power. The notion of the categories in any realist sense is rejected. Indeed, there is an emphasis on divine omnipotence throughout the propositions about God.[126] These limitations are apparent with respect to secondary causes. The notion of secondary causes, that there are causes immanent in nature, which although created by God can be understood by reason without direct reference to the divinity, is central to the natural philosophies of Albertus Magnus and Thomas Aquinas. For Aquinas, God is the primary cause of all things not only of their coming to be but also in their continuity in being. Nevertheless, within nature there are causal relations which have regularity and can be understood immanently with respect to the relation of cause and effect.[127] Condemnation 56 condemns the following proposition: 'God is not able to immediately know contingent things, if it is not by [the intermediary of] an other particular and proximate cause [*Quod deus non potest immediate cognoscere contigentia, nisi per aliam causam partiuclarem ex proximam*].'[128] This thought is reflected in a number of the condemnations, namely, that the positing of secondary causes is in effect opening up a domain for philosophical investigation independent of theology (and implicitly, too, this means that a number of the condemnations are directed at Magnus and Aquinas).[129]

The question as to whether the charge of double truth is a correct one or not is a matter of intense scholarly debate.[130] For our purposes, however, the crucial issue is that this event of 1277 set out starkly as a matter of fundamental debate the possibility of reason free of theology and faith. It thereby opened the door (probably unintentionally) to a theology freed from the constraints of philosophical reason. In this way it set up a gap between divinity and nature, sacred and secular, which will continue to develop with fundamental implications for the relation of God, nature and human in the centuries to come.[131]

As the 1277 Condemnations makes clear, a key problem with any synthesis of Aristotle (or Greek thought generally) and Christianity is the idea of an all-powerful God. Not only was Greek divinity plural (polytheism) but even when thought monotheistically (as arguably is the case in Aristotle and less clearly in Plato), God was thought in terms of the world – as *cosmos*. It is a Christian innovation to conceive all-powerfulness as the first and, in a sense, only divine name. It is characteristic of those theologians of the *via moderna*, first Duns Scotus but then more forcefully William of Ockham, that this way of understanding God explodes the citadel of reconciliation of Christian and Greek thought. Once the distinction between *potentia Dei ordinate* and *potentia Dei absoluta* – between what was actually ordained by divine power and that which is possible for divine power – becomes a central thought, as it does for Ockham, then worldly correlates become merely provisional and inherently reversible. While Ockham maintained the law of non-contradiction as a limit on the absolute power of God,[132] as was soon observed, this was really an arbitrary stipulation. In effect, Aristotle's priority of actuality over potentiality is thus inverted and a domain of speculative thought concerning the first principles of things is opened up, which is prior to, and (in principle) unlimited by, the world.[133] Possibility unlimited by actuality is prior to and independent of the world. This idea is already found in Avicenna who understood the world as it is, the world of creation, as one possible – albeit the best possible – world. As

Rémi Brague points out, this has the unintended effect of relativizing the world to a will exterior to it and understands the being of this real world as having its source in a good that does not coincide with it.[134] Worldly relations become radically contingent on the will of a God untouchable by the world. The world can now be thought not from itself but from a possibility, of which it is only a contingent actualization, the contingency of which has no worldly correlate. Lacking a worldly correlate, the relations of humans to nature and to God lose their grounding in the unity of those relations; the relations themselves become secondary, provisional and redactable.

A relation which can not only be broken but also be undone, the very basis of its prior reality subverted, loses any ontological sense of fundamental relationality. The relationality of things, embeddedness in lines of sense in which purpose, value and understanding gain intelligibility, is essentially constituted by trust. Relation is both dependence and confidence – otherwise it is simply an arbitrary juxtapositioning – and as such trust is essential to relationality. Trust, as the already accepted being towards and with entities as they appear, grounds the communicability of the being of things as intelligible – possibility as already contained in the actuality of the relations themselves. But as Louis Dupré states, 'the trust in the essentially rational quality of nature that had supported traditional epistemology had collapsed'.[135] Nominalist Voluntarism understood entities as significant not in terms of their place in a relational whole but as owing their being singly to a source beyond all order, namely, the divine will.

While Heidegger is indeed right that the Medieval account of being is in terms of *ens creatum*,[136] it is crucial to see how the account of what that means shifts dramatically with the Nominalist critique of Thomist metaphysics. While for Aquinas the creative act of God brought into being a teleological world, that is, a world in which entities had a purpose and meaning in terms of their own natures, natures which existed within a harmonious horizon of all beings,[137] for Ockham God created singular beings each time, whose purpose was not of their own nature – understood as the genus and species to which they belonged – but rather was external to them.[138] For Thomas, to be created was to be in the world; for Ockham, it was to be a singular entity that derived its significance not from its relation to other entities but to that which was beyond all worldly entities: God understood in terms of his inscrutable will. To be is to be willed into being. No entity contains its being in itself, and the relation of any entity to another can in no way be accounted for in terms of the entity in question.[139] Nothing *is* in relation to anything else, that is, there is nothing in the nature of any thing which places it necessarily in any given relation. Relation is nothing positive but is rather pure difference.

Understood voluntaristically, however, if the principle of things is in an origin prior to and radically incommensurable with the world, if the ordered unity of things which is experienced as world has no necessary ontological connection to the principle of being, then the world becomes for all practical and indeed theoretical purposes a human creation – a creation indeed of signification, first of language and then of mathematics.[140] At the concrete level, entities opened up in this way can be experienced and understood in abstraction from their worldliness. Hypothesis replaces categorical syllogism as the mode of reasoning appropriate to things as they appear,[141] and as such 'world' appears not as what has been, what is always already there, but rather as that which is projected by a (human) mind as a suggested context for proof.

When the will displaces intellect as the highest faculty, as that faculty through which God relates to things and in consequence the human being as *imago Dei* (image of God) is a willing being, this opens up to infinity the realm of possibility and potentiality. The *imago Dei*, goes back to the book of Genesis and the idea that the human being contains the divine image and likeness within itself.[142] In Aquinas the image of God is to be found in the intellect, through which the human being 'can best imitate God in his intellectual nature'.[143] Augustine understands the human as imitating God in his Trinitarian nature through will, intellect and memory.[144] The relation of imitation here allows for degrees, and for both Augustine and Aquinas, through the Fall the human has lost some resemblance to the divine. The reconfiguration by which will, rather than intellect or memory, is understood to be that image of God has important implications. If the will is the divine image in the human, then it is within its freedom that the human resembles the divine. But in that case, it is the very divinity in the human that leads to a turning away from God. Furthermore, a God understood as primarily will hides within himself the fundamental principles of being and knowledge. Again, this is characteristic of the will: To know the will of another is only possible from the inside; to understand divine will it would be necessary to become God. God becomes necessarily inscrutable as the inner source of all things and that inner source is darkened. Of this 'dark' God nothing definitive can be said, except that his power has no limits.[145] Such power as absolute is understood as pure possibility – not even divine actuality can limit the potential of his will. Conversely, the actual, the realm of real experience, becomes radically contingent as that which finds the source of its being and its significance in an act removed from all pasts and claiming power to enact any possible future.

As Arendt points out, when from Aquinas and Scotus onwards the question becomes whether intellect or will is the dominant cognitive faculty first in God and then in the human, the third Augustinian faculty, that of memory, is lost.[146] For Augustine, memory is crucially important in the human imitation of the divine and it gives access – in quasi-Platonic fashion – to the absent object of desiring love:

> And it [the mind] remembers the Lord its God. ... Not because it recollects having known Him in Adam or anywhere else before the life of this present body, or when it was first made in order to be implanted in this body; for it remembers nothing at all of all this. ... But it is reminded, that it may be turned to God, as though to that light by which it was in some way touched, even when turned away from Him.[147]

The occlusion of this place of memory has consequences not only for political philosophy (which Arendt stresses) but also for theology in the understanding of the Trinity and First Philosophy in the understanding of God with respect to creation: To conceive cognition without memory is to conceive it as initiating, as radical beginning. But such a radical beginning is ultimately arbitrary as it goes out first towards its object without first precognizing the object in its own self-relation. As such, the primacy of the will is already prepared by Aquinas in the undervaluing of memory. This consequence is not seen by Aquinas, however, and for him the intellect is higher than the will because of its presence to itself: The intellect in possessing its object finds fulfilment in reflecting truly and absolutely that object.[148] The will, on the other hand, begins in lack – in the lack of desire – and as such is lost with the possession of its object. The divine relation to things is that of the intellect, one of pure self-possession. But such self-possession requires memory as the relating of the self of God back to himself in his own possession of the object of his intellect. While intellect and will are identified in God, for the human, will is characterized by lack. This is to identify will with desire and implicitly love with eros.

With Ockham, this identification, which, as we have seen, lies at the core of Augustine's account, is broken. In this, Ockham reintroduces a Stoic thesis of the indifference of the will. Will for the Stoics is first and foremost the capacity to negate, that is, dispel all positivity from anything given to it: 'Instead of automatically assenting to [frightening] impressions … our wise man spurns and rejects them.'[149] That means two things: first, that the will is indifferent to things, and all things are equally negatable, and second – but this implication only became clear in the Voluntarist appropriation of the Stoic will – that the will relates to things in the singularity of their own being. If all things are equally negatable, then so is any resemblance between them, such that the will is capable of isolating the singular being from all other things (*determinatio est negatio*). For the will so understood, the world is pure spectacle: The world is a stage and the will can stand back from the differential relations of things in the world and view them in terms of a fundamental conflict between the claims of justice and of self-interest. Will is distinct from desire; its freedom lies in not being motivated.[150]

Will in this sense defeats hierarchy and affirms singularity: Through its negativity it posits the singular being as singular. To understand divine creation from divine sovereignty is to understand God as both ultimately indifferent to things, that is, as related purely contingently to them and to have as his creative object the singular being. Hierarchy falls into question: Hierarchy refers to the beginning or first principles in the holy (*hieros – arché*). If that holy beginning is lodged in an inscrutable divine will, then the route back towards it is obscure. An order without hierarchy, that is, a world understood in terms of creaturely equality (as all infinitely distant from the Creator), can be seen in certain Patristic writers who emphasize creation as beauty: Gregory of Nyssa relativized the difference of super- and sublunar realms as equally sharing in divine providence; for Tertullian the smallest flower or insect displayed divine providence as much as the elements of the world, and for Augustine the flea shares the same benefit.[151] But any such account depends on a prior dynamic of love and beauty. Understood from the indifference of the will, love becomes an option of the will and loses any ontological character, as indeed does beauty. Furthermore, this also has clear implications for the Church as a body understanding itself as mediating between the 'people of God' and the divine. The hierarchical structure has a very real and concrete pertinence, which Voluntarism unintentionally called into question.

'World' can thus be understood as a merely human creation between the singular entities of experience and the inscrutable principles of their being and intelligibility, a guide for action perhaps but not corresponding adequately to the source of their being. Truth becomes not of the world but is either empirical (concerning singular entities as such), a matter of pure thought (logic) or a matter of revelation and known on faith. Faith here does not simply mean the acceptance of certain mysteries (the Incarnation, the Trinity, the Resurrection, for example) as true, but rather a mode of existence in a world without guarantees, a world in which reason, if faced with a revelation that opposes it, can do nothing other than to accept the incongruity of that revelation as something excepted from its (reason's) proper domain.[152] In that case, theology cannot rightfully be termed a science at all, and indeed Ockham recognizes this consequence.[153] It follows *a fortiori* that theology can no longer claim to be foundational for the sciences. Indeed, Ockham claims that the conflict between reason and revelation lies not in any weakness of reason but in the exceptional nature of revelation. The shift that is occurring here can be seen in the manner in which the idea of miracles evolves in this period. Franz Rosenzweig sees the change in the understanding of miracles in terms of a suspicion of testimony,[154] but the change has a much earlier and more fundamental source where the miraculous is understood as an expression of divine will rather than as confirming the ordering principle of divine intellect. For Augustine, a miracle is not a break in the rational order of things but rather confirms that order in a way which is mysterious for the human mind.[155] The mystery here, though, does not indicate any break, any moment of irrationality, but rather shows the weakness of the fallen intellect. The fallen intellect is already cut off from the source of its being, but through divine grace it can find indications in the world of that source. There is a strict isomorphism between the human and divine intellects; their difference has its source in the human turning away from God towards the world. But again that turning is not one which points to a disjunction but rather to a hierarchical order: World is to be used in reaching the divine, which is to be enjoyed. Once, however, the source of being is found in the inscrutable will of God, an obscure darkness falls over the order of things. There can be no guarantee anymore that the order of experience reflects the order of things as presently ordained. In relation to the divine will, in relation to the absolute power of God, the order of experience can understand things only in terms of a power in which everything is possible. As such, the miraculous becomes that which is extraordinary in terms of human experience. The testimony of a miracle is the testimony of the extraordinary, perhaps the monstrous. It is an interruption of the order of things as presently, but not necessarily, given.

The revolt of the *via moderna* against the *via antiqua* faced Western thought perhaps for the first time in a position of deep ontological uncertainty, occasioned not by the weakness of human cognitive capacity alone but by an infinite and potentially capricious source of being. Understood as emanating from such a source, being is divorced from cosmology, in the sense of a discourse on an ordered, beautiful and finite being. What is opened up is a 'chaotic' disorder of entities in the sense that each entity is understood singularly and not in is cosmic relations, singular and unrepeatable expressions of divine will, which – as the new science of the seventeenth century makes clear – are not even bound by finite boundaries. At the level of experiment, the reduction of entities to quantification, already in Galileo and then more fundamentally in Descartes, discloses world as an infinite space of mechanical motion, a space in which the human being either becomes naturalized or withdraws into a non-worldly domain.[156]

1.4 The self and crisis

The crises out of which Modernity emerged were manifold and concerned the life conditions of those living through it in diverse ways. They had both intellectual and concrete manifestations, including war, social and economic disruption, and dislocation. The breakdown of the old order in these many ways brought forth anxiety and fear. But at the same time the religious movements of reform had in common an appeal to the individual Christian vocation of all, the rejection of the mediating function of the Church in the face of the singular relation of creature to Creator. If the individual can no longer appeal to the authority of set ways of being and established economies of salvation, where does she turn? Where does the human being find its place in such a boundless sea?[157] The predominant philosophical and to a large extent theological response to this question was: turn within. This characteristically Augustinian response took, however, many forms. The revivals of Stoicism and Scepticism in responding to these crises embodied this inward turn in different ways. The common characteristic of both is the distinction drawn between what is in the self's control and what is not, coupled with a certain intellectual, moral and affective ascetic practice of limiting the will to those things within its control. This is so because the very boundary between that which is in, and which lies outside, the self's control appears threatened by the passions. The account of the passions and how the self ought to be with respect to them depends on the understanding of the ultimate goal of the self. If in Christian terms it is to love God, then there can be no question of suppressing the passions but rather of cultivating those passions and their mode of directedness which most fulfils the self's calling. Increasingly, however, as the self is thrown back on itself in early modernity, the fault lines of the passions becomes those of the boundaries between self and world.[158]

The move within becomes apparent in the form of a kind of therapeutic Stoicism. The disposition of doubt was preceded by a mood of anxiety. This anxiety concerned the very place of the human being in relation to God, nature and other people. What the re-emergence of Stoicism offered was a response to this anxiety through self-discipline and self-assertion. The point of this is not to find a model in nature, of existing human communities or in God – each of these relata being in question – but rather creating a world through the individual use of reason and thereby establishing a second nature.[159] This ambiguous situation tends to be understood in terms of the passions: It is the passions (both the self's and other's) which threaten, and it is reason which can defend. So we have both dualism and constructivism: Nature is dualistically divided between reason and passion and reason is understood not as intuiting truth in nature but in constructing a truer nature out of the its own (natural) potential.

Here is manifest the loss of trust we spoke of earlier, and indeed, one of the main works of the so-called Neo-Stoics of the sixteenth century, Justus Lipsius's *On Constancy*, begins with a note of distrust: The country is ravished by war, no place is safe, the only answer seems to be to flee.[160] The response, however, to this breakdown in trust is not to flee – because nowhere else is going to be safe and in any case the problem is not with the situation but within the self: 'For you shall still find an enemy in you ... You carry war with you.'[161] The enemy is his passions. The constancy Lipsius is seeking is not going to be found in the world but within himself through a rational mastery of his passions. The Stoic motif and much of the Stoic technique of control of the passions is retained here, but at the expense of the Stoic understanding of the world as ordered and geared towards human good. The world is chaotic, the only order that can be found is within. This move within, however, takes the form of self-assertion. The self in this view finds itself in a dangerous and threatening world, beset by contingencies, without any assurance of a rational structure either in nature or in politics.[162] In this sense, Neo-Stoicism tends rather towards a Gnostic than an Ancient Stoic view of the universe. Human beings can find no consolation in nature nor in politics; in neither is there any hope of constancy. But that path within does not lead in Augustinian fashion to a sense of the height of divine mercy and grace but rather seeks in Pelagian fashion to the assertion of the self's own capacities. In particular, early modern Stoicism emphasized the virtue of self-preservation. Being an individual means being capable of preserving oneself, and this requires the rule of reason within the self. As Lipsius puts it, 'being regulated by the rule of right reason is the very root whereupon is settled the high and mighty body of that fair oak constancy. ... Virtue keeps the mean, not suffering any excess or defect in her actions, because it weighs all things in the balance of Reason, making it the rule and squire of all her trials.'[163]

There is probably no figure from Antiquity whose influence was so widespread and as diverse in early modernity as that of Augustine.[164] Yet, for all that, the nature of his influence remains elusive. The Augustine of the sixteenth and seventeenth centuries takes many forms, some in direct contradiction with each other. The question here, however, is not one of the authenticity of these appropriations but rather the manner in which a certain Augustinianism arose in response to a certain Pelagianism or Semi-Pelagianism. The crisis of world brought with it a renewal of the Pelagian debate of late Antiquity, albeit in a new key.[165] This can be seen in Luther's debate with Desiderius Erasmus, in the controversies surrounding Calvin, in the disputes between the Jansenists and the Jesuits.

Philosophically, the Augustine-Pelagian debate – in its original occurrence, but also in the manner in which it was renewed in Modernity under different guises – is significant because it addresses what became fundamental philosophical questions in Modernity, namely, that of the autonomy of reason, the nature of the will and the project of mastery of nature, all of which in one way or another centred on the understanding of freedom. Furthermore, the working through of this debate in early modernity and later was informed by the Stoic and Sceptical motifs, such that one can speak (among other variations) of a self-denying Augustinian 'scepticism' (in Pascal, for example) and a self-mastering Pelagian Stoicism (Descartes and Spinoza). Paradoxically, however, the Augustinian arguments often hide Pelagian assumptions, reflecting, and reflected in, the shift in the understanding of Scepticism and Stoicism.

The Modern crisis of world involved a sense of the radical contingency of world. As radically contingent, the world depends fundamentally on that which is outside of itself. Furthermore, the contingency of world is a contingency of the inner relation of the human, nature and God, and in consequence a sense of the impotence of human reason and will in finding or achieving the inner meaning of the living relation to nature and God. Beginning from such a premise, an either/or tends to present itself: *Either* the meaning of the world and of human existence in that world is a matter of the divine will *or* the prospect of meaning arising from either God or nature is foreclosed and the self-creative capacity of the human is emphasized. Therein lies a potentially radical dualism of reason and faith, activity and passivity, being and nothingness, nature and grace. The latter terms, 'nature' and 'grace', name theologically and politically explosive themes in this time. Philosophically, the questions which underlie these debates are crucial, first, because of the common assumptions underlying both sides – assumptions which served to transform the terms of the debate – and, second, because of the different modes in which the crisis of world was expressed in each, and these modes served to mould the manner in which the Sceptical rethinking of faith and reason developed at the emergence of Modernity. The Voluntarist challenge is one that affects both Augustinian and Pelagian accounts. For Pelagius, to do what is right is to do the will of God, and only in knowing the will of God can anyone follow his will. As Pelagius puts it, 'it is impossible for anyone to please someone, if he does not know what it is that pleases him ... just as doing the will of the Lord is more important than knowing it, so knowing is prior to doing'.[166] The will of God for Pelagius is communicated in the Laws and in the example and doctrines of Christ. For Augustine, the will of God is known through Scripture too, but that knowledge is made possible through the grace of God who gives faith: To simply understand the words of Scripture is not to have faith; rather, to have faith is to love God as the 'author' of those words: 'Faith is not that which is believed, but that by which it is believed.'[167] Furthermore, through grace the human mind comes to participate in the mind of God. The very basis of his doctrine of grace is the understanding of that relation in Platonic terms as a participation which is at once ontological and epistemological, because it is first a matter of *caritas*, love. If, however, the divine will is inscrutable, if an ontological gulf, indeed an *aporia*, separates divinity and humanity, then the very basis of both Augustinian and Pelagian accounts of salvation is threatened.

The gulf opened up here removes the human from the divine and in consequence nature from grace. But while the claim to such a gulf runs counter to both Augustine and Pelagius and rather shares presuppositions of radical dualism with their common foe, Marcion, nevertheless, Pelagius points in this direction, in a manner quite foreign to Augustine. This is so even though one can already see the traces of Voluntarism in Augustine's theology of love, as Dupré points out.[168] Indeed, the hidden heart of God is the object of Augustine's quest. However, with Augustine, love is always in relation to understanding and remembering, as the unity and common being of the three reflect the Trinity. The place of memory is particularly important here, as it allows Augustine to refer the self back to that which is prior to its own will and indeed (paradoxically) to its own remembering. Hence, those responding to this crisis, from Luther to Pascal even when they invoke Augustine, do so in terms of a question which he not only did not pose but also strongly resisted, the question being whether freedom *or* grace. This question assumes, on the one hand, an opposition in terms of responsibility between the radical abdication of responsibility to God, in the fundamental rejection of freedom, and, on the other hand, the radical assumption of responsibility in the self, set against divine grace. In his debate with Erasmus, Luther opposes again and again the idea that God commands the impossible and the claim to free will. According to Luther, the divine commands, far from implying free will, faces the self with its utter dependence on God.[169] Once that is the question, a Pelagian solution suggests itself (paradoxically in respect to Luther) in the form of Stoical self-assertion. Yet, the Augustinian admonition of humility forms a response to this situation that strikes a Sceptical rather than Stoical note.

For Ockham, grace is subject to the will of God not simply in the sense of election but also in the sense that God could choose another manner to save. Grace is neither ontologically rooted in the being of the human nor does it have any more than a relative basis in the nature of God. Removed as will is from love and goodness, where God cannot will badly because he has no obligations that he can break, grace is made contingent not simply on the electing will of God but also with respect to nature as such. This allows for an account of nature as sufficient to itself, sufficient that is to fulfil its own ends. Grace in such a concept is superadded onto nature, but superadded as a contingent possibility of divine will. While Ockham contends that human actions can make a person meriting of divine grace, this, he argues, in no way conditions the actual granting of grace.[170]

No further language of responsibility or irresponsibility can be employed in speaking of God: God is in Ockham's terms beyond good and evil, beyond responsibility and irresponsibility, beyond justice and injustice, beyond love and hate. The Augustinian account of the human being willing the good freely through participating in the divine being is rooted in an understanding of divine nature as good, responsible, just and loving. The gratuitousness of the gift derives not from a radical unconditionality of divine power but from the fundamental wretchedness of fallen human nature, on the one hand, and the overflowing splendour of divine love, on the other. Once the basis of that ontology is undermined, the gratuitousness of grace must be reconceived. As Henri de Lubac states the problem, in the 'modern' theory of Voluntarism an end cannot be given freely unless the recipient of that end already had another end that was actually realizable.[171] The supernatural becomes in that way radically distinct from the natural, and the world becomes detached from God and potentially from the human being qua recipient of grace. According to Francisco Suarez, the withdrawal of supernatural finality was one of the punishments for the Fall. As such, fallen humanity was left in a natural state, not called to a supernatural destiny. The supernatural beatitude amounted to a radically contingent rupture in the natural order of things.[172]

The natural human being is one who has natural responsibilities, indeed one who can read her responsibilities from nature, from the world around her. Such a being, to the extent to which she lives happily, lives in unity and harmony with her own nature and the nature of the world around her. To this 'pure nature',[173] the ideal of the Stoic sage grants a large degree of self-understanding. If the nature of the human being appeared as that which is and can be understood prior to any relation to revealed truth, prior then to the God of grace, it follows that a life could be lived in virtue, in the control of the self, in its being in nature. Such a self can be responsible for itself within the limits of the world that God has ordained. The world which appears, the world of harmony and unity, is one that gives the guide and model for natural virtue. Such virtue is common to all, and Christians have no particular claim on it. The nature that so appears is hierarchically ordered in terms of natural goods, and similarly the human self finds within herself a hierarchy of mind and body. The ethical endeavour is to be true to that hierarchical order by subjecting the body to the mind.

Such Stoicism had strong Pelagian elements. Faced with a world in which the principle of being was detached from apparent being, no power seemed present except the power found in the self-awareness of the individual, the awareness that is of his own powers. On the other hand, the omnipotence of God meant that there was no guarantee that the fulfilment of these powers could or would merit salvation. This is a blind Pelagianism, striving to merit salvation from a God who is unknown and unknowable. Separated radically from the divine and unable to read from the world anything of his salvation, the Humanist response was to move within the self and see creation of meaning – creation of world – as the purpose of language and life. This dual movement of interiority and creation prevailed in the major literary, religious and scientific revolutions of the period.

Pelagian and Stoic ideas became interwoven with Augustinian motifs and claims. A case in point is the figure of 'Augustinus' in Francesco Petrarch's *The Secret*. Discussing his conversion, Augustinus is made to say, 'Then after I desired completely to change, I was instantly able, and with miraculous and most welcome speed I was transformed into another Augustine.'[174] In the passage of the *Confessions* to which Petrarch is alluding, however, what Augustine describes is not so much a heightened desire as an increased state of misery and self-doubt; he is engaged in tearful prayer, in calling out to God to help him and expressing his utter dependence on divine grace.[175] The actual conversion is in Augustine's account occasioned by such grace – the voice of a child, which he understands, on the basis of a similar account in the life of St. Anthony, to be a divine command: 'Pick up and read.' The text he reads is from Paul's letter to the Romans, which declares happiness and salvation to be in Christ.[176] What in Augustine is an account of divine grace that rids him of anxiety, which is – as he puts it elsewhere – a physician for his soul that gives him relief in his nature for a desire that he is incapable of fulfilling, in Petrarch becomes an account of a conversion resulting from the will of the person to reach a meritorious state. Augustine becomes – or at least comes close to being – a Pelagian! While Augustine hoped for the impossible, that is, to obey God's commands with divine help, and polemicized against the Stoic account of fate,[177] Augustinus states, 'Stop hoping for the impossible … accept your fate as a human being.'[178]

Petrarch's Augustine becomes a Stoic insofar as he speaks in this text of reason eliminating desires and states that he has nothing in common with his body, that visible things are dirty.[179] This renunciation of the body is at odds with Augustine's deepest insights: The point is not to renounce the body but to turn desire in body and soul, in its wholeheartedness, towards God. While Augustine privileges the heart, Petrarch's Stoic reading of him privileges a self-sufficient will.

The Stoical/Pelagian Augustine which we find in Petrarch is one whose self-withdrawal from the world is a self-exploration that ends with the power of self-expression of that self. This power of self-expression is one which finds in itself, as a singular being, through the voice of its conscience, a realm of self-awareness in which the relations to God and nature are radically separated. In this realm, world and self are disjoined. Petrarch ends *The Secret* with an either/or: care of the self *or* desire for the world.[180] But self-knowledge here is knowledge of the self as he struggles to find a place with respect to nature and God. The self that engages here looks forward to the day in which the call of the world is silent, but this silence does not allow it to hear another call but rather to care for itself. The self which is here at issue is a self beyond all conditions of the world, a self which is an expression of its own will. The goal is not self-knowledge in Augustine's sense, where the knowledge of self goes hand in hand with a knowledge of God, where indeed to know himself he must first love God, but rather a process of self-creation through which he can aim towards his own perfection. In the silence of the world and the silence of the inscrutable divine will, the self is free to express its own being as for the first time.

The very idea of self-formation becomes transformed through the Modern Age, from the classical account of self-discipline in relation to reason or exemplary figures or in the love of God, to the concept of 'self-creation'. The latter term comes quite late; indeed, it seems as if it was only first attested in the nineteenth century, the very notion of human creation itself being even then an apparent oxymoron. Nevertheless, the idea that the self can form itself such that it becomes its own 'creation' can be seen particularly in the writings of Pico della Mirandola. In his 'Oration on the Dignity of Man', della Mirandola emphasizes the exceptional human indeterminacy of nature. This thought of the human as indeterminate in nature is not new, of course. It forms the basis of the Prometheus myth, whereby there were no qualities left for the gods to give humanity, and therefore Prometheus made the human walk upright and gave to the human the possession of fire. In Christian thought, fallen humanity finds itself between an angel-like fulfilment and falling lower than the 'beasts'. What is new with della Mirandola is the manner in which he stresses the freedom which comes with such indeterminacy. He has God say to the human, 'We have made you neither of heaven nor of earth, neither mortal nor immortal, so that you may, as the free and extraordinary shaper of yourself fashion yourself in whatever form you prefer.'[181] What this means for della Mirandola is to 'become what we wish to be'.[182] There is little trace of Augustinian humility nor Sceptic doubt here. But while the will is free, della Mirandola retains a classic account of a vertical relation of lower and higher; indeed, he speaks in this respect of a 'ladder'. The self makes itself in terms of that vertical scale. It is drawn down by 'the impulses of our passions' and the 'darkness of reason'. Through 'natural philosophy' the self can purify itself in order to fulfil its 'efforts to imitate the angelic way of life'.[183] Such Stoic discipline through philosophy is that which allows the self to know and to overcome nature. Early in the 'Oration' he has told us that the self should 'spurn the terrestrial, disdain the celestial [i.e. astronomy and astrology], disregarding all that is of the world, hasten to the otherworldy court that is near the most eminent Divinity'.[184] The knowledge of nature is a step on the way to the supernatural, where 'we shall be made perfect with the felicity of theology'.[185] The theological is literally not of this world; philosophy is that which by its use of its will the self can employ to transcend the worldly and then as a fulfilment of its efforts, be made perfect by God's revelation of himself. In opposition to Stoicism, della Mirandola affirms that philosophy does not give peace; that can only come from 'her mistress, that is, of the most holy Theology'.[186] Only God can give peace, but he does so in response to human effort. This effort ends in a somewhat Gnostic fashion, with initiation into divine mysteries.[187] The dignity of man is here not proclaimed as an egalitarian thesis but rather as that which can be attained by the few, who can make themselves into worthy recipients of divine mysteries.

The fundamental difference of Augustine to any Stoic or Pelagian discourse lies in his rejection of self-assertion – or indeed self-making – in the order of fulfilment for the self. The fulfilment that arises through this means, that of *apatheia*, Augustine understands as a resistance to the love of God.[188] *Apatheia* cannot function as an ideal for Augustine because the will is not sovereign and freedom cannot be detached from desire. Freedom in a Stoic sense requires a non-temporal self, a self which is capable of reaching *within itself* an atemporal moment: *Apatheia* implies *achronia*. This is inherent in the Stoic will, a will to assent and dissent. To will or nill, to be in that between of willing and nilling, is to stand before not only the world but also the self and to cut a caesura in the being of world and self. Such a withdrawal is a movement beyond time to an eternal presence, the *nous* as divine within the self. For Augustine, however, the self in all its actions simply reinforces, reaffirms, its own temporal being, as the states at the end of his long discussion of time in Book Eleven of the *Confessions*: 'You, my Father, are eternal. But I am divided between time gone by and time to come.'[189] It does so because its every act and thought pursues a movement of desire within it, which leads the self either outwards to the objects of its carnal desires or inwards to the self which finds itself precisely as and when it finds God within itself. The 'within' here is understood in a radically anti-Stoical manner.

The Pelagian/Stoic/Augustinian response to the crises of world, reason and faith gave various possibilities for understanding the self. The picture, however, is incomplete without including the final face of selfhood, namely, the Sceptic. Indeed, the Augustinian, Stoic and Pelagian variations of the self helped form the basic presuppositions which made Scepticism attractive in Modernity. World as the intersection of human, nature and God rooted in the gratuitous act of creation and characterized by fundamental events of the Fall, the Incarnation and the Second Coming was for much of the Common Era anchored in Platonic and then Augustinian terms or Aristotelian/Thomistic ones. Each assumed an inner harmony of these three elements and each assumed that reason infused or supported by grace could in principle come to an understanding of the fundamental principles governing the interrelation of these different relata of world. The meaning of each of these terms was dependent on these relations, at least from the human point of view, and human responsibility lay in its mode of response to the revelation and nature (in it and around it). Voluntarism undermined this inner harmony, and the movements of self-knowledge, of self-responsibility and of self-assertion all gave voice to a crisis of world which resulted. The Sceptical response to this crisis marked the literary, religious and scientific discourses of the period.

What occurs in this period is a strange and unexpected Christianization of Scepticism.[190] This Christianization is unexpected because from Augustine through to the fifteenth century, Pyrrhonianism was practically unknown in the West. What was known of Ancient Scepticism was that of the Middle Academy – transmitted through

Faces of the Self in the Emergence of Modernity

of Cicero's account.[191] In Ancient Christianity certain common ... between Scepticism and Christianity, in particular their ... pretensions to knowledge. Augustine was deeply influenced ... thought and understood it as a necessary corrective to human ...ions he rejected above all because they ended in pride, which hid ...manity on God. But it is precisely in this respect that Augustine ... to reverse the Sceptical move. He puts it in *De Utilitate Credendi*: 'I ...th was hidden except insofar as the means for searching for it was ...ins should be taken from some divine authority.'[192] In *Against the* ...ms the philosophers of the Middle Academy enemies of knowledge, ...eeking illumination through God, they remain satisfied to stay in ...tion he traces psychologically to fear of error, which in the end ...pping the limits of the self's own powers of cognition.[193] At issue ...tanding of wisdom. For the Sceptic, wisdom is achieved through the suspension of belief where there is no evidential basis to assert ...true. As such, the wise man refuses to assent to the non-evidential and ...instead in a state of *aporia*. Living in that state is one of peace, tranquillity (*ataraxia*). Such a state cannot give the Christian tranquillity according to Augustine (and orthodox Christianity generally) because he seeks salvation as a gift from that which lies outside himself, that, in other words, which precisely transcend his cognitive powers – the divine authority referred to in the passage quoted above. The Christian in such a view seeks eternal salvation through faith and good works. Nonetheless, to the extent that Scepticism limits the claims of human reason, Augustine's account of grace can be understood as a Sceptical gesture towards the claims to the capacity of human nature. This is all the more so if we remember that the real is hidden or non-evident (*adéla*), according to Sextus.[194] He does not reject the being of the real; indeed, he assumes it. However, that being is hidden from the perceiving self. Similarly for Augustine, God is affirmed but cannot be known in himself. Like the Sceptic seeking after truth, the Augustinian self strives to be with God, while being absent from him. In its Modern transformations, this absence of God becomes radicalized to the *deus absconditus*, whereby no traces of the divine are to be found in nature, they emerge only through grace.[195]

As we have seen, however, Augustine's theology of grace had been stripped of much of its basic assumptions by the theologians of the *via moderna*, and it is precisely this ungrounded Augustinian Christianity which formed the basis in which a renewal of Scepticism, in the form of a Christianized Pyrrhonianism, was possible. What occurred here was momentous and its effects far-reaching, nothing less than the vacating of the ambition to harmonize reason and faith (with respect to Christianity) and the transformation of an eminently worldly philosophy into virtually a propaedeutic to revelation (with respect to Scepticism).

To speak here of Christianization at the origins of Modernity invites comparison with certain theses concerning secularization that we have already discussed, suggesting not so much secularization as the de-Hellenization of Ancient philosophy. The basic intuition of an underlying *logos* in the world, which is shared across almost every school of Ancient philosophy, is lost at the origins of Modernity. In contrast

to Blumenberg, my claim here is that early modernity was n᎒
to the collapse of belief in providence but rather to the radi
providence¹⁹⁶ – such that self-assertion (as stressed by Blu᎒
response only in competition with a quasi-Augustinian faith i᎒
here is not so much the filling of an empty space (Blumenberg) but ᎒
of the world and humanity in the face of deep uncertainty. The t᎒
Scepticism responded to, and fortified, a sense of world loss and led
sense of self-responsibility. However, that self-responsibility only gradua᎒
mantle of autonomy and even then wore that mantle often uneasily.¹⁹⁷ As I ᎒
later chapters, Montaigne, Descartes, Pascal, Hume, Rousseau and Kant all s᎒
express this transformed Scepticism, and in doing so in varying degrees tend ᎒
Pelagian autonomy but fail to escape Augustinian intuitions regarding respons᎒
As in any case of transformation, it is important to see what gets lost here and whe᎒
what is lost remains somewhere beneath the surface.

The transformation of Scepticism is ontological as much as it is epistemological, or rather the epistemological consequences were drawn from an ontology rooted in theological uncertainty. The epistemological consequences themselves are entwined with ethical ones. From Montaigne through Pierre Gassendi, Descartes and Pascal and then on to Hume and Kant, the issue of Scepticism was understood in terms of a distinction of appearance and being, in which the being of things was hidden due to its origins in the mind of God. The origins of things, their inner nature, was that which was created by a God, whose ideas were closed off to human reason. Scepticism, by remaining at the level of appearances, provided a discourse that allowed this to be thought. If the origin of things is hidden, if the nature of things cannot be perceived, appearances signify nothing of the world but rather of the one perceiving. Thus is opened up the vista of a worldless subject facing an alienated nature created by God, but vacated of any divine presence. The issue of responsibility here is not first a Sceptical, but rather a theological, question concerning will and grace, to which Sceptical answers become possible. But these are answers to questions fundamentally different, indeed radically removed from, the questions to which Ancient Scepticism, especially Pyrrhonianism, was an answer.¹⁹⁸ The extent of this difference is already manifest in certain key issues of translation and interpretation at the very beginnings of the appropriation of the texts of Sextus.

Works of Sextus were first translated into Latin in the sixteenth century by Henricus Stephanus in 1562 and Gentian Hervet in 1569. A number of issues in these translations are significant regarding the reception of the Pyrrhonian Scepticism in Modernity. When in the Greek Sextus uses the term *aporia*, or the verb *aporein* or derivative terms, the translations systematically translate with *dubitare*, *dubitatio* and its derivatives.¹⁹⁹ When, for example, Sextus speaks of the Pyrrhonian being in a state of *aporia* concerning everything, 'ten peri panton aporian', Herveti translates, '*dubitationem de rebus ominibus* (doubting of all things)'.²⁰⁰ This is an important shift in meaning. Sextus uses the term *aporia* to refer to the state of having no way through, a state in which we find ourselves when we cannot decide between two contrary arguments. The translators transform this into the state of doubt. While *aporia*, at least as Sextus accounts for it, can lead to tranquillity, doubt is beset by anxiety.

When Sextus speaks about living without belief (*pistis*), the translators tend to change his meaning. In place of belief they translate *dogma*: Living without belief becomes living without dogma.[201] For the translators of Sextus the consequence of Sceptical arguments is not to live without belief but to believe non-dogmatically, to live that is with beliefs while accepting them to be without sufficient rational grounding, to be matters of faith. To live without belief would be to live without faith, but precisely this is what remains unthinkable for them. Related to this is a further issue of translation. Sextus distinguishes sharply between *hypokeimenon* and *phainomenon*. *Hypokeimenon* would have been quite familiar for his sixteenth-century translators through reference to Aristotle's Greek, generally translated as *subiectus*, but was often understood as equivalent to *substantia* – substance. *Phainomenon* was translated by *apperentis* – appearance. But in understanding Sextus, this distinction was routinely understood as one between inner experience and the external world.[202] This followed from understanding *aporia* as doubt and *pistis* as dogma. It betrays a certain Augustinianism in the reading of Sextus, where the place of faith becomes the inner domain and living without dogma becomes understood as not requiring external validation. But it involved a reading back into Sextus's text concerns which were not his. He was concerned with how to justify the inference from the way an object appears and that object as it is in its own nature.[203] This corresponds to the distinction he draws between the phenomenal and the noumenal. There is no claim here to an inner domain somehow different from or otherwise than the external world of appearances.

So we have here a transformation whereby those who for Sextus do not doubt become known as doubters (which for Sextus were the Academic Sceptics) in Modernity. A superficial reason for this is that differences between Pyrrhonian and Academic Scepticism were ignored and the Pyrrhonians read in terms of the Academics with which (through Augustine and Cicero) his translators and early interpreters were already familiar. The more fundamental answer, however, has to do with concerns relating to conflicts over the content of faith. The letter of dedication to Cardinal Charles of Lorraine, which Hervetus wrote for his translation of the *Outlines of Pyrrhonianism*, recommended this book as a weapon in the critique of Calvinism: The overly rationalist claims of the Calvinist could be countered by a critique of the very pretension of reason to decide on matters of faith.[204] But also for those who were troubled by these religious conflicts such as Montaigne, Erasmus and Gassendi, Scepticism offered equanimity in the face of conflict: They showed that the certainty with which both sides held their positions was misplaced. The Pyrrhonist argument against criteria to decide disputes leads potentially to a total breakdown: Between the criterion of individual conscience and that of the Church authority there is nothing to choose. In the Catholic response to this situation, the argument then becomes one of conservatism: In the absence of compelling criteria, it is simply presumption to argue for change. Equally, however, such a consideration can bolster the argument for reform: The authority of the past cannot itself serve as a criterion better than any other.[205] The response to such a situation was not one of *aporia* and living without belief, but rather one of choosing without sufficient reason, choosing namely through faith. The point was not one of reaching an aporetic state of tranquillity but of 'annihilating his judgment to make more room for faith', as Montaigne puts it.[206] In this sense one can see a movement from Scepticism as a way of life (as it was for Sextus) to an instrumental employment of Scepticism in the conflict of faiths.

The Christian Sceptic cannot find tranquillity in *aporia* for two fundamental reasons. First, the Christian is seeking salvation and as such hopes for a presence beyond the limits of her own experience. This hope is justified by faith in the witness of the Gospels and as such requires an affirmation, an act of assent whether through faith or through reason. In an Augustinian and Thomistic framework, where faith seeks understanding, this assent can be justified by reason, albeit reason infused with grace. The Voluntarist revolution and the related Pelagianization of Augustinianism leads to a separation of faith from reason and grace from nature, and this leads to a receptivity to the Pyrrhonist refusal of a move from appearance to truth – thus from nature to grace, from rational argument to claims of knowledge of God – and at the same time deafness to the Pyrrhonian message of a tranquil life this side of appearance, reason and nature. Rather, the life lived in response to Pyrrhonism had strong Stoic elements – a life of self-control, ascetic restraint and a certain resignation but at the same time a life lived in the hope of grace, understood as a gift from elsewhere, as an intervention in the life of responsible and self-knowing beings. Second, the separation of faith and reason makes doubtful the rationalist presupposition of an underlying cosmology, an underlying order of the world. The Ancient Sceptic does not doubt this *logos* but simply critiques the assumption of having transcended the *logos* manifest to the self to the *logos* of things as such; the Modern Christian Sceptic, on the other hand, makes no such assumption: The very *logos* of the world is in question. Paradoxically, it is precisely in response to the loss of belief in that assumption of order – a belief which allows the Ancient Sceptic to reach his state of tranquillity – that motives the Christian turn to Scepticism.

The formation of the Modern self responds to a situation of collapse. Finding the maps of the past out of focus with new realities, wandering through lands with the same place names but no longer appearing as their inherited pictures still represented them, it was necessary to piece experience together again anew. The four faces looked out towards a not yet written history and projected God, Nature and Humanity into new relations of verticals and horizontals. This was a long process, and starting with Montaigne, philosophers turned to face an uncertain future and in so doing reformed the self and formed something that had not been possible before this: a self ontologically distinct and independent, living anxiously or contentedly in a world where God remained hidden.

2

Montaigne: Sceptical alterity

If Descartes is the 'father of Modern philosophy', Montaigne is the father of the Modern self. In his work, for the first time, the self is the central concern. With him arises the idea of the 'essay', the probing, testing, piece of writing, which in his hands was a means of both discovering and inventing his self.[1] His essays can be understood as both autobiography and a fundamental questioning of the possibility of *auto*biography. He faces his reader and does so not with a 'perfect face' but with his own. However, this is a face which changes constantly.[2] There is no master narrative of this self: 'I do not portray being: I portray passing', and he goes on to claim that he is doing something unprecedented: 'I am the first to [communicate with the people] … by my entire being.'[3] While Augustine begins and ends with creation – hence with the whole of God's domain of which he is but a small part – yet in doing so draws a coherent, linear narrative of himself, Montaigne goes out from himself only to return to himself; nothing is spoken of which is not in relation to he who speaks and writes of it, but what we have is a fragmented, temporally complex, patchwork: not so much of a life as of a point of view on life.[4]

In Montaigne we find a sustained, if enigmatic, attempt to practice in the texts of his *Essays* a Sceptical reflexivity, an exercise in self-exploration in a 'world' of radical difference. He achieves a form of tranquillity, a tranquillity found not through philosophical reflection, not through aporetic stasis, but rather as the atmosphere in which he moves, an open reflection on himself and the world carried out in 'learned ignorance'.[5] For Montaigne, the claim to knowledge – in the sense of a comprehensive understanding of its object, or in the sense of grasping truths which we can know to be true, or even of representing something in the world as it is – is presumptuous in the specific sense of asserting a privilege not only for the self's finite experience but also for an experience at one time over another. The undoing of such a claim is achieved not on the basis of experience alone but rather through the self-reflective power that reason has given the self, the exercise of which affirms the Voluntarist thesis concerning the limited efficacy of human efforts and the omnipotence of God.

Montaigne writes in the midst of turmoil and civil war, where religious pretext can incite friends, family members and servants to become his enemies. Montaigne withdraws to his castle, but the nature of the war is such that he cannot know where he might be in danger. He turns to face such danger with a countenance which is open and frank, stating that defence is the start of war. In the face of enemies or potential enemies he does not attempt to disguise himself but rather to approach all with an open face and heart.⁶ By not treating the other as enemy, he recognizes the difference between friend and enemy but refuses to engage that difference with enmity. He presents his self to others in its changing aspects, not as a fixed identity. In doing this he takes up Epictetus's motif of the stage;⁷ however, he stresses not the role of the director (as Epictetus does) but that of the actor, specifically how the parts he plays relate to the inner self. In playing many parts on the stage of life – as a judge and landowner, as advisor to the future king, Henry of Navarre, as husband, son, father, master and so forth – Montaigne seeks to unmask himself and show the self which plays these parts in a way that is both specific to himself and yet exemplifies what it is to live life where the efficacy and the legitimacy of the roles the self plays are questioned and jeopardized. The self which emerges is a self in a time of crisis, or a self which the crisis of the times discloses. Indeed, while the term 'crisis' would have been known to Montaigne only in its medical sense, as the point in the illness which is decisive for recovery or not, the self Montaigne probes and explores decides only provisionally, playing its roles while never forgetting the vulnerability of being a self without certainty or guarantee.⁸

Readers of Montaigne are often puzzled by certain apparent inconsistencies: He claims to suspend judgement, yet makes judgements; he claims to be Christian and yet seems to relativize Christian claims; he demonstrates often extreme credulity about stories of fabulous events and yet claims to be a Sceptic. Indeed, the texts of the *Essays* are replete with contradictions. Such contradictions are, however, deliberate. They are not to be explained away but rather can be seen to lie at the core of his Sceptical project. The world as he approaches it is a sea of contra-dictions, of statements and counterstatements, of beliefs true and heretical, of countenances faced off in conflict. His reflections, those as he terms them, of an 'unpremeditated and accidental philosopher',⁹ are an acceptance of the relativity of points of view and an openness to the validity of such diverse and multiple viewpoints as the world of his birth is disintegrating around him.

Pyrrhonian Scepticism as we saw in the previous chapter tended to be employed in the defence of Catholicism, and this is true of Montaigne. Many commentators do see in him only an outward acceptance of Catholicism masking an agnosticism, if not atheism,¹⁰ forgetting what Lucien Lefebvre has shown, namely, that the sixteenth century has neither the philosophical nor scientific resources for such unbelief.¹¹ Such commentators also require us to read Montaigne as continually insincere.¹² In examining how Montaigne explores and constructs his self, what we find is a novel and daring transformation of the Graeco-Roman and Christian models of the self, but one that is self-consciously developing a way of being: a Christian self, but one which could no longer live in terms of the world of Medieval Catholicism, while refusing the path of the Reformation. Having said that, the Montaigne who emerges in these *Essays* is not, as many have claimed, a fideist.¹³ Even ignoring the anachronism of the term itself, the *Essays* do not bear out a radical split between faith and reason. There is for Montaigne a reasonableness in faith (and a fidelity in reason), but one which can no longer be supported by scholastic systems. Reason and faith are deeply personal issues for Montaigne. They concern the ways in which the self understands itself and the world around it, how the self lives in uncertainty, doubt and hope. In this,

Montaigne's concerns are not simply theoretical. He is seeking to understand himself and the world around him in order to know how to live in a world that can no longer be understood philosophically as *cosmos* – as an ordered space of entities – but rather as the space of competing and contradictory customs, beliefs, viewpoints and, above all, anthropologies. The exploration of the self is crucial because he – and each of his readers – can no longer appeal to any unquestioned authority.

This chapter is divided into five sections. The first concerns the difference between the own self and the stranger that is fundamental to Montaigne's Sceptical thinking (2.1). Underlying the discussion and employment of this difference is an understanding of experience, which is the theme of the second section (2.2). Throughout the *Essays*, Montaigne understand the self as a linguistic being. Montaigne's account of the linguistic being as the recipient of grace will be discussed in this third section (2.3). For Montaigne, philosophy is concerned with how to live a life, and in this regard questions of happiness and virtue are of central importance. The fourth section discusses these themes in relation to the fundamental sense of the contingency of things, the passions, the body and the goal of tranquillity (2.4). The most enigmatic but central essay of the whole book is the 'Apology for Raymond Sebond'. The concerns of that essay, namely, the relation of faith and reason, are examined with respect to the figure of the Sceptical self (2.5).

2.1 Openness to the strange

The Sceptical movement of Montaigne's thought begins in a refusal to take himself as a measure for the other. The *Essays* centre around his self, yet his thought gives no privilege to the self or the same. 'I do not share the common error of judging an other by myself,' he says.[14] Yet, he also states, 'The opinion I give of them [things about which he speaks, specifically books in the context of this remark] is to declare the measure of my sight, not the measure of things.'[15] The only measure he has is that of his own sight; he can only measure things as he finds them, as they appear to him. He makes a judgement, according to his own measure, but he cannot trust his own judgement. As such, the common error is not to judge an other by the measure of oneself, but rather the failure of a self-reflexive corrective that recognizes the fallibility of such judgement, its inherent weakness. Such fallibility pertains not only to Montaigne but also to the 'we' with whom he identifies – Christian Europeans: They have as little right to claim to be a measure of other cultures. His famous essay 'On Cannibals' is a masterly exercise in undermining the claim to cultural superiority.[16] The barbarism of the 'savages' is more than matched by the barbarism of the 'civilized' in his account. This essay (and these sentiments are repeated in other essays) is a Sceptical denial of the certainty Europeans felt in their claims to be the measure of true humanity. The point for Montaigne is not to establish such a universal measure but rather in its anarchic absence to challenge the basis of his own judgements, thereby showing up the limits of his own world and experience. Implicit in Montaigne's account is the claim that any appeal to a neutral measure is either delusional or disguises the appeal to oneself as measure. It is delusional insofar as it claims a viewpoint beyond the specificity of the self that only God can have or it is a disguise because it subjects the strange to the customary, which of course is customary only for a specific self and the people to whom he belongs. He states, 'Not that experience has since shown me anything surpassing my first beliefs, and that through no fault of my curiosity, but reason has taught me that to condemn a thing thus, dogmatically, as false and impossible is to assume the advantage of knowing the bounds and limits of God's will and of the power of our mother Nature.'[17]

What is a measure of things for the self is not derived from a divine-like judgement but rather is based on his 'first beliefs', those beliefs inculcated in him by his background, which arbitrarily limit the range of the true and possible. Montaigne begins with a sense of heterogeneity, of diversity, and refuses either a claim to unique truth in his own range of understanding or any route to fulfil such a claim. The most rational response to such a situation for Montaigne is the Pyrrhonian one:[18] to suspend judgement. In introducing their 'sacramental word' *epoché*, Montaigne parses it as meaning: 'I hold back, I do not budge'.[19] The withdrawal is itself an assertion, in stepping back from judgement the self asserts a position. This ambiguity is central to understanding how the Pyrrhonian is the gateway to the self for him. The withdrawal from judgement is at the same time a withdrawal from the world. The philosophical attitude requires a stepping back in which the comedy of the world becomes apparent. Life is more comedy than tragedy, because the self is more worthless than wretched. This is so because the self continues to hide its own vulnerabilities through the vanity with which it enacts roles in the theatre of life.[20] Viewing all of this as comedy, the Sceptic sees the self as it makes itself in its movement of position-taking towards the world. This is a poetic power in the self, which understands the place of the self as being in a world without a preordained trajectory.[21] In taking up a position, the self comes to see that its judgements, while claiming to be valid for all, are in fact expressions of itself. But, as he states, 'either we can judge absolutely or we absolutely cannot'.[22] To judge absolutely is to judge from a non-relative position, precisely that divine place unavailable to the self – the self is an actor, and if also an audience member this is so only from its own position as actor. Its judgements then are not statements of truth but rather statements of how things appear to it. To judge by appearance is to judge in terms of the impression on the self, not the object itself. The diversity of opinions is for Montaigne – following the Pyrrhonian trope – demonstrative of this claim about judgement. If it were the case that the 'original essence of things' imprinted itself on each person as it is in itself, then there would be no plurality of opinions.[23] But, in fact, things appear to us relative to our judgements and desires: 'Things in themselves (*les choses à part elles*) may have their own weights and measures and qualities; but once inside, within us, she [the soul] allots them their qualities as she sees fit.'[24]

The self knows things as they appear to it. That appearance is the product of both the qualities of the things appearing and the self's own receptivity to those qualities. Montaigne never calls the real appearing of things into question; the trope of illusion is brought up only once and then with respect to miracles, and when he speaks of dreams it is not in the context of a Sceptical argument.[25] He rarely disbelieves his senses, nor the testimony of others. This is quite consistent: Things are only as they appear to him, his account begins from that relation to things through their appearance. The thing as it is in itself remains hidden and unknown; what is known to him is the thing as it appears. The philosophical question concerns how the appearance is. A fundamental duality in appearance is between inner and outer, with respect to the self, other selves and things in a more general sense. When Montaigne says that strangers only see the outward appearance in us,[26] this statement can also be reversed: We only see the outward appearance in the stranger. Indeed, Montaigne states this somewhat paradoxically: 'A sound intellect will refuse to judge men simply by their outward actions; we must probe the inside and discover what springs set men in motion. But since this is an arduous and hazardous undertaking, I wish fewer people would meddle with it.'[27] These sentences come at the end of an essay on the 'inconsistency of our actions'. The self is a self-contradictory being, if understood as having an unchanging identity. In fact, Montaigne argues, experience shows us both in ourselves and in others that we are buffeted both by circumstances and our own 'unstable posture' such that 'anyone who observes carefully can hardly find himself twice in the same state'.[28] Inner and outer, self and stranger, mirror each other[29] in terms of such fundamental inconsistency: The outward appearance shows the response of a fleeting self to changing circumstances. While I cannot know the stranger, neither do I know myself, if knowledge means something solid and constant. Nonetheless, the self has a certain priority: in the end it is the self which experiences and I am aware of myself experiencing. Montaigne can aim at his thoughts (*pour visée à mes pensées*) and 'follow a movement so wandering as that of [his] mind ... penetrate the opaque depths of its innermost folds.'[30] Nevertheless, 'there is no witness so sure as each man to himself'.[31] Indeed, he asserts 'that no man ever treated a subject he knew and understood better than I do the subject I have undertaken'.[32]

All things are in flux, including his self, for Montaigne. That he understands himself better than anything else does not mean that he has come to a full understanding of himself. Rather, Montaigne's point is that all claims to knowledge are rooted in those appearances, which are the products of a happening of appearance here in this self that he is. All other claims to knowledge are derivative from this fundamental level. However, the self is not transparent to itself. The soul's actions of allotting qualities occurs behind the back of the self in its normal dealings. This is because the self is normally engaged with things, orientated towards them and the goals at which it aims. In Husserl's terms, the self is in the 'natural attitude'.[33] Montaigne states, 'The world always looks straight ahead; as for me, I turn my gaze inwards.'[34] This inward gaze is not to be mistaken for a turn towards ideas in the mind, as later with Descartes and Locke. The inward gaze, rather, goes hand in hand with the primary method of the work, namely essaying: taking forays into diverse topics and testing himself in those forays. The self-testing involved is a letting free of his fancies, through the encounter with foreign matters. This form of inquiry Montaigne understands as doubt, in the sense that it implies no privileged standpoint and indeed is a Sceptical stance: 'If to philosophize is to doubt, as they say, then to play the fool and to follow my fancies as I do is all the more to doubt.'[35] This is doubt because it questions the claim to ultimacy of any given position. There is an implicit normative claim here, that such 'essays' allow the self to encounter that which is strange to it in its strangeness – which is not to say in itself (as its strangeness is in relation to the perceiving self) but as a claim to be which is no more or no less valid than the self's own. Montaigne's 'credulity' in acceptance of testimony, sometimes quite bizarre and incredible, far from being an exception to his Scepticism, actually confirms it.[36] This is so because Montaigne begins from the premise – stated in the context of a discussion of testimony – that 'it is a dangerous and fateful presumption to disdain what we do not comprehend'.[37] Presumption is the cardinal sin for Montaigne; it is the closest he comes to affirming an original sin: a fundamental failing within human nature. It offends against humility and characterizes a basic dishonesty or insincerity, namely, when we claim the capacity to judge beyond our own powers. 'The man who is presumptuous of his knowledge does not yet know what knowledge is.'[38] This is so because what presumption ignores is the source of the claim to know in that happening of appearing between self and thing known and within the self in the operation of its imagination and desires.

Each self and each collectivity of selves (cultures, peoples, religions, etc.) produce ideas, fancies, which seem true to them. In such a context, Montaigne avers that 'there is no fancy so frivolous and so extravagant that it does not seem to me quite suitable to the production of the human mind. We who deprive our judgment of the right to make decisions look mildly on opinions different from ours; and if we do not lend them our judgement, we easily lend then our ears.'[39] In making judgements, the self is stating that something appears to be thus for it. This is not a claim to know; indeed, Montaigne states, 'There is virtually nothing that I know I know.'[40] Reason teaches him not to consider what is outside his own experience as false and impossible, when it is testified to by others, because to do so would be to claim knowledge of the thing from the point of view of God and nature. Where Montaigne does express incredulity he does so by a drawing of limits which is prudential but can never be evacuated of all traces of arbitrariness, through the use of the formula 'they say …, but I think …'

Strange and familiar, then, are relative terms which refer not to the nature of things but rather to the effects of habit: Habituation makes the strange seem familiar, and through habit customs are formed. Montaigne asks rhetorically, 'Is there any opinion so bizarre … that habit has not planted and established it by law in the regions where she saw fit to do so.'[41] What was strange now may in time no longer appear so: 'Habit has led me not to perceive the strangeness of this action'.[42] Significantly, so understood, habit functions in tandem with nature. Habit functions through a making similar of the dissimilar, making the bizarre – the strange – seem normal. Such differences are themselves the product of nature for Montaigne: 'Nature has committed herself to make nothing separate that was not different.'[43] There is no nature or naturalness against which to compare and measure custom, because custom is instituted out of habit, which is a mode of being with and in nature.[44] Nature in this view is opposed to custom in a very specific sense: Custom delimits actions as allowed and as not, while there is nothing out of harmony with nature.[45] Montaigne makes this point with reference to monstrosities: What is monstrous is so only from the partial view of custom, but 'I do not see the whole of anything; nor do those who promise to show it to us'.[46] This applies to actions as much as to singular entities. We cannot appeal to any nature, either anthropological or cosmological, to guide our actions. The only guide we have is custom (the laws of conscience themselves are born there[47]). Nature functions as a negative idea: Nature is the realm of difference and possibility. It is a constant producing of possibility in and through difference. But the self's actions as delimiting one set of possibilities over others is always partial, always customary in the sense of being enacted within a dialectic of familiarity and strangeness.

'There is nothing that custom will not or cannot do.'[48] This statement recalls the words of the book of Genesis, that there is nothing which is impossible for God.[49] Montaigne understands possibility in a highly fecund sense. The world is full of possibilities and there is no absolute limit to the realization of possibilities. This is a fundamentally anti-Aristotelian position, whereby in effect Montaigne reverses the priority of actuality over potentiality in Aristotle and in so doing transforms potentiality into possibility.[50] An actual entity has potentiality, has capacities which are inherent in it, natural to it, and are realizable according to the nature of that entity. Basic to this is the notion of telos and form. Montaigne rejects both accounts: The purpose of things is known only to God. However, Montaigne suggests that the very idea of purpose in the Aristotelian sense is mistaken. He forms himself, and that self formation is the result of his own natural inclinations and the circumstances in which he finds himself: 'By long usage this form of mine has turned into substance, and fortune into nature.'[51] At a more basic level this is true of all things: They are moulded and mould themselves through the circumstances in which they find themselves. There is no telos and no form in things, because all things are particular and singular. The only truly universal quality is diversity.[52] No later Modern philosopher is more forthright than Montaigne in his rejection of any notion of a final cause.[53]

Beyond the play of familiarity and strangeness is God, to whom alone the 'knowledge of causes belongs'.[54] God is understood by Montaigne in terms of will; the divine will is opaque to human beings. Doubt is the appropriate stance of philosophy because it takes place in the face of the authority of the divine will: 'My master is the authority of the divine will, which ... has its place above these vain human wranglings.'[55] The divine will stands as the unreachable measure of truth: In the face of its authority, philosophy can only have the negative task of doubting, not in order to deny truth nor to reach the tranquillity of aporetic stasis but rather to develop a self-reflective sense within the self of its own contingency and finitude.[56] Because of this there is a flattening out of the relation between human and divine. Nothing in the world gives privileged access to God, but by the same token everything is potentially a sign of the divine. The closest to a polemical tone in the *Essays* comes in his discussion of miracles. This simmering polemic arises a number of times with surprising forthrightness in the context of discussions of the Imagination ('Of the Power of the Imagination'), Custom ('Of Custom' and 'Of Experience'), Truth and Falsity ('It is Folly to measure the True and False by our own Capacity'), the Ordinary ('Of the resemblance of children to fathers') and Deformity ('Of Cripples'). The tone and content of the discussion remains constant. He does not deny the testimony regarding miracles but rather the understanding of what is being described as miraculous. He does so because to speak of something as miraculous is only possible on the basis of a claim to know nature. Hence, when he states that 'miracles arise from our ignorance of nature',[57] he does not mean that what appears miraculous can be explained by scientific laws but rather that what appears miraculous is simply that in nature which is beyond what we are accustomed to experiencing and beyond that for which reason can account.[58] Thus, the miraculous and the monstrous have the same origin, namely, the self's response to that which is beyond its ken.[59] Here again the problem is a lack of self-reflexive attention. Familiarity simply makes the self blind to what is wondrous all around it: 'I have seen no more evident monstrosity and miracle in the world than myself. … The more I frequent myself and know myself, the more my deformity astonishes me, and the less I understand myself.'[60] Reason seeks causes and in so doing places things including the self in relation to form and ends, but in attending to the thing as it appears, what we find is that which no account in terms of form and ends can explain. For Montaigne this is the sign of the divine: Things in the world including himself cannot be accounted for except by God; the point of philosophy is to learn how to live in a world grown strange to his sight.

The possible as the really possible, as that which has been made possible, is for Montaigne not what we can conceive of but that of which we have credible testimony. On the basis of such testimony we can engage in what Husserl calls 'free variation' of the real.[61] However, this variation does not lead us back to essences (as it does for Husserl) but rather multiplies difference. The basic principle of Montaigne's logic is to distinguish:[62] Things and states are related not in their similarity but in their difference. What the self encounters in its experience of the world and in reflection on its own states is difference. Nothing presents itself which does not contain in itself some difference.[63] In reflecting on these variations – both in the self's own experience and in the testimony of others – what we find are contradictions: incompatible ways of doing and perceiving. Indeed, these contradictions are found not only between different customs but also within the self between past and present. Such contradictions should not offend reason; they only do so when reason makes presumptuous claims. It is rather so that such contradictions confirm a fundamental experience of reason: 'There is no reason which does not have its opposite, says the wisest school of philosophers [namely the Pyrrhonists].'[64] In an earlier essay, 'Of Custom', he states, 'Human reason is a tincture infused in about equal strength in all our opinions and ways, whatever their form: infinite in substance and infinite in diversity.'[65] The claim here is that reason is infused, is something external and like a tincture changes the quality of that into which it is infused. In other words, for the one habituated to a particular custom or set of customs the reasons for them do not arise: It is in the encounter with the stranger that she has either to give reasons for her actions or seeks to find such reasons. Customs do not derive from the reasons; rather, the reasons are like foreign substances used to explain them. The reasons, though, are not arbitrary; they make it possible to discourse about a custom, but by the same token they are infinite: For every possible custom there are possible reasons, often in contradiction with one another. Nor are these reasons to be confused with original causes, which do not so much make the custom intelligible as they weaken it. Furthermore, customs change over time. Speaking of the custom of dress and fashion, Montaigne states, 'One and the same judgment [about a the place of a doublet], in the space of fifteen or twenty years, may be so incredibly inconsistent and frivolous as to adopt two or three opinions that are not merely different but contrary.'[66] The philosophical task is to explore such differences, not in order to unify them into systematic coherency, but rather to show the impossibility of such systematicity. Montaigne's style reflects this fundamental claim to difference: 'I may indeed contradict myself now and then; but truth, as Demades said, I do not contradict. If my mind could gain a firm footing, I would not make essays, I would make decisions, but it is always an apprenticeship and on trial.'[67]

For Montaigne, the Sceptical does not contradict truth but presupposes it in its movement of self-critique and openness to the strange.[68] As such, reason has only a negative relation to truth: Employed correctly it shows us the limits of our capacities. This is as much in political and ethical as in epistemological affairs. Reason is anything but self-grounding for Montaigne: It is based on experience, and experience is diverse. For every reason we can give for a belief or an action, the opposite can also be found. He is true to the Pyrrhonian injunctions to suspend judgement (*epoché*), and this brings him to an *aporia*. But he does not rest with this *aporia*.

Throughout the *Essays* Montaigne speaks of three stages of learning, from ignorance to cleverness and finally returning to a reverential ignorance. The most unstable stage is the middle one: It is dangerous because learning can instil false confidence; it is unphilosophical because it does not doubt itself; it is irreligious because it questions all authority. The first stage is dogmatic, but is so not in the philosophical sense, but rather simply as an acceptance of inherited dogmas. The second stage, which arises out of doubt, is similarly dogmatic, but this time culpably so as here is displayed overconfidence in one's own reasoning. This is the stage of error for Montaigne, error in the sense of closedness: despising those who 'stick to the old ways', but failing to see the limitations of one's own capacity for judgement. Error here is not a matter of specific mistakes or misunderstandings, but a self-reflective error: the failure to reflect on the finitude of their own perspective.[69] The Sceptical movement of thought arises in this middle region, but when carried through, it brings us to the third stage. With respect to the passions, the middle realm between the 'noble impassibility of the Stoics' and 'plebeian stupidity' 'harbors tempests'.[70] While Montaigne modestly speaks of himself as belonging to the plebeian and ignorant group, his essays clearly seek to move through the middle realm to reach a philosophical state. In Paul Ricoeur's terms we could speak of this as a movement to a 'post-critical' or 'second naiveté',[71] a state of return to the pre-philosophical living in the immediacy of things, but now non-dogmatically, in recognition of the contingency of the world.[72] The *aporia* that opens up through Sceptical reflection between the first fruits of dogmatic reasoning and the familiar beliefs he has inherited arises in the shadows of the example of those 'at the extreme limit of Christian intelligence',[73] who return to the familiar, not however any more experienced as familiar, but rather as that which continues to inspire the mind to reverence and obedience. The Sceptical becomes in this way a moment in a dialectic of return whereby the strangeness of the familiar is recognized. The familiar is no longer the self-evident; it is in some instances the absurd. There is no reason to choose it; Sceptical doubt leaves the mind in a state of indifference. For Montaigne this state of indifference can be maintained, but wisely only to a limited degree. Custom, he says, is that from which I should withdraw myself in thought but not in action.[74] But such a withdrawal in thought is not absolute; it rather marks a certain mood of equanimity in which the wise take a mental distance from custom, not out of presumption but rather out of the recognition of contingency. Montaigne is refusing both the presumption of cleverness and the indifference of the *aporia* because the nature of experience is such that neither can give him tranquillity.

2.2 Experience

The concluding essay of the third and final book of the *Essays* is entitled 'Of Experience'. It can be understood as the essay which recapitulates the movement of his thought and amounts to a meta-reflection on the progress of the work. He commences the essay with an allusion to the beginning of Aristotle's *Metaphysics*: 'There is no desire more natural than the desire for knowledge.'[75] This desire is operative and seeks whichever means available to it. If reason fails, then experience is employed. Ironically, Montaigne states this in the same breath as he says that experience is weaker than reason. But the 'weakness' of experience is that it is led by example, while reason Montaigne understands in Pyrrhonian fashion as supplying grounds for both sides of an argument. In the essay 'Of Presumption' in Book Two, he states, 'The reasons [supplied to justify an argument] have little other foundation than experience, and the diversity of human events offers us infinite examples in all sorts of forms.'[76] Experience is characterized above all by diversity and variety.

Against the Stoic claims about the indifference of the will, Montaigne invites his readers to attend to things in experience and to see 'that nothing presents itself to us in which there is not some difference, however slight; and that either to the sight or to the touch, there is always something extra that attracts us'.[77] Sceptical doubt, as openness to experience, is not simply a seeing of difference but also subject to the allurement of difference. Seeing similarity at the expense of difference is a kind of erotic failing; it is a failure of openness to what appears in its distinctiveness and its relative power of attraction. To be blind to such difference is to use past experience as a measure of the present, to allow familiarity to blunt desire. To blunt desire in this way is to undermine knowledge because 'nature has committed herself to make nothing separate that was not different'.[78] Following this characterization of nature, Montaigne immediately turns to the example of law and says, 'There is as much freedom and latitude in the interpretation of laws as in their creation,' and then in relation to the meaning of the Bible, he dismisses the claim that disputes can be resolved by 'recalling the direct words of the Bible' and exclaims, 'As if there were less animosity and bitterness in commenting than in inventing!'[79] Nothing can simply be read off the objects of experience; the hermeneutical task of interpretation and commentary is in principle no different from the productive task of creating and inventing.

Experience, then, is an intervention that by its nature temporally differentiates and distinguishes. It marks difference, which can be covered over by habit and custom, but the reflective movement of Montaigne's thought is to uncover and track these traces. Experience conflicts with law for Montaigne, because law can never match the variety of human actions: Multiplying laws to match this variety is pointless as law needs always be finite, the diversity of human actions infinite. Law, then, needs to be general and simple – to be the opposite of experience, so that it can apply to most experience through its very formality. Such generality would allow for the specific circumstances of the case to be taken into account 'without being bound by precedents, past or future'.[80] The openness to difference is an openness to that which may appear in the present, an openness to novelty which law undermines. Above all, law offends against justice. The law takes on the form of justice, but 'laws remain in credit not because they are just, but because they are laws'.[81] Justice is not contained in law, and it is a mistake to obey a law on the presumption that it is just. Justice, like truth, remains for Montaigne a negative principle: In the same way as I recognize that my own judgements fail to reach the truth, so too do I see that my actions and the actions of judges (of which Montaigne was one) fail in the goal of justice.[82] That failure, however, is not cause of despair. On the contrary, such failure spurs the mind to further research and exploration, while teaching the mind its 'weakness in general and the treachery of my understanding'.[83] He goes on, 'To learn that we have said or done a foolish thing, that is nothing; we must learn that we are nothing but fools, a far broader and more important lesson.'[84] But this lesson in humility is learned through a dynamic relation of self-overcoming: 'A spirited mind never stops within itself; it is always aspiring and going beyond its strength; it has impulses beyond its powers of achievement ... Its pursuits are boundless and without form, its food is wonder, the chase, ambiguity.'[85]

Experience is a transcending of the past, of immutable laws, of the self, in the events of appearance. But such transcendence testifies not so much to the capacity of the self but rather to its incapacity: Its judgements cannot avoid foolishness as they attempt to give definite form to that which is endlessly deferring coming to form, the passing moments of experience. Self-knowledge in that context is a self-understanding of experience which, however, is only possible if directed towards the negative and empty ideas of nature, truth and justice: negative because unreachable, empty because our judgements always fall short of their goals. As such, the ideas of nature, truth and justice open up for Montaigne the space of possibility, in which there arises novelty. Incapacity leads to self-transcendence which follows nature, not as a fixed domain, but as the source of diversity and variation. Habit can function either positively or negatively in this respect, either making the self blind to novelty and hence to experience, or shaping it 'for change and variation, which is the noblest and most useful of its teachings'.[86] Experience, though forever new, remains by its nature habitual. Habit functions in a double manner: It allows the self to change from one mode of behaviour to its opposite, and it 'imprints its character on me' by making certain practices very difficult to change. In both cases the self becomes habituated to one form of behaviour such that its body takes on that behaviours as its own, but the body as subject to habituation is malleable in different ways.

Experience is embodied and Montaigne pays particular attention to its carnality in terms of desire and of aging. The two are related as one of the signs of aging for him is a cooling of his desires, particularly sexual. There is, however, no aspect of bodily experience that he despises. Quoting Augustine on the vanity of despising the body, he goes on: 'There is no part unworthy of our care in this gift that God has given us; we are accountable for it even to a single hair.'[87] To be is to be as given, as gifted, and there can be no disparaging of any aspect of that gift. Philosophy makes itself ridiculous when it seeks to separate the mind from the body, something which he points out, Socrates 'her [philosophy's] tutor and ours' did not do.[88] Elsewhere Montaigne identifies this as a specifically Christian insight: 'Christians have their own special teaching about this bounding [of body and soul] ... and that God sees the deeds of the whole man, willing that the whole man should receive rewards or punishments according to his merits.'[89] This gift is that of being a creature of nature. Such nature is a guide, but again nature as the maker of difference. What counts for Montaigne is the process of learning in and from such difference, learning to be in the novelty of the specific eventual situation in which the self finds itself. That process is no less bodily than mental, no less habitual than surprising. The measure, such that it is, is in the moment, conditioned as it is both physically and mentally, both by the earthiness of our origins and the anticipation of celestial calling. Against all dualisms of mind and body Montaigne affirms, 'Between ourselves, these two things I have always observed to be in singular accord: supercelestial thoughts and subterranean conduct.'[90] The ironic and conspiratorial tone here simply reinforces Montaigne's concern to avoid all dogmatic claims, while directing thought to the moment and the circumstantial.

Montaigne's concern is an ancient one: to limit the human to the realm of the human and to understand experience in those terms alone. It is madness, he thinks, to attempt to escape from our own humanity. In doing this, 'instead of changing into angels, we change into beasts.'[91] Human experience of difference, variety and change is measured by the negative ideas of nature, truth and justice, but this is no reason to flee this state. On the contrary, it is the ideas of nature, truth and justice which allow us to understand that state correctly, and to understand our place in it with humility. Such humility is one of self-relation: the self-relation of Sceptical honesty, which in its process of self-transcendence never attempts to transcend its own being (as self-transcending). This self-relation is one of enjoyment – 'it is an absolute perfection and virtually divine to know how to enjoy our being rightly.'[92] Such self-enjoyment comes out of a satisfaction with ourselves in the very difference and variety of our own being. Human life in its celestiality and rudeness is not without contradiction, but those contradictions Montaigne understands counter-pointedly as harmony. 'Our life is composed, like the harmony of the world, of contrary things, also of different tones, sweet and harsh, sharp and flat, soft and loud. If a musician liked only one kind, what would he have to say? He must know how to use them and blend them.'[93] To live a life is to live a composition always in progress. It is a self-creative process, but one which creates out of the situation in which the self finds itself, rather than as an imposition on that situation.

We find here what Ann Hartle calls the dialectic movement of Montaigne's thought.[94] Experience is always of a situation and that situation is the self's own. The presumption to escape that situation arises from an over-confidence in the power of reason. Reason is embodied and situated; as self-reflective the self sees both the contingency and the inescapability of its situatedness. This is true also, indeed especially, of religion. Montaigne states, 'We receive our own religion only in our own way and with our own hands and not otherwise than as other religions are received.'[95] He goes on to say, 'We are Christians by the same title as we are Perigordians or Germans.'[96] Two things are being said here: first, that religion no less than nationality is contingent on the self's own realm of familiarity and, second, that this contingent situation is inescapable. It is both contingent *and* necessary that Montaigne is a Christian. The indifference of the will, implicit in the Sceptical *aporia*, is for Montaigne only a moment – albeit and important one – in the movement of thought, because it fails to appreciate that the self is committed before it can ever make a choice. Self-formation is always a self-relation to the familiar and the strange and as such can never abstract itself from what it has received at the origins of its being. Self-relation returns to the familiar, but it returns in the knowledge of its own contingency and limits. This dialectical movement is forever characterised by the Sceptical distance of the *epoché*.

2.3 Language and self

Language functions for Montaigne in two distinct but related ways. On the one hand, his whole project is the linguistic articulation of himself in a text. On the other hand, language fails to reach being or to reach God. The actual language – French – in which he writes is significant. French was not the language of philosophy in the sixteenth century but was developing in this time as a language of literature. Montaigne was not writing philosophy as it was written in the schools. Yet, unlike the schoolmen, Latin was for him his 'mother tongue', having spoken Latin exclusively until the age of six.[97] French was his second language, so in writing of himself he was writing in a language that is not closest to his own heart. In situations of extreme emotion, such as when his father fell in a faint, the 'first words from the depth of [his] entrails' were in Latin.[98] French does not have the force of nature in him but is rather a second nature, habituated in him after leaving his family to go to school. It is in this language, however, that he expresses himself in a book, which for him is not simply a work produced as by an artisan but is 'consubstantial' with him.[99] He shares a being with the book, such that he has no more made the book than the book has made him. Yet, there is an 'I' which has made the book, an 'I' which is doubled in reflecting upon itself. The book incarnates that self-reflection, such that one cannot be without the other. The use of the term 'consubstantial' immediately suggests the formulation of the Nicene creed: '*Deum de Deo, Lumen de Lumine, Deum verum de Deo vero, genitum non factum, consubstantialem Patri* (God from God, Light from Light, true God from true God, begotten, not made, consubstantial with the Father)'. Just as the Father has not made the Son, so too Montaigne has not made the book; he has rather engendered it as a son. Indeed, he uses this metaphor of parenthood elsewhere to describe his work. The relation of Montaigne the man to Montaigne the book is, it is suggested, analogous to that of the Trinity. If that is the case, what is the analogy of the Holy Spirit? In terms of the *Nicene Creed*, the Holy Spirit is '*vivificantem, qui ex Patre Filioque procedit* (the giver of life, who proceeds from the father and the son)'. In Montaigne's terms this would mean desire, the desire to reveal himself, which animates his work and in turn animates him. This is a desire at once for self-knowledge and self-exposure. The strength of the animating desire is evident in his outright refusal of custom, which he otherwise exhorts to follow, even at the cost of presumptuousness: 'Even if it were true that it is presumption … to talk to the public about oneself' he will do so and 'to say what I think about it, custom is wrong.'[100] If this is so, then the linguistic act of writing creates a world while opposing the norms of the world, makes possible salvation in that world and is infused with an animating love. Montaigne would have been familiar with Augustine's analogy of the Trinity, from the *City of God*: 'We resemble the divine Trinity in that we exist; we know that we exist and we are glad of this existence and this knowledge.' This is followed by the famous argument against the Academic Sceptics, who ask how he knows he is not mistaken about his existence: 'A non-existent being cannot be mistaken; therefore I must exist, if I am mistaken.'[101] Similarly, Montaigne never doubts his own existence, rather affirms this as that of which he is most certain. His *Essays* are a continual restatement of his existence, a striving to know that existence and an expression of his enjoyment of it.

For Augustine, his existence is not simply that of an entity living in the world but more fundamentally a being which desires salvation, an everlasting, posthumous, life with God, its maker and saviour. Death is indeed a constant theme of the *Essays*: The very project is inspired by the death of his friend Etienne de La Boétie, and the initial message 'To the Reader' speaks of the purpose of the *Essays* as leaving behind something of himself to his relatives and friends after his death.[102] The relation to death is not, however, one of Christian hope in immortality. Indeed, quoting Augustine's statement (without naming Augustine himself) that only what comes after death could make it an evil, Montaigne on the contrary understands death in its own actuality.[103] The linguistic universe of the *Essays* is an immanent Trinitarian structure, where the significance of death lies in the manner of dying. Indeed, Montaigne states that 'never did a man prepare to leave the world more utterly and completely, nor detach himself from it so universally, than I propose to do'.[104] Sceptical detachment and preparing for death go hand in hand, because the *Essays* are Montaigne's continual reminding of himself of his own finitude. The only salvation which he can find for himself in that universe is acceptance of death and the recognition that virtue is its own reward. The two go hand in hand, because death is something that is endured in life, living well is the art of dying well and this has no reward outside of itself. With respect to death, Montaigne takes up a resolutely Stoic attitude and the Christian expectation of an afterlife receives for him no philosophical purchase. This is so because it is not pertinent to death. The point for Montaigne is that learning how to die is to no longer be a slave: the threat of death no longer carries any leverage.[105] The belief or otherwise in an afterlife is a matter of faith in miracles, which he resolutely opposes. But Montaigne goes beyond the Stoics in seeking an animal-like ignorance of death, an ignorance paradoxically practiced through his own experience of being as good as dead following an incident of being attacked during a skirmish in the civil wars. This essay into death has shown him that all anxiety regarding salvation is misguided, as the 'experience' of dying is one in which body and soul both descend together into passivity.[106]

Montaigne's living and dying being is consubstantial with his essays, which, however, live on after his death. The linguistic universe of Montaigne's self-formation is written for others, specifically those who will experience his death, who will 'recover' him after his death. This self which lives on beyond his death is 'naked'; indeed, the *Essays* is a work of self-exposure to others.[107] Yet, paradoxically, this exposure will only be partially understood by others, while he is totally exposed to God in a manner that is beyond all language. In speaking to an other, Montaigne's is dependent on the other to pick up what he wants to say. 'Speech belongs half to the speaker, half to the listener.'[108] There is a tone in speaking, not only in the spoken word but also in the text. He speaks through the text of his essays in order to be understood; he does so in the expectation that others can learn from his experience of himself. But the singularity of each self means that the *Essays* will be understood differently by each one. Montaigne cannot control this, he must let the work, as an expression of his love for himself, find a resonance in each self, in their own self-relation. While Augustine writes his *Confessions* to God and allows the reader to look over his shoulder, so to speak, Montaigne writes to the reader, while acknowledging their common distance from God.

Words, Montaigne maintains, add nothing to the being of the thing; they are rather sounds which signify, extraneous to the things they designate. Yet, he is immediately mindful of a long-standing issue in Christian theology namely that of divine names. And although he states himself 'hardly versed in' theology, he pushes the Nominalist account of God to its doxological conclusion: The divine names do not designate God, do not reach his nature or even his existence; they do, however, function to give 'blessing and praise … to his external works'.[109] Divine names function to glorify God. Such giving of praise and glory is justified with respect to God because he transcends humanity and the human world in which we find ourselves; yet within that world the divine origin can and should be praised. These words of praise are human words, but ones which appropriately aim not to understand but to give thanks. In relation to God, then, communication, whether in prayer or in divine revelation, does not function to fix its object in terms which contain the sense of that object, but rather acts to express praise, blessing, love, value. Nature may be a guide, but it does not reveal to us the truth God alone can know. 'The things that come to us from heaven have … alone the stamp of truth; which also we do not see with our own eyes, or receive by our own means.'[110] We cannot know the world around us in terms of its originating principle and significance. The stamp of the maker must, indeed, be on things, but our 'imbecility' makes us incapable of seeing it; nonetheless, the invisible operations of God are manifest in the things which we can see. These manifestations are, however, seen only by faith and human reason and argument is 'heavy and barren matter', to which only divine grace can give form.[111] Language functioning simply as the expression of such heavy barren matter lacks all liveliness.

In discussing the Sceptical use of language, Montaigne suggests that the apparent self-refutation of Scepticism is due to the limitations of language: While language functions positively, that is, propositions affirm certain things to be so, the Sceptic would be better served by a language of negation. It is in that context that we must read the famous sentence from the conclusion of the 'Apology for Raymond Sebond': 'We have no communication with being.'[112] The concluding paragraphs of that essay were copied almost word for word from the French translation of a text by Plutarch,[113] but while in Plutarch we read 'we have no participation in being', Montaigne substitutes 'participation' with 'communication'. It is for Montaigne an issue of language here, of the articulation of thoughts, which by its nature will fail to grasp their essence. These words, rather, express a way of seeing things, the manner in which things impress themselves on the self, impressions that are fleeting and passing. If, then, words do not communicate with being, their function is to express the self's own experience, which testimony can enrich the experience of others: The limits of reason seen in humility before an all-powerful God opens the self to the testimony of others.

The language of praise, of thanks, of prayer, is expressive of the Sceptical situation because it both expresses the externality of language and the self-transcending movement of incapacity. Montaigne clearly distinguishes human and divine speech, claiming for himself nothing more than human speech 'human speech has lower forms, and should not make use of the dignity, majesty and authority of divine speech'.[114] Human speech is a matter of opinion not of faith. Human speech as a communication of sounds has a pragmatic function of expressing meaning or intent but as such can claim no special authority. There is only one exception to this, for Montaigne: There is only one form of speech that is more than the expression of meaning by a self – the Lord's Prayer.[115] This prayer, which Christians believe to come directly from God, is not only superior to other prayers but in contrast to them transcends the uncertain level of opinion and experience. The language of the tongue Montaigne contrasts with the language of conscience,[116] a contrast which parallels that of reverence and irreverence. The language of the 'sacred mysteries of our belief' should not be spoken except with a reverence that involves a disposition of both body and mind.[117] Things of nature are objects of experience, without special authority and requiring no particular reverence; nature and God as beyond things have authority and are due reverence. While the strangeness of things is to be respected, as that which is spoken about, they become vain and banal; but when faced with divine grace, the language we employ is not our own but the words of thanksgiving 'dictated word for word by the mouth of God'.[118]

Language is itself split between the words of reverence and the words slipping into banality. In short, as a linguistic being, the self finds itself in its very speech between grace and nature.

2.4 Contingency and constancy

Tranquillity is a constant theme in Montaigne's *Essays*. It is not so much the goal of his self-exploration as the mood that makes them possible, such that 'either reason is a mockery or it must aim solely at our contentment'.[119] He does not *seek* tranquillity; it is manifest in the activity of his thought. In this he refuses two possible avenues to tranquillity, the Stoic and the Pyrrhonian, but finds it already manifest in a Christianity poised between Augustine and Pelagius.

Tranquillity is not to be found in philosophy but rather in himself. He states, 'All the glory that I aspire to in my life is to have lived it tranquilly – tranquillity not according to Metrodorus or Arcesliaus or Aristippus, but according to me. Since philosophy has not been able to find a way to tranquillity that is suitable to all, let everyone seek it individually'.[120] The context here is a discussion of glory and specifically the distinction between acting for the sake of virtue and deeds which aim for glory and fame. The final sentence of the essay states, 'Any person of honor chooses rather to lose his honor than to lose his conscience'.[121] This brings to a heightened conclusion the paradoxical nature of glory itself. We seek glory in the eyes of others, yet the success of our deeds is the result more of chance and fortune than our own worth: 'It is chance that attaches glory to us according to its caprice.'[122] Nonetheless, even philosophers such as Epicurus care about their reputation, and Montaigne's project of self-analysis is directed to others, seeks to be pleasing to his readers.[123] He does seek glory and is a man of honour, and he is and acts in relation to those who are his witnesses. But if great deeds often go without witnesses, and if conversely it is to abandon ourselves to wickedness to do good only when such deeds might be exposed to witnesses,[124] then within virtue is marked the difference between inner and outer. Nothing happens in secret, for Montaigne, because he is always his own witness; his actions are subject to his conscience. So the true glory which is not simply the result of the caprice of fortune is the glory of an act appearing to conscience. Life as glorious is lived without the reproach of conscience, without the reproach of my own self-witness: 'I do not care so much what I am to others as I care what I am to myself.'[125]

Although we rightly translate the French word *conscience* here as 'conscience', we could with almost equal correctness translate with 'consciousness'. Indeed, we can look at Montaigne as a philosopher of consciousness. What is at issue is the self-relation as opposed to the relation to strangers, who, he tells us, see only 'outward appearances … .do not see … [his] heart … only [his] countenance'.[126] The self-relation at issue here then is a relation which is one of the heart. The heart is the realm of feeling – of self-relation as self-love. In his loving self-relation, Montaigne appears to himself as he is; love here is not blind but rather open and free of dissimulation: 'A generous heart should not belie its thoughts; it wants to reveal itself to its inmost depths.'[127] The heart thinks, its thoughts and feelings are one. Thoughts are not abstractions, are not tools for manipulation, but are rather expressions of the self. These expressions are witnessed by the self in its inner awareness of itself – conscience/consciousness – and in its generosity that self should never falsify its thoughts: 'We must not always say everything for that would be folly; but what we say must be what we think; otherwise it is wickedness.'[128] The openness to the strange of which we spoke in the first section, is also a being open *for the stranger*. In not judging the other by myself, neither does the self judge itself by the other, that is, by its reputation. It is rather the case that the gap between self and other, of inner and outer, is overcome when the self opens itself to the other in generosity, as it is open to itself in conscience. Although it may not be fully achievable, for Montaigne the ideal self is one which shows its heart, hence itself in loving relation, to the other. Such a self is truthful and its greatest enjoyment is friendship.[129] This self is both thematic in the *Essays* and operative in the very movement of essaying, testing itself in the face of others.

Tranquillity is a being in relation to a witness: first the self and then the other, most notably the friend. Such a relation to the witness is not secondary to virtue, is not simply a relation to the observer of virtue, but rather is the essence of virtue: 'Truth is the first and fundamental part of virtue. We love it for itself. He who tells the truth because he has some external obligation to do so … is not sufficiently truthful.' The love of truth here is not the love of true knowledge. In other words, the striving here is not one for seeking truths about things; it is rather the love of telling the truth, of wearing no masks.[130] The virtue of truth is the virtue of sincerity. Being sufficiently truthful is placing one's heart before the other. It is an openness *for* as well as to the stranger. Virtue is not for the sake of something else, but for its own sake. To do something *for its own sake* is to do it: 'Those who run after ... a hare do not run.'¹³¹ The truth of an act is that act itself, to sincerely profess it is to do it for its own sake alone. All other purposes hide the act, hide the self-presence of the self in its being towards the other who witnesses it. This only appears to contradict Montaigne's constant emphasis on change and passing: the self-presence of the self in being towards others is its self-presence in the moment of its passing, refusing the 'precedents' of past or future.

Hiding oneself is a dividing of oneself from others, a separation of the inner and the outer. Virtue, though not for the sake of its appearance to another, is openness for the other. Such openness is loving in its care for the other. Not judging the other by myself, neither do I place myself before the other. In this context, Montaigne turns to the question of capacity and the relation of habit and nature. Each individual is born with certain natural inclinations, certain of which are inclinations towards goodness. But virtue means something greater than a natural inclination whereby souls are led 'gently and peacefully in the footsteps of reason'.¹³² Such is nature as calm and untroubled, nature as good. Montaigne suggests that God is good in this sense. To turn the other cheek, however, following being 'outraged and stung to the quick by an injury' requires a conflict with 'this furious appetite for vengeance' and a mastery of such passion. Only the one who goes through such conflict and is tested by it can be said to be virtuous. In this sense the *Essays* themselves can be said to be exercises in virtue, testing the self's resolve in different situations to follow what its reason dictates. In doing so, Montaigne is testing his own capacities, his own natural dispositions, and trying to habituate them to follow the right course.

The greatest capacity he can find in himself is the capacity for change. Against the Stoic ideal of constancy of will, which for Seneca comprised all wisdom,¹³³ Montaigne affirms the reality of inconstancy rooted in changes of circumstances and irresolution. In a Heraclitean tone, Montaigne says that he is concerned 'with passing [*le passage*] not becoming'. In other words, the concern here is not with a coming into being, not with an emergent order, but rather with a radically temporalized world in which change occurs minute to minute. Such change has its source in two things: 'various and changeable occurrences [*divers et mutable accidents*]' and 'irresolute and, when it so befalls, contradictory ideas [*d'imaginations irresolu et ... contraires*]'.¹³⁴ Somewhat loosely, but speaking to the matter that Montaigne is dealing with here, I would translate 'various and changeable accidents of fortune' and 'not yet determined and contradictory figures in thought.' The 'occurrences' are accidents of fortune in the sense that they are outside the control of the self. They happen to the self and affect that self, but affect it in terms of the figures of the imagination through which it thinks. Such thoughts are of the heart and cannot be distinguished from the passions and appetites. Against the Stoic ideal of constancy, Montaigne points to the 'ordinary practice ... to follow the inclinations of our appetite'. To ignore this is to falsify a human life, placing constancy where there is none. 'Irresolution seems to be the most common and apparent defect of our nature,' he states. Again, the emphasis here is not on resolve as much as on indeterminacy. The nature of human beings remains undetermined; this is a 'defect' only when we try to see human actions 'as a whole and in the same light'.¹³⁵ But a human life is always less than determined; indeed, he speaks of himself as 'very ill-formed'.¹³⁶ In tracing his own life, he is tracing changes, mutations, contradictions.¹³⁷ The human life is one of constant change and constant formation and re-formation. Two questions arise here. The first is the relation of such appetites to reason, to the figures of thought which themselves are varied and at times contradictory. Second, having spoken of being 'ill-formed' at the beginning of the essay 'Of Repentance', Montaigne continues that he will portray himself 'whom I should really make very different from what he is if I had to fashion him over again'.[138] If the self changes with its appetites and with its circumstances, then what is its relation to its past, and more concretely what is its responsibility for its past and itself? I will address both issues in turn.

Montaigne, as we have seen, is suspicious of any attempt to separate the mental and the carnal, the celestial and the terrestrial. Reason is as varied as experience and its relation to passion a complex one. Admitting it to be a 'monstrous' thought, he states, 'I find ... more restraint in my morals that in my opinions, and my lust less depraved than my reason.'[139] He has from nature a horror of most vices. If that horror were lacking, he would easily have been led by his reasoning to exercise license in morals. There is an element of modesty here, particularly given the distinction drawn between virtue and natural disposition to morals earlier in this same essay. Nevertheless, something else is operative: Reason alone can lead not to goodness but to evil, goodness requires an affective openness – a nobility (*generosité*)[140] – which makes him dislike all cruelty to humans and animals. All of this he attributes to nature. His nature is manifest as feeling; in recognition of this he – like Augustine, but for different reasons – resists the Stoic ideal of *apatheia*.

Montaigne pleads against the unnaturalness of reason abstracted from appetite, an unnaturalness resting ultimately in its closing off of the heart and its fostering of an ideal of indifference. In the process he does not so much choose goodness over virtue but transforms the meaning of virtue: 'We should have given virtue the name of pleasure ... not that of vigor, as we have named it.'[141] The 'hedonism' expressed here develops organically from his Sceptical concern with self-reflexivity, as well as from a strong Epicurean influence. Virtue is only possible in the relation of the self to itself, in its awareness of itself, in conscience. But this self-relation is affective, is the relation of the heart, is pleasure. A fully virtuous life Montaigne sees as unobtainable. But if the enjoyment of virtue is pleasure, then the quest cannot be 'rugged and disagreeable', since 'in all the pleasures we know, even the pursuit is pleasurable'.[142] The relation to ends is a self-relation in the means. If, however, reason is opposed to pleasure, then this turns the human into a 'miserable animal', turned against its own natural powers, its own relation to its own natural capacities for pleasure.[143]

At issue here is the relation of reason to appetite, virtue to desire. The Stoic *apatheia* assumes the indifference of the will, which can insulate itself from the drives of appetite and desire. Taken to its logical conclusion this would mean that the mind can be equally balanced between competing desires. To desire is to be desiring, so such a concept would imply a self capable of being desiring in respect of two things equally and hence divided against itself. This can be understood in two aspects: in terms of equal appetites (Montaigne's examples are the appetite to drink and to eat) or in terms of equal qualities in the object (one crown pieces).[144] To imagine such indifference is to imagine the self – both in itself and in its object – confronted with absolute equality. But this is to abstract from the circumstance of the objects, which always present themselves to the appetite of a self with some difference either to the sight or touch 'which attracts us, though it be imperceptibly'.[145] Although this is an argument against the Stoics, it also attacks the basis of *epoché* – the self is never in a position, in which an indifference of the will is possible. For Montaigne, the self is always relating to things in their difference and that means in the variation of their attractiveness for its appetites. Living in the *aporia*, living without beliefs, is thus impossible for Montaigne, and the *aporia* is only an abstract reflective moment, because in its self-reflexivity the self is always in a state of attraction and appetite; virtue is pleasure, not vigour, because it is a being with itself in its appetitive being towards that which attracts it. While we may suspend judgement, the self is always inclined by its appetite towards one side or the other – the suspension of judgement is a second-level act which expresses doubt as to the absolute validity of that inclination.

The self which Montaigne portrays in himself in his openness to an other provoking his appetites is a self related to itself in its self-reflexivity and which in its self-reflection brings its self-relation to literary expression. If he cannot make judgements about others, if he cannot judge others by himself, can he at least judge himself by himself? In what sense is he answerable for himself (the second question noted above)? A comparison with Augustine brings out the issue here. Montaigne's project of self-exploration has certain parallels to that of Augustine's *Confessions*, although there is no evidence that he actually read that work. Both Augustine and Montaigne speak of themselves, both find fault with themselves, both understand the self in them as constituted through desire and love. But equally the differences are clear. Augustine begins and ends the *Confessions* with creation: Augustine's own life is important only in its journey to the Creator. The account of that journey is linear up to the point of his conversion and the subsequent death of his mother. When that conversion to the Catholic religion is complete, Augustine's turns to knowing God: 'May I know you, who knows me.'[146] Montaigne's account, on the other hand, is non-linear, and it begins with diversity of human experience and ends with a plea for finding himself within himself. For Augustine, the self finds God within himself through a long journey ending in conversion; for Montaigne, the self discovers itself through a constant return from the strange to itself. Permeating Augustine's discourse is his relation to the history of salvation as a 'little piece of creation'.[147] The pleasure he is seeking is not in the tranquillity of his self-relation but rather in praising God, a pleasure stirred not by the objects of his appetites but rather by God as Creator of such objects. Moreover, Augustine's predicament is itself fore-structured by the history which precedes him, specifically the Fall of the human and the sinful state which only the grace of God can remove. Not only his own past but also the past of all humanity weighs upon him, but this weight can be lifted through grace that allows him to truly repent his past: that is not simply to regret it but to overcome his past self and to overcome also the past of humanity, which is the 'stain' of original sin. While he does speak of natural propensities to evil, in particular with respect to presumption, Montaigne avoids all reference to the discourse of the Fall. In this respect he takes up a Pelagian position, whereby any account of a prelapsarian state is without relevance to the condition of the self in the world. It is significant in this respect that baptism is mentioned by Montaigne in a few contexts whereby its customary rather than sacramental significance is to the forefront. Furthermore, although as we have seen, he begins his essay, 'Of Repentance', by stating that if he had to do it over again he would fashion himself differently; he then adds, 'But now it is done [*Meshui c'est fait*]'.[148] He cannot undo what was done, the self is what it is. While Augustine looks to God to undo his past, to forgive him his past transgressions, throughout this essay there is no mention of forgiveness.

Montaigne self-consciously writes 'Of Repentance' from the point of view of an aged man (although much of it was written when he was only fifty-three) looking back on his life. In looking back on his life he does so with a particular 'deficiency', a specific refusal and in a tranquil state: a deficiency of memory, a refusal to repent and with a 'conscience content with itself'.[149] These are all related closely to one another. His denial of a good memory is one we find throughout the *Essays* and cannot be taken either as an act of modesty or simply as disingenuous.[150] It is rather the case that he is here making a specific point about memory, which he alludes to in introducing the assertion that he rarely repents. He claims memory to be different from understanding and to facilitate both vengeance and lying. In relation to the latter, his lack of a good memory gives him a natural disposition towards goodness and towards virtue (truth). His lack of a good memory is nothing for which he should be blamed, as it is a natural defect, for which he is not responsible. This is an accident of nature, an act of fortune. But this act of fortune is an ambiguous one. His lack of memory makes him less reliant on others: Those with good memories remember what they have read and use those ideas instead of their own. However, Montaigne's essaying into the strange is to test himself; to simply memorize what one has read or heard substitutes the words of another for one's own. Memory in this sense extinguishes the life of that which is remembered. It remains either as a dead idea or as a resentment, inciting vengeance. The lack of memory means that he 'remembers injuries received less' and conversely 'the places and books that I revisit always smile at me with a fresh newness'.[151] Lacking a good memory is a natural disposition which makes Montaigne more open to novelty. By speaking in these terms, and not by making Sceptical arguments against memory, Montaigne is not so much denying the veracity of memory as he is questioning its value: To remember is to return to the past rather than portraying the passing. Furthermore, a good memory facilitates untruth: A liar needs a strong memory. Without a strong memory, Montaigne is naturally disposed to truthfulness and hence to virtue.

The experience of the past as past, as already experienced, is a deadening and potentially corrupting influence for Montaigne. The past is a weight; one might say that the past is being for Montaigne and that being is that which is completed, finished, fully formed. Being in this sense is death. Living is dying for Montaigne, it is a passing into death. There is no liveliness in the past as such – such liveliness comes from the apprehension in the present of a place or book as new (to him). Experience ideally would be without past, would be a pure apprehension of the moment. This is paradoxical of course, because novelty cannot exist in the vacuum of past experience and indeed Montaigne is speaking of representational and cognitive memory, habit as we have seen is always operative. So the newness of a place or book is facilitated by a weak memory as his former perceptions or interpretations respectively are not alive in him at the moment. The liveliness of his experience comes from the manner in which it breaks with his habitual expectations in the now-moment. It is in the light of this account of memory that we need to read his refusal of repentance.

It is striking that he asks the reader to excuse him on this issue: 'Let me here excuse what I have often said, that I rarely repent and that my conscience is content with itself.'[152] He does not speak of forgiveness, yet seeks the forgiveness of the reader for saying that he rarely repents and that his conscience is content. It is the saying, not the said, which needs to be forgiven: The apparent claim is that he has rarely done wrong and that his conscience is clear. But he does this in submission, he opens himself up to the standards of others: 'common and legitimate beliefs' to 'even false and erroneous opinion'. He seeks the judgement of others not in the sense of having a good reputation but rather in the sense that he will stand up to the scrutiny of anyone who will see into his soul and will not find him guilty. The testimony of his conscience will be attested to by any other. He adds, nevertheless, an important caveat, namely, that his conscience is 'not of an angel or a horse, but … the conscience of a man'.[153] The conscience of a man is his self-awareness, his judgement about himself as a man, not as an animal without mind or an angel without body. That awareness of is of himself as a human being, subject to the capacities of that being. As we have seen, such a being is one for which memory is if anything a tendency towards vice.

To rarely repent is to rarely seek forgiveness: This is not to deny wrongdoing but rather to deny the efficacy of forgiveness. Repentance far from eradicating the effects of vice, is itself an effect of vice. 'Vice leaves repentance in the soul, like an ulcer in the flesh which is always scratching itself and drawing blood.'[154] Repentance shares with memory a retrospective structure. To repent is to retrospectively return to and rethink a past act. This is an act of reason, which engenders repentance. Such an act of reason again seeks to abstract from appetite, from desire and inclination, repeatedly scratching at the self, repeatedly irritating the self in its own nature. Montaigne distinguishes here between vices contingent upon specific circumstances and those which are characterological. Those vices which 'take us by surprise and towards which we are driven by passion'[155] can be disowned and retracted, hence repented, but precisely because they are not ours, they have overtaken us from without. But to repent those vices, 'which by long habit are rooted and anchored in a strong and vigorous will cannot be denied',[156] would be to place oneself outside oneself, to take up a position of abstracted, disinterested, indifferent reason and will. To take up such a position is dangerous and potentially destructive: In disavowing the past self, both virtues and vices are disowned, something which is destructive both on an individual and on a societal level. Montaigne denies repentance for similar reasons that he objects to overturning custom: The presumption to stand outside the flow of time, the presumption, that is, to privilege an abstract moment over time and history, is based on the delusion of a self-grounding reason. Montaigne distinguishes here between the act in itself and the act as part of a particular life. In his example, a thief, who in old age uses his ill-gotten wealth to compensate the descendants of the people he robbed, is not repenting his past acts but rather accepting them as his own and trying to compensate for them. In short, Montaigne's basic claim is that reformation of self is impossible. The self is always changing, is always different from itself, but that change is a passing, which occurs largely beyond the self's own power of control. The natural inclinations which it inherited can be strengthened by education, but they cannot be rooted out, only concealed. Nature will always win out: 'Nature surging forth and expressing herself by force, in the face of long habit.'[157]

Montaigne does speak of imploring 'God to completely reform me and to pardon my natural weakness. But this I ought not to call repentance ... any more than my displeasure at being neither an angel nor Cato.' This is not repentance because repentance concerns that which is in his own power. He can *regret* not having another nature, but not repent it. His nature is one; his actions are the expressions of his whole self, both in its virtues and its vices. There is then no overcoming or overturning nature and by the same token he is not responsible for the vices of his nature. To receive divine pardon for the weakness of his nature is to have his nature elevated above itself. Such an elevation is a gratuitous gift to a nature which can only be understood in its own terms. His actions are the result of his nature and the forces of fortune. He can take responsibility for neither. For Montaigne, then, the truly wise self accepts both her natural condition and her powerlessness with respect to fortune. In both respects, neither repentance nor regret are appropriate because not only can the past not be changed, but it also could not be otherwise: 'For this idea takes away the pain; that they [past affairs] were bound to happen thus, and now they are in the great stream of the universe and in the chain of Stoical causes. Your fancy, by wish or imagination, cannot change a single point without overturning the whole order of things, and the past and present.'[158]

The repentance which may come in old age arises not from a strength of reason, but a failing of appetite. Repentance in old age comes from the cooling of desire and appetite (especially sexual), which gives reason the illusion of abstraction. But this illusion would soon be dashed for Montaigne if 'reason were confronted with my former lust'.[159] Old age is not a cure, it is rather a 'powerful malady'; what seems like repentance in old age, is simply the weakening of that nature.

The 'fallenness' of human beings is completely naturalized here. There is no original sin. There are inherited vices, but these are facts of nature, for which the self has no fundamental responsibility. As a natural being, the self's responsibility is one of conscience, of self-awareness and of truthfulness about itself. The greatest vice Montaigne is suggesting is that of dissimulating towards others regarding his own nature: The problem here is in social relations through which the fundamental vice of falsehood arises. It is for this reason that Montaigne withdraws from public life and is generally disparaging regarding it. Comparing Alexander the Great and Socrates he says,

> The shortest way to attain glory would be to do for conscience what we do for glory. And Alexander's virtue seems to me to represent much less vigor in his theater than does that of Socrates in his lowly and obscure activity ... If you ask the former what he knows how to do he will answer, 'subdue the world'; if you ask the latter, he will say, 'lead the life of man in conformity with its natural condition'; a knowledge much more general, more weighty, and more legitimate.[160]

The response to the human condition is a Socratic one, of know oneself – to know oneself in one's natural condition. There is in the human condition nothing further which can be said. However, that does not mean the last word. The last word is not human, but divine. We have already seen how he implores God for reform and pardon, and later in the essay he states, 'God must touch our hearts [*il faut que Dieu nous touche le courage*]. Our conscience must reform by itself through the strengthening of our reason, not through the weakening of our appetites.' This marks the intervention of divine grace which is found within the self-reflexivity of the self. God touches the heart by giving it courage, the courage to reform itself. Grace here functions to strengthen reason, to give the soul a way of reaching beauty in 'despising and fighting sensual pleasure'.[161] Divine grace is the infusion of a supernatural courage towards a pleasure of the self in its relation with itself in conscience. This claim lies at the heart of the enigmatic essay, which literally forms at the centre of the *Essays* the 'Apology for Raymond Sebond'.

2.5 Faith and reason

Pyrrhonism for Montaigne is an openness to the strange, a rebuke to the presumption of reason and a doubt regarding the absoluteness of judgement. It is neither aporetic nor is it tranquil in itself. Tranquillity is the 'natural rejoicing' of a 'conscience … content with itself'.[162] Conscience is the self's witness of itself. The self, though, finds itself in its own self witnesses giving witness for itself. To be truthful to oneself is at the same time to be truthful to another. The very secrecy of the heart is open to God. God for Montaigne is the ultimate witness, and when he invites others to look into his heart, he is asking them ultimately to take the place of God. That place, however, is not simply the place of witness but also the place of grace. While conscience is a human conscience and as such is limited to human capacities, specifically to the human tension between reason and sensual desire, that voice of reason which points human beings beyond the human, that voice which is most manifest for Montaigne in Stoicism, is answered in Christianity by divine grace. He states, 'It is for our Christian faith not for his [Seneca's] stoical virtue to aspire to that divine, miraculous, metamorphosis [of rising above humanity].'[163] What binds Sceptical doubt and faith in grace together is the thought of a heterogeneity between experience and being, human and divine, habit and nature, judgement and truth/justice. In each case, however, Montaigne assumes hidden mechanisms whereby the inner coherence of world is maintained, such that the ideas of being, God, nature, truth/justice operate to make sense of the finite, fragmentary and ultimately individual life he was portraying. This domain of the specifically possible, that is, the possible of the world of his experience, could be understood as a product of difference – indeed, we can say a product of a play of differences – because reason in perceiving that world in its fragmentary finitude contained ideas of justice, truth and nature. The source and necessity of these ideas for Montaigne lie in the nature of experience itself: The impression on the self of the strange marking in the self both that of which it is conscious and that which as foreign indicates the transcending of its possible awareness. Implicit here also is a certain temporality: The self which experiences knows itself to be a habituated self, a self which is constituted as an arbitrary limiting of the infinite possibilities of differential relations in nature. It knows itself as both a foreclosing of the future and an openness towards possibilities of the future. The self in this understanding is both a closing and an opening but in each respect subject to nature as a mechanism of infinite pasts and infinite futures. The self which repents in the wish for a different past and a different future does so only because of the infinite possibilities that reason can perceive in nature. The mistake, however, is to see these possibilities in the abstract and think of reason as transcending the actual possibilities it is living. In living those actualities, it is living in the order of its own experience but is incapable of reaching nature as anything other than an empty idea.

Reason relates only negatively to this infinity: It perceives it in its self-reflection on the world, but as itself subject to the infinite variety of experience, any positive idea of nature will be a distortion. Montaigne speaks, as we have seen, of nature and God in one breath. God is the source of this variety, the name for nature in its infinite richness. But at the same time God is the name for justice, which again functions as an empty idea for Montaigne. Binding these two aspects together is that notion of grace. If the ideas of nature and justice are empty, that does not mean that they are unreal. On the contrary, Montaigne speaks of nature and God as real, but unknown. The 'Apology' is structured (as is 'Of Prayers') in terms of a dichotomy of human and divine. 'We must ... accompany our faith with all the reason that is in us, but always with this reservation, not to think that it is on us that faith depends, or that our efforts can attain a knowledge so supernatural and divine.'[164] This dichotomy, far from conflicting with his Scepticism, supports it: The world appears to the self as it impresses itself upon her, but for it to so appear to her, it must also appear in itself. It appears in itself as nature. This divine relation to things is understood as a relation to the things in themselves, while the self's relation to them is one of the impressions they make within her. Thus, the Sceptical claim leads Montaigne to understand appearance not so much as a property of the thing, but rather as an inner state of the self. This is a secondary inflection for Montaigne from the more fundamental distinction of human incapacity and divine potency: to know things as they are would be to know them from the will of God.

The dichotomy of human and divine is so fundamental that no special claims can be made for Christianity over any other religion: 'We receive our religion only in our own way and with our own hands, and not otherwise than as other religions are received.'[165] This in effect is a variant of Sextus Empiricus's second mode, 'based on differences between human beings'.[166] If certain people are Christian and others Mohammaden, the same techniques can be employed – threats and promises – the same type of things are present – 'hope, trust, events, ceremonies, penitence, martyrs' – but all in the service of (in certain respects) contrary beliefs. What this indicates for Montaigne is variations in the type of people, particularly their modes of reception. Religions, however, are human articulations, and Montaigne distinguishes (not always terminologically, but nonetheless conceptually) religion from faith: Religion is a matter of human difference in reception; faith is in 'a divine and supernatural clasp, *having only one form, one face and one aspect*, which is the authority of God and his grace.'[167] Faith relates to religion as form to matter: 'Our human reasons and arguments are as it were the heavy and barren matter; the grace of God is their form.'[168] As we have seen, he had said a little previously, 'We are Christians by the same title as we are Perigordians or Germans.'[169] Religion is contingent. There is nothing in the things themselves to make him prefer Christianity over Islam or even over the religion of the Aztecs. But this does not mean, as some have interpreted him, that faith for Montaigne is simply lukewarm conformity or even insincere and opportune compliance.[170] The emphasis here is on the capacity to receive: divine grace is limited to the capacity to receive it, which itself is conditioned by the customs and history of the people in which a self happens to be born. Religion, to the extent to which it is rooted in revelation, must recognize the limits of its own capacity to understand what is revealed: that can be given shape only by faith.

The attempt to give a rational account of religion based on nature is doomed to failure (and to the extent to which this is Sebond's project, Montaigne's 'defence', undermines its very foundations). Nature's operations – which Montaigne refers to more than once as a 'machine' – are invisible. As such, the marks of the 'great architect' are also not perceptible.[171] While Montaigne puts this down to 'our imbecility', in fact, it is for him fundamental to nature as such. In this he takes the Voluntarist conclusion a step further and in effect evacuates nature as perceived by us of any positive indication of God. What nature does teach us of God is his infinity, but this is precisely what remains incomprehensible to us. Hence, what we perceive as monsters are not monsters for God, 'who sees in the immensity of his work the infinite forms that He has comprised in it'.[172] What is at issue here is the claim of reason to make normative judgements regarding nature. Such judgements for Montaigne are presumptuous not only because of the limits of any particular individual's experience but also because of the basis of reason in the constitution of one being amongst others. Montaigne naturalizes human reason: It is a faculty of a particular being, which functions relative to the capacities of individuals. The naturalization, however, is not complete: The ideas of truth, justice and nature are, so to speak, regulative ideas which communicate being, but they do so in an empty and formal manner. In its concrete and positive articulations, human reason is a form of expression of human experience and nothing more. It binds human beings to creation, rather than placing them above it: The coupling of 'gods and men' Montaigne characterizes as impudent.[173] It is on this basis that he engages in the account of animals in the 'Apology'.

The strategy is rooted in Sextus's first mode, the difference between animals and human beings.[174] But it goes to the heart of not only philosophical but also Christian thinking: Far from being in the image of God, far from intellect being the 'spark of the divine', human beings are simply 'miserable and puny creatures'.[175] The human being is a part of nature like any other: 'Nature has universally embraced all her creatures; and there is none that she has not very amply furnished with all powers necessary for the preservation of its being.'[176] The accounts he gives of elephants having 'some participation in religion'[177] are not the signs of 'credulity' on Montaigne's part but rather are part of an account which attempts to show that there is no specific difference which elevates human beings above animals, but that animals as much as humans can and do perceive the beauty of creation and give thanks for it. This giving of thanks and praise is not directed at the God of revelation but rather at nature itself. The religion of animals is a natural religion; as natural beings, human beings too give thanks to God for the bounties which nature gives: being 'favoured by God and nature'.[178]

Montaigne devotes much discussion to this question because he seeks to place the human within nature as a creature with no particular claim to participation in the divine. He does this not to deny participation in the divine but to show it to be both supernatural and beyond human capacity. 'The participation we have in the knowledge of truth has not been acquired by our own capacities.'[179] Montaigne quotes in this context 1 Corinthians: 'I will destroy the wisdom of the wise.'[180] Whatever participation in truth is possible comes through a gratuitous divine gift. What the self contributes to it is obedience and submission.[181] The gift is not given on the basis of moral worth or intellect but rather on the basis of humility. The gift of grace, the gift of faith, is something which is cut off, separate and incommensurable from the world of experience and the workings of reason. The gift can be received only through the recognition of those limits. It is here that Montaigne sees common cause between St. Paul and the Pyrrhonians.

In the 'Apology', he sets out the threefold division of philosophy to be found in Sextus: those who have thought they have found truth and certainty (Peripatetics, Epicureans and Stoics); those who despair of ever finding it (Clitomachus, Carneades and the Academics); and those who are still in search of the truth (Pyrrho and the other Sceptics or Ephechists [from *epoché*]).[182] At issue here is the nature of ignorance itself. As we have seen, Montaigne understands the end of human inquiry not in terms of knowledge but of learned ignorance. This he reaffirms here: 'Ignorance that knows itself, that judges itself and condemns itself, is not complete ignorance: to be that, it must be ignorant of itself. So the profession of the Pyrrhonian is to waver, doubt and inquire, to be sure of nothing and to answer for nothing.'[183] The Pyrrhonian in employing the *epoché* does not deny experience but rather understands the proper limits of all claims made on the basis of experience. The soul, he says, has three functions: the imaginative, the appetitive and the consenting or judging. These three functions concern decisions and judgements. The imaginative Montaigne understands as a form of empathy – of placing oneself in a situation, of recognizing possibilities: 'a strong imagination creates the event'.[184]. This capacity to see possibility is tied to appetite, as we have seen. The Pyrrhonian in suspending judgement refuses to give assent to one inclination over another: He accepts it as his own but can equally argue for the opposite. 'They use their reason to inquire and debate, but not to conclude and choose.'[185] He goes on to conclude, 'There is nothing in man's invention that has so much verisimilitude and usefulness [as Pyrrhonism]. It presents man naked and empty ... fit to receive from above some outside power; stripped of human knowledge, all the more apt to lodge divine knowledge in himself, annihilating his judgment to make more room for faith ... a sworn enemy of heresy.'[186]

Sceptical practice presents a 'blank tablet' to God, which is open to divine grace.[187] To receive such divine knowledge it is necessary to annihilate judgement. However, judgement as annihilated does not – as for Sextus – bring the thinker to the aporetic state in which he finds tranquillity but is rather opened, ready for divine knowledge. The tranquil state of indifference and autonomy has been reversed. The Sceptic now is one who makes himself vulnerable, indeed absolutely vulnerable – 'naked and empty' – to a totally heterogeneous source of knowledge and being. The world of appearance is now placed in opposition not to the noumena, that is, not to the real as thought, as ideas, but to God as the inscrutable origin of that world and as the one who can write in the soul from without. The goal of the Sceptic to arrive at tranquillity is overturned – if the *epoché* makes the soul vulnerable to the God, it makes the soul vulnerable to that beyond itself, that beyond its capacities – Pyrrhonism leaves the soul, it would seem, in a state of high anxiety.

Montaigne does not draw that last conclusion, however. The God that he discusses is both omnipotent and benevolent. Nonetheless, the vulnerability of the human towards that God is clear. In a telling passage he asks, 'Is it possible to imagine anything so ridiculous as that this miserable and puny creature, who is not even master of himself … should call himself master … of the universe?'[188] But tranquillity for the Sceptic and the Stoic arises as the human being becomes master of herself. If that mastery is denied to her, where can she find happiness? Only beyond herself. But then the source of happiness becomes deeply uncertain, the appropriate and compelling mood in which to face this is one of doubt, doubt which may easily slide into anxiety.

Montaigne warns against anxiety in the *Essays*. The anxious fear towards a hidden God is foreign to him. God may be hidden, but the task of life is that of living. The country may be in turmoil, but human beings have experienced worse. The power and capacity of his self is limited, but he must enjoy what he can and live as best he can. Nature may sometimes be frightening, but it is full of wonders for a finite self open to its mysteries. This first gambit of thinking the self at the forefront of philosophical concerns gives us an initial synthesis of Augustine and Pelagius, the Stoics and Sceptics (with more than a little Epicurean emphasis on the immediacy of pleasure). Despite all the turmoil around him, despite the spectre of an darkly hidden God, Montaigne philosophized on the basis of tranquillity, living with beliefs, accepted on faith but with a self-reflexive, corrective reasoning. He lived in a confidence based not on the world – either as it is or as it should be – but rather on a self-discipline and self-understanding, which will cope with whatever comes. This noble synthesis, gave an initial ideal, a reasonableness without certainty, the calmness of a mountaineer surefootedly defying the abyss beneath him. But within a generation of Montaigne's death, this calm acceptance of uncertainty seems a world away; the relation of self, God and nature falls deeper into crisis. In that new, emerging world, Descartes and Pascal play exemplary and complementary roles, and it is to them that we must now turn.

3

Descartes, Pascal and the ambiguity of the self

Inhabiting the world as it is, with all its wonders and dangers, Montaigne taught himself to live peacefully with uncertainty. That serene mood gave way by the time of Descartes and Pascal to an anxious self, searching for relief from inner and outer turmoil. A sense of rebirth and renewal gave way to one of dissolution and a sense of ending. The self in the works of Descartes and Pascal emerges in response to a world of threat and unease, where neither the past nor the future can be taken at face value: The rupture with the past seems unbridgeable, and the future can only be that which the present makes for itself. There is no world more to inhabit, but rather all around are the ruins of a world inspiring melancholic despair or the will to create and build anew.[1]

The crisis of meaning splintering the Medieval world accelerated in this period, evident politically in the emergence of absolute states through the wars of religion and philosophically in the terminal decline of Aristotelianism. But while Montaigne viewed earlier manifestations of this with a degree of comic detachment, Descartes and Pascal lived it with intensity. Furthermore, while for Montaigne the wars of religion and the new discoveries of other worlds could be incorporated into a world in essence commensurate with Antiquity, Descartes and Pascal saw themselves as living in a new epoch. Nevertheless, the philosophical questions which Montaigne raised about the self and about reason were, if anything, more pressing in the middle of the seventeenth century than they were a half-century before. Montaigne's challenge was to live a Christian *and* Sceptical life – fragmentary, incapable of ultimate grounding, finding the diversity of the world mirrored in himself. The presupposition of ultimate harmony can guide reason only as an act of faith in a hidden and inscrutable God. Nature and grace, in his view, are separate domains, such that human beings are incapable of communicating with God, but, conversely, human nature is distinct and separate from divine grace. Reason is not autonomous, but it is set adrift in the world and incapable of reaching universal truths. Both Descartes and Pascal responded in different ways to these challenges posed by Montaigne's *Essays*. For both the Sceptical was inescapable but not ultimate; for both the fragmentation of Montaigne's self and world posed the challenge of thinking this relation of self and world in its origins; for both, philosophy concerned nothing less than the question of how to live a happy life, which they understood as impossible without knowledge of truth and goodness.

The claim that for Descartes and Pascal philosophy aims at happiness may seem at first surprising given Descartes's supposed exclusively theoretical orientation in philosophy and the melancholia associated with Pascal. However, this is to lose sight of the manner in which they both understood the relation of self and world. For Descartes and Pascal, the unity of self and world was originary, lost but recoverable, and this was the precondition of human happiness.[2] This unity they understood to be originary, because neither truth nor goodness could be the result of historical processes but had to be rooted in the ontological constitution of the self's place in the world; recoverable, because though this ontological condition was hidden to human consciousness, traces were evident in a basic fault in the self, where the very recognition of this fault indicates a perception of some lost perfection. For both Descartes and Pascal, the Sceptical is a fundamental, but relative, *moment*: It is symptomatic of a recognition of loss but by the same token points beyond itself. The Sceptical moment indicates a fallenness that can only be overcome through a transformation of the conditions of human existence. Neither the diagnosis of that origin nor its overcoming can be achieved by reason alone. In seeking for grounds, reason can conceive loss only as negative, as a failure, which must be diagnosed and cured. Only if within the self another mode of being towards itself and the world is present, which can both guide reason and help it to see its own limits, can the Sceptical moment be traversed and an original unity be recovered. For Descartes this is to be found in the will; for Pascal, in the heart.

Descartes and Pascal develop anthropologies in reaction to Scepticism and its fragmentary effects, which emphasize the non-rational (as opposed to irrational) in the human being, that element of human nature that transcends the limits of reason. In so doing they draw on strong Augustinian motifs – the self-certainty of the self beyond all reasoning and the fallen state of human nature. Descartes's response to this situation is ultimately (but not unambiguously) a Pelagian one: to restrict the will to the limits of the intellect, hence to discipline it and gain a capacity of self-assertion in a state of self-esteem and endeavour for the common good, which he terms 'generosity'. Through this act of restriction, Descartes opens up a domain – that of human capacity – which is without any *definite* limits. For Pascal, this Cartesian attempt only serves to deepen the delusional effects of the Fall: The lesson of loss is not that human capacity needs to be disciplined but rather that the human capacity is itself corrupt. The response needs to be one that follows the reason of the heart, a contradictory reason, which is captured by Christianity.

Pascal response to Descartes's 'Pelagianism' has strongly Jansenistic tones.[3] In 1640 a lengthy theological treatise, *De Augustinus*, was published in Leuven in the Dutch Republic. It had been written by a Catholic bishop, Cornelius Jansen, and was to spark the Jansenist controversy that lasted in France until the French Revolution. In effect, this book rearticulated and reinterpreted Augustine's doctrine of grace and double predestination. It responded both to the Calvinists, by attempting to show that the Catholic faith remained truer to Augustine than Calvin, and to the Molinists, who advocated a form of semi-Pelagianism. The history of these debates is complex, but the motifs, which are at play in them, are central to understanding the manner in which a new account of the self begins to emerge in the seventeenth century. The battle concerns the place of Augustine, particularly the later Augustine, within the intellectual framework of early modern Europe. Jansen and his Port-Royal supporters emphasized the sovereignty of God and the fallenness of the human being. The gulf between God and his creatures was unbridgeable except through grace. By understanding nature as fallen, Jansen marked the separation of human beings from the nature in a manner which meant a clear break between theology and physics. That break splits through the human self, as a being which is at once belonging to nature and created by God. The work of salvation then becomes a saving *from* nature. Jansen wrote partly in opposition to the sixteenth-century Spanish Jesuit theologian Luis de Molina,[4] who limited God's sovereignty, first, with respect to eternal truths of mathematics and logic, and, second, in relation to the human self: The latter is given grace – sufficient grace – to be worthy of salvation, such that God rewards the effort of that self. The complexities of the discussions concerning grace – particularly the multiple adjectival modifications of grace refining and defining ever more circumspectly the different forms of God's gratuitous action – should not obscure the fundamental issue in question: the nature and limits of the self's agency and of divine sovereignty. The Molinists believed in human progress, in the capacity of human beings to cultivate their own nature and earn salvation. In Pascal's terms, they understood the human being to the masters of their own salvation.

The relevant issues of the Jansenist/Molinist dispute can be understood in terms of their respective attitudes: first, to the body, where the Jansenists fall under a Gnostic temptation,[5] while the Molinists are closer to a Aristotelian affirmation of embodiment; second, to freedom, where the Jansenists understand the will as turned either by the fallen nature of the self or by God, while the Molinists affirm the will's freedom of choice; third, to the world, as threatening hence requiring ascetic withdrawal, according to the Jansenists, as the messy arena of life, which in the end is God's creation, for the Molinists; and fourth, to the nature of God, as sovereign king showing gratuitous incomprehensible mercy to the few for the Jansenists, and as the loving father, seeking the salvation of all, for the Molinists. Descartes and Pascal cannot be unambiguously be placed on either side of this debate, but Pascal has clear and explicit tendencies towards Jansenism; Descartes less clearly and certainly not explicitly tends towards Molinism.[6]

The history of the reception of the relation between Descartes and Pascal is a complex one. Léon Brunschvicg speaks of an 'integral opposition' between Descartes and Pascal; Victor Giraud contrasts the calm curiosity of Descartes, unconcerned with human destiny, with 'all passion, ardour and impetuousness' of Pascal.[7] But these seem both to embody caricatures and to fail to recognize the deep commonalities between both thinkers. The Descartes who emerges in this chapter is deeply concerned with human destiny and not always calm, while Pascal's passion goes hand in hand with a rigorous intellect and a probing engagement with the self as it finds itself in a Cartesian universe.

This chapter will open with a comparison of Descartes's account of the will to Pascal's account of the heart (3.1). The second section will trace these two anthropological accounts to their accounts of Scepticism (3.2). The third section will discuss the way in which this reflects their rival accounts of the beginnings of philosophy (3.3). The fourth section then develops the comparison between Descartes and Pascal with respect to God as Creator and as saviour (3.4). The final section turns to their respective ethical accounts (3.5).

3.1 Cartesian will / Pascalian heart

Descartes and Pascal share a common concern: to understand human life and the pursuit of truth, wisdom and goodness where their conditions are hidden, their origins lost. For both, neither truth nor goodness can be discovered in the world, because (as for Montaigne) the ancient idea of *cosmos* – of world as given order, legible to human reason – has been undermined for them by Voluntarism. The world remains silent to all inquiries regarding the objects of knowledge, the good conduct of life and the nature of God for human reason and faith in their natural states.[8] The path to truth and goodness can ultimately be found only through tracing the mark of that origin, the mark of God, which can be found only obscurely in the world, but most clearly within the human being itself. In contrast to Montaigne, both Descartes and Pascal return to the motif of the book of Genesis of the human being made in the 'image and likeness' of God.[9] The unbridgeable distance to God is overcome through a denaturalization of the human being, a bringing of the human out of nature and back towards the 'impudent coupling' (Montaigne) of God and human. This self discovers God in its own relation to truth and goodness, because in that relation the insufficiency of human reason alone is demonstrated. The Sceptical problem is the problem of that insufficiency. But it is resolved differently by Descartes and Pascal due to their respective understandings of a fallen state, a state, namely, in which desire outstrips capacity, where the human being is both driven by nature to know and yet not granted by nature (alone) sufficient means to reach that knowledge. The Pyrrhonian solution of *aporia*, of tranquil non-belief, is made impossible for both because they understood the Sceptical, in the unstable and ambiguous condition of doubt, as itself a symptom of fallenness: To rest with that condition would be to fail to move beyond the diagnostic stage. Montaigne through his naturalizing anthropology and the limits he sets to reason could retain a Pyrrhonian openness, if not *aporia*; both Descartes and Pascal rejected his anthropology, but they did so in different ways, thus arriving at very different accounts of the relation of faith and reason.

Descartes recognizes the self Montaigne charts. He recognizes the Sceptical in that self as not simply an epistemological strategy but as a mechanism of self-constitution. Clearly, Descartes's autobiographical accounts, above all in the 'Discourse', are stylized, yet precisely for that reason they can be read as his attempt to account for the manner in which a self constitutes itself as most human, that is, as wise.[10] The account Descartes gives is of a child deprived from the outset of that which would make its life both good and truthful, that is, the full use of reason so as to be guided by it alone. The child is endowed with reason, but without the capacity to use it. That capacity is not given to it naturally. Rather, its nature inclines it in ways that are harmful to it. So long as the natural inclinations are not under the guidance of reason the child has no criteria of its own by which to make judgements as to truth or goodness. The only criteria which it can have are those which it is taught. The child is under the authority of its parents and then its school masters.[11] Descartes points to a kind of *spontaneous* Scepticism, a self-reflexive movement of reason against those propositions, which he was asked to entertain: '*I found myself beset* by so many doubts and errors that I came to think I have gained nothing from my attempts to become educated but increasing recognition of my ignorance.'[12] The self finds itself in a situation of doubt; doubt befalls it. Hence arises a spontaneous Sceptical[13] in the response of the self to the process of learning and comes before any systematic Sceptical doubt. The Pyrrhonian crisis arises from within the self-relation of the self.

This spontaneously Sceptical movement of thought arises in response to – indeed, in reaction against – the teaching which he received not only through nature but also through his education. It is striking that in the 'Discourse' (as opposed to the 'Meditations') the first target of the Sceptical movement of thought is this learning, not the senses.[14] Descartes's awareness of his own self, in the sense of an authoritative centre for knowledge, arises out of his sense of the failure of the authority of learning, a potentially perverse failure: It is good to engage in learning not for any intrinsic value in the subjects been learnt but rather 'to guard [oneself] against being deceived by them'.[15] The Sceptical is ultimately a movement of self-defence against deception. The first movement of thought that forms the self as an authoritative centre is a negative one: That which was being taught as truth is not being investigated for its truth but is being examined for its potential betrayal. But where does this betrayal arise? Until he speaks of the evil genius at end of the 'First Meditation', Descartes does not locate this betrayal in a deceiver or a will to deceive, and there is certainly no suggestion that his teachers at Le Flèche deliberately deceived him. But if the source of deception remains at first elusive, the target of the deception is clearly his own self. In being deceived, he had been led to assent to an untruth. However, assent is an act of the will. Hence, to be deceived is to will that which deceives; it is to will on the basis of a desire or inclination in such a way that falsity seems more attractive than truth.

The will is thematized only quite late in Descartes's oeuvre. And yet operatively, his early work, the 'Rules for the Direction of the Mind', are governed by the will seeking to lay out the field of knowledge in such a way that reason can proceed unhindered. The will to order pervades that work in the sense that the success of method depends on a setting forth of objects in a series from simple to complex within the field of vision of the 'mind's eye'.[16] In setting up the field in this way the mind places objects for the intellect to examine, to attend to. The will directs the attention of the intellect. The problem of the misdirection of the will, its subjection to deception, becomes a more pressing issue in the 'Discourse' (though not thematically so) and the 'Meditations'. At issue in both these works is how the will can free itself from inclinations towards that which is false. The sciences presumably – with the possible exception of the 'false sciences'[17] – aimed originally at the truth in their different domains. If that were the case, how do we explain their failure? The pervasiveness of this failure indicates that it is not simply a matter of a lack of proper methodological development – as Descartes suggests in the *Rules* – but something more fundamental. Descartes's project of a method, already implicitly in the 'Discourse' and explicitly in the 'Meditations', is metaphysical in the sense that it aims to overcome a fundamental constitutive failing in human beings with respect to truth and goodness. This failing is constitutive in the sense that there is in human beings a fundamental tendency to deception, despite their original calling to truth and goodness. This situation is reflected in Descartes's account of method.

Method is fundamental for Descartes as a means to achieve this end. The place of method reflects the ambiguity of the fallen situation in which he finds himself. For all the rigor of the method, which he sets out first in the *Rules*, he denies it functions prescriptively. Rather, his method is simply describing how the intellect *already* operates: 'Nothing can be added to the clear light of reason which does not in some way dim it.'[18] Hence, in effect the method he is proposing is a reflection of the intellect on itself: the intellect by virtue of its own operations attempting to set the limits of these very operations. Yet if the clear light of reason functioned simply naturally, there would be no need for a method, or that method would be known intuitively by all. Again, he begins the 'Discourse' by saying that all people have good sense (*bon sens*), yet the very project of the 'Discourse' would be meaningless if that good sense was exercised by those who possessed it. Descartes is assuming here a logic of fallenness: The self is called to truth and goodness and yet, systematically and historically, fails to reach either. As with Montaigne, Descartes avoids explicitly raising the question of original sin,[19] but again, similar to Montaigne, he approaches it in diagnosing the tendency to presumption. In a letter to Hector-Pierre Chanut, he speaks of the love of God as the most 'useful and delightful passion possible' but warns against 'absurdity of wishing to be gods, and thus mak[ing] the disastrous mistake of loving divinity instead of loving God'.[20] As Geneviève Rodis-Lewis points out, this passage alludes (almost certainly consciously) to the text of Genesis. 3.5: 'You will be like gods, knowing good from evil.'[21] The further symptom of this fallenness being more than simply a contingent failure is the classically Augustinian one of disunity and disobedience within the self, between will and desire, a conflict which for Descartes is rooted in the relation of body and mind.[22] As the reality and origin of this conflict are not recognized, it is manifest as a conflict of the passions, through which the will can only employ representations to excite opposing passions.[23] This is the fallen state of the human being, one in which the relation of body and soul has not been brought into a harmonious relation and the self is subject to a conflict of the passions. What is lacking here is a purity of judgement,[24] judgement that is unclouded by error. The fallen nature of the human being then is one in which the soul is ruled by the appetites of the body. Descartes's response to this situation is, however, radically anti-Augustinian: not the appeal to grace, but the employment of method. So understood, method functions both positively and negatively: Negatively it frees the mind from the deceptions of which it has been subject; positively it guides the mind not simply towards truth and goodness, but to being certain of itself in its truth and goodness. Indeed, the goal of the method is to guide the human nature to its highest perfection; a claim which Descartes planned to announce in the title of the 'Discourse on Method'.[25]

The initial spontaneous Sceptical movement then is one that recognizes – albeit obscurely – that the falsity of its judgements is based in the congruence of two related influences: the twin governance of teachers and appetites, of society and nature.[26] For Descartes there is no question of a choice between one and the other, neither rejecting nature for the benefits of civilized society nor rejecting society in the name of nature. Both nature and society are equally complicit, hence the need for a metaphysical meditation, a move away from and beyond both nature and society, a movement within. This movement within arises out of the spontaneous Sceptical movement but is for Descartes the precondition of any systematic Sceptical reflection. This is not simply a concession to the Sceptical[27] – as we have seen (in Chapter 1) this inward movement is absent from the ancient Sceptics and I have argued that it is only ambiguously present in Montaigne (Chapter 2) – rather, the inward movement arises from Descartes's diagnosis of human fallenness as a fallenness into corporeality. The latter can be understood metaphorically in terms of society and nature, but it also has specific meaning in Descartes's work, which marks a reaction against Montaigne's account of the self's embodied understanding of itself and the world. While – as we will see – he shares Montaigne's conservatism regarding custom (at least in a certain context), Descartes restricts the scope of Montaigne's account of habituation. The inward movement is one away from the body as external and as subject to the time in its externality. The time of habit is the time of the past in the present, moulding the present in terms of the past; the inward movement is a liberation from that time. It is a movement out of the external relations of time in the causal connections of past and present, towards a domain in which all those forces and connections can be bracketed out and left in abeyance. This temporal indifference, this foreclosing of past and future, makes possible the will's indifference, operative in systematic doubt. This temporal foreclosure is possible for Descartes only through an inward movement which resists the body, which in thought, if not in actuality, attempts to undo the fallenness into the body and by that token fallenness as such.[28]

Descartes understands 'will' as the action of thought to affirm or deny, pursue or avoid: The will affirms truth and pursues the good.[29] But the will is dependent on that which is given to it by the senses or the intellect. The will as such is empty; the infinity which Descartes claims for it (to which we will return in the next section) is its emptiness, and alone it is powerless, even to want the benefit of the embodied soul. The passions function to bring the soul to the proper disposition, namely, of 'wanting the things which nature deems useful for us'.[30] The will is dependent on the passion of wonder, without which it remains blind.[31] In transforming his spontaneous Sceptical movement into a systematic Sceptical meditation, Descartes seeks to reduce the givenness to the will to nothing – 'resolutely to guard against any falsehoods'[32] when nothing can be willed which may not be false – to allow the will to begin again in nothingness. As such, a space is opened up in which the self can build itself as if *sui generis*. Descartes argues that the indifference of the will is the first and commonest form of freedom;[33] operatively it appears to be constitutive for the will as such. In the third 'Replies to Objections Raised against the *Meditations*', he states that indifference arises when the person does not see clearly enough to allow for no doubt. But in that case the Sceptical will is indifferent in its operations, such indifference reflecting precisely the limits of the self's power in the exercise of doubt. The non-indifferent will, the – in Augustinian terms – truly free will, which turns towards the good and the true, is only possible as a sincere, philosophically justified exercise of the will due to its having passed through the Sceptical stage of indifference and restricting itself to indifference towards what is beyond its knowledge.[34] The point for Descartes is to 'convert', so turn around, to that which the intellect perceives clearly. This turning is not for him, as it is for Montaigne, a result of being attracted by one aspect or other of the object, but rather involves the will disciplining itself to remain within the limits of clear and distinct perceptions.

The strongest souls are those in which the will most easily conquers the passions.[35] In conquering the passions, the will first curbs the bodily consequences of particular passions, for example, running away in the case of fear, but then further controls the passion itself.[36] This latter task is only possible through firm and determinate judgement concerning truth and goodness.[37] Such judgement is possible to the extent to which the soul assents to that which is clearly perceived by the intellect. Furthermore, while the intellect is an instrument in this task, the will is that which governs: The will for Descartes needs to both control the passions and guide the intellect; indeed, these are one and the same task. While this account of the will has clear Stoic antecedents, particularly in the indifference of the will and the need to train it to control the passions, the will itself is, as we have seen, itself dependent on the passion of wonder. We will return to this point in the next chapter. For now, though, it is important to see that the method which Descartes develops brings the will into harmony with reason not to suppress the passions but rather to guide them in the interests of the self as a whole, consisting in both body and soul.

In agreement with Descartes, Pascal's diagnosis of the human predicament also finds that neither society nor nature can resolve it. Much more explicitly than Descartes, Pascal places this discussion within the discourse of the Fall but in doing so seeks to show that the fallenness of human nature can be understood initially *without* reference to Genesis. The trace of this fallenness is to be found the fundamental contradictions of being human. For Pascal, 'he [the human self] has within him the capacity for knowing truth and being happy, but he possesses no truth which is either abiding or satisfactory'.[38] If this were simply a contingent state, such that a self has not *yet* found that truth, there would be no contradiction here. The contradiction lies rather in the fact that the capacity it has for truth and happiness (hence goodness) is one which the self is incapable of realizing. Yet, it is nonetheless a capacity: It is directed at truth and goodness, and reaches some truths and some goods, but finds itself constitutively incapable of finding that truth and happiness that, as a capacity, it is directed towards. A capacity is a natural power, a power to fulfil something. As such, it implies a natural relation of capacity and the object of that capacity, such that the being with that capacity has a fixed nature. The fallenness of the self is indicated for Pascal precisely in that lack of fixed nature. The human self is defined negatively for Pascal: He is neither a beast nor an angel. The self-consciousness of his fallenness is that of not believing himself to be equal to the beast or the angel, but knowing both as poles of his own existence.[39] The human being is caught between the baseness of his actions and the greatness which he can perceive as his end. For Pascal, this is the natural state of the self. The self discovers in himself a mass of contradictions; he is to himself a 'monster that passes all understanding'.[40]

At play here for Pascal is the 'paradox' of the fallen state:

If man had never been corrupted, he would, in his innocence, confidently enjoy both truth and felicity, and, if man had never been anything other than corrupt, he would have no idea either of truth or bliss. … We possess an image of the truth and possess nothing but falsehoods, being equally incapable of absolute ignorance and certain knowledge; so obvious is it that we once enjoyed a degree of perfection from which we have unhappily fallen.[41]

A symptom of this state is the power of concupiscence in the self. In this, Pascal follows Augustine, but more explicitly than Descartes. While in Descartes the lack of a harmonious relationship between mind and body was a symptom of fallenness with respect to truth and goodness, in Pascal the yearning and desire for worldly things, particularly with regard to sexual satisfaction, results from a fundamental disorder in the human self, which – again following Augustine – he associates with original sin. Pascal understands concupiscence as threefold, being of the flesh, of the mind and of the will.[42] In each case, the self is driven by a desire for pleasure in those objects which it seeks to appropriate. The concupiscence of the will Pascal understands as self-love, manifesting itself in pride. The will is driven by pleasure for Pascal and in seeking pleasure comes to dominate the mind and overcome the power of reason. But this seeking is itself restless and cannot find satisfaction. This Pascal diagnoses as the source of the boredom (*ennui*) and the need for diversion. The pleasure the self takes in diversions he traces back to what we are diverting itself from, namely, the contradiction of the capacity for truth and goodness and the inability to fulfil that capacity: 'Not having been able to conquer death, wretchedness (*misère*), or ignorance, men have decided for their own happiness not to think about it.'[43] The diversions of life give us a means to escape for a while from such thoughts. But if these distractions are taken away, the human being falls into boredom. Boredom then is not an incidental mood but rather one in which the self comes face to face with its own emptiness. This emptiness is in its nature. As such, boredom is symptomatic of the paradox of fallenness: In boredom the self in feeling its emptiness has a sense of a higher destiny but finds itself incapable of reaching that destiny. This leaves the self in a 'state of unbearable sadness'. While for Descartes sadness is a passion of the soul and intellectual sadness arises from the belief that we have some evil,[44] Pascal understands it as revealing a fundamental element of human existence, namely, the contradiction between capacity and capability: between a natural capacity for truth and goodness, on the one hand, and being incapable of fulfilling that capacity – so of actualizing the potential (in Aristotelian terms) – on the other.

In the face of this condition of paradox and contradiction, Pascal rejects both a movement without and a movement within. The former he associates as a mere attempt to find happiness in diversions. In this he is expanding the idea of diversion well beyond his usual examples of gaming and gambling. Diversion for Pascal is closely related to curiosity: It attempts to displace the question of human wretchedness by seeking to find distraction in things which arouse curiosity. Pascal understands curiosity as the concupiscence of the mind, which is to say a perversion of a natural inclination of the mind. The capacity for knowledge gives rise to a desire for truth, but curiosity is for Pascal a corruption of that desire. This is so because the curious seek to attain truth, which is ultimately beyond their capacity to attain. It is a blindness rooted in a desire for that which can only be attained through divine grace.[45] But at the same time, an inward movement does not break out of the state of contradiction; it simply returns the self to its own incapacity. The (Stoic, but implicitly also Cartesian) promise of peace in the self is thus an illusion. The way within is a way beyond the passions, it is a way which, in the Stoic guise at least, involves a suppression of the passions and with Descartes a ruling by reason of the passions. This again assumes that reason has a capacity for truth which is constant and satisfying. What such an ambition ignores is the manner in which reason itself is undermined: 'Reason and the senses mutually mislead one another.'[46] The senses mislead reason with false appearances, but reason through the passions of the soul gives the senses false impressions in turn. Reason for Pascal cannot be disassociated from the passions of the soul, because it arouses these passions. What is at stake here is the relation of body and soul. Pascal, like Descartes, understands fallenness in terms of their relation, but he understands this relation as indicative of an incapacity in the human soul to negotiate its own ontological fixity: Echoing Montaigne, Pascal holds that the attempt to renounce passions is to seek to become God, the attempt to renounce reason is to seek to become beasts, and he concludes that neither course is possible.[47]

The place of method in Pascal's account is quite instructive here. As we have seen, for Descartes method is internal to reason: If we think rationally, that is, in accord with method, we arrive at the truth. Pascal – and in this he is following the Port-Royal logic – understands reason as the faculty for perceiving the connection between ideas and as more or less independent of the truth.[48] The role of method in such an understanding is ancillary to reason itself and allows reason to correct itself. Method plays more of a rhetorical role in Pascal; it is a function of communication, of making clear the terms of an argument and in so doing facilitating the judgement of good or bad reasoning. Crucially, Pascal understands reason as capable of going astray. It does so partly out of its own weakness but also because it is subject to the will. We find reasons to justify that which is most attractive to us. Due to this situation, reason, will and the senses are each incapable of recognizing the contradictory state in which the self finds itself. To see the contradiction as such is to see that which offends, indeed humiliates, reason and yet in turn gives reason its due place. Such sight requires a faculty to see beyond both the objects of the intellect and those of sense. For Descartes, the will assents or not to that which is presented to it by intellect and sense. What this account neglects, for Pascal, is that the will lies at the origin of belief in a more fundamental, and from the Cartesian point of view, problematic level: Things appear aspectively, the aspect that appears to a self is that aspect most pleasing to it, that which most attracts it.[49] The will is orientated towards that which attracts the self and as such it directs the mind to one aspect over another, in terms of preference. The will does not await the intellect nor is it in any straightforward sense in an a posteriori relation to sense: The will directs the intellect and the senses towards the object, but it does so in a manner which is pre-structured by desire. Thus, will and knowledge function aspectively and uncertainly.

In certain cases the mind does grasp its object immediately and with certainty. This is not a matter of the will or of knowledge alone but rather their unmediated unity. The faculty responsible for this Pascal terms the heart.[50] Through the heart, the self is directed towards the world and has an immediate sense of the reality of the world and its place within it. But at the same time the heart is a perspectival knowing, a knowing which is always locatable. Furthermore, the heart is a desiring knowing, a longing to know. It knows certain things immediately, but most things are closed to the heart. This lack is made up by reason, but reason fails to achieve the same immediacy as the heart. The heart shares the structure of the paradox of fallenness and uncovers the order of love in this paradox.

Pascal's account of the heart recaptures key elements of Augustine. As James Peters puts it, 'as Augustine conceives of the mind as both cognitive and passionate, so Pascal conceives of the heart as a unity of cognition and will'.[51] In the heart Pascal seeks to capture both that which is constitutive of the nature of the self and that which at once reveals the limits of its capacity and its receptivity for what is beyond its nature. This is reflected in the manner in which Pascal understands the heart to stand outside Descartes's conceptual distinction of mind and body. The heart is not, as for Descartes, simply an organ of the body, nor is love what it is in Cartesian terms, namely, a confused thought, which the mind experiences as a result of the movement of the animal spirits impelling the soul to join itself willingly to objects that appear agreeable to it.[52] For Pascal, one of the failures of Cartesian philosophy is not to have been able to understand the mixed nature, body and soul, of the human.[53] This failure has the corollary effect of misunderstanding love. The love of God, of which Pascal speaks, is ambiguous in its effects. It is through this love that the self recognizes the difficulty of his predicament, and yet when this love is faced up to, it opens up the only possibility of happiness. The heart is the organ of love: It is both of the soul and of the body; it is the organ of feeling and of understanding. The heart mediates between will and instinct, between that faculty which threatens to escape altogether into a transcendent nature and the earthly feeling shared with animals. The movement of love is one in which the self feels its own being most fully.

Love and knowledge are closely related for Pascal and are entwined in the heart. Human beings know not only through reason but also through the heart. This is so because the objects of knowledge in each case are different. In the case of the heart the object of knowledge is that which cannot be made evident and cannot be proved. What is known by the heart, however, is not simply contingent and peripheral but rather consists in first principles. What we know through the heart is not subject to an exhaustive causal account. This is so because it is known through feeling rather than by reasoning. Pascal gives examples of such objects: that we are not dreaming, that there are three dimensions in space, that there is an infinite series of numbers, that there is time and that there is movement.[54] In each of these cases the feeling halts any infinite regress: I do not need a further argument to prove that I am not dreaming, not because it is already proven but because it is a category mistake to try to prove it. 'The principles are felt, and the propositions are proved, both conclusively, although by different ways.'[55] What is felt in this way is a reality which is recognized prior to reason and to causes.[56] The first principles are felt not proved as is the case with love, which does not seek proof. The heart is the organ of trust, which as such grounds the human beings natural belief in the truth of the first principles and his love of God. What binds all these together is the basic movement of trust, which for Pascal is foundational to the endeavours of reason. Such a movement of trust requires a basic humility – a recognition of finitude, situatedness and the relation to what transcends such finitude: the relation to an object of trust which cannot be fully known, but which appears as felt in the sensibility of the heart.

3.2 The sceptical moment

For Descartes and Pascal, the Sceptical is a both inevitable and relative moment: inevitable to the human condition as embodied beings but relative to a certain way of being embodied. Will and heart, respectively, allow the Sceptical to be overcome.

The movement of Descartes's thought in the 'Discourse' is from a spontaneous Sceptic to an inward movement, which in turn spontaneously comes up with a thought regarding unity and diversity. These two spontaneous movements are significantly different. The self comes to a Sceptical attitude through the noticing anomalies: the opposition of appetites (nature) and teachers (society), cultural diversity and so forth. These bring forth Sceptical doubts onto the self. However, alongside those thoughts come the question of the greater perfection of the works of one or those of many. This is spontaneous in the sense that he has not encountered perfection, and even those things that are produced by one man really contain manifolds within them (the single architect alone does not build a city), yet he is directed towards this Godlike thought.[57] While Montaigne employed Scepticism self-reflectively to expand the self through its encounter with strangeness, Descartes's strategy from the beginning was to discover the inner unity at the origins of apparent diversity. In the 'Discourse' he tells us that when he began to reflect as a result of his spontaneous Sceptical thoughts, the first thought that came to him had to do with the one and the many, unity and diversity. He employs here architectural, political and ecclesiastical images. The city, its laws and its religion are products of a diversity of hands. Descartes's initial point is that, irrespective of truth and falsity, the products of one is greater than that of many. The products of more than one hand rely no less than the latter on the senses and presumably also on teachings from the past. But they have the advantage of being without contradiction. Being the result of one mind they bear the imprint of that one mind and have an inner source of unity. Hence, the first step to counter the spontaneous Sceptical movement of thought is to remove the diversity of viewpoints on which it is based. In this Descartes is not only countering Montaigne but also engaged from the beginning in a strategy of countering the very Scepticism he purports to be employing.

The Sceptical movement in the 'Discourse' concerns initially neither the natural inclinations, nor the sense of sight, but rather the sense of hearing. Hearing the diverse claims of teachers, the claims which are internally inconsistent, Descartes in his inward movement thinks from himself of the superiority of unity over diversity. In other words, he no longer listens to the voice of his teachers but rather listens to an inner voice within himself: The thought which he can find in himself alone will be superior to what he can find from a diversity of external sources. This is so because it defeats one of the main Sceptical strategies of arguing from diversity for a lack of a criterion of truth.[58] He is at the same time refusing the richness of Montaigne's Sceptical openness and in doing so taking the course Montaigne warns against: 'the common error of judging an other by myself'. Indeed, Descartes states this in what is most probably a conscious repudiation of Montaigne, that he felt 'free to judge all others by reference to myself'.[59] Arguably, though, he is mindful of Montaigne's admonition: before judging the other by himself he is seeking to secure his own judgment from any possible error.

What is striking here, however, is that the images of architecture, law and religion suggest a concern with the practical as much as the theoretical, and the 'Discourse' is quite explicit on this: Descartes's philosophical reflections 'opened my eyes to the possibility of gaining knowledge which would be very useful in life, and of discovering a practical philosophy which might replace the speculative philosophy taught in the schools'.[60] This is ironically reinforced by the care Descartes takes to forestall any political implications which derive from the doubt he prescribes and the images he uses. In effect, his images can be read as an attack on custom, reflecting the ambiguities of Montaigne's account of the customary: on the one hand, neither true nor just; on the other, better maintained than risk the chaos of its overturning. Descartes position here has a similar implication: Custom is to be maintained because of the difficulty and uncertainty of any attempt at reform. Like Montaigne, this conservative caution goes hand in hand with a concern for the self: 'My plan has never gone beyond trying to reform my own thoughts and construct them upon a foundation which is all my own.'[61] But this statement cannot be taken at face value. The foundation is to be a foundation for the sciences, which are precisely not all his own but rather common to all who can think clearly. Furthermore, these sciences are not merely theoretical but practical also: involving physics, medicine and morality.[62] While Descartes does not include political philosophy under morality, it is hard to avoid the conclusion that it must be contained therein. The reform of the sciences would need also be a reform of our understanding of politics (of which, with the exception of brief responses to others on Thomas Hobbes and Niccolò Machiavelli, Descartes furnishes us with very little). As such, the Sceptical movement of thought while allowing an outward observance of custom logically entails a lack of inner commitment to a polity which is not reconstructed in line with the 'highest and most perfect moral system'.[63] I will return to these questions in section 3.5; what I wish to point out here is that the Sceptical movement of thought directly concerns the self's moral being. Descartes will often discuss the desire for truth and for goodness as closely aligned. The Sceptical movement of thought makes the self painfully aware of this desire, precisely in showing its lack of indubitable criteria for judging either truth or goodness: Again the fallen state is apparent here, one in which criteria are lacking for that which the self most strongly desires.

The metaphysical task is to give systematic expression to this spontaneous Sceptical, to transform it into a methodical and universal Sceptical investigation, so as to find a way to overcome Scepticism or to gain clear insight into the fallen state and find a way of overcoming it. This he achieves only in the 'Meditations', and he does so through a radical and hyperbolic movement of doubt. Descartes understands systematic Scepticism as an exercise in doubt – he entitles the 'First Meditation': 'What can be called into doubt'. He begins with a completed Scepticism, so to speak, with a Sceptical *aporia* in Sextus Empircus's terms and then attempts to show the reducibility of this *aporia*. The *aporia* with which he begins is that between his received opinions and those beliefs arising from his critical self-reflection. From the beginning, however,

Descartes resists the force of the *aporia*: He speaks of finding received beliefs false, but this is an empirical, non-metaphysical falsity. At this early stage in the 'Meditations' he cannot, from the metaphysical point of view, legitimately claim certain beliefs to be false. In effect, in terms of what he can claim, he is beginning from opposing beliefs for which he has no criterion for deciding between them. He then takes the opposite course of the Pyrrhonian Sceptic: Instead of pursuing a dialectical strategy of putting forward contrary positions and then demonstrating the failure of all criteria to decide between them, he claims that the lack of such criteria indicates falsity. In other words, Descartes immediately goes about demolishing the *aporia* by curbing from the outset the possibility of conflicting beliefs: What is doubtful is taken as false. This is what the strategy of doubt allows him to do: Any claim to truth for which the criterion of truth is contestable – the senses, the waking state, sanity, a benign Creator – all of these are brought under the one homogenous category of doubtful and what is doubtful is taken as false. There are in such an account no conflicting positions, because the possibility of conflict, namely, two opposing claims to truth, is disallowed due to the lack of criteria: While between claims to truth there can be conflict, between two falsities there can be none.

Descartes not only translated the Pyrrhonist strategy of *epoché* into one of doubt but also placed from the beginning a criterion of truth in terms that escape any possible *aporia*, namely, a truth *sui generis*. While the Pyrrhonist does not speak in his own voice, but rather self-confessedly remains a parasite upon dogmatic theses, Descartes's 'Scepticism' involves the destruction of all such dogmatic theses. The difference here is crucial. The Sceptic offers himself as a self-reflective moment in all dogmatism. This self is radically dependent on others: He invents nothing himself but feeds off the words others give him. Such a self is a radically responsive self and can justify himself only in terms of his own empirical self: He *is* only as a being which experiences and does not believe, hence which lives only and always on the surface of his own being. Descartes, by seeking to 'demolish everything and … start again from the foundations',[64] has destroyed the very possibility of Sceptical argument, in Pyrrhonist terms. The truth *sui generis* is a truth to be found – if at all – not in dogmatism or Scepticism but rather at that extreme point where the very conditions of the dialectic of dogmatism and Scepticism have been taken away. That point emerges clearly with the deceiving genius: It is the point at which Descartes neutralizes the fallen state. The relation of creature and Creator whether pre- or postlapsarian is here at issue.

The question from the beginning of the 'First Meditation' is not simply whether he is mistaken in his beliefs but whether he has been deceived (the case of insanity is the exception, as there he does not think himself as deceived, but by that same token it can be excluded from consideration). The senses deceive (*falleret*), in sleep I am deluded (*delusum*), I delude myself (*me decipio*) and finally, of course, the deceiving demon deceives me (*fallere*).[65] In all these instances what is crucial is whether or not the self can trust: Can the self trust the testimony of its senses or of the sciences? Left without any basis to make such assent, its former beliefs are traced to its credulity (*credulitati*). The seeking for certainty is seeking for the trustworthy. The issue for Descartes is not one of withholding belief from that of which one cannot be certain; it is rather one of seeking for what one can trust. This has an ambiguous effect: On the one hand, the self is secured against error, but, on the other hand, is mired in uncertainty such that it can trust nothing or no one. It is, then, not surprising that in contrast to the calmness of mind which the *epoché* leads the Ancient Pyrrhonist, at the end of the 'First Meditation' he is left 'in dread' and 'amid inextricable darkness',[66] at the beginning of the 'Second Meditation' he speaks of being in a 'whirlpool … so that I can neither stand on the bottom nor swim to the top'.[67] Far from tranquillity, Scepticism has brought him close to despair.

That Descartes overcomes despair in the discovery of the cogito and then the proof of God's existence is well known. Central to both arguments is the question of origin or authorship (authority): the cogito as the author of its thoughts and God as the author of the idea of the infinite.[68] Despair is overcome only through a restoration of trust. That final restoration in the figure of the good, Creator God is responded to by Descartes with an outpouring of reverence.[69] The latter needs to be taken seriously: The Sceptical movement of thought, first spontaneous, then systematic, is finally overcome only through the recognition of the self as existing in a relation of benign dependence on God. This relation of dependence can be understood as grace, but a grace which has been affirmed as rational and comprehensible. But this trust is at once a trust in the self, a trust in the testimonies of that self and in the source of all truth and goodness. Descartes refers to this trust in terms of faith (*fidam*) in the natural light (Third Meditation) and lack of faith in the natural impulses (Sixth Meditation).[70] The restoration of trust at the same time offers a cure to the fallen state itself: Once trust is placed in the natural light then it needs to be kept free from all corruption. If the fallen state is one in which the body clouds the mind, then in this fallen state the natural as such cannot be trusted. A clear distinction in trust – in natural faith – needs to be drawn between the natural light of the mind and the natural sense which comes through the inclinations of the body. The movement is from deception to trust (faith), a movement mediated by reason. But reason alone does not achieve this transformation; it is at its basis a movement of the will.

The issue for Descartes is not that of reason alone, where it would be a question of truth and falsity, but rather one of what the self can assent to, which is a matter of the will, that of a self which is 'unwilling to be deceived'.[71] When Descartes comes (in the Fourth Meditation) to ask what the source of his errors are (and as such what the source of his vulnerability to deception is), he finds this source in the lack of correlation between his will and his intellect. The will that assents to what the intellect does not clearly perceive turns aside from what is true and good and this leads to error and sin.[72] Indeed, he argues that the will and the intellect have two different natures in human beings: The one is finite and the other infinite. It is quite consistent that while he talks of the intellect as *created* by God, Descartes refers to the will as *given* to him by God.[73] The human will is not created by God, because anything created lacks in perfection. The will as indivisible can only be given in its perfection. The created being is made by the inscrutable will of God. The will now is to be found on the other side of that divide. The human will is not a creature but rather is something of the divine given to the human. The will is free, but its freedom does not lie in arbitrariness. On the contrary, to the extent to which the self tends towards something because she recognizes it as good and true, the more free she is. In effect, Descartes is outlining a freedom modelled on the nature of divine nature: the unity of will and intellect. If this unity was present in the self in a pure form, then I would not have to deliberate as to how it should judge but would rather immediately perform a free, true and good judgement.[74] But precisely because he has been given only the divine will and not his intellect, the human is prone to error. Here Descartes alludes to the fallen condition: With a trace of the infinite prelapsarian condition, the human being cannot exercise it because of its clouded understanding. Hence, the limiting of the will is in fact its true expression. This requires a discipline limiting the will to assent only to that which the intellect can perceive clearly and distinctly.

The will is the mark of the divine, because like God it is infinite. In discussing the human possibility for true judgement, Descartes repeats the Creator God through his discussion of truth and falsity in terms of intellect and will. It is characteristic of the human being that the indissoluble unity of will and intellect in God is broken. Indeed, in its will and intellect, the self has two distinct natures, one finite, the other infinite, one created, the other uncreated. Through the unity of will and intellect Descartes restores unity in the self of these two natures, returns the self to a prelapsarian condition and offers it the possibility to avoid repeating the Fall, namely, by recognizing in the will that which is not subject to the weaknesses and vulnerabilities of created beings. The Sceptical is not simply traversed but can be systematically suspended so long as the human being retains a harmonious relation of will and intellect (and as we will see of desire and power). If the will does not depart from the clear and distinct perceptions, human judgement cannot fall into error.

We can understand the movement of the 'Meditations' as one from Pyrrhonian Scepticism to a form of Pelagian Stoicism, but only with a number of caveats. First, as I have shown, Descartes never takes the Pyrrhonian position seriously: He employs a limited number of the Pyrrhonian *topoi* and does not engage in the dialectical movement of equally compelling arguments. That equality of reason and its resulting *aporia* is fundamentally denied by the account of reason which is at the heart of Descartes's project. Second, while the self which emerges from the 'Meditations' is close to that of a Stoic sage, it is one which – as I will go on to show later in more detail – does not so much suppress the passions as employs them to rebuild the world around him. This is a fundamental divergence with both the Sceptic and Stoic accounts of the self: The self which emerges in Descartes's 'Meditations' is one which in mastering itself strives to master nature.

Both Descartes and Pascal recognize the limits of reason and for both reason reaches its limit in the infinite: as with Duns Scotus the fundamental ontological distinction is that between the finite and the infinite. But while for Descartes, as we will see, infinity is a quality of God, for Pascal nature itself is infinite. What this means is that in the domain of nature – in the discourse of physics – no universal statements are possible. In this sense, Pascal returns to Montaigne's Sceptical openness to experience: No rational statements about nature can defeat experience because nature is beyond human reason.[75] Descartes seeks to secure the knowledge of nature from all Scepticism and give us a way for thought immune from error (or sin). For Pascal (following Montaigne) this is a greatest presumption: Far from allowing the human being to escape its fallen nature, it simply accentuates one symptom of that fallenness and indeed one cause of it, namely, pride and arrogance. Similarly to Descartes, Pascal relates the Sceptical to the fallenness of human reason and to its embodied state. The Sceptical is true and will remain true because of human fallenness. While for Descartes the Sceptical can be overcome through a metaphysical method, for Pascal the Fall cannot be undone by human effort alone and as such the Sceptical is a legitimate, but partial, philosophical response. He states, 'The one [Stoics] seeing some traces of its [humanity's] initial greatness and ignorant of its corruption treated nature as healthy and in no need of a healer ... the other [Pyrrhonians], experiencing the wretchedness of the present age and unaware of the dignity of its inception, treats nature as inevitably weak and incurable.'[76] This line comes in Pascal's conversation with the Isaac Le Maître de Sacy, one of the leading presences in the Port-Royal community and known for his antipathy to philosophy. One of the striking features of that discussion is that there is no mention of Descartes, although it probably took place in 1655 when the Cartesianism was central to philosophical discussions, not to speak of the fact that Descartes's *Principles of Philosophy* introduced Pascal to philosophy. Descartes is surreptitiously present, though, as some of the account of Montaigne in that conversation was in effect a summary of the 'First Meditation'. That Descartes does not appear in his own voice may be explained, according to Vincent Carraud's analysis, by the fact that Descartes does not fit easily into the divide of Stoicism and Pyrrhonism by which Pascal attempts to explain philosophy. This 'ambivalence of Descartes' is such that he plays both the part of the Sceptic like Montaigne and that of the Stoic like Epictetus, not just in the 'undeniably Stoic themes of his ethics, but even more in the thought of the greatness of thought [*des thèmes indéniablement stoïciens de sa morale, mais surtout comme pensée de la grandeur de la pensée*]'.[77] But this ambivalence is fatal for Pascal, because what we have here are two paths of reason which cannot be united because they are mutually exclusive and destroy one another. When reason is considered only in terms of its own capacities, all are 'sunk in one or the other' of these two paths.[78] The only recourse is through the Gospels, which teach that all weakness is to be found in nature and all strength in grace. By attempting to navigate from the Sceptical to the Stoical, Descartes is in Pascal's terms suggesting that the self may be able to ultimately overcome its own fallenness and reach humanity's primordial greatness. In so doing he is denying the agency of grace and is taking up a Pelagian or at least semi-Pelagian position. For Pascal the point is not so much to overcome this abyss of the fallen condition but tc live in it, not to knock down and rebuild the buildings but to find a proper mode c dwelling within them, not to reconcile contradictions but to accept the 'paradox of th fallen state'. The human being who can do this is one guided not so much by the w as by the heart.

Pascal follows Montaigne's 'dialectic' of the three forms of humanity much clc than Descartes did. He states,

> Knowledge has two extremes, which meet; one is the pure state of natural ignoran<
> of every man at birth, the other is the extreme point reached by those with not
> souls who, having explored everything man is capable of knowing, realize th
> know nothing and return to their original state of ignorance. But it is a v
> ignorance of self-awareness. Those who are in between, who have discarded t

original state of natural ignorance but have not yet reached the other ... presume to understand it all. They upset the world, and judge everything badly.⁷⁹

As with both Montaigne and Descartes, this progression begins in ignorance and for both also is a progression of self-awareness. Furthermore, all three agree on the dangers of the middle state. However, Pascal (similarly to Montaigne) sees the end of this progression in an acceptance of ignorance. For Pascal this acceptance (as also for Montaigne) is rooted in the acknowledgment of the infinite distance from God.

While both Pyrrhonism and Stoicism are limited perspectives on human fallenness, Pascal remains closer to the Pyrrhonian. This is so because the Pyrrhonian in Pascal's account has the virtue of humility. The Pyrrhonian recognizes that the goal of certain knowledge, the goal of a purely rational account of the real and of human life is an illusion. As such, the Pyrrhonian poses the objection to the Stoic, which he (along with all 'dogmatic' philosophers above all the Cartesians), cannot answer: 'From the uncertainty as to our origins derives uncertainty as to our nature'.⁸⁰ Fallen nature is uncertain because it has no natural knowledge of its former greatness. Lacking such knowledge means being radically alienated from its origins. The Pyrrhonist has seen this alienation most clearly and the Sceptical moment is a moment of its realization.

Pascal follows Montaigne in affirming the inescapability of diversity. The relation the soul to that which appears to it, the relation then of the self to the world, is er unambiguous: 'The same things makes us cry and laugh.'⁸¹ We are affected by vorld in ways which do not allow for simple unity or classification. Things appear vs which touch us at different levels and in different ways. This is so much the at 'I have never judged anything in exactly the same way. I cannot judge a ile doing it: I have to do as painters do and stand back, but not too far. How Guess [devinez].'⁸² The self changes, its past experience of a thing itself the way it perceives it now, such that the judgement is never the same. e, what is given is so in a situation, in which the self is engaged. Even ds back to reflect on that situation, there is nothing in the situation itself ow it is truly to be judged. What we are faced with here for Pascal is not m but a riddle: Deviner means more than simply guess, but to divine e. The secret here is the proper way to be towards things with which d, when it cannot reach the origin of its own knowing. Judgement that which is clearly perceived but rather a contingent assent to in a particular manner, but which has and will appear otherwise. arises the diversity of custom, indeed, custom itself. If nature he natural laws were clear and when clear were followed, then for a second nature in the form of custom. 'Habit/Custom is stroys the first.'⁸³ But even this first nature Pascal fears to be There is no natural access to our nature because 'instinct about it.⁸⁴ 'Experience' is a word rarely used by Pascal. stinct and reason. Here he is understanding experience in e are accustomed. Only instinct can break through that ct rarely gives us unalloyed access to things. There are, t our reason is too corrupted to know them. Living in custom we cannot avoid the customary, but we should follow custom only because it is custom, not because it is just or true.[85] The origin of all laws and customs is to be found in usurpation. Yet, this origin needs to be hidden or laws will lose their authority. Hence, the Pyrrhonians are right that custom is to be followed not because it is true or just, but because human beings have no access to a standard of truth and justice by which to measure it.

The Sceptical gives expression to a fundamental truth of human experience. It does so, however, as a corrective: Pyrrhonism is true only because there are non-Pyrrhonians:[86] It is (as we have already seen) fundamentally parasitic on dogmatic claims. Outrageous claims are made – such that human beings are not by nature steeped in inevitable weakness – and this provokes Pyrrhonian arguments. The clear implication is that Descartes's claim to find certain truth does not overcome the Sceptical but provokes it.[87] This is the case because both Descartes and the Sceptic share the one principle, which Pascal wishes to contest, namely, that the fundamental truths are to be discovered by reason or not at all. The Pyrrhonist denies that certainty is possible and suspends judgement, the dogmatist claims that he has found certainty, but in both cases the measure is certainty. Pascal's argument against both is that the very claim to certainty as a measure fails to account for the peculiar, indeed, contradictory place of the self. The key to overcoming the Sceptical then is not to seek certainty, because this will remain unachievable and hence will simply perpetuate unhappiness, but rather to probe deeper into the source of unhappiness and the mode in which it is perceived. Unhappiness for Pascal is something felt; felt not as a discrete state, but rather as a fundamental condition. Within this feeling of unhappiness is discovered a truth that reason can only find if it listens to that feeling itself. But in doing that reason discovers its own limitations.

Unhappiness indicates the between state of being human: Human beings sense in themselves both greatness and wretchedness. These relate to each other in an 'unending circle' which Pascal states as follows: 'Thus it is wretched to know one is wretched, but there is greatness in knowing one is wretched.'[88] Pascal is perhaps responding to Montaigne's denial of wretchedness, the latter's taking up of a comic rather than tragic attitude. But for Pascal, to know oneself as wretched is to recognize a higher state within oneself which has been lost: not to know one's true place but to know that one has fallen from it and has no capacity to return.[89] This is both the source and the limitation of the Sceptical moment. The self finds itself in a non-place, suspended 'between two abysses of infinity and nothingness'[90] or between angels and beasts. This non-place is one in which no repose is possible and as such the Pyrrhonist promise of tranquillity is a vain one.[91] It is so because the suspension of judgement simply reflects the state of unhappiness: The *a-topos* of human being is an *aporia* considered in terms of reason alone, because it is embodies a contradiction at the level not of logic but of practical reason – the contradiction between desire and capacity. Faced with this contradiction, to suspend judgement is in effect to limit desire to the self's capacity to satisfy it. But the capacity in question is that of reason, and desire teaches reason not simply of its incapacity but of the presence of a higher capacity, which is the capacity of reception rather than action, that, namely, of the heart.

Pascal's final judgement on the Sceptical moment can be seen in his account of the wager, which is nothing other than a refusal of the Pyrrhonian ideal of *ataraxia*. In effect, Pascal introduces the situation of the wager in terms of a classical Pyrrhonist *aporia*. This is a situation of a finite being before the infinite. We know that there is an infinite, but not its nature. God can be known neither in his existence nor in his essence. By natural light then we are faced with an *aporia*: We can argue for the existence of God and against, but we have no absolute criteria by which to judge between these two accounts. 'Reason cannot make you choose.'[92] Faced with this situation the Pyrrhonist suspends judgement and finds 'by accident' tranquillity. It is the voice of the Pyrrhonist which asserts itself here: 'The right thing is not to wager at all.'[93] Pascal sweeps this objection aside: 'You have to wager. It is not a matter of volition, you are already embarked [*C'est n'est pas volontaire, vous êtes embarqués*].'[94] In other words, the state of *aporia* is not a possibility; as an existing being the human is already engaged in the play of dice. The wager concerns volition, concerns choice; indeed, for Pascal it concerns the ultimate choice, but that choice cannot begin at the beginning, it must begin *in medias res*. The necessity to choose is not dictated by reason: 'Reason is not hurt by choosing one or the other'[95] and presumably is not hurt either by choosing neither one nor the other. The discourse is at the level of reason, natural light, not faith, but, nonetheless, the starting point is not in reason but rather in sentiment, feeling. It is the heart which is already committed, because the heart does not require certainty and yet must commit itself. It is the heart that perceives wretchedness and it is the heart which disallows any escape from the game. Hence, the wager takes place through reason, but is made necessary by the heart.

Here then the Sceptical moment is overcome on two levels: The Sceptical remains on the level of reason where it remains unassailable, but that level is never ultimate; and furthermore, the stakes of happiness make the decision without sufficient reason inescapable. Reason can only know the finite, but the infinite is at stake, and in such a case reason and Scepticism have to be overcome, or rather are always already overcome. The choice is one in which, Pascal affirms, the only rational response is to decide for the infinite, to decide to believe.

For neither Descartes nor Pascal can the Sceptical *aporia* be ultimate. But for Pascal, if we were to remain at the level of reason it would be ultimate, whereas for Descartes it is only through reason that we arrive at the state in which will and intellect operate harmoniously to avoid error. The projects of transcending reason, on the one hand, and of rebuilding science and indeed human life generally in terms of reason, on the other, reflect divergent understandings of what philosophy is, what its ends are and its origins with respect to being a self in the world. It is with these questions that we can delve deeper into the related but in fundamental terms opposing views of the how and why of philosophy.

3.3 The beginnings and ends of philosophy

In the Preface to the French edition of the *Principles of Philosophy* Descartes gave the following account of wisdom:

... a perfect knowledge of all things that mankind is capable of knowing ... In order for this knowledge to be perfect it must be deduced from first causes; thus ... we must start with a search for first causes or principles. These principles must ... be so clear and so evident that the human mind cannot doubt their truth when it attentively concentrates on them; and ... the knowledge of other things must depend on them.[96]

Implicit in this understanding of the principles, the beginnings, of philosophy are the twin operations of intuition and remembering, the contribution of the two faculties of intellect and memory. Memory is that which, as Descartes says, 'connects the present with what precedes it'.[97] It is in this very connection, however, that fundamental philosophical difficulties are to be found. In ways that resemble Montaigne, but with almost opposite consequences, Descartes expresses a deep suspicion of memory. Memory is governed by a logic of similarity or resemblance: What resembles the present is found in the past; the connection between present and past in memory is hence one of gradual difference. It is not by accident that Descartes in the first line of the *Rules* attacks both this logic of resemblance and the influence of habit.[98] Therein we see the danger of memory: Memory is not merely the deliberate act of recalling but rather is for the most part habit, that is, the forming of ways of thinking and acting, treating the present case in terms of its similarity with past cases. For Descartes, however, similarity is vague and uncertain; the movement of thought is in the opposite direction, in seeing differences. But such differences are precisely what habit covers over. As set out in the *Rules*, then, habit has none of the flexibility to variation which Montaigne suggested but is exclusively the becoming familiar with something, the overcoming of distance, indeed, in a real sense an incorporation. While for Montaigne, too, thinking was seeing differences, such a seeing occurred as embodied and situated. Habit articulates the ambiguous nature of such situatedness: both limiting and opening up. By equating memory and habit Descartes guards against any such ambiguity. The incorporation inherent in habit is also a stretching back to the initial encounter with what has become habitual and a stretching forth beyond the present in the taken-for-grantedness of certain ways and ideas. The suspicion of habit is in fact a suspicion of the past, which shows itself only in resemblances (e.g., images). The beginning is a setting out of the beginner's limits on herself, a cutting off of that which has already begun from any standard other than its own limits. Through this reflection Descartes discovers that there are two operations of the intellect: intuition and deduction.

While Descartes is careful in defining intuition to delimit it from the imagination and sense perception,[99] this is not possible in the case of deduction and memory. While it is *prima facie* possible to understand intuition as an act of the attentive mind, neither tied to sense perception nor employing images, it seems evident that memory is necessary for deduction, given that deduction involves a series of steps, in which every past step must be kept present in the mind.[100] Because Descartes defines intuition as a momentary insight of the mind, but must account for the fact that science consists in the connections between what individually can be grasped intuitively, he is forced to recognize an operation of the intellect which 'in a sense gets its certainty through memory'.[101]

The radical punctuality of intuition, which allows Descartes to break with any logic of similarity or resemblance, and hence with the past, supplies him with an atemporal, or, better, adurational, access to first principles.[102] The *deduction* from such first principles requires the aid of the faculty of memory, hence of duration. But there is nothing in the intuition which allows for such a temporal duration. The intuition once made can either be repeated or remembered. If it is repeated, then deduction can never get started; if it is remembered, then the source of its certainty, namely, the *act* of intuiting, is lost. The problem in the first instance is not the uncertainty of memory but rather the requirement to ground knowledge on the certainty of a momentary and indeed adurational act. Hence, deduction receives 'in a sense' its certainty from memory but loses its basis in intuition.

Faced with this difficulty, Descartes attempts in 'Rule 7' to collapse deduction and intuition. He does so, however, by, in effect, teaching his intellect to acquire a habit of thinking. Faced with a deductive series, the thinking self passes through this series several times, each time imprinting the series deeper on her mind, so that eventually memory is left with little or no work to do. The self does not need to make the effort to recall the series: Once it starts the series in its mind it can 'swiftly' run through it to the end. In this way I '*seem* to intuit the whole thing at once'.[103] This appears so because the operation of the mind occurs *as if* no time passes, as if everything were grasped at once. In effect, however, intuition is being supplemented by habit, but habit which has been spiritualized, purified of any bodily element. A new habit has been acquired, through which the intellect no longer requires an act of recalling for its certainty but rather has formed the habit of combining, along with a particular intuition, a series of deductive steps.

The crucial step here is that of suggesting that it is possible *simultaneously* to intuit a relation and to pass on to the next. The moment of intuition is being understood as allowing for passing away; implicitly it is being understood not as a adurational moment (*nunc stans*), as it first appeared, but rather as a passing moment, a moment in time. As a passing moment it is already becoming past, it is a beginning which does not grasp itself but rather is occupied with what has *already* begun. Memory has not been overcome; rather, it has been merged with intuition.

To begin at the beginning is to begin in such a way that one's own past in the sense of all former habits of thought have been crossed out. This cannot be achieved at the methodological level of the *Rules*, because the problem of memory remains unresolved at this level; in the 'Meditations', method is treated metaphysically. A similar concern with habit and a similar ambiguity regarding memory can nevertheless be found in the later work too; both are centred on the problem of intuition. The Sceptical moment, in its first spontaneous and later systematic instantiations, arises in part from a suspicion of habit: Opinions which since childhood have been habitual and unquestioned are put in doubt. What is crucial is not the falsity of some of his prior opinions but rather that their origins remain unclear. Some of the opinions which derive from his teachers or indeed his natural inclinations may be true; what is crucial is to find the principle on which he can base his certainty. Such a principle will be the beginning of philosophy.

Descartes finds this principle in the certainty of the ego's existence, in the intuition of the necessary relation between I think (*cogito*) and I am (*sum*), thinking and being. But if this does mark the beginning of philosophy, is the way of doubt itself philosophical? In his *Conversation with Burman*, Descartes refers to the stage of the 'First Meditation' as 'beginning to philosophize' and as 'pre-philosophical'.[104] But if philosophy begins with first principles and if indeed without them the very possibility of philosophy is left open, then the beginning of philosophy and the beginning of philosophizing are different things. To begin to philosophize is pre-philosophical because, while it is a turning away from nature and society in their unquestioned validity, the first principles, upon which alone philosophy can be built, remain as yet undiscovered. The method of doubt goes 'straight for the basic principles on which all ... former beliefs rested'.[105] Thus, the philosophical concern with principles, with true and certain beginnings, is already foreshadowed, here though those first principles have not yet been discovered.[106]

What he intuits in the cogito is already implicit from the start of the 'Meditations', to the extent to which he begins with doubting, that is, with thinking. What has been gained is a new *beginning*, not any*thing* new. The new building will have the same bricks as the one which has been knocked down. But this recouping of that set aside in the 'First Meditation' is by no means guaranteed at the beginning of the 'Second'. On the contrary, the destruction of doubt has left a nothingness. At the start of the 'Second Meditation' all that seems to be left is a phantom, the evil genius. Out of this nothingness arises something totally different (*diversum*)[107] from all that has been 'destroyed'. It is totally different, because it is not part of the world the self has known or could know, in other words, not part of the created world. It is something *un*created. Central to the cogito argument in the 'Second Meditation' is the figure of God. It is the Voluntarist God as omnipotent Creator in the guise of the evil genius, who brings doubt to the hyperbolic level. The emphasis is on this God who creates all things, even rationality itself. All that he creates is imperfect and must remain open to doubt. It is for this reason that in the created realm nothing of certainty is to be found. The created realm extends beyond the actual existent things. Descartes's God is the Creator of the eternal truths.[108] Hence, no essence can be free of doubt. But what Descartes finds in the cogito is a pure existence, an existence without essence, neither a thing nor an idea but rather the existence of the I in the act of thinking. The I is not an enduring substance independent of the act of thinking. The certainty of the cogito depends on no reference to anything created by God. This can be seen in the very necessity of the cogito itself. Nothing created is absolutely necessary as even the truths of mathematics depend on the divine will and could have been otherwise. The existence of the I that thinks is, however, necessary in a way which is not dependent on that will. Descartes later states that the rational soul was created by God, but this can only be subsequently affirmed. The cogito argument would break down if God created the I think in its self-transparency, because it is not yet shown that God does not deceive. The place of the cogito is beyond creation. But this means that the ego is without past and without future; it is merely in a momentary act. Descartes recognizes the full implications of this in the 'Third Meditation' where he makes the very duration of the ego dependent on the creative act of God.[109] This creative act is irrelevant for the certainty of the ego, however. The certainty excludes the creative act of God and is based on that exclusion.

The issue of the relation of philosophy to the pre-philosophical remains unresolved at the level of the cogito. At this level, the identity of the I which thinks with the I which decided to doubt cannot be established. Indeed, in terms of the 'Second Meditation', such an identity of the cogito with the meditating self, though assumed, plays no constitutive role in the development of the thought of the thinking thing. In relation to the doubt of the 'First Meditation' nothing is gained in the sense that none of the three main areas doubted, sense perception, self-awareness and rationality, finds any foundation in the certainty of the ego. As at the end of the 'First Meditation', in the 'Third' all he can do is examine the implications of his idea of God. The difference in *mood* between the meditating self at the end of the 'First' and the beginning of the 'Third Meditation' is, however, immense: The certainty of existence has tempered the passions that were most vocal at the end of the 'First' and the beginning of the 'Second Meditations'. This is not due to suppression of the passions but to a redirection of thought to thinking alone, where the wider issues of the self and its well-being have been bracketed.

Having found a certainty in the uncreated realm of his own ego, he can find no guarantee for anything durable, as the cogito has no duration in itself. It is not the structure of consciousness then which grants the notion of duration; the inward movement is a movement away from duration. What he is left with, however, is empty: a certainty of himself as uncreated, but adurational, excluding the possibility of progression necessary for knowledge. The question is now not what I can know for certain to be but rather what it is which makes knowing, as philosophy, at all possible. This question is an ontological one; it asks of the being of that which allows something to be, of the first being, the beginning. The adurational cogito needs to find a source of justification for its temporal connections in order to be a foundation for knowledge, in order for something to begin.

It is such motivations which bring Descartes to ask about the limits of his own capacity, about the possibility of a gift from elsewhere, the possibility of a source of fulfilment outside of himself. The latter point is crucial: The movement of thought from the 'Second' to the 'Third Meditation' is not from the self to the world by way of God but rather a deepening of his knowledge of himself. He begins the 'Third Meditation' by withdrawing all sensory engagement with the world, conversing with himself and attempting to 'achieve little by little a more intimate knowledge of myself'.[110] He is seeking to come to an intimate and, indeed, adequate knowledge of himself. The idea of God within him is an idea for which he does not have an adequate capacity; an idea which as infinite and perfect must, he tells us, come from that being which implanted the idea in him. The self, he states, can only understand itself as a doubting being and hence as lacking certainty, on the basis of the idea of God, because only this idea gives him the sense of a perfection which he is lacking.[111] Hence, the idea of God as Creator can be seen to ground the thinking of the 'Meditations' from the start.[112] From the intuition of the cogito, the certainty of which cannot depend on God, its duration as a *res cogitans* cannot be derived. From the fact that I exist in this moment there is no necessity that I will exist in the next.[113] If, as Descartes argues, he has not derived its being from himself or from his parents, then only from God can he be said to derive it. But for there to be a substance at all it must endure, it must have duration. Hence, it is the very substantiality of the *res cogitans* that is at stake here. Only if the cogito is preserved from beyond itself can its identity and duration be assured. Hence, the cogito which appears as self-sufficient in the 'Second Meditation' is revealed as radically dependent on God in the 'Third Meditation'. The nature of the human being is one of which we can speak only abstractly, only in the moment of thought, as independent of God. Once we speak of it durationally, once we wish to understand it as temporal, then its radical dependence on God is revealed.

This dependence, however, which is gratuitous from one moment to the next, is an act of grace in the Pelagian sense, grace as creation, except Descartes understands creation as continuous. Philosophy in its beginning must recognize divine grace, that is, the recognition of the cogito, that although it is self-certain in its self-reflexive being, the cogito's own existence as an enduring being is dependent on creation. This is a subtle shift in the self-understanding of the cogito, from an assertion of its own radical independence to an acknowledgment of itself as a dependent, created, being. But there is no contradiction between these two forms of self-relation; rather they refer to distinct aspects of itself: in its own adurational self-certainty and its temporal being through the grace of God, manifest in the divine trace, the *imago Dei*, in the mind of the cogito-self.

The certainty of the clear and distinct ideas as such does not depend on God, rather that this certainty is maintained over time only God can guarantee. While intuition is the beginning of philosophy, that which begins and endures does so only through God's preserving will. To secure the unity of these two beginnings, however, Descartes must show how the human and divine on the level of thought and the level of being reflect and complement each other. To achieve this, Descartes, as already pointed out, returns to the idea of the human as bearing the mark of God. As we have seen, that mark is to be found in the will, because the will is like God infinite. The attempt to repeat the beginning in God requires the limiting of that faculty in which man resembles God the most, namely, will. Only through a reconstitution of that original unity in God can philosophy begin at the beginning.

It is in this context that near the close of the 'Fourth Meditation' Descartes collapses deduction into intuition as he attempted already in the *Rules*. Once more he appeals to the possibility of acquiring a new habit, the habit, namely, of not erring[114] or, positively stated, of uniting intellect, will and intuition. This new habit in effect preserves the cogito as the certain beginning of philosophical knowledge. The incomprehensibility of God rests on his relation to the beginning: The creation of eternal truths differs fundamentally from the human relation to them. The latter rests on their 're-creation' out of a nothingness, which, however, was reached through the destructive force of doubt. The preserving act – in God one with the creating act – is only possible through habit. Once this habit has been established, however, the incomprehensible relation of God to the beginnings of things in the eternal truths has been replaced by a fully comprehensible one, that, namely, of the clarity of the idea of the ego cogito.

It is a criticism which is as old as the first responses to the 'Meditations'[115] that while the cogito is true and certain because it is a clear and distinct idea, the certainty that anything clearly and distinctly perceived is true can only be justified by recourse to God's existence, which in turn is known to be true because we have a clear and distinct idea of it. Faced with this objection, Descartes makes the distinction between intuition and memory.[116] Corresponding to this distinction, Pascal distinguishes between heart and reason.[117] The heart like intuition in Descartes does not function through steps, and does not depend on memory. It is an immediate felt relation to the real. It is a relation which, however, again like intuition can be prepared for. There are obstacles to the heart, which through reflection can be removed. Reason, on the other hand, like deduction in Descartes requires memory. For Pascal, too (taking this parallel a little further), the beginning of philosophy has to do with this relation of heart and reason. But it is precisely in exploring that relation that the fundamental difference between them emerges.

The heart does not judge according to the measure of certainty; it has no time to wait. The heart knows that I am awake, although it is not at all certain. I might be dreaming, but I cannot convince my heart of that.[118] For a self to entertain the possibility that it is not awake would require it to suspend its heart, to, so to speak, put itself on life support. The seeking after intuitive certainty is only possible through such a suspension of life. This suspension is not indifferent; it is possibly fatal for the self's future happiness, for Pascal. In making its judgements, the heart does not depend on the intellect as a gatekeeper to supply it with that on which it is to judge; the heart is already committed. The heart discloses the human dependence on the real. It denies Sceptical *aporia* as much as Sceptical doubt by showing the irreducible dependence on nature and on God: Reason cannot escape the fundamental trust in those principles which appear to it, nor can it escape the contradictions of human existence which the heart reveals.[119] In that situation philosophy cannot claim a foundational position; it cannot claim to rebuild but can only find a way of inhabiting those buildings which already exist. Philosophy for Pascal is a mode of inhabiting not of building. It begins therefore not with foundations but with the inescapable realities in which the self finds itself. The buildings are necessarily unstable; the self inhabits them in anxiety and with a sense of urgency. 'To have no time for philosophy [*se moquer de la philosophie*] is to be a true philosopher.'[120] To have time for philosophy, not to mock it, is to be in Descartes's heated room.[121] It is to be in abstraction from situatedness, allowing for purely rational reflection. Such a philosophy of the mind, however, is impossible for someone who has no such secluded time, whose time remains the time of the heart, the time of the lover, who is uncertain that he will be here in one hour.[122] While for Descartes the cogito is not certain of the future, it does not require that certainty because it has in the moment a sort of eternal insight, an adurational glimpse into the foundations of being; for Pascal the uncertainty of the future concerns nothing less than the possibility of death without wisdom and a destiny of eternal damnation. To be a true philosopher is to mock philosophy's claim to a time abstracted from mortality.

The beginning of philosophy for Pascal takes place in the shadow of death, the shadow of the uncertainty of the next hour. The delay which Descartes speaks of, the waiting for an appropriate time to reflect, is premised on the assumption that each moment can be viewed *per species aeternitatis* in the moment of intuition and as bound together through the creative act of God, who preserves the world in being from moment to moment. This radical dependence on God has to do with the will of creation, which affects the thinker not so much in his personal being, which is certain, as in his participation in the temporal being of the world. But Pascal's thinker is faced not with the dependence of things on the creative will of God but rather with the reality of his own death and the question of his mortality. In the face of the contradictions of human existence, the first, and in a sense the only, philosophical question concerns the immortality of the soul. This question is inescapable, because it opens up the possibility of redemption in the face of fallenness.[123] Philosophers who neglect this question are undermining the very project of philosophizing itself. Pascal does not mention Descartes directly in this regard, but Descartes despite the centrality of the immortality of the soul in the title of the first edition of the 'Meditations', admits in his 'Replies' to Arnauld that he had failed to prove it and drops all mention of it from the title of both the subsequent Latin and French translated editions.[124] The question for Descartes is not ultimate, because philosophy is not concerned with death (as it is in different ways for both Pascal and Montaigne) but rather with survival: Being masters of nature for him could lead also to being masters of our own bodily nature – death is a failure of the organism, which, with advances in medicine, could be expected to be greatly delayed.[125] While Descartes did acknowledge divine providence in this regard, that irrespective of advances in medicine the human being was subject to divine will, philosophically this was not a matter of concern. Philosophy, and the self which philosophizes, is concerned with that which is within its own capacity and with the extension of this domain.[126] If philosophy can cure the effects of the Fall, then it might also cure death depending on whether or not death was a result of the Fall.[127] In short, as Pascal suspected, for Descartes the human being is the master of his own salvation.

The only way to be happy is to become immortal, Pascal states.[128] This is to say that happiness is beyond the self's capacity to achieve. Death, ignorance and wretchedness belong together as the three conditions that the human being cannot overcome: The human self sees immortality, knowledge and happiness within herself, but she cannot reach them. She seeks to find happiness through diversions, but this cannot make her happy because they come from outside.[129] In common with Augustine and also with the Stoic and Sceptic accounts of happiness, Pascal understands independence from outside effects – broadly speaking from chance or fortune – as a necessary conditions of happiness. To seek happiness in the world is to look in the false domain; only an inward turn can lead to happiness, but that inward turn finds a self incapable of achieving happiness, who nonetheless yearns for it. The way to show this is to face that which is least in the self's power, namely, death. Death is not generalizable in its existential import: My death concerns me in a manner which is exclusive to me. Faced with death, the question of the afterlife cannot be set aside from philosophical reflection (as both Montaigne and Descartes attempt to do) but becomes central and 'all our actions and thoughts must follow such different paths, according to whether there is hope of eternal blessing or not'.[130] Pascal offers no positive argument for the immortality of the soul; the yearning for happiness itself transcends mortality. A secret instinct 'left over from the greatness of our original nature' tells the self that its true happiness lies in rest.[131] All the striving which the self engages in is useless to its happiness and that includes philosophy. It is in this sense that Pascal says of Descartes that he is 'useless and uncertain'.[132] While philosophy can teach about nature, it stands in an ambiguous position regarding happiness and salvation: 'It is no good philosophers telling us: Withdraw into yourselves and there you will find your good. We do not believe them, and those who do believe them are the most empty and silly of all.'[133] The injunction to withdraw into the self is not in any way empty or silly. It is what Pascal himself advocates. What is foolish, rather, is the idea that philosophy can achieve this withdrawal and can find the good within. This is so because the ultimate philosophical question concerns the immortality of the soul, but when we pose that question philosophically, what we find, for Pascal, is that it is both unavoidable and unanswerable either by reason or by the heart in their natural states. The human self is faced with mortality and with the question of its destiny. The unhappiness of the present state of being in the world indicates something beyond the world; beyond that is the mortal existence which the human being knows. Reason cannot respond to this unhappiness, because it is rooted in a contradiction. Reason seeks to take one side or other of the contradiction but in doing so argues in circles. Reason responds in this way to the heart which feels the contradiction and suffers from it. The heart recognizes the contradiction as being unsurpassable and as such if reason is to follow from the intuitions of the heart it cannot begin from itself. It has to rather begin from that which humbles it, namely, its failure to find a fundamental unity, a starting point of pure presence. The starting point which the heart reveals is one of disunity and of loss. In this sense philosophy is both an inevitable pursuit for the self and is yet impossible. The philosophical begins in a situation that calls not for reconstruction but for elucidation of the condition in which the self finds itself. The goal of philosophy, then, is to think back to that beginning which always comes before it and which is essentially hidden from it.

Both nature and God are obscure to human reason, such that there is no way from one to the other: The 'sky and the birds' do not prove God.[134] Similar to Descartes (and Montaigne), and opposed to Augustine, Pascal understands nature non-teleologically. There is no telos to be read in nature, because in nature we find only the absence of God. This absence is shown in human misery, and the only cure is that which no argument from nature can demonstrate, namely, grace, which is for Pascal the only way beyond the misery which philosophy shows but cannot cure. The function of thinking, the goal of philosophy, then, is not the accumulation of knowledge and not the justification of science or the reform of society or the betterment of the human condition, but rather the contemplation of the paradox of the Fall in its reasonableness.[135] It is in this respect misleading to speak of Pascal as a Sceptical fideist.[136] For Pascal, philosophical thought needs to be guided by reason, but by reason which reflects the situation in which humanity finds itself, rather than covering it over. Reason can be more or less reasonable and its reasonableness consists in the manner in which it perceives its own limits. But while with Descartes reason when allowed to take its natural course – that is following its own true method – will always understand its own limits, for Pascal it must encounter them as a shock coming from beyond reason, but emerging within the self.

The relation of heart and reason operates on two levels, the natural and the supernatural. Religion is present at both levels: 'The way of God ... is to implant religion into our mind through reason and into our heart through grace.'[137] Religion, as the understanding of the Fall and the need for salvation, is implanted in human nature. This is crucial for Pascal, that the human predicament and its possible resolution is something which is dependent on revelation; indeed, revelation only makes sense through responding to it. The task of philosophy, then, is to make people think the religion of the mind, but to do so as a preparation for the religion of the heart. The religion of the heart, supernatural faith, has, however, no human or natural source. It is a gift of God.

The intuitions of the heart and the thinking of reason remain distinct for Pascal: One is felt, the other is thought. But the reality which is felt and thought is the same: It is a symptom of the Fall that they are separate for human beings. At both the supernatural and natural levels there is an interlocking relation of both, but while at the natural level this interlocking can be accomplished by human capacity, it remains frustrated at the supernatural level without the gift of God – natural faith does not lead to supernatural faith, because the latter is that of which the heart is receptive but for which it has no capacity.

3.4 God: Creation and salvation

The relation to God is complex in Christianity because God is understood to be beyond nature, while nature is his creation and he becomes incarnate within nature (Jesus Christ); the world is understood as totally dependent on God, and yet there is evil in the world for which an all-good God has no responsibility despite being all-powerful; the one God creates the world, all of nature, and through an act of grace redeems it, and in particular redeems human beings. Augustine grappled with these contradictions, and the keystones of his account are human culpability for the Fall through his free will and the utter gratuitousness of God's love that saves some of humanity, by bringing them back to himself. Pascal's denial of the 'God of the philosophers' is not a fideistic claim to truth contrary to all reason but rather an Augustinian affirmation of the irreducibility of revelation and of the contradictions which seem associated with the revealed God. God, for Pascal, cannot be spoken of truly in abstraction from religion. The true God is to be discovered within the doctrines of the 'true religion'. For Pascal, then, the problem of knowing God is that of knowing the true religion and the problem of talking about God is a problem of talking with those who do not share that true religion. To be Christian as one is a Perigordian (Montaigne) is do fail to recognize that Christianity is not a human construct but rather the divine answer to the human predicament.[138]

It is striking that both Descartes and Pascal begin from the recognition that non-Christian believers could not be convinced by arguments from Scripture, because of their innate circularity. In this letter to the Sorbonne Descartes states,

> It is of course quite true that we must believe in the existence of God because it is the doctrine of Holy Scripture, and, conversely, that we must believe in Holy Scripture because it comes from God; for since faith is a gift of God, he who gives us grace to believe other things can also give us grace to believe that he exists. But this argument cannot be put to unbelievers because they would judge it to be circular.[139]

Faith is a gratuitous gift of God, but reason can suspend that gift as it were and prove the existence of God by natural reason alone. The God so proved will be theologically neutral and will not be a God subject to theological disputes based in Scripture but a God in whom any rational person must believe. Pascal is concerned with the same problem: That which is known by the gift of faith alone will convince only those who have already received that gift. But to respond to this situation in the Cartesian manner is at best to bring the person to a rational acceptance of God, something which is 'nothing but human and useless for salvation'.[140] Pascal's strategy is rather to diagnose the contradictions of the human condition and to show that only Christianity can respond to those contradictions. The unbeliever is brought in this way not simply to an understanding that God exists but more importantly to recognize the true relation of God to humanity, a relation which gives the possibility – for Pascal the only possibility – of happiness in resolving the contradictions of the human condition. The difference between Descartes and Pascal centres around their different approaches to God and the correspondingly different relations of propositional knowledge and passionate, loving knowledge.

For Descartes the power of God is absolute. God's way of making, of creating the world, was entirely *ex nihilo*: It did not rely on the truths of geometry as an architect does. It is, Descartes tells Marin Mersenne, blasphemous to claim that the truths of mathematics are merely recognized by God,[141] because if that were so, God would not have created out of nothing. Descartes is following the Voluntarist understanding of God here. It is a God very different from Plato's demiurge; it does not create on the basis of a template but creates the template of all possible creation. This God is both the poison and cure in the account Descartes gives in the 'Meditations': The most radical step of doubt is to question the truths of mathematics and this can only be done on the assumption that these truth and the rationality at their base are created by God, not simply used by him. The 'true God' is, similar to the deceiving God, conceivable beyond the truths of mathematics: 'The existence of God is the first and the most eternal of all the truths which there can be and that one alone from which all the others proceed.'[142] It is not a matter for Descartes of speculating on the Christian God but rather of seeking the divine that which lies at the foundation of physics. That foundation remains incomprehensible. It does so, however, because of the heterogeneity of beginning. If reason relies on cause, it reaches its limit in the cause which has no cause but is rather a *causa sui*. God is not subject to the laws of mechanics; indeed, he created them and as such preserves them constantly in being. His creation is a special kind of cause. It is not just the first cause in a series, as if God, so to speak, 'set the ball rolling'. Rather, God is an 'efficient and total cause'.[143]

God is a beginning in which there is no difference between his being and the beginning which happens in his being. This is clear when Descartes states that in God, will, understanding and creation are one; neither precedes the other, not even logically.[144] Not only does this mean that the eternal truths cannot precede God, but it also leads to the conclusion that God does not precede the eternal truths. That is not to say that the eternal truths were necessary, only that it was necessary – it is in God's essence – to create eternal truths. That this is the God which is at issue in the 'Third Meditation' is clear. The argument goes from effect (infinite idea in the thinking self) to cause (the most perfect being). Furthermore, the argument purports to prove this God to be the cause not only of this idea but also of the very being of the self. It is the wonder of creation that is fundamental here, and it is this wonder which inspires his reverence at the end of the 'Third Meditation':

> I should like to pause here and spend some time in the contemplation of God; to reflect on his attributes and to gaze with wonder and adoration on the beauty of this immense light, so far as the eye of my darkened intellect can bear it. For just as we believe through faith that the supreme happiness of the next life consists solely in the contemplation of the divine majesty, so experience tells us that this same contemplation, albeit much less perfect, enables us to know the greatest joy of which we are capable in this life.[145]

Faith and reason tell the same thing. They are not in conflict. This is so because the proof of God's existence is clear – only his nature remains obscure. This God is infinite and cannot be approached by any gradual increase in knowledge.[146] There seems, therefore, to be an unbridgeable gap between the world of the self's natural faith and its faith in God. Furthermore, the outcome of the 'Third Meditation' is in fact a negative one: God does not deceive. All that is left is to contemplate 'the true God in whom all the treasures of wisdom and the sciences lie hidden'.[147] But such a contemplation will never get beyond the hiddenness of such wisdom, given that as Descartes makes clear 'there is considerable rashness in thinking myself capable of investigating the <impenetrable> purposes of God'.[148]

The claims regarding the incomprehensibility and hiddenness of God recall Pascal's constant reference to the hidden God, the *deus absconditus*. This, though, is the common Voluntarist starting point for Descartes, Pascal and indeed Montaigne. The crucial question is, rather, given the hiddenness of God, how can the self relate in knowledge and in action to that God? For Descartes the hidden God is the God who *created* all things for purposes that cannot be grasped; for Pascal the hidden God is one who *saves* the self from its own folly for reasons that cannot be understood.

The human predicament, for Pascal, is such that the self is prey to two fundamental moods: arrogance and despair. These two moods disclose the human predicament but only one-sidedly: Arrogance discloses the greatness of the human in his philosophical proofs of God, despair his wretchedness in his atheism. The God of Christianity is the incarnate God, who redeems, and as such is a God which can unite these two moods. It is for this reason that Pascal says that the human knows himself through God. The God of redemption is the God which gives sense to the Fall and the human predicament. The Fall and its effects remain a mystery, but only through an engagement with that mystery can the self make sense of its predicament. Humanity is more inconceivable without the mystery of the transmission of sins than that mystery is inconceivable to humanity.[149] Humanity can only be understood in terms of this mystery because it gives an account of that which cannot be comprehended. The Fall cannot be comprehended because the state of Adam is so different from ours that we cannot make sense of it.[150] Only the redeemer God can bring these two realities together.

The redeemer God is not to be found at the source of things but rather only appears to those who seek him. The God who may appear to such a seeker is the God who shares in absolute form the two natures of humankind: who has the height of greatness and descends (in Christ) to the depth of wretchedness. The truth of Christianity, for Pascal, consists in its teaching the principle of greatness and of wretchedness together. In teaching that contradiction, it teaches of a God which human beings resist but whom they are obliged to love. While the hiddenness of God for Descartes reflects the unbridgeable gulf of his transcendence, in Pascal's terms, this hiddenness takes on much the form of seduction: This God is a God of redemption, who attracts those who are to be saved. The relation to this God is one of the will (and the heart) not the mind.[151] This is so because the relation to God is, for Pascal, one through which the self comes to recognize its own wretched situation and dependence on God for a return to a greatness, which was lost with Adam. The recovery of a prelapsarian state is as much for Pascal as for Descartes the goal of philosophy, but that recovery is only possible through Jesus Christ.

For this reason Pascal opposes both Montaigne and Descartes on the incomprehensibility or incommunicability of God. 'If God is incomprehensible we would have no relation with him.'[152] 'He dares to say that God cannot make him [man] capable of communicating with him, and why he believes that God cannot make himself knowable and lovable to him since man is by nature capable of love and knowledge.'[153] These fragments addressed respectively to Descartes and Montaigne amount to the same point: God does relate to human beings and does communicate to them, but in ways that neither Montaigne nor Descartes acknowledged, that is, through the heart. In terms of the heart, God is comprehensible and his being is communicable, but we need to find the proper mode of perceiving his being and the proper language to express it. This means, on the one hand, seeking God sincerely and openly and, on the other hand, adopting an ambiguous mode of expression which can think the presence and non-presence of God at once.

The God of Christians is the God of love and consolation.[154] This is a God who loves without reason – in the lapsarian state no human being has a good reason for being loved by God. But by the same token this God challenges the self-assertion of the human being – the unjust and unfair claim to be loved. This is a God, then, who both teaches the self its wretchedness and promises its salvation. A true relation to such a God cannot be either arrogant or despairing. As such it allows the human being to transcend the abysmal contradictions of his fallen state. The dialectic at play here is one of loss and redemption: The human being needs to recognize her being lost in order to accept her redemption. Such a dialectic cannot occur in the mind, which in the autonomy of its own reason will never reach the knowledge of God and will neither understand its own fallenness nor its need for redemption. The knowledge of God through the heart, on the other hand, can accept the ambiguity and paradox of its situation. The truth of religion is thus necessarily obscure: This obscurity is itself revealing, in the sense that it brings the paradox of the human situation to expression. The double contradictory truth of the human situation – being both wretched and great – is that which the God of Christianity communicates. This is incomprehensible only if one remains on the level of one or other of these truths. Humanity is 'at once unworthy and capable of God: unworthy through their corruption, capable through their original nature'.[155] It is this which the obscurity of religion reveals.

The God which is revealed is not a God beyond reason in the sense of one to be believed simply on blind faith. On the contrary, this God reveals that without which the human condition would remain mysterious. Trust in this testimony is reasonable for Pascal, although it undermines the very attempt of reason to find a sufficient ground. The God which this religion reveals is a God that calls the autonomy of reason into question.[156]

3.5 Evil, ethics and the passions

The self is both soul and body, and the relation of these two aspects of the self is problematic for both Descartes and Pascal. They both stand in ambiguous relation to a certain Gnostic tendency in Christian thought. This tendency to diminish the body in favour of the soul, to despise nature in the interest of spirit, finds clear echoes in their work. Nevertheless, the self which emerges in their writings is undoubtedly both of body and soul and is one for which the relation to nature is essential. Truth and goodness are intertwined for both Descartes and Pascal: Happiness is in a necessary relation to truth; goodness is informed by knowledge. Central to happiness, goodness and truth is the relation of to the passions. The unity of body and mind is played out in the passions, there is no human life without them. They both follow Montaigne in rejecting a fully Stoic goal of suppressing the passions, while being both alive to their dangers. In approaching these questions, I will begin with the notion of practice. Both Descartes and Pascal are often understood as advocating a withdrawal from the concerns of practice to theory and contemplation respectively. However, both of them think the self as inescapably addressed by ethical demands which are exacting and make the question of the passions of central philosophical significance.

The Sceptical thoughts that trouble Descartes in principle affect his account of the good as much as of the true: In respect to both, neither the authority of his teachers nor the inclinations of his nature are certain. He consistently pursues an investigation of the basis of each. Yet, with respect to his *practice* of the good and the true, he finds that he cannot suspend belief. Although he speaks of a provisional moral code,[157] in effect it is a provisional *practical* code, a code of how to act while investigating the grounds of the opinions on the basis of which he acts. There are two concerns here, regarding the place of thinking and the happiness of life. Descartes speaks in this regard of a place for thinking, a capacity to judge decisively and the ability to live happily. The provisional moral code supplies for him nothing other than the goal of his scientific endeavour, but in a provisional manner. The rational basis is not yet in place, but the code expresses the main elements of the way of life to which he is seeking to give a rational foundation. The mistake is to think that this provisional moral code simply expresses a code of life that has no relation to the content or goal of the scientific process itself. On the contrary, the goal of that process is to achieve a way life in which we can live in dwellings of truth and goodness that are certain, where we can make decisive judgements regarding the true and the good and where we can live happily. While it is certainly true that

Descartes never worked out a fully fledged morality, the moral code itself concerns the way of life, implicit in the totality of his philosophical work.

The provisional moral code pre-structures the way of life of someone who is aiming through an indubitable method to reach a clear understanding of the true and the good. It is in place through two distinct processes, that of tearing down and of building up the house of his beliefs. While tearing down the house of his beliefs he in practice needed to accept some guidance as to how to act. Faced with this situation he accepts the authority of custom as custom.[158] He accepts the customs of his society not because he judges them better than those of other societies but simply because they are the customs into which he was born. This acceptance is provisional on a number of levels. In the first place, Descartes (in common with Montaigne and Pascal) recognizes the arbitrariness of custom: What is customary is neither true nor just but is rather the mode of life of a particular place – a country in Descartes's terms. Within any society there are more moderate and more extreme opinions and modes of action. In beginning his way of Sceptical doubt, Descartes has no reason to accept his own opinions, nor can he be certain of making true judgements regarding what is moderate and what is extreme. In the face of this he looks towards the opinions of others, specifically those he judges to be the most sensible of those amongst whom he lives. The second maxim is to be firm and decisive in his opinions and in everyday life to act on the most probable opinion. By employing such constancy, he can free himself of regrets and remorse.[159] Third, he commits himself to trying to master himself rather than the order of the world. He alludes here to the Stoics as 'those philosophers who in earlier times were able to escape from the dominion of fortune and, despite suffering and poverty, rival their gods in happiness'.[160] Finally, he reviewed the various occupations open to him and decided to 'devote my whole life to cultivating my reason'.[161]

While at first sight this 'moral code' may appear quietistic, a manifesto for withdrawal into unworldly contemplation, it is important to read it as dynamic, as containing within itself the outlines of a path to a more perfect morality and practice. The first maxim is heavily qualified by declaring promising to be excessive.[162] In this way the very basis of his commitment to such customs and opinions becomes provisional. The declaration of the excessiveness of promising undercuts the apparent conservatism of the first maxim. While Montaigne sees little reason to change customs, Descartes understands the present acceptance of custom as entailing no obligation into the future. What this means is that his very membership of the community is provisional, he makes no promises to his fellows. His freedom is ultimate and without condition. Hence, although he speaks of his own lack of confidence in his opinions and his deference to the most sensible, this has currency only for the time being.

As his judgements become more perfect they will become more resolute. But in practice he cannot wait for this development. Hence, the second maxim is in effect to imitate the final definitive morality already in his judgements. In practice he needs to judge without sufficient justification, but his judgement cannot reflect this lack of justification, because he cannot wait for the time when his judgement will be justified. Having to act now he has to do so with a decisiveness that he can only justify pragmatically.[163] What occurs here is the inverse of the denial of the *aporia* which Descartes practices in his systematic doubt: What is doubtful is treated as if certain.

This is justified only by the practical consideration of having to act. If the self follows this course of action, she will not be subject to regret or remorse. In setting out on one course of action, she should follow it to the end, not because she knows it to be good but because that was the course she chose. In the 'Passions', Descartes shows – as Montaigne did – a resistance to repentance, but he does not totally deny the validity of feelings of remorse and repentance. In the case of remorse, we doubt that what we have done or are doing is good; in the case of repentance we are certain that what we have done is bad.[164] Both have the function of bringing about change. What the self should be aiming for, however, is a state in which what it does is never evil, a state of firm resolution. While irresolution gives the self time without commitment to make a choice, this time should be limited. In the case of 'too great a desire to do well' an excess of irresolution results.[165] While Princess Elisabeth[166] feared that only an 'infinite science' would give us knowledge of all the circumstances influencing the outcome of our actions leading to a state in which remorse and repentance were no longer necessary, Descartes does not deny contingency and limits of knowledge in practice, but he is suggesting that the self who lives in such a world should train itself to act *as if* in a world of certainty.[167] The underlying assumption is that society can be made increasingly rational and as such that the contingencies with which the self must deal gradually diminish. Important here is the emphasis on habit: The self must 'become accustomed to form certain and determinate judgements regarding everything that comes before [him], and to believe that [he] always do[es] [his] duty when he do[es] what he judge[s] to be best, even though [his] judgement may perhaps be a very bad one'.[168] What is being practised here is constancy of resolution. The self is developing the habit of judgement, which is necessary to a good life of one who has reached certainty. The possibility of bad judgement is acknowledged – the source of this would not be the passions because Descartes is in the process of showing how the wise man can control his passions. The source of error is rather external circumstance, and virtue depends on nothing outside the self.[169]

The self which Descartes is setting forth here owes much to Stoicism, reminiscent of Lipsius's account. For Lipsius, the self stands in relation to divine providence; he is silent, however, regarding grace. Understanding divine providence as being always directed towards the good, Lipsius advocates a reorientation of the mind from listening to opinion to listening to wisdom and reason. Thereby he finds constancy within and does not allow himself to be buffeted by passions provoked by the circumstances in which he finds himself. Constancy is 'a right and immovable strength of mind, neither lifted up nor pressed down with external or causal accidents. By strength I understand steadfastness not from opinion, but from judgment and sound reason.'[170] Such constancy originates from patience which he defines as 'a voluntary sufferance without grudging of all things whatsoever that can happen to or in a man.'[171] Similar to Lipsius, Descartes seeks such constancy through self-mastery and faith in divine providence. In agreement with Lipsius too, Descartes understands such Stoic self-discipline to imply not quietism but active struggle for the good.

As the will limits itself to the intellect, so too in morality desire is limited to the possible: In morals as much as in theoretical life error and sin derive from overreaching the power of the self. The point is not to change the world but to limit desire to what is within the self's power. Only its thoughts are fully within its power. Again, though, while at first sight this maxim seems to imply a deep conservatism, the inner dynamic is evident: Limiting desire to that which is within the self's power means limiting desire to that which he can fruitfully engage in pursuing. The thoughts which are within his power are precisely the thoughts through which he rebuilds the buildings of his knowledge. The results of that building are already evident in the essays attached to the 'Discourse', and such knowledge may make us 'the lords and masters of nature'.[172] The key to this whole quest lies in the honing of desire, motivated by the goal of knowledge of nature: 'I could not have limited my desires, or been happy, had I not been following a path by which I thought I was sure to acquire all the knowledge of which I was capable, and in this way all the true goods within my reach.'[173]

Capacity, power and possibility are not limited by any pregiven nature for Descartes but rather indefinitely expandable by the power of the will and intellect. The self as such is capable of goodness and truth and requires a method to help him reach this potential. It is important here to note that alongside this code, Descartes sets the truths of his faith beyond systematic Sceptical doubt. Again, though, the truths of his faith prefigure the result of his 'Meditations'. Descartes never considers that the fruits of his reflection will conflict with the truths of his faith. Revealed truth and reason are not in conflict but rather mirror one another. The God which reason discloses is the God of revelation, but it is the God of creation rather than of redemption. This does not mean that Descartes rejected the God of redemption but rather indicates that he took a Pelagian or at least semi-Pelagian view of the relation to redemption. This is not accidental: The very project of science that he sets out was premised on the human capacity for self-betterment, the fulfilment of which a good and just God could only reward.

In the 'Fourth Meditation' Descartes states, 'Neither divine grace nor natural knowledge ever diminishes freedom.'[174] Against the Augustinianism of Luther and the Jansenists, Descartes understands divine sovereignty and natural necessity as working in harmony with human freedom. In a letter to Princess Elisabeth he states that 'while faith teaches us about grace, philosophy suffices to know that not the least thought can be in the mind without God willing it'.[175] The analogy to grace here can be understood at first in a Jansenistic manner: Thoughts like grace are willed by God and cannot be resisted. Yet, far from this meaning that the human freedom is thereby diminished, Descartes understands grace and freedom to be compatible.[176] It is important here to note that thoughts, as Descartes understands them, originate both in the mind as innate and through the body from the senses and the imagination. Thus, his understanding of freedom needs to account for the relation of body and mind; specifically he needs to show that the body, although symptomatic of human fallenness, can be purified of this fallen state and become an instrument of freedom. In Part 1 of the 'Passions', Descartes states that 'the soul is really joined to the whole of the body [*l'âme est véritablement jointe à tout le corps*]'.[177] The soul is really joined to the body and this joining is not local, not in a particular place, but concerns the body in its totality. The body is a unity, an indivisible unity – not in the sense that it cannot be divided (an arm can be amputated, for example) but in the sense that it has a normative unity. The soul relates to the body as such a normative unity, or a self. The agitations of the body are nothing which can be localized with respect to the soul: They concern the soul as effecting the whole self. Such agitation, such passions, Descartes terms 'emotions of the soul', because, as he explains – alluding the root of the word in *emouvoir*, 'to stir up' – 'of all the kinds of thought which the soul may have, there are none that agitate and disturb it so strongly as the passions'.[178] While God may will the thoughts in the mind, freedom demands that the passions be brought into harmony with reason, such that these thoughts are most fully directed towards the well-being of the self, which is acting in accordance with divine providence by expanding its own powers over itself and through extension over the world around it.

The emotions are actions on the soul that dispose it to want certain things. Wonder is the first of the passions, because it is through wonder that something in the world commands our attention in its novelty or difference. The difference which is perceived here is one not directly related to the object itself but to the benefit or harm that it can have for the body. This emotion opens up a space of irresolution: It is indifferent to good or bad. As with the indifference of the will, Descartes is ambiguous here with regard to irresolution: There can be no novelty without a suspending of resolve, but when that suspension becomes too prolonged it gives rise to the twin vices of curiosity and irresolution. Wonder is a kind of stasis; unique amongst the passions, it is not accompanied by any change in the heart or in the blood, according to Descartes.[179] This is so because it does not disclose its object in terms of good or bad but simply as novel. There is here a constitutive ignorance in wonder and a lack of concern for the body. The brain is engaged, but the object is viewed in its indifference to the body. It is significant that for Descartes the prolongation of wonder has negative implications. It ends in blind curiosity. The curious are, so to speak, addicted to wonder and are not spurred on to know and hence do not come to distinguish between things in terms of what are more or less useful.[180] The self that emerges out of wonder learns to relate to the objects appearing to it, first in wonder with respect to their novelty and then though acquaintance with them with respect to whether they are beneficial or harmful to it. Such a self loves and hates, and these passions are directed towards benefit or harm in terms of good and evil. Desire is a passion directed towards a future good and avoiding future evil.[181] The emotions of joy and sadness arise through a reflexive movement, whereby the self considers itself with respect to a present good or evil, which it finds within it.

If we now read backwards from this account of the 'primitive passions' in the 'Passions of the Soul', to the provisional moral or practical code and to the movement of the 'Meditations' from doubt to certainty, what we find is an attempt to regulate passions through uncovering the true power and capacity of the self, first as soul then as body.[182] Although Descartes may have modified his position in response to Princess Elisabeth's probing questions and scepticism,[183] these works are best read in relation to each other. The self of the 'Meditations' is from the start an embodied self, which is evident in the passions, which that self displays. The 'Meditations' are, as Amélie Rorty says, an exercise not the description of a project.[184] In relation to the self they are an exercise of freeing itself from its worldly engagements mediated by the body, in order to know the real distinction within itself between its body and mind. Cartesian method is a lived method, doubt is a lived doubt. It is for this reason that Descartes is particularly anxious to deny that the real distinction of mind and body had been established until the 'Sixth Meditation'.[185] The self that doubts is an embodied self; it is a self that does not cease being embodied while it doubts the existence of the body. It is a self that knows itself only as embodied but cannot justify that knowledge until the 'Sixth Meditation'.

The self that emerges out of the spontaneous Sceptical moment is a desiring self; the loss of its former beliefs is painful to it. The seeking after certainty is a passionate seeking; it is a seeking which aims not at pure knowledge but at contentment. Such contentment is not achieved by the soul alone but rather by the soul in relation to its body and the material world around it. This self is driven forward to find justifications through its desire for certainty. It is for that reason that Descartes describes himself as oscillating between anxiety and despair, on the one hand, and hope and confidence, on the other.[186] The references to these passions are not simply literary devices. These passions arise precisely when desire seems to go beyond the self's own powers. The results of the 'Meditations' calm these passions to the extent that it demonstrates that knowledge of truth and goodness is after all within the power of the finite intellect. Understood in this way, the whole project is one of finding tranquillity, not through Sceptical *aporia* but rather through establishing of the conditions for resolute judgement and happiness. Those conditions are met, however, for Descartes only when the power of cognition is adequate to the object of desire. This is not present at the beginning but only at the end of the process. In other words, the dynamic structure of the moral code corresponds to his project only to the extent to which the third maxim is understood in such a way that change occurs neither in the world alone nor in the self's desires themselves but in the capacity of the self to fulfil its desires.

The whole process of philosophical reflection is one of coming to see and thereby developing the self's capacity for knowledge. Nothing can prescribe this as the self cannot know except what it can justify to itself. The mastery of desire becomes a matter of directing it towards its true aim. This true aim can be found once two conditions are met: that desire proceeds from true knowledge and that desire is for that which is within the self's power. True knowledge is knowledge of what is good.[187] Desire based in true knowledge is a desire for that which is good. Once that thing is within the self's power to possess, then there can be no limit to the ardour of the self's desire,[188] directed at nothing other than the good of the self. The goal of philosophy is true knowledge of that good. Once that is achieved then the thought that 'the truth of which we are so firmly persuaded, appears false to God or to an Angel and hence is, absolutely speaking, false' is beside the point.[189] It is beside the point because the task of philosophy is precisely to build a space in which the true good for the human being can be aimed at without limit, a space in which truth and falsity can be decided in those terms without the absolute certainty, which only God possesses.

Wisdom, then, for Descartes means an acceptance of this state of living in relative, not absolute, certainty or living with complete but not adequate knowledge. Living in that state, the self has a clear sense of that for which it is and can be responsible. This means living within the realm of its own free will. The exercise of free will makes the self Godlike in the sense of being self-responsible. Only through the twin restrictions of the will to what is clearly shown by the intellect and desire to what is within the self's power can that free will have sovereignty. Such sovereignty is Godlike because it remains within the domain of its own capacity. The passion of generosity functions in a manner complementary to the contemplation of divine providence: In the case of the latter the self not only reflects on its own powerlessness to change the world but also recognizes that the world is as it is through divine care; in the case of the former the self is caused to esteem itself to the extent it deserves, that is, to the extent to which it is contained within the limits of its own free will. Generosity is the passion that discloses to the soul its own true exercise of free will and consists in knowledge and feeling: knowledge that nothing belongs to her but the free exercise of her will and the feeling of a firm resolution to use it well.[190] The passion of generosity in effect combines the second and third maxims of the provisional moral code. In this is combined knowledge and feeling – indeed, one could term it a knowing feeling or a feeling knowing – in which the self knows itself as body and soul and knows itself in the exercise of virtue. The self which is generous in this sense is the self that deserves praise and depends on nothing or nobody else. It is a self that recognizes the limits of its own capacity but in that recognition does not respond by acknowledging its dependence on anything or anyone beyond it. It rather strives to extend the boundaries of its capabilities indefinitely.

The generous self has self-esteem, loves itself and is humble only in the sense of recognizing that this capacity for self-esteem is one which the self shares equally with all others: Anyone capable of free will is potentially worthy of such self-esteem.[191] Descartes is not denying possible depravities in the self, but as the passion of generosity clearly demonstrates, he thinks the proper understanding of the self in its mind/body relation and the establishment of a good order between mind and body gives the self cause for self-esteem. For Pascal, on the contrary, the self is hateful and unjust.[192] The fallenness that Scepticism sees is radical for Pascal; the self that would attempt to bring itself out of such a fallenness even by means of its self-limitation is destined simply to reinforce that state. The Cartesian attempt of a provisional moral code is self-defeating in Pascalian terms, because it is rooted in the illusion that the self is capable of happiness.

Like Descartes, Pascal states custom should be understood as contingent, but while for Descartes this is simply a recognition of the relativity of cultures, for Pascal it arises out of a rejection of the claim of custom to justice. Laws are customary and result from past usurpations. Their claim to justice dissimulates their inherent injustice: It is lawful to kill a man across the river because that is enemy territory and it has been ordered by the king, while it is unlawful to do the same on this side of the river. Hence, if justice were known then it would not be laid down that one should follow one's own customs.[193] There is no consistency in customs; they contradict each other and are arbitrary, while justice is none of these things. We do not know justice, according to Pascal, because of the weakness of our reason, but we are then locked in a lie: If people did not believe their laws to be just they would not follow them. But this is simply imaginary. Hence, to follow custom is not the starting point of the development of true moral principles as it is for Descartes but rather affirms an injustice, namely, the claiming of a place in the sun.[194] Diversity for Pascal is not simply a sign of relativity but rather the indication of usurpation and injustice.[195] The point, then, is not to deepen this usurpation but to seek redemption from it. The continual expansion of the Cartesian self is opposed in Pascal by the thinking reed: 'A thinking reed. It is not from space that I must seek my human dignity, but from the ordering of my thought. It will do me no good to own land. Through space the universe grasps me and swallows me up like a speck; through thought I grasp it.'[196] Pascal starts here from a Cartesian opposition between thought and space (extension). But while Descartes, even in the 'Meditations' and clearly in the 'Passions', seeks to emphasize the unity of body and mind, such that self-esteem is an esteem the self owes itself as an embodied being, for Pascal the self's only dignity comes from controlling its passions through thought. The thought of this dignity arises for Pascal in the manner in which the self is confronted and threatened by the universe around him: 'A vapour, a drop of water is enough to kill him [the thinking reed]. But even if the universe were to crush him, man would still be nobler than his slayer, because he knows that he is dying and the advantage the universe has over him. The universe knows none of this.'[197] Here again is the centrality of death: The self understands the dignity of thought in the face of death.

Descartes, despite his critique of it in the *Rules*, rejoins the more positive account in Montaigne of habit, as enabling as well as restricting, in the 'Passions'. The same can be said of Pascal when he is concerned with the manner in which the self can open itself up to faith. To see this it is instructive to return again to the wager passage.[198] This begins with the soul as 'cast into the body'. It is as if in a prison, and in this state the soul thinks only in the terms of physics – number, time, dimension. Nature is all it knows and it can believe nothing else. This it would seem is the Cartesian self for Pascal. Descartes's proofs of the existence of God do nothing else than make the soul forget God. When Descartes tells Burman that he should not spend much time on metaphysics but concentrate on physics, he is advocating what Pascal here condemns.[199] In effect, despite setting out the real distinction of mind and body, Descartes is for Pascal enslaving the mind to the body. We can only know through the body for Pascal, which means that all we can know is that which has extension. As God is both infinite and has no extension, we cannot know God's existence or his essence. But he goes on, 'By faith we know his existence, through glory we shall know his nature.'[200] With respect to God, then, there is only faith through grace. The soul 'cast in the body' cannot rise above extension; only God can raise it above the material.

The wager argument that follows, as we have seen, is not so much an argument which should convince the reader but one which describes the situation beyond all Sceptical *aporia*. In this situation, for Pascal what holds the unbeliever back is his passions. Hence, he has to cultivate new habits. The unbeliever should behave as if he believes: 'taking holy water, having masses said'. This will 'make you believe quite naturally and will make you more docile [*abêtira*]'.[201] This passage has been the subject of much scholarly debate. The word *abêtira* literally means to become beast-like. The way to overcome reason is to become like beasts. This is a remarkable conclusion particularly when we consider that in other fragments Pascal has understood the human being as having fallen from God-like nature and being without grace to be as a beast[202] and that to be as a beast is to be governed by passions. But like Descartes, Pascal understood the route to happiness to be through governing the passions, but the Stoic path was one which he rejected as presumptuous and self-defeating. The body can only be controlled by its own nature, which Pascal, following Descartes, understands as mechanical. The self can only be a fallen self, hence she must habitualize herself to welcome divine grace. Again we see here how Pascal adopts Cartesian costume, but in a very different drama. The mind needs to be convinced by reasons 'seen only once in a lifetime' like Descartes's meditator and like the Cartesian self, the mind is united to an automaton which can only be brought to belief by habit.[203] He goes on to say that we must put our 'faith in feeling'. Through habit the body can be moved to incline towards God. But the habits are precisely those which clear the body of those attachments to things and empties it in preparation for divine grace: 'The law obliged men to have what it did not give: grace gives what it obliges men to have.'[204]

These habits direct the body away from the world, while the habits of the Cartesian body allow it to maximize the well-being of the self in the world. The difference here we see most clearly in their respective accounts of concupiscence. Descartes addresses this question in Section 81 of the 'Passions'. The distinction, as Descartes understands it, is between that love which prompts the wish for the well-being of the beloved and that love which seeks possession of the object. This distinction Descartes does not see as essential because he understands love to be that which 'impels the soul to join itself willingly to objects that appear agreeable to it'.[205] In love, then, there is a relation between the soul and another in which the self assents to consider itself as joined to another in such a manner that it imagines them both to be part of a greater whole.[206] Descartes distinguishes between three forms of love depending on the relative relations of esteem between the self and its beloved within this imagined whole: where the self esteems itself more than the beloved (affection), where the self esteems itself equally to the beloved (friendship) and when the self esteems the beloved greater than itself (devotion). These distinctions Descartes understand in terms of their effects along a sacrificial scale: whether the self is willing to sacrifice itself or the beloved so as to preserve the greater part of the whole.[207] It is this coupling of love and preservation that Pascal rejects. The self in love recognizes rather its own nothingness, opens itself to annihilation, not in order to preserve the beloved – God – but because the love of God shows the self in its own nothingness. The sacrificial scale which Descartes employs places God on the same level as king or country. In this sense the devotion Descartes speaks of is not true love for Pascal, because it places all beings along the same measure, an economy of esteem. At the root of such a view Pascal would diagnose concupiscence: 'Concupiscence and force are the source of all our actions. Concupiscence causes voluntary, force involuntary actions.'[208] The benevolence of which Descartes speaks is but an effect of concupiscence. 'Man's greatness even in his concupiscence. He has managed to produce such a remarkable system from it and make it the image of true charity.'[209] The picture of benevolence is however only a covert disguise for the underlying concupiscence. Pascal anticipates here the 'hermeneutics of suspicion' of Nietzsche and Sigmund Freud,[210] seeing beneath the surface of benevolence unacknowledged motives rooted in the lust for earthly things and pride in the self's own capacities.

For Pascal we cannot know the true good or just.[211] This is the case because human reason and human will is unable to know the good for the human being. To know the human good is to know what the human being is for, but this knowledge lies locked in the Creator. For this reason, with respect to God and by consequence with respect to the good, love comes before knowledge. The question which not just comes first but in its extent exhausts all other questions of human practice is what ought the self to love. Pascal's response is unambiguous: She ought to love God and hate herself, and the corollary is that there are no reasons why she should be loved. That God loves her and that she has the gift of faith to love God are both gratuitous gifts of God. But for all Pascal's emphasis on the self's love of God, God is more a merciful king than a loving father in his account. Hence, even God's love does little to affirm the self and certainly does not lead to self-esteem; indeed, the very freedom to strive for the good, as a freedom rooted in the self's own capacity, is called radically into question by Pascal.

Leszek Kolakowski understands Pascal and Jansenism as defending an Augustinianism that stood between the Catholic Church and Modernity.[212] But this is questionable. For one thing, the doctrine of grace and human incapacity to achieve salvation shares many common elements with Calvinism, which was the religion of much of the rising bourgeoisie in Europe. But more fundamentally, Kolakowski is assuming Modernity to be distinct from Jansenism. This is to read history with an idea of the Modern, rather than finding the Modern within the epoch itself. With respect to the formation of the Modern self we find between Descartes and Pascal two accounts that, for all their similarity of themes and questions, diverge on the question of human capacity. Understood in those terms, Descartes is Pelagian with strong Stoic elements, and Pascal is Augustinian with significant Pyrrhonian commitments.

Kolakowski completes his account of Pascal with the striking sentence: 'All his [Pascal's] protestations about the happiness of those who 'have found God' notwithstanding, [Pascal's religion] was a religion for unhappy people and was designed to make them more unhappy.'[213] He had earlier denied that it could be termed tragic, because 'the tragic impossibility of a morally good choice is the situation, not [the actors'[214]] inherited guilt'.[215]. Kolakowski's denial of the tragic in Pascal's case is the inverse of the standard claim that Christian theodicy as the death of tragedy, due to its supposed optimism of the Christian account of redemption.[216] But that is much truer of Descartes than it is of Pascal and Pascal's closeness to Augustine gives his thought a tragic hue. Jeremy Worthen states the case with respect to Christianity and tragedy in this way: 'For Augustine ... why some are abandoned to the full consequences of such sin, to die forever in the flames of eternal hell, and some plucked out, burning brands, to enjoy their Saviour forever, is entirely past finding out.'[217] Pascal gives us a tragic diagnosis of the situation in which the self finds itself, beset by the contradiction of its own sense of greatness and the wretchedness of its situation, unable out of its own capacity to act well, incapable of commanding its own destiny and yet finding a certain dignity in its situation. Thinking, in giving the self dignity, discloses its own wretchedness to it, but in thinking that wretchedness, the self is raised above nature and given a special place between angels and beasts. The source of happiness is willing what God wills; the tragedy is to be incapable of this without divine grace.

Descartes, writing to Princess Elisabeth, states, 'Provided we know how to use our will well, we can make everything which depends on it good and thus prevent the evils that come from elsewhere, however great they may be, from penetrating any further into our souls than the sadness which actors arouse in it when they enact before us a tragic history.'²¹⁸ In an earlier letter he speaks of the negative physiological effects of such sadness, the manner in which sad imaginings can be detrimental to health.²¹⁹ While truth is higher than joy for Descartes, the two are not in necessary conflict: Selves acting in concert, so long as they are acting from reason and governing their passions, can limit the evils coming from without. Such as self works on two levels, first, to be less affected by reversals of fortune and second, acting in concord with divine providence to build a society of human happiness, one in which even the life span of the self can be increasingly subject to his will.

Montaigne's comic viewpoint is closed off to both. Descartes is aware of the tragic but seeks to build a world and form a self in which all tragedy will be at one remove, will affect the self as viewer not as actor. Out of the ruins of the past a new world can be built, of which we can dream of establishing a new heaven and a new earth under God's benevolent and rewarding gaze. But such building for Pascal is simply digging deeper in the morass in which we find ourselves. The injury which the self bears within itself can be cured by no medicine or no physics of human origin, but in recognizing the contradictions of its own formation, the self can only look with gratitude towards truth as Christian revelation, in faith and according to the reasons of love.

4

Spinoza and Hume on the good life

Pascal affirmed the Cartesian universe of nature following mechanical laws, but for him such a world is habitable only through directing the self at transcendence, manifest in the release of the self from this world at death. Spinoza and Hume responded to the contrary that the world disclosed and being built by the New Science of the seventeenth century was one in which the self can aim to live truthfully and happily. They shared a common project of allowing the self to dwell within a world limited to the structures of its own understanding and practice. Both reduced the space of transcendence to a minimum and philosophical reflection to understanding and navigating an immanent world. Unlike Descartes and Pascal, they both pursued a consistently naturalist account. In doing so, they both appealed back to the Ancient Epicurean Atomists, especially Lucretius, and they both self-consciously worked from Stoic and Sceptic positions, respectively. For both Spinoza and Hume we find an energy immanent to the world, very unlike the world of Descartes, which needs an external God to keep it in motion. They both respond differently to this world, Spinoza finding contentment in a Stoic acceptance,[1] Hume finding tranquillity in a Sceptical distance.[2] For both, however, the inner power they perceived in nature was inescapable; there was no place for the human beyond nature. To be a self was to find oneself as a natural being, but one defined by a certain freedom. Being free as a natural being for Spinoza is to express as much as possible one's own nature, the self's nature as an individual being; for Hume, freedom is to respond to impressions as both constitutive of the self and as fallible signs of a reality of which the self can only ever have a partial view.

Spinoza is as a philosopher of *expression*,[3] Hume a philosopher of *impression*. Early in the 'Ethics' Spinoza speaks of the relation of substance and its attributes as one of expression; Hume begins the *Treatise* speaking of impressions as 'our sensations, passions and emotions, as they make their first appearance in the soul.'[4] The underlying reality is that of pressing (*premere*), whereby nature is a dynamic relation of pushing and pulling, out of which, and in relation to which, their respective accounts of the self as a power-enhancing agent and an information-processing pleasure seeker emerge. These accounts are of selves for whom freedom, social and political life and the knowledge necessary to live well are vital concerns. While less explicitly than their Stoic and Sceptic orientations, Spinoza and Hume take up themes of distraction, fallenness, desire, autonomy and grace from the Augustinian and Pelagian controversies. Spinoza's account is one of a conversion of the soul from its fallenness into passions towards love of God and is an account, which – in a remarkably Augustinian fashion – is driven by desire which can only be fully satisfied in the eternal. While autonomy in Spinoza is in the end indistinguishable from heteronomy, Hume in Pelagian fashion understands the human being as striving towards an autonomy, which though limited by the finitude of individual capacity, requires nothing beyond those capacities to reach virtue and goodness.[5]

This chapter will begin with a discussion of the aims of philosophy for both Spinoza and Hume. The practical goal of human happiness is common to both. For Spinoza, though, philosophy plays a positive role, it is the royal road to happiness; for Hume the role is more negative: philosophy needs to be curtailed in its pretensions in order to allow the human to find a natural happiness (4.1). The next section will explore the genesis of ideas in Spinoza and Hume, working through their respective discussion of adequate and inadequate ideas and the relation of impressions and ideas (4.2). This then brings us to a core issue between them, the nature of substance and cause, which is discussed in the third section (4.3). A core concern for both thinkers is the role of the passions in human happiness, which is discussed in the penultimate section (4.4). The final section then turns to Spinoza's and Hume's respective accounts of God and the political place of religion (4.5).

4.1 The aims of philosophy

Spinoza and Hume share a common belief in the practical significance of philosophy. The outline of their two major works, the 'Ethics' and the *Treatise*, is remarkably similar: the 'Ethics' begins with metaphysical questions (Part 1), goes on to issues of epistemology in (Part 2), to the passions (Parts 3 and 4) and finally to human happiness (Part 5). The *Treatise* begins with epistemology and metaphysics, goes on to the passions and ends with morals.[6] For both Spinoza and Hume, the fundamental philosophical question is how to be happy. In order to respond to that question effectively, both aim to understand three factors: the self's nature, the nature of the world and the optimal relation possible between self and world. For that reason a certain philosophical anthropology is central to their concerns: For Hume all sciences are 'dependent on the science of Man, since they lie under the cognizance of men and are judged of by their powers and faculties';[7] for Spinoza, having shown the essence of God, the fundamental theme becomes 'the knowledge of the human mind and its highest blessedness'.[8]

At the close of the 'Ethics', Spinoza states that the wise man possesses *aquiescentia animi*, which, following Donald Rutherford,[9] I will translate here as 'contentment of mind', and Spinoza then goes on, 'But all sublime things are as difficult as they are rare [*Sed omnia praeclara tam difficilia, quam rara sunt*].' Describing what he has discussed in the pages of the 'Ethics' as a way (*via*), Spinoza urges on the reader to take up this path towards wisdom, towards becoming one of the wise (*sapiens*).[10] Beneath the surface of the geometric method he employs, Spinoza lets glimpse a path, which the attentive reader can (and is encouraged to) pursue herself. Similarly in the Appendix added to the *Treatise*, Hume states, 'The annihilation which some people suppose to follow upon death, and which entirely destroys this self, is nothing but an extinction of all particular perceptions; love and hatred, pain and pleasure, thought and sensation. These therefore must be the same with self; since one cannot survive the other.'[11] That self is both the self which the *Treatise* affirms and the self which must recognize itself as operative already in Hume's text.

There is a circularity at the heart of both major works. With respect to the 'Ethics', the self that we find at the end of that work – that self which loves God – is the self that can think God as a necessary being. While it is true that the very structure of the 'Ethics', progressing step by step through propositions, axioms and definitions, is carried out in terms of what Spinoza calls the 'second form of knowledge', the motivation of the self which carries out this process is one of love: love of that which increases its power to the point of transcending time itself. This love Spinoza understands as the highest knowledge, the 'third form of knowledge'. This loving knowledge Spinoza identifies with wisdom and sees it in Stoic fashion as the justifying end of all human desire. As he puts it in his 'Treatise on the Emendation of the Intellect', happiness and unhappiness are dependent only on the 'quality the object to which we cling with love'.[12] Reaching the love of the eternal is hindered by disturbances of the mind arising from 'avarice, sexual desire and love of fame'. The path of thinking, therefore, is turning away from such disturbances, using objects for moderate enjoyment but above all for enjoying the rational life, an enjoyment that has its end in the joy of the love of God. Spinoza employs these Augustinian terms (*uti* and *frui*) in a less dichotomous manner than Augustine but with a similar trajectory: In the Appendix to Part 4 of the 'Ethics', Spinoza states that 'things are good only insofar as they aid man to enjoy (*frui*) the life of the mind'.[13] He then goes on to say,

> It is permissible for us to avert, in the way which seems safest, whatever there is in nature which we judge to be evil or able to prevent us from being able to exist and enjoy (*frui*) the rational life. On the other hand, we may take for our own use (*usum*), and use in any way, whatever there is which we judge to be good, or useful (*utile*) for preserving our being and enjoying (*fruendum*) a rational life.[14]

Augustine stated the relation in this way: 'To enjoy (*frui*) something is to hold fast to it in love for its own sake. To use (*uti*) something is to apply whatever it may be for the purpose of obtaining whatever you love.'[15] The whole journey of the Augustinian soul is one from enjoying what should be used to enjoying God and using all else for this purpose. Spinoza follows a similar trajectory, and his critique of Stoic *apatheia* also reflects that of Augustine. It goes further, however, because Spinoza understands enjoyment to admit of degrees, such that the lesser things that are used to reach enjoyment can themselves be enjoyed, but only insofar as they are useful. Furthermore, this movement for Spinoza is one of return of each human being to his own nature, which has within itself the power to strive for self-fulfilment.

For Hume, on the other hand, the self, which can understand itself as nothing but a bundle of ideas, cultivates the calm emotions of Sceptical distance through its own auto-affective realization of itself.[16] The process of philosophical thought accustoms the self to Sceptical reflection, curbing those impulses which lead to superstition, enthusiasm and speculative excess. The difference in styles between Spinoza and Hume reflect the difference between the selves which normatively are presupposed in their thinking. The geometric method of the 'Ethics' presupposes a Stoical self, who thinks of herself as a constituent part of nature; Hume's conversational style is that of a Sceptical self finding tranquillity through suspending judgement about the world.[17] Respectively these selves must be thought with differing concepts of freedom: Spinoza is Augustinian (but crucially an Augustinianism of a self-sufficient nature) in thinking freedom as acting through one's own nature as that which takes its essence from elsewhere (as a modification of the divine substance), undistracted by the passionate attachments to things in the world, driven by a love of God; Hume is Pelagian in his belief that the source of all confusion and error is in habituation and that the self through habituating himself to virtue overcomes vice and reaches calmness and tranquillity.

Neither Spinoza nor Hume begin with the self but rather with the situation in which a self emerges, a situation which on first reflection is bewildering for the self. Apart from the authorial voice, the first voice which makes itself heard in the 'Ethics' is that of the one 'who judges about things in a confused way'. Furthermore, such people, as Spinoza pictures them, live in a kind of dreamlike state: 'For those who do not know the real causes of things confuse everything and without the least mental repugnance they picture trees no less than human being speaking, and imagine human beings to be formed from stones no less than from seed, and any forms to be changed into any forms whatever.'[18] But to avoid this confusion it is necessary to know the cause of things. Part 1 of the 'Ethics' attempts to chart an account of this, but as he make clear in the Appendix to that Part, his arguments may not be clear to his readers. As with both Descartes and Pascal, for Spinoza the reason for this disconnect lies in the prejudices of his readers. Spinoza agrees with Descartes on the role of society in fostering these prejudices, stating that 'but all have one common nature. Only we are deceived by power and culture'.[19] But there is a deeper prejudice, which is an inherent tendency within that common nature, namely, that of seeing all things on the basis of one's own human nature, hence, for example – but the example is crucial – thinking of God as acting to fulfil certain ends and as expressing passions. This prejudice does not stand up to rational scrutiny as it is based on the fact that people take 'for things that which is really the modification of [their] imagination'.[20] But while he states that a little reflection will dispel these prejudices, the goal of the 'Ethics' relates directly to the journey necessary to achieve this. In an earlier work he states, 'It is necessary to understand of nature only as much as is sufficient for one to acquire a human nature of this kind [i.e., one of constancy].' Furthermore, he states that he 'wish[es] to direct all the sciences toward one end and goal, … that we should achieve … the highest human perfection'.[21] Spinoza is here affirming the superficiality of Sceptical claims to relativity, as cultural specificity hides that common nature which we need to follow and further that this nature needs to be refined by proper thinking to achieve that Stoic goal of constancy.

In a related manner, Hume begins the *Treatise* by showing the self that it is not what it thinks itself to be. The prejudice Hume is encountering is one to which Spinoza might also be subject, namely, the affirming of occult presences beyond experience. The first part of the *Treatise* seeks to show that the self is not a substance and that what gives us the illusion of a substance are in fact laws of association through which ideas are bundled together. Again that great confusion is to be overcome through a proper account of the self. That account needs to show how the self comes to be and how we are misled as to the nature of that self that is so intimate to us. Hume's strategy from the beginning of the *Treatise* is to reconstruct the mechanisms forming epistemological and moral selfhood. The Sceptical approach he takes allows him to disassemble both the 'vulgar' and philosophical accounts of this self in order to dispel common confusions.

The confusions which Spinoza and Hume identify are different – indeed, each could fall under the other's category of 'confused' – yet essentially the confusion is the same: thinking of the self as its own substantial being. Hume rejects this because neither this nor any other substance appears in experience; Spinoza rejects it because there is only one substance, namely, God. The source of the difficulty lies in tendencies of thought. Thinking has the tendency to go astray, and the task of philosophy is to redirect it out of confusion into clarity in a way which both aims towards a new account of the self and depends on that newly articulated self for its realization.

For both Spinoza and Hume, philosophical reflection needs to take place within the context of society as they experience it and Spinoza outlines a version of Descartes's 'provisional morality'. He sets out three principles:

1. To adapt as much as possible to the 'capacity of the vulgar [*captum vulgi*]'.
2. To enjoy luxuries insofar as they are necessary of health.
3. To copy the customs of the state as much as possible.[22]

This 'provisional morality' shows Spinoza's distance from a key aspect of much of Stoic thinking, namely, its individualism and distrust of political society. Indeed, as we will see, Spinoza rejects Stoic 'cosmopolitan' approach as a veiled withdrawal from the political. For Spinoza the practice of philosophy requires *libertas philosophandi*, that freedom to philosophize which only a stable political constitution can provide. Similarly, the external goods necessary for health are crucial to the power of the self and hence to its flourishing. The capacity of the vulgar is not simply that of those with whom the philosopher lives but also within the philosopher himself: The vulgar capacity is also the capacity of any self living in society, and the philosophical pursuit is always in relation to the normal human existence underlying it. To be sure, the capacity of the vulgar is lesser than that of the philosopher, but it is only on a basis of a commonality between both that adaption is possible. These commonalities include those things which are used, such as luxuries and the customs of the community, which make living together and cooperation possible. Hume shares a similar view. He too works with the distinction between the vulgar and the philosophical and again for him this distinction is found within the philosopher too. But for Hume in a manner very similar to that advocated by Montaigne, the goal of philosophical reflection is more to inhibit its own tendencies to speculation and in a certain sense to return the philosopher back to the vulgar, freed of the credulity of the latter but sharing their faith in appearances. The true philosopher is distinct from the vulgar and yet shares with them a dependence on custom and a distrust of abstract theorizing. The philosopher's Scepticism refuses the metaphysical, while at the same time taking an ironic distance to the credulity of the vulgar. For both Spinoza and Hume, the 'theologically minded' form a kind of middle group. They are educated beyond the vulgar but have an ambiguous role: ideally to teach the vulgar to obey reason, for Spinoza, and sharing with the philosopher a Scepticism about reason,[23] but to be kept away from philosophical reflection, for Hume.

Philosophical reflection for both Spinoza and Hume needs a method to find its way towards its goals. Spinoza distinguishes four modes of perception (*modos percipiendi*), which he ranks between hearsay and intuition.[24] The manner of proceeding through these modes, which are hierarchically arranged, Spinoza explains by analogy to the use of tools: through a gradual development, starting with instruments 'supplied by nature' ending with 'complicated mechanisms', 'in the same way the intellect, by its inborn power, makes intellectual tools for itself, by which it acquires other powers for other intellectual works, and from these works still other tools, or the power of searching further, and so proceeds by stages, until it reaches the pinnacle of wisdom'.[25] The goal of wisdom is achieved in this way, starting from nature and working through a refinement of nature, that is, a refinement of oneself. In this context Spinoza understands the intellect as going beyond the mere employment of truths it does not adequately understand (he uses the example of a tradesman resolving a mathematical problem 'because they have not yet forgotten that procedure which they simply heard from their teachers, without any demonstration'[26]). Nevertheless, implicit through this analogy is a certain historicity of knowledge and a refusal of the Cartesian Sceptical step of suspending the validity of all learned truths.

While for Spinoza experiment is secondary to theory as merely confirming but not discovering truths,[27] Hume understands the 'only solid foundation' of science is experimental: one 'laid on experience and observation'.[28] Despite his references to Isaac Newton and Robert Boyle in this regard, Hume's method is less that of experiment in the natural scientific sense and closer to what Husserl will later term 'imaginative variations of the real'.[29] Hume tests philosophical claims against the observation of experience and does so by varying the factors in such experience to see whether the claim can be accounted for by experience. The self that engages in such 'experiments' is Sceptical in the twin senses of rejecting all speculations which escape the boundaries of any possible experience and of seeking (*zetic*) for truth through observation.[30] Humean wisdom is more negative than positive, more an insight into the weakness of dogmatic claims than the affirmation of solid truths. At the end of Book One of the *Treatise*, unable to respond positively to philosophical questions, Hume finds himself in a stage of 'philosophical melancholy and delirium', and nature draws him back to the vulgar – dining, playing, conversing, merrymaking.[31] It is only when he exhausts such pleasures that a certain intellectual curiosity and ambition draws him back, but this is tempered by a repugnance at superstition and the dogmatic claims. The violent emotions emerging here are ones he wishes to oppose with 'mild and moderate sentiments'.[32] The point is not, however, one of ascetic withdrawal. On the contrary, the philosophical could do with 'a share of gross earthy mixture' (i.e. of vulgar amusements and recreations). The wisdom being sought never allows the philosophical to break free of communication with the vulgar and everyday. Indeed, the point of philosophical reflection is to habituate the mind to forms of thinking that will remain as dispositions in his everyday life. As Philo puts it in the *Dialogues concerning Religion*, the effects of the Stoic's reasoning will appear in his conduct in common life, and through the whole tenor of his actions. ... In like manner, if a man has accustomed himself to sceptical considerations on the uncertainty and narrow limits of reason, he will not entirely forget them when he turns his reflection on other subjects. ... To philosophise on such subjects is nothing essentially different from reasoning on common life; and we may only expect greater stability, if not greater truth, from our philosophy, on account of its exacter and more scrupulous method of proceeding.[33]

The end or goal of this process of achieving wisdom is happiness for both Spinoza and Hume, and in this sense they both share a eudaemonistic account of the self. Spinoza speaks of contentment of mind both in his letters and in the 'Ethics'. In a letter he states, 'I realise (and this gives me peace of mind [*mentis tranquillitatem*]) that all things come to pass through the power of the most perfect being.'[34] The intuition of all things as the expression of this perfect being is the third kind of knowledge in the 'Ethics', which is a knowledge indissolvably connected to intellectual love of God. The goal for Spinoza is salvation.[35] Salvation from ignorance and from the play of passions, salvation from a fallenness, which is not to be understood as that of a fallen nature, but rather as the fall from natural understanding, that is, from an understanding of nature as it is. This fallenness is twofold: from an intellectual understanding, using reason, and from a true obedience through the power of the imagination. The story of the Fall in the book of Genesis is, according to Spinoza, one of limited knowledge of God: Adam thinks of God's commands as ruling out of fear, while in fact 'God commanded Adam to do good out of love for the good rather than fear of evil'.[36] Salvation is the coming to a true love of God, one which is not simply gained through intellectual conviction but through an affective turning of love towards God: 'The more the mind is suited (*aptior*) to understanding things by the third kind of knowledge, the more it desires to understand them by this kind of knowledge.'[37] To become suited the mind must share being with its 'object', namely, nature or God.[38] It does this through developing its clear and distinct ideas, working on itself to think all modifications clearly and distinctly, and in so doing coming to see all things under the species of eternity. This is not simply a transformation of thought but a transformation in being as the mind loses in this way any partiality for itself and even for temporal relations. The self comes thus to recognize its own eternity. This recognition does not take place through recollection – the very movement of recollection through images formed through the body is governed by time and duration – but rather through a feeling. 'We feel and know by experience that we are eternal. The mind feels those things that it conceived in understanding no less than those it has in the memory.'[39]

Remarkable is the emphasis on feeling, which we find also in Hume. The feeling of eternity is something that the mind senses immediately. But this immediate sensing is made possible by a prior process of turning the self away from all that distracts it, ultimately away from the actuality of things including its own body towards these as expressions of the divine. The point here is not a turning away from things towards God but rather a turning away from them in their temporal actuality towards seeing them as timeless, necessary expressions of the divine. Hence, understanding a singular thing under a species of eternity is understanding God.[40] In this way the self lives its own life as a modification of the divine and understands its own striving for being as nothing other than the divine striving in it. This becoming eternal is not the Christian idea of an afterlife. It is rather the case for Spinoza that the self-illumination involves the loss of self through its incorporation in the greater 'self' of nature. As Firmin de Brabander notes, this marks a 'tragic element' in Spinoza's 'Ethics'.[41]

For Hume, the goal of philosophy is happiness and is also a certain kind of salvation. Philosophy needs to be rescued from its own speculative excesses, the self who can do this is guided by feeling, but by a feeling which is moderate and sympathetic. For him the Fall is not so much one of ignorance as one of deafness to those fundamental feelings that can guide the human being more surely than reason. In this sense, for Hume, wisdom requires a recognition of animality at the core of the human. In each book of the *Treatise*, Hume is at pains to show that not only in reason, passions and morals is there no difference in kind with animals but also that the human self has much to learn from observing animals. In Book One, in clear reference to Descartes, Hume states that 'the beasts are endowed with thought and reason as well as men'.[42] We observe animals behaving as humans do when seeking to preserve themselves, to achieve pleasure and to avoid pain, and, knowing that we use reason and design to do these things, we can infer that they act through a like cause. Without experiencing what it is like to be a non-human animal, Hume can only infer analogously from the similarity of behaviour to a similarity of cause. The actions of animals become unintelligible if we do not allow for reasoning on their part. Hume reverses the common explanation of instinct on the part of animals, saying that 'reason is nothing but a wonderful and unintelligible instinct in our souls', it operates in human beings as in animals through the force of habit, which is 'nothing but one of the principles of nature, and derives all its force from that origin.'[43] Scepticism regarding reason allows us to recognize the utility of normal reasoning processes in bringing us pleasure, avoiding pain and preserving our being.

Spinoza and Hume understand the goal of philosophy to be happiness. For Spinoza, happiness or blessedness is the equivalent of being: It is strictly speaking impossible *to be* unhappy, as unhappiness is a privation of being. Evil is 'every kind of sadness and especially what frustrates longing'.[44] Each being is concerned with increasing its power to be and in so doing its joy, which affectively expresses goodness for it. But such increase of being is not to be understood as necessarily conflictual: As each being is the expression of the divine being which is all there is, the true expression of the self's being cannot be in contradiction to the being of all there is. As such, on a purely rational level the expression of the self's being is an expression of the universe in it. For Hume, happiness is always going to be partial to each individual self. The self cannot make claim to a significance of being going beyond that which it can sense and experience – beyond that which impresses itself upon it. The feeling of eternity which Spinoza appeals to is something that Hume can accept as a belief – an intensity of feeling – but one which takes us far beyond the phenomenal level and by implication that level at which we can communicate with one another. Hence, what is the goal of philosophical thought, for Spinoza, lies, for Hume, beyond that which is philosophically accountable.

4.2 Genesis and nature of ideas

'By Idea I understand a conception of the mind which the mind forms because it is a thinking thing,' states Spinoza.[45] The reference to and distance taken from Descartes is clear here: A thinking thing is a thing which has ideas, but ideas are not images in the mind (as Spinoza states more explicitly later); they are rather a conception of the mind (*mentis conceptum*), which he immediately defines as an action of the mind (*actio mentis*). Ideas are to be understood here not as simply representations, but as conscious acts expressing the nature of the mind to a greater or lesser extent; the mind itself is thus a process.[46] In contrast, Hume understands ideas as perceptions (which in the 'Ethics' Spinoza explicitly denies due to the implication of passivity with this term) and as images, indeed, 'faint images'. They are not even faint images of things but rather of impressions, of the marks made by the manner in which things affect the body.[47] Beginning with impressions in this sense entails a rejection of any claim to knowledge that cannot show its source in the things appearing in sense perception. This is implicitly a doxastic starting point, which entails a Scepticism regarding any claim to kataleptic impressions. The distinction between impressions and ideas is understood by Hume in relation to a number of contrasting terms: immediate/mediate, primary (first appearance)/secondary, original/image, lively/weak, feeling/thinking. He then introduces a distinction encompassing both impressions and idea, between simple and complex. Both impressions and ideas are divisible into simple units, which can be added to one another. Whereas ideas express the nature of the mind for Spinoza and are as such active, in Hume the emphasis is on the passive, the manner in which ideas depend on impressions. At a fundamental level for both ideas are the mind's manner of encountering the power of nature: For Hume, the idea reduces that power and liveliness, through converting the impression into an image resembling it; for Spinoza, the idea is how the mind affirms its object, far from diminishing liveliness the idea asserts the power of the mind.[48] What we find here are two manners of understanding how the mind can be in a world of a plurality of sources of power and how order is possible or not within such a world.

For neither Spinoza nor Hume does the thinking of ideas, their production and combination, originate in a thinking self. For Hume, the thinking self, in the sense which it would be meaningful to speak of such, comes later, arises out of a prior process whereby ideas emerge out of impressions and are combined by association; for Spinoza, ideas are indeed products of a mind, but they are products of the mind of God, which express themselves through the human self as a mode of the divine attributes of thought and extension.

Spinoza explicitly separates image and idea, imagination and intellect. Indeed, it is for him a basic confusion to fail to make this distinction.[49] An idea does not resemble something and is not a mere word but rather affirms an object as existing. This is the act of the mind, but one in which volition and intellect are one in the same. So the corollary of separating intellect and imagination is to deny the distinction between intellect and will: To think an idea is not to have 'mute pictures on a panel'[50] that the mind can then affirm or deny through an act of the will, but to affirm something about the world. We can see this, Spinoza thinks, if we consider ideas of non-extended things: These cannot be images of bodily impressions (to use Humean language), because they do not refer to bodily motions. The nature of ideas refers directly to their origins. If the idea does not come from bodily motions, it cannot be an image, it cannot simply resemble something else. For Spinoza the idea as a product of the mind testifies to the power of the mind. This is so because Spinoza understands the idea as expression: 'The formal being of ideas is a mode of thinking (as is known through itself), that is ... a mode which expresses, in a certain way, God's nature insofar as he is a thinking thing.'[51] Indeed, Spinoza explicitly rejects the view that ideas can be understood in terms of impressions: 'The ideas ... of singular things admit not the objects themselves, or the things perceived, as their efficient cause.'[52] The idea of a circle and the object circle do not differ in kind; the idea is rather the objective aspect of its object. In tracing the nature of the idea it is necessary to seek the one who thinks it and then to understand the function of the idea in terms of that originating relation. Immediately upon introducing the notion of ideas, Spinoza qualifies it with the feature of adequation – *idea adaequata* (adequate idea).[53] To a scholastically trained reader this would suggest the notion of truth – *adaequatio rei et intellectus* (correspondence of thing and intellect). Yet, Spinoza immediately frustrates this implication by stating that an adequate idea as an idea 'considered in itself without any relation to the object' qualifies as true. An idea is a conscious act but – when adequate – is an expression of the mind which thinks it, that is, a self-sufficient act. Adequate ideas express the self as mind and as active. Such a self has mastery of itself, but only through an understanding of its own nature. At the same time, the self is never simply an intellect thinking conceptually; the mind also has inadequate ideas, that is, ideas which do not originate (fully) as expressions of its own nature. To this respect the mind is passive, subject to something else outside itself.[54]

Hume, as we have seen, begins not with an expressive being but rather with the ways in which the human mind is impressed upon by the world around it. This human mind is not considered in its agency within this world but in its passivity: It is that on which things are impressed, stamped, pushed upon. If we deny the reality of the expressive being of the mind in Spinoza's sense, then Hume's account of the origin of the ideas follows. Effectively, in Spinoza's terms, Hume's account is of inadequate ideas, which indeed (again from Spinoza's account) is suggested by Hume's designation of ideas as images rather than pure concepts. Ideas for Hume arise automatically for the most part from impressions.[55] They are pictures showing – in a less vivacious manner – the impressions. So with ideas there is a decline in the liveliness of the being, which is having them, that energy of liveliness is being lost. Yet by the same token the liveliness of the impression is being stored, retained albeit in a weakened form. The human mind is in this sense primarily a mechanism and functions as all nature does in a mechanical manner. Despite the fact that there is a falling off in energy with ideas, through this mechanism they produce new things, which may or may not correspond to nature as it impresses itself on the mind. The very lessening of vivacity in the idea allows this to happen: While in memory the ideas remain in their order tied to the impressions, as they lose vivacity they become more susceptible to manipulation through the imagination. Hume states, 'Where-ever the imagination perceives a difference among ideas, it can easily produce a separation.'⁵⁶ Yet, the functioning of the imagination is itself governed by a mechanism of association. The mechanisms of separation and combination appear to have a certain order, not merely a matter of chance.⁵⁷ In speaking of the imagination, Hume is not referring to an agent, a thinking subject, but rather a faculty of the mind, which operates according to a 'uniting principle' by which simple ideas are connected to one another through resemblance, contiguity and causation. This mechanism is not a conscious one but rather one without which there would be no conscious subject, because there would be no connection of ideas. As Gilles Deleuze puts it, 'the ideas are connected in the mind – not by the mind'.⁵⁸

By understanding ideas as images and their combination in terms of association in the imagination, Hume opens up – in principle if not in fact – a space of pure possibility. The relations of contiguity and resemblance are so broad that we cannot rule out any particular combination of ideas. While originating from impressions, the order of impressions does not govern the order of the ideas, which may be combined in many different ways. As such, ideas are removed from things in a double manner: They are themselves images of impressions and are combined not in terms of the order of impressions but in terms of a mechanism of association governing the mind. Furthermore, Hume works on the principle that anything that can be distinguished can be separated and that the proper philosophical method is precisely to separate and then reconstruct. Paradoxically, Hume in emphasizing that passivity is methodologically much more constructivist that Spinoza would claim to be. This may seem strange given Spinoza's geometrical, and Hume's much more discursive, method. But the geometrical order is understood by Spinoza to reflect the order of things, while Hume from the very beginning of the *Treatise* cannot rely on any order except that which emerges out of the mechanism of ideas. This mechanism understood only in terms of resemblance and contiguity could not form, however, a coherent world. For this to arise there must be a third relation: causality. In his discussion of causal relations, Hume brings out the consequence of understanding terms independent of their relations. This is his basic atomism: Nothing in any of the terms determine the relation, so nothing in one idea allows the inference of another. For any such inference to occur, we need experience.⁵⁹ The details of Hume's critique of causation will be discussed in the next section. For now, what is important is to examine the preconditions in the mind for that experience that allows for inference. First and foremost, this is memory. Hume's understanding of the mechanism of perception starts with vivacity that is then retained in ever weakened forms (there are exceptions to this general rule as we will see, but these need not detain us here). The first retention and weakening occur in the translation of impressions into ideas through a process of imagining. The process is twofold: a loss of vivacity but a temporal gain; the impression is retained beyond itself in its image. We can say that it is here that memory begins and through memory the notion of causation is possible, and with this is gained a sense of personal identity and selfhood.⁶⁰ Memory allows the mind to preserve past impressions (albeit with reduced vivacity) and to return to them under the principle of identity as being one and the same as the present object. Hume tends to conflate memory and recollection: Memory is only apparent in the act of recalling. He states, 'what is memory, but a faculty, by which we raise up the images of past perceptions?' He goes on, 'The memory not only discovers the identity, but also contributes to its production, by producing the relation of resemblance among the perceptions.'⁶¹ As Hume sees it, this is as much an operation of producing identity in the self as it is in the things perceived. But while memory is crucial to identity it does not exhaustively produce it. This is evident in the fact that we extend our identity beyond our memory, in the sense of identifying ourselves both with that entity which existed before we can remember and with that being whose day to day past life we can in many instances no longer recall.⁶²

Imagination is crucial to this process. The senses alone do not give us sufficient grounds for ascribing external existence to what we perceive because for Hume our perception is inherently internal. All perception is related back to impressions to which the self relates auto-affectively: My principle relation is not to the appearing paper on which I write but to the impressions which I feel in myself. Hume refers in this context to the hypothesis of a double existence of perception and object which he terms the 'monstrous offspring' of two principles: the one of the imagination which 'tells us that our resembling perceptions have a continued and uninterrupted existence' while 'reflection tells us, that even our resembling perceptions are interrupted in their existence and different from each other'.⁶³ It is the imagination which goes beyond the discrete data of impressions to postulate external and continuous existence of objects. In this sense identity is fictitious. To say it is fictitious is not to say that it is non-existent or a matter of mere fancy but rather that it is a construct of the imagination that cannot be justified epistemologically or metaphysically. Something similar is true of personal identity.

Hume employs the experimental method introspectively in asking about the self. The self he is investigating is the Cartesian self discovered in the *Discourse* and the *Meditations* by an inward movement of thought. Through a method of experimental variation, Hume can find nothing to justify the Cartesian claim to a substantial self. What he finds when he inspects his consciousness are rather ideas and impressions. As he famously concludes, 'when I enter most intimately into what I call myself, I always stumble on some perception or other … I never can catch myself at any time without a perception, and never can observe any thing but the perception'.⁶⁴ There is no impression corresponding to the self, because such an impression would have to persist through all the sensations.⁶⁵ As such, when we do ascribe identity we are speaking either 'of something invariable and uninterrupted or of something mysterious and inexplicable'.⁶⁶ What happens here is that imagination transcends what is given to it through the impressions. In doing so nothing in principle more is done than what we find in the normal processes of association. The imagination is a transcending faculty that operates to create fictions of identity in excess of what is perceived. The imagination has a 'natural propensity' to do this.⁶⁷ In this section of the *Treatise*, Hume does not tell us why it has this propensity, but it would appear that the imagination is motivated by a kind of desire for 'greater regularity than observed in our mere perceptions'.⁶⁸ Constancy, coherence and identity are fictitious constructs which give a regularity to experience based on the association of ideas but going beyond it. The imagination somehow brings with it metaphysical principles of identity and independent existence. These metaphysical principles though have real practical efficacy, relating directly to temporality.

For Hume, time is a matter of the mind not the object; more specifically, time is a 'manner, in which impressions appear to the mind', that manner namely of them 'succeeding each other'.[69] In this sense, time or duration is not properly applicable to unchangeable objects; indeed it is not applicable to objects at all but rather is projected onto the succession of changeable objects. In maintaining identity over time in the object the self supposes the agent of change to be time rather than the object. To say that an object is identical with itself is, according to Hume, to say that the object 'existent at one time is identical with itself existent at another time'.[70] In this sense an identity over time is maintained, whereby despite the lack of continuity of perception, a sameness in the object is upheld. In placing, so to speak, the responsibility for change onto time, the mind is following a tendency to 'repose', not exerting itself to do anything other than to maintain the same idea of the object as before. The relation of identity maintains an equilibrium, requiring the continuation of the same action rather than the emergence of a different one. There seems to be a tendency in the mind for an 'easy transition'. The mind, Hume is suggesting, is faced with a contradiction between two principles: that of identity arising from the imagination and that of difference arising out of the experience of interrupted perception. It seeks to reconcile this contradiction through sacrificing difference for identity.[71] Difference, for Hume, is not a relation but the negation of all relations. The sacrifice of difference is the manner in which the mind displays its need for relation. We could say that relations express the mind in the face of the difference of impressions. What they express is not the self but rather that process of the imagination below the self, productive of the self. Furthermore, relations serve to maintain the vivacity of impressions. Hume's claim is that this principle of identity is established by which new impressions remain connected to the same idea – the same identical idea plays the role of representing a plurality of impressions.

For Spinoza, duration is pivotal in terms of knowledge. Of the three forms of knowledge he outlines, the first is vague, dependent on signs and on the imagination, while the third is intuitive knowledge. The second form of knowledge is based on adequate ideas understanding the 'common order of nature and the constitution of things' in causal terms.[72] Spinoza understands cause in a fundamentally positive way: A cause brings something about; only indirectly does it negate the existence of something else. This is tied to his notion of endeavour (*conatus*) but also to that of duration which he defines as the 'indefinite continuation of existing'.[73] Every entity, whether as a thing or idea, has within itself a force, an endeavour, to maintain itself in existence over a duration without prescribed limit. In other words, ending – or mortality more specifically – is contingent upon external causes. As such, the duration of anything is fundamentally rooted in a distinction between inner and outer causes. In this sense the impression of something external upon a thing ultimately bears the seeds of its demise. Like Hume, Spinoza understands memory as a form of imagination, but what this means for him is that memory remains at the surface of identity: It simply records the sequence of modifications of the body through external things but does not involve 'the ideas which explain the nature of the same things'.[74] This is not to say that memory is unconnected to the intellect: Spinoza is clear that the more intelligible a sequence is the more easily it will be remembered.[75] However, memory is susceptible to the 'force with which the imagination ... is affected by some singular corporeal thing [*rei singulari*]'.⁷⁶ Memory, then, retains both intelligibility and the singular finite thing, both of which are understood by Spinoza in terms of an association of ideas, or more properly of images.

'If the human body has once been affected by two or more bodies at the same time, then when the mind subsequently imagines one of them, it will immediately recollect the others also.'⁷⁷ The self imagines when the body is affected and disposed in a certain way. Such affection originates in external objects affecting the body. The imagination is that function of the mind which concerns the manner in which a thing appears to the body. The imagination is a form of knowledge in this sense, but knowledge of particular things only, the 'first kind of knowledge'.⁷⁸ This knowledge is of inadequate ideas, as it depends on particular appearances of things. It is here that for Spinoza falsity is possible. Imagination presents objects as present, the 'affections of the human body whose ideas present external bodies as present to us'.⁷⁹ As he introduces the theme, Spinoza mentions three terms: *impressiones*, *vestigia* and *rerum imagines*. *Impressiones* and *vestigia* are used rarely by Spinoza. In this context they are being used synonymously to refer to the traces of objects which are retained by the body. In Part 2 he speaks of the body as a complex of individual parts which make up a particular corporeal entity and those parts for Spinoza are of three basic types: fluid, soft and hard.⁸⁰ Traces are impressed on the body through the changing fluid part having been determined by an external object that 'impresses [*imprimit*] on [the soft part] certain traces [*vestigia*] of the external body striking against (the fluid part)'.⁸¹ Impressions in this account are not discrete but are traces (*vestigia*) caused by a frequency (*saepe*) of contact. In other words, there is already a pattern established in the very process of leaving an impression through traces in the soft part of the body.⁸² Thus, affection is also disposition; it is a taking up of a position with respect to the external object. This disposition is not discretely dependent on the presence of the object and as such does not indicate its present existence.⁸³ There are no innocent impressions for Spinoza; the impression is a pattern of motion within the human body that at once involves both the nature of the external body and the nature of the perceiving human body.⁸⁴ As such, the human body is temporally constituted, and what is regarded as present through the imagination is so because of the manner in which the mind retains past affections and continues to be disposed in terms of them. For this reason the mind may regard as present that which is not present and does not exist.⁸⁵ Memory and recollection are not distinct from perception; they are all species of the imagination. They function through association. So if two objects are associated together, they will continue to be associated in the mind. For Spinoza, memory is nothing other than a certain connection of 'ideas which involves the nature of things outside the human body'.⁸⁶ They are not ideas which explain the nature of those things, as they do not concern the cause of those things, but simply the manner in which they were impressed upon the body. The manner of such impression has to do with events, the events of affection, disposition and impression, which can be purely arbitrary in terms of the nature of the things associated.

The associations formed are specific to the individual experiencing them, because they are contingent on their temporal constitution more generally, that is, on the general context of their lives. Spinoza understands this as custom, as being accustomed to a certain way of connecting images. So a soldier and a farmer, when they see the traces of a horse's hoofs in the sand, will associate this affection with different images depending on their different life experiences.[87] Spinoza's account through all of this is remarkably similar to Hume's discussion of imagination and habit. But, for Spinoza, all of this happens in the first form of knowledge. This form of knowledge is closed off to the ultimate end of happiness in the intellectual love of God.

We cannot move from the impression to existence, because the impression is the pattern of affection and disposition of the body towards the externally affecting thing, which may no longer exist. To experience it as no longer existing requires a contradictory affection, which excludes that body from existence or from being present.[88] For Hume, on the other hand, the idea of existence is connected with the thing of which we have an idea or impression. To perceive or think something is to affirm its existence. This is true only of simple impressions and ideas: These can be combined to form the idea of non-existent, imaginary things, such as the New Jerusalem with pavements of gold and walls of rubies.[89] The idea of being is not itself grounded in any impression and as such has no independent reality: The idea of existence 'when conjoined with the idea of any object, makes no addition to it. Whatever we conceive, we conceive to be existent.'[90] This has the consequence for Hume that we have no access to the question of existence beyond the impressions and ideas which we form: The existent object is nothing other than the impression or idea which we have of it. Following Berkeley, Hume affirms that general ideas are nothing other than 'particular ones, annexed to a certain term, which gives them a more extensive signification, and makes them recall upon occasion other individuals, which are similar to them'.[91] In defence of this position, Hume states that 'nothing of which we can form a clear and distinct idea is absurd and impossible'.[92] Later in speaking about geometrical ideas, Hume states that clear and distinct ideas imply the possibility of existence.[93] Hume's use of such a rationalist phrase, 'clear and distinct ideas', is interesting particularly in this context. His fundamental point is that general ideas understood as abstract cannot be clear and distinct. The actual ideas we have of abstract entities are particular. To the extent that these ideas are clear and distinct, they are ideas of possibly existing things. In this way, Hume uses the rationalist principle against itself, by insisting that the possible existence of ideas is a matter of their particularity not their abstractness. For Spinoza, clarity and distinctness is tied to adequacy: A clear and distinct idea contains the cause of the thing.[94] As such, the ideas of affections of the human body, so the imagination, cannot be clear and distinct. For Spinoza, clarity and distinctness indicate necessary, not possible, existence.[95] Spinoza and Hume, however, both share the view that all ideas are particular. An adequate idea cannot be general or abstract, for Spinoza, because it is a particular expression of the divine attribute of thought. To know it, is to know its cause, that is to know it as it manifests the divine essence. A general idea through abstraction is a function of the imagination, a prop based on cognitive limitations in the human being. Spinoza and Hume share a common Nominalism that forms the backdrop through which we may investigate their respective accounts of substance and cause.

4.3 Substance and cause

According to Hume, it is possible in the imagination to separate the idea of beginning from that of cause and hence it is not necessary in terms of knowledge for something to have a cause.[96] Furthermore, to say that something exists without a cause is not to say that it is its own cause; it is to deny the necessity of the causal relation in understanding anything.[97] Clearly, the last point concerns the *causa sui* and the notion of God inherent in it. Hume consistently rejects all a priori arguments for God's existence, while Spinoza begins the 'Ethics' precisely with the cause of itself, whose essence involves existence.[98] Hume denies both aspects of this: that something existing must have a cause and that we can move from essence to existence. The fundamental philosophical decision separating Hume and Spinoza here is that for Spinoza all things are relational, and nothing is outside of the relation in which it is, while for Hume anything that can be distinguished can be separated, such that relations are in this sense secondary to their terms. For something to be, for Spinoza, is for it to be in a causal relation either with itself, with God or with things external to it; for Hume, that which is distinguishable by the imagination can be separated in fact. Spinoza is guided by the Stoic insight of the interconnection of all things such that happiness comes from the acceptance of the self's place within that totality; Hume employs Sceptical reflection concerning reason in questioning the absoluteness of such relations, showing that they can all be analysed and reconstituted. In metaphysical terms this leads to fundamentally different accounts of the laws of nature. Natural necessity is eternal for Spinoza; for Hume there is no contradiction in saying that in the future the same cause could have a different effect.[99]

It is striking, nevertheless, how often Hume invokes the agency of nature. To give just a few examples: 'Indulge your passion for knowledge,' says nature, 'but seek knowledge of things that are human and directly relevant to action and society'; 'nature has kept us at a distance from all its secrets, and has allowed us to know only a few superficial qualities of objects'; 'nature may certainly produce whatever can arise from habits'; 'nature by an absolute and uncontrollable necessity has determined us to judge as well as to breathe and feel'.[100] In his discussion of miracles he talks about the violation of the laws of nature.[101] The fundamental intuition is that shared with Spinoza: Nature acts and does so with necessity, a necessity which encompasses the human along with everything else.[102] Both Spinoza and Hume understand the human self ruled by necessity, yet what for one is a fundamental ontological category is for the other unknowable. What is unknowable for Hume is still operative – he speaks of cause and necessity – but he can only speak of them as constructs of the imagination.

Spinoza and Hume share the understanding that knowledge is not simply the registering of an occurrence but is rather the placing of the object in a necessary relation to something else. However, Hume states that no particle of matter implies another.[103] This is so because matter itself is unknown to us. We can only know qualities; to suppose these qualities to inhere in a material substance is to transcend the facts of experience. In this sense 'matter and spirit, are at bottom equally unknown'.[104] What this means is that both materialism and idealism are naïve: Both claim to know that which remains unknowable and in so doing appeal to both substances and the causal power of substances, which remain hidden to the perceiver. The originating principle of cause, he says, cannot be shown as there is no adequate idea of power.[105] Hume is being quite consistent here. If ideas are images, then there cannot be an idea of power but only of objects which are the putative effects of power. He is not denying the appearance of causal relations but rather is seeking to account for them through nothing more than what in fact appears. 'Experience alone can point out to him the true cause of any phenomenon,'[106] he states in the voice of Philo. We go wrong for Hume both when we appeal to powers beyond what is experienced to account for these relations and when we make analogies from the causal relations which we experience (like the making of human art) to the actions of a designer God (as Cleanthes wishes to do). For Spinoza, nature is intelligible only in terms of power, yet he never actually defines 'power'. Unknowable for Hume, power is a basic unanalysable concept for Spinoza. They differ only in that for Hume such basic concepts can be employed but indicate nothing known, while for Spinoza knowledge begins from the concepts which are evident in terms of the propositions that we derive from them. He speaks of 'power' as the capacity to bring something about and follows ultimately from the essence of God. In effect, according to Spinoza, for something to be, it must have a reason to be and the reason is its cause. As such, nature has two aspects, the power of bringing about and that which is brought about – *natura naturans* and *natura naturata*. In all things, both aspects are there as the external appearance and the internal dynamic of its coming to be.

Both Spinoza and Hume begin with an intuition into the continual change in things. Nature is a realm of continual change, made up of individual things. The human self faced with this world seeks both understanding and stability. The seeking after stability has political aspects, and is also fundamental to their respective accounts of the passions, as we will see. Ontologically, however, both are seeking to answer the question of how in a world of change there can be stability and continuity. For Spinoza, this is based in the understanding of all that is as expressions of the divine substance; Hume appeals to experience, which tends to indicate a 'kind of pre-established harmony between the course of nature and the succession of our minds'.[107] Hume goes on to say that it is through custom that this correspondence has been effected. It is striking how Hume expresses in a Sceptical key this rationalist term, 'pre-established harmony', which he is taking from Leibniz but which also is implicit in Proposition 7 of Part 2 of Spinoza's 'Ethics' ('The order and connection of ideas is the same as the order and connection of things'). But this is in line with the Pyrrhonian orientation of much of Hume's Scepticism: denying dogmatic claims in favour of the phenomenon, philosophizing in terms of appearance. Hume is affirming the appearance of harmony between nature and mind, while rejecting that we have sufficient reason for claiming it. Indeed, this Scepticism does not preclude Hume from making strikingly speculative statements. Having rejected any analogous transfer from experienced things to the actions of the Deity, Hume says of the universe, in the voice of Philo, that

> it bears a great resemblance to an animal or organised body, and seems actuated with a like principles of life and motion. A continual circulation of matter in it

produces no disorder: A continual waste in every part is incessantly repaired: The closest sympathy is perceived throughout the entire system: And each part or member, in performing its proper offices, operates both to its own preservation and to that of the whole. The world, therefore, I infer, is an animal, and the Deity is the SOUL of the world, actuating it, and actuated by it.[108]

This account has much in common with Spinoza's as it rejects a body/mind dualism and understands the order of the universe as immanent to it. As matter and spirit are equally unknown to us in their essence, we have no more reason to affirm matter than spirit, but what we can affirm is the apparent order of things. We cannot affirm this order to be in the world, but we can affirm that there appears to be an isomorphism between the mental ordering and that of appearances, one seems to fit the other. The use of the term 'sympathy' here is striking. The neo-Platonic resonance is evident, but above all an invocation of an intrinsic vital relationality between all beings in the universe. Despite a theoretical atomism, Hume stresses the phenomenal relationality which again indicates his Pyrrhonism. In any case, the fit between mental ordering and appearances is not a priori; it is not a transcendental condition but rather arises through custom and habit.

Our everyday lives and our science is premised on the belief that the future will resemble the past. It is this which gives the self a sense of stability both in its life and its claims to knowledge. The collapse of such stability, due, say, to traumatic events, would have a devastating effect on the self's capacity to exist. Hume does not speak of trauma, but he is well aware of how precarious stability is, given recent (for him) European history and how stability is premised on the perception of causal relations. Cause is pivotal to stability but is never actually perceived. To show this, Hume asks us to consider how without knowing its past effects, viewed purely in and of itself, an object cannot give us any clue as to its causal efficacy.[109] Causal relations are read backwards and are so through repetition: When we see two events occurring in sequence a number of times, we form the habit of anticipating the same sequence to occur in the future. While the repetition of the conjunction of two things following one from the other lead to belief in the causal relation between them, this belief is made uncertain by what he calls 'contrariety in our experience and observation',[110] that is, occasions where the same effects do not follow from the same causes. While the 'vulgar' in such cases appeal to chance, philosophers seek to defend cause through appeal to causes which are hidden in nature. There is here an appeal to that which is unknown to support knowledge: If the causal relations appear uncertain, that is because of causes (yet) unknown. According to Hume, though, the 'vulgar' and the philosopher make inferences of the same kind. The first element of this is the arising of awareness of cause in the first place: When there is a frequent repetition of the conjunction, the mind is 'determined to pass from one object to the other' – when, however, this repetition is interrupted by exceptions, that facility to move from one to the other, is weakened.[111] In either case, the basic assumption is that the future will resemble the past. When there is a contrary event, breaking with that which the self is habituated to expect, it brings with it uncertainty and doubt.

The assumption that the future will follow the past, and the wider assumption that nature has laws which are constant and consistent, are based in belief. Hume understands belief in terms of vivacity: 'An idea assented to *feels* different from a fictitious idea, that the fancy alone presents to us: And this different feeling I endeavour to explain by calling it a superior force, or *vivacity*, or *solidity*, or *firmness*, or *steadfastness*.'[112] Such liveliness derives from custom or habit: 'As we call every thing custom, which proceeds from a past repetition ... we may establish as certain that all the belief, which follows upon any present impression, is derived solely from that origin.'[113] In recognizing causal relations we think backwards rather than forwards, towards the past rather than the future, but that retrospective movement of thought opens up the possibility of future action and thinking within a stable universe. As we have seen, memory is crucial for the self, but what grounds memory is repetition working through custom and habit. Custom and habit, Hume says, 'has the same influence as on the mind as nature'.[114] While an idea is a weakened image of an impression, it nonetheless holds onto some of the vivacity of an impression; a self without ideas, with only impressions, would have no sense of the future; without impressions he would have no sense of reality. Habit opens up the future and which allows for continuity. In this context Hume distinguishes – following Joseph Butler[115] – between active and passive habits: While passive habits result in a loss of vivacity, the active repetition of an action leads to increased facility and more tendency towards engaging with the world according to that habituated action.

On Spinozistic grounds, Hume is right to deny causality, if we begin with discrete impressions. However, to begin there for Spinoza would be to begin with an abstraction. Spinoza, as we have seen, understands habit already at the level of the impressions and the imagination. But for him the idea of causation is of another, rational, level. We are here at the second level of knowledge, where things are known in terms of their cause. We can think this if we take seriously Spinoza's account of the individual, which is the basis of his account of the self, of all things that are and of the universe as such. A complex individual is a unity of individuals which are in relation to one another and are individuated by a specific dynamic relation which identifies it. The crucial term here is 'relation', which translates the Latin *ratio*. This word has many meanings – reflecting in many cases the Greek *logos* – account, plan, method, reason and so forth, but what is common to all is a certain relation between parts which give unity to the whole.[116] The individual is defined by the relation, not the relation by the individual. It is worth quoting the definition in full:

> When a number of bodies, whether of the same or different size, are so constrained by other bodies that they lie upon one another, or if they move, whether with the same degree or different degrees of speed, that they communicate their motions to each other in a certain fixed relation, we shall say that those bodies are united with one another and that they all together compose one body or individual, which is distinguished from the others by this union of bodies.[117]

An individual body in this view is that in which there are contained a number of bodies which, however, communicate reciprocally in terms of a relation that defines them, that is, makes them part of one individual entity. On a basic level, this can be understood as the human body which in each individual has parts remaining in reciprocal relation to one another. These individuals can in turn join together to form an individual containing them. But ultimately each individual is related to one another in the universe as a whole. As Spinoza puts it, 'if we proceed ... to infinity, we shall easily conceive that the whole of nature is one individual, whose parts, that is, all bodies, vary in infinite ways, without any change of the whole individual'.[118] For Spinoza, then, to start with impressions on the body of one individual is an arbitrary starting point; it is also a partial one in both senses of the word: It displays a partiality to a specific viewpoint, which can only capture a very partial number of affections. Furthermore, understood as part of a wider individual, experience while having a partial validity, can never reach the standpoint of understanding cause and causal relations.

The issue between Spinoza and Hume is cause rather than substance. As the early Christians were accused of atheism because they rejected all (but one) of the gods, Spinoza evacuates the world of substances leaving only one behind. The self, specifically, is not a substance for Spinoza any more than for Hume. There is nothing self-sufficient in the world, no entity which can be given substantial presence. For Hume, to speak of such an entity would mean to have an idea which is based in an impression – an impression of a substance would have to persist through the whole life of that substance. When he enters 'most intimately into what I call myself, I always stumble on some perception or other'.[119] I will return in the next section to discuss how this account is premised on the experience of 'something he calls himself'. For now, what is crucial is that there is nothing 'simple and continued' there, only what he had earlier termed 'nothing but a heap or collection of different perceptions united together by certain relations'.[120] For Spinoza, too, there is no substantial self; there is nothing behind the perceptions, in the form of a substance. The individual self is nothing but that which is held together by a certain relation. But again that which is held together is only in and through the relation, which forms the self into an individual. That relation is cause. For anything to be is for it to bring things about. Being is causal efficacy, such that a thing increases or decreases in being depending on the effects it brings about. What we call a self is nothing other than its causal history, the history of its effects and its endeavour through that efficacy to preserve its own being. The habitual, for Hume, is that which forms a continuity and constancy; that same continuity is maintained by the endeavour to preserve its being, without which an entity would not be. That continual repetition, which can both increase and diminish the thing (passive and active habit), is, in Spinozistic terms, cause that either increases or diminishes the power of the entity.

The essence of each thing is its own history of causal efficacy (horizontally understood), but vertically each individual is its singular relation of parts to whole. At one level, for Spinoza, there is only one individual, nature itself, which is common to all that is and is the highest form of knowledge, intuition, grasps that individual as eternal, that is, as containing outside of all duration the infinity of all its causal relations. Yet, as nature is singular, so too are all individuals within nature: The monism of substance carries over into the singularity of the modi of that substance. The singular is a singular instance of nature. But for it to be, for it to have causal efficacy, it must have something in common with that which it effects. This Spinoza understands as 'common notions'. At the most fundamental level these are the notions of the attributes of extension and mind, and in terms of bodies, movement and rest.[121] The relations between these are infinite, such that each singular being is essentially itself to the extent to which it forms that which is common to all bodies into singular relations. Understood as common to all these things, common notions can only be understood adequately, because they are common to both the singular body and external bodies. The difference between internality and externality is irrelevant at this level.

'It is in the nature of reason to regard things as necessary, not as contingent.'[122] The corollary of this is that if we were basing our thought only on the imagination, we would regard things as contingent. Again here we see Hume inverting Spinoza: If all we know is the external appearance of the thing as it impresses itself on the mind, there is only imagination and in that case there is only contingency. Again, on Spinozistic grounds Hume is quite consistent. Through the association of ideas, the solidification of these associations through habit and finally through a transcending of such custom to set out the principle of identity,[123] Hume understands that we have such ideas as substance, God, identity, cause for which there are no impressions and which can only be understood as products of the imagination.

Spinoza advances a Stoic account of substance and causality, but in arguing for monism, he rejects the Stoic understanding of matter as passive. He need not appeal to reason independent of matter to explain material motion because matter has its own motivating force. Furthermore, the divine substance has no end other than itself. It is not adapted to human beings; indeed, Spinoza rejects any appeal to final causes. His reason for doing so arises from his account of the eternity of the world: There is no end to which nature is aiming; it acts simply out of the necessity of its own being.[124] For Hume the ordered universe indicates an omnipotent mind constantly directing everything, but this omnipotent mind cannot be invoked to explain motion, although the phenomenon of order strongly indicates such a being. In reality, Hume states, philosophers have affirmed that 'matter ... operate[s] by an unknown force' and we cannot simply then postulate an idea of force.[125] The Humean Sceptic does not reject the idea of God, but he does reject any *deus ex machina*. If the notion of God itself names an unknown origin, Hume is consistent to remain ambiguous towards it. The God, which the order of the universe seems to indicate for him, is neither the theistic God of Judaeo-Christianity nor a Lockean Deistic God but rather something more akin to Spinoza's as a divine principle which names as much the essence of matter as it does that of spirit. In any case, Hume as much as Spinoza rejects any notion of final cause as inconsistent with causal relation as the 'constant conjunction of two objects'.[126]

Spinoza and Hume can each be read consistently of the basis of each other's metaphysics/epistemology. This is so because they both start from nature as that which is pressing, a dynamic relation in which the self can only be if it affirms itself with respect to that network of pressing: impression and expression. By thinking 'pression' from expression or from impression, both self and world appear otherwise. It is in this context that we need now to explore their respective accounts of the passions and community made manifest in the state.

4.4 The passions and tranquillity

Having denied the notion of the self in Book One of the *Treatise*, Hume begins Book Two ('Of the Passions') by affirming it. The passions of pride and humility are reflective ideas representing the most common of impressions, that which everyone has of 'himself'.[127] This seems all the more strange as Hume had explicitly denied that we have an impression of the self. However, as we alluded to in the last section, Hume does in effect employ the idea of himself, indeed, calling attention to the intimacy of that idea for him, in the very act of denying the self. He was not so much denying the self-relation inherent in the notion of self, as he was contesting a particular theoretical approach to establishing that self. The self of epistemology – the substantial, thinking thing – is to be replaced, by an account of the self as passion. Again here he appeals to intimacy: We have an 'intimate memory and consciousness'[128] of this self, or better, this intimacy *is* in some sense the self. In the passions of pride and humility the self is concerned with itself or with objects as they relate to itself. However, the impression of the self is not an immediate one, produced by an external object; it is rather a reflective impression produced by the idea of pleasure or pain reflecting back on the soul. The self is produced in this very self-reflexivity, which is there from the first paragraphs of the *Treatise*. It is precisely as a being that can experience pleasure and pain with respect to its sensations that the self arises. Already in section 2 of the first book of the *Treatise*, Hume introduces an auto-affective process: An idea of pleasure or pain 'when it *returns upon* the soul, produces a new impression of desire and aversion, hope and fear, which may properly be called impressions of reflexion'.[129] Here there are impressions that are caused by no thing but rather by ideas. What is being posited is a being that can receive impressions both from things and from ideas, both from that which is other than it, and from itself. Only on the assumption that the identical being is that which receives both sets of impressions does the talk of return or indeed of reflection make any sense. This process of return is one by which this identical being affects itself, and does so repeatedly: 'These [impressions of reflection] are *again* copied by the memory and imagination, and become ideas, which perhaps *in their turn* give rise to other impressions and ideas.' Clearly, Hume understands the impressions of sensation and of reflection being distinctly different in character. While the first is the domain of the anatomist, that is, can be understood as a purely physical process, the latter is that which can best be understood by the moral philosopher.[130] This is so because in the latter case what we have is the relation of the soul to itself. It is, therefore, by definition true for Hume that there will be no impression (in the first sense) of the self: The anatomist will never discover anything resembling the self, because anatomy analyses into discrete physical components, while the self is a relation, that is, an auto-affective relation. It is for this reason that it is only in the second book of the *Treatise*, when he comes to look at the passions, that Hume encounters the self thematically.[131]

Hume understands the basic ideas brought about by the impressions under binary rubrics: pleasure/pain, thirst/hunger, heat/cold. Of these, pleasure/pain seems to be the most general. As these ideas affect back onto to the soul, passions arise that share this binary nature: beauty/deformity, love/hatred, grief/joy, pride/humility. While ideas as copies of impressions were understood as weaker copies that could reasonably be understood as potentially diminishing their intensity towards zero, reflective ideas regain intensity within the auto-affective process. Indeed, passions are divided by Hume into passions 'properly called' and emotions,[132] along a trajectory of violence (passions) and calmness (emotions).

Spinoza begins his discussion of the affects by affirming that they can be understood in terms of natural laws and that 'nothing happens in Nature which can be attributed to any defect in it'.[133] Having stated this, Spinoza gives three definitions of cause, action and affect, in each case governed by a dichotomy working along an axis of self and other. Just as ideas can be self-sufficient or not, that is, adequate, clear and distinct, or inadequate, confused, so too can cause and for similar reasons. The direct relevance of this to the question of the self becomes immediately clear when Spinoza defines action and passion. Two aspects are important here. First, he understands action and passion in terms of the cause that brings something about and hence, a being can be the adequate cause of something when that thing follows from its own nature. Its own nature is that singular nature (essence) that makes it what it is in the universe (existence). The self is not responsible for her nature; she did not bring it about, but to the extent that what she does bring about is the effect of her nature, then that effect is the expression of her nature. Passion, on the other hand, is that which the self suffers (*pati*) and when the self suffers something then he is not wholly the cause of it. He is still partially the cause: It expresses someone's nature to break a window due to his weight even when he is pushed into the window. Second, Spinoza introduces here a distinction common to the Stoics and Sceptics between what is in the self's power and what is not. Spinoza is signalling the factor common to the distinction between adequate and inadequate cause. He articulates this distinction in terms of inner and outer – 'in us or outside us [*in nobis aut extra nos*]' –[134] a distinction crossing over the difference between action and passion. Spinoza goes on to define affect and does so in relation to power. Having distinguished between action and passion, he understands both in terms of affect. While Hume distinguishes between calm and violent passions, Spinoza understands affects as either those that increase the power to act of the body or those that diminish such power, calling them action and passion respectively. In this sense both Spinoza and Hume distinguish, within the affective domain more generally, between passion and that which is not a passion, be it understood as an emotion or an action. What this points to is the understanding common to both of the agency of affection, which reflects the rejection on both their parts of the notion of free will. Spinoza rejects the Stoic account of will as governing the passions.[135] He is closer to Augustine in affirming the disjunction between enslavement to the passions (what Augustine terms the 'flesh') and love of God. But in negotiating this disjunction neither grace nor free will is available to the self. As a natural being the self is torn between actions (emotions in Hume's terms) that aim towards its benefit or passions that are destructive of it.

Hume begins with the violent passions and more specifically with what he terms the 'direct' and 'indirect' passions. The direct passions he understands to be those which arise directly from good and evil, pleasure and pain, while the indirect involve some other quality. The key difference here is that the indirect passions involve society, involve, that is, some comparison with others, such that the self is directed as much at herself as at others. Without explicit justification Hume begins with the indirect passions, in particular pride and humility. These passions are auto-affective and quite general: All actions can to a greater or lesser extent evoke pride or humility in the one who has initiated them. Indeed, Hume immediately speaks of the self as the object of pride and humility: 'Whatever other objects may be comprehended by the mind, they are always considered with a view to ourselves.'[136] Hume is careful to distinguish the object of these passions and their cause: They are directed at the self, but the self does not cause them. In pride and humility the self is affected by itself, but only as it is in relation to some quality which it perceives itself to possess. As Hume makes clear, there are a multiple of qualities of the mind, the body and of objects related to the self which can give rise to pride or humility. As such, the causal nexus of these passions is a complex one involving positive or negative qualities in their relation to the self. Crucially, a passion is not a representation, but rather an impression: It is not an idea which points beyond itself but rather an impression made on the soul, which is complex in that it is an impression of a relation.

Feeling is constitutive of passion for Hume. That feeling is directed at the self in relation to some pleasure or pain experienced. As a feeling it does reference some quality in the world, say, that of beauty in the home of which a self is proud, but the feeling itself expresses nothing other than the self's own relation to that quality. That relation is quite uniform, Hume affirms, is based on nature, but the passion itself relates only to the self experiencing it. Similarly for Spinoza, affect is closely tied to the imagination as passions arise through the imagination, through the ideas of external things acting upon the self. In that sense passions are not confined to the human mind but rather are related to all singular things to the extent to which they are acted upon.[137] This is important because in effect Spinoza is universalizing the basic distinction from which he begins, between action and passion. For all things they are either acting or being acted upon in the specific sense that they are either expressing their own natures or (in part) expressing another's (by expressing their own reaction to another). It is for this reason that Spinoza, in beginning to speak of the affects, speaks of power: the power of expression. Hume starts from the feeling of power also and strives to find, if not the aporetic state of indifference, at least a calming of the passions. For Spinoza this is not available to us because the fate of all things is to strive to increase their own power and restrict the diminishment of that power.

In this sense two of these philosophers' most famous statements can be brought into dialogue with one another – Hume: 'Reason is, and ought only to be, the slave of the passions, and can never pretend to any other office than to serve and obey them';[138] Spinoza: 'The striving [*conatus*] by which each thing strives to preserve [*perseverare conatur*] in its being is nothing but the actual essence of the thing.'[139] First, we should note the mixture of descriptive and normative statements: Reason *is* the slave of the passions, and this is as it *ought* to be; the striving to preserve in existence contains a normative claim that it is right to do so. In both cases what we have is an account of the self as it is and as it ought to be. Second, in Spinoza's terms Hume's claim to the subordination of reason to the passions would amount to a statement of the necessary diminishment of the self and hence go against the *conatus essendi*, while in Hume's terms the striving to preserve its being as a fundamental principle would be contrary to the goal of tranquillity better achieved by contemplating the shortness of life and comparing our lives to others especially those inferior to us.[140] Most of all for Hume, it is best to keep in mind that 'human life is more governed by fortune than by reason',[141] while for Spinoza fortune is that which does not follow from our nature, should be borne with equanimity, but in any case follows from 'God's eternal decree' and as such is not opposed to reason.[142] Here again Hume sceptically restricts philosophical affirmations to that which can be shown in appearances: It may be the case that what appears as fortune to us is guided by divine reason, but this is to appeal to unknown causes. It may be the case that the order of the universe indicates a divine mind, but in the situation of ill-fortune this is neither apparent nor for Hume does this thought have any power to affect the passions responding to this situation.

As things impress themselves upon us, they can do so in ways which cause pain or pleasure, and from these arise our passions of pride and humility, love and hatred, benevolence and anger, and so forth. The self seeks pleasure and is repelled by pain. Pleasure leads the self to approve and pain to disapprove of an appearing thing.[143] In relation to ourselves and to others we see these motives as fundamental. Here again Hume is appealing to experience: In judging a present situation we appeal to past experience[144] of how people act, and what we find there are motives based in the increase in pleasure and the diminishing of pain. Against any appeal to free will, Hume understands the motive to act in humans as well as animals as indicative of the power to act: The power to act is the relation of the motivations of the person to the circumstance in which she finds herself. Hume sets up a square of emotions, in four quadrants – Pride, Humility; Love, Hatred – divided into sets of self and other, where pride and love are agreeable or pleasurable and humility and hatred disagreeable or painful.[145] There is in each case a double relation of ideas to the object of the passion and impressions to the passion. There are objects which have no relation to any of these passions, which are affectively neutral and the effects on the passions increase with the degree of relation to the object and the feelings of pleasure/displeasure they elicit. Crucial here for Hume is that the power of the passions diminish as we move from ourselves to others and increase in the opposite direction. He says, 'If a person be my brother I am his likewise: but though the relations be reciprocal they have very different effects on the imagination.'[146] The context here is that virtue or vice in my brother will cause love or hatred, and this will be 'transfused' into pride or humility due to my relation to him. But the same transfer does not occur in the other direction: My pride or humility of my own virtue or vice does not lead to love or hatred of my brother. As such, there is a natural transition from pride or humility to love and hatred but not in the other direction. Hume's explanation of this is that our intimate consciousness of ourselves is such that our sentiments and passions have greater vivacity for us than the ideas of them in other people. This liveliness captures the imagination and makes it transference to another difficult, while the movement from the 'obscure to lively ideas' is much smoother. Vivacity in this sense has an attracting power, fixing the attention of the imagination, and the self's own auto-affective sensations attract its feelings from elsewhere, that is, the self has a natural tendency to feel itself in relation to the passions it has for others, those passions being along a trajectory of love and hate.

While Hume begins with pride and humility and moves outward to others through love and hatred, Spinoza in Augustinian fashion understands all affects as rooted in love. Joy and pleasure accompany love, but love is the motivating force: 'One who loves necessarily strives to have present and preserve the thing he loves.' Spinoza defines love as 'joy with the accompanying idea of an external cause'.[147] In other words, love is directed outwards towards the other, that other, namely, that the mind imagines to preserve its being. When Spinoza does speak of self-love he changes from speaking of *amor* to *philia* and adds the synonym *acquiescentia in se ipso* (contentment in himself).[148] The striving outwards towards external causes is a movement of desire for that which will give the self such love of itself. The latter is reflected in God, whose love of himself (*amor* in this case) is one of that which has no cause outside itself. The intellectual love of God aims to find that self-sufficiency not through an independence from external causes but through identifying of the self with nature as such. It is significant here that Spinoza affirms what Hume denies (self-love) and also denigrates what Hume places centrally in the passions, namely, pride. Hume is not entirely terminologically consistent here: He denies self-love but then goes on to speak of self-love in the sense of self-interest. It is undeniable that people act out of self-interest for Hume, but the passions are always directed towards objects which impress themselves upon the self. The self-relation itself never becomes an object of passion. For Spinoza, in contrast, the self in experiencing itself as a modification of the divine reaches blessedness. In this sense, the self in its self-relation fully comes to that self-relation only through thoroughly embedding itself in its relatedness to others and in the third form of knowledge to others as manifesting nature as such.

Reason then can never motivate an action for Hume because we act in order to achieve pleasure, while for Spinoza action as opposed to passion is a seeking after self-sufficiency. Again in quasi-Augustinian form, Spinoza sees self-sufficiency as achievable only through heteronomy, albeit a heteronomy which – as with redeemed nature for Augustine – discloses itself as expressing better the self than any autonomy could; Hume, on the other hand, remains strongly Pelagian in his understanding of the self as capable in itself of finding its ultimate end. Reason in that sense remains for Hume strictly instrumental: We do not reason about ends, only about the means to achieve those ends. The ends are given to the self by its nature, or rather its nature responds to the impressions received through the passions to maximize pleasure. Hume states, 'It is as little contrary to reason to prefer even my own acknowledged lesser good to my greater, and have a more ardent affection for the former than the latter. A trivial good may, from certain circumstances, produce a desire superior to what arises from the greatest and most valuable enjoyment.'[149] Reason and passion do not oppose one another because they operate on different levels. However, if reason can show that the passion rests on false presuppositions or is employing insufficient means to reach its goals, then passion yields to reason. But in terms of ends, it does not. The only way of countering a passion is by another passion. There is a remarkable consistency between Montaigne, Descartes, Pascal, Spinoza and Hume (among others, including Hobbes) on this point. Spinoza states it in this way: 'An affect cannot be restrained or take away except by an affect opposite to and stronger than the affect to be restrained.'[150]

The sense of the emergence of an explosive dynamic of passions, religion and politics can be seen in the emergence of words such as 'enthusiast', 'fanatic', 'zealot' and 'fervor' from the sixteenth into the eighteenth century. These were expressions of an unease with the manner in which passionate commitment to religious beliefs appeared to be contributing to political instability in Europe. The transformation into a new world in this period brought with in not only insecurity but also intense conflict as to the orientations of this new world with respect to the self and the manner in which the self lived in community with others. Tradition and established forms of government no longer seemed to have sufficient authority to contain the passions of 'subjects', making the very origin of communal living itself a key issue of political philosophy. With respect to the self, a fundamental question was the place of the passions; for the philosophical formation of the self, the controlling of those passions both in the self and in others became an issue in which politics and theology, religion and question of state intersected.

Both Spinoza and Hume give a normative account of the self that entails the restraining and moderating of the passions. For Spinoza, this is necessary in order to increase the power of the self; for Hume, precisely because reason is the slave of the passions, happiness is only achievable, if the passions are moderated. The restraint and moderation of the passions can occur, for Spinoza, only through the coalescing of imagination and intellect. The self is affected by external things acting upon the body. It is aware of these things through images and the imagination posits these things in different modalities: as actually present, as contingent, as possible in the future, as necessary. Affects grow or diminish in intensity to the extent to which the self imagines them as proximate to it. The manner of directedness of such passions is orientated towards knowledge of good and evil, that is, the knowledge of each being of its own good or evil. Good and evil are not absolute but rather comparative terms, for Spinoza, relative to the being of the entity involved.[151] What follows from this is that 'the knowledge of good and evil is nothing but an affect of joy or sadness, insofar as we are conscious of it.'[152] However, such joy or sadness is the affective recognition of an increase or diminution of power to act. Knowledge of good and evil is a guide at the heart of affectivity towards rational self-interests. Nonetheless, this is unstable because of the inconstancy of the imagination, which is swayed by the strength of external causes stronger than the self. The only way to restrain the passions is through another affect or rather another mode of affect, namely, reason. Reason, for Spinoza, is not simply instrumental but rather is expressive of the nature of each individual and of nature as such. The self is its own self-expression in a world of expressing beings. Its power is diminished to the extent to which it is determined by the expressions of other beings and increased to the extent to which it expresses itself in adequate ideas. The actions which arise in this way[153] express the desire of a human being, which is its essence. Desire is the complete striving of the human being, its 'impulses, appetites and volitions'.[154] The desire which arises out of reason is that desire that seeks to increase the power of the self and diminish its dependence of external causes. Here again we can see Hume as inverting Spinoza: Reason as a peculiar instinct of the human being is that instinct to find a means to achieve its ends; for Spinoza, on the other hand, instinct as arising out of reason is that impulse to fully express the nature of human being.

While reason is a slave of the passions, for Hume, calm emotions resemble the work of reason because of the lack of agitation of spirit in them. This observation is important in understanding that though reason ought to be slave to the passions, the self is generally best motivated to act in accordance with the calm rather than the violent passions. This distinction has long roots; indeed, it can be understood in terms of Stoic psychology.[155] It is a subtle distinction, regarding which there is little consensus in the secondary literature.[156] In our context, what is crucial to recognize is that the cultivation of calm emotions is in the overall self-interest of the self and is most conducive to her happiness. Any attempt to classify particular passions as violent or calm is to miss a vital point in Hume's account. In introducing the distinction he sees the calm emotions in the 'the sense of beauty and deformity in action, composition and external objects', while violent tendencies are more evident in 'the passions of love and hatred, grief and joy, pride and humility'.[157] But he immediately states that this is a 'vulgar and specious' distinction and is 'far from being exact'. The fact that, as Hume emphasizes, one passion can transfuse into another, suggests strongly that what we need to be looking for here is the mode of movement of energy to and away from the passions and the circumstances which lead to this. It is in this context, not accidental, that he puts together aesthetic and moral emotions in exemplifying calm emotions. The sense of beauty can involve a certain detachment and distance, while love, hatred, grief, joy, pride and humility tend to involve an intense partiality. But this is only a clue, and as Hume makes clear, violent raptures are possible in reading poetry and calm moderation in the experience of love.

Crucial here is that Hume is understanding tranquillity as essential to happiness. 'Calmness and tranquillity'[158] are associated with calm emotions. This is the equanimity Pyrrhonians seek. Significantly, Hume doubts that a state of indifference is really possible. In this respect he shares with Spinoza a doubt about the capacity of the mind to reach that state of either aporetic indifference or passionless *apatheia* and for similar reasons: The human being is always in a state of being affected by fortune. Furthermore, the energy of the passions can neither be reduced to zero nor indeed would it be desirable for them to be so, as the passions are what give us those ends for which we strive. The passions move between calmness and violence, leaving little room for indifference: 'The connexion is in many respects closer betwixt any two passions [violent and calm], than betwixt any passion and indifference.'[159] The violence of a passion is characterized by Hume in terms of agitation of the mind. The source of that agitation is instability and uncertainty. Violence here is being understood as disruption. For this reason security and despair are both states in which passions are moderated: Despair and security are two forms of certainty, Hume states. In both cases the mind is not susceptible to agitations. What this indicates, however, is that the lack of violence is not sufficient for tranquillity. Certainty in this context means stability. Calmness is achieved through the development of stability in the mind. Hume understands this capacity to cultivate calm passions and control violent ones as the virtue of 'strength of mind', the virtue which brings about 'the prevalence of calm passions above the violent'.[160] In the *Inquiry concerning the Principle of Morals* he shows not only that strength of mind is essential to happiness but also that they involve deciding for long-term interests rather than immediate pleasures.[161] Strength of mind is that capacity of the self to understand itself as it is, namely, in two respects: as a being existing over an extended temporal duration (identical with itself) and as a being with others (in community with other selves).

In exploring this theme, it is important that Hume distinguishes with respect to the passions between calm and violent, on the one hand, and weak and strong, on the other.[162] A calm passion is not for that reason without motivating power. People are often motivated by violent passions, but this is not always the case, and indeed there is an implicit normative claim that happiness depends on being motivated as much as possible by calm rather than violent passions. The normative claim here concerns that self which is operative in Hume's texts: It is a self which is not pulled back and forth by the momentary passions but rather one in which 'a passion has once become a settled principle of action'.[163] Such a self looks to the distant rather than the present good: 'The same good, when near, will cause a violent passion, which, when remote, produces only a calm one.'[164] In each of the typical cases he mentions with respect to calm passions – benevolence, resentment, love of life, care of children and moral and aesthetic sentiments – the self views its actions in relation to a settled goal, the ultimate good of his own happiness, and acts accordingly. But what facilitates this is habit. As Hume states, 'Nothing has greater effect both to increase and diminish our passions, to convert pleasure into pain, and pain into pleasure, than custom and repetition.'[165] The other side of this is that novelty excites us, puts the 'spirits in agitation',[166] and this novelty adds more pleasure and pain than what is natural to the object of that passion. The state of mind consequent on this situation is ambiguous: On the one hand, novelty is agreeable, but, on the other hand, it is agitating. Novelty, no matter how pleasurable, inevitably brings pain too. So, for Hume, the role of repetition is to moderate such novelty, to calm the passions (ultimately to the level of being almost imperceptible) and give the self a sense of its own stability over time. Custom operates in a twofold manner bestowing facility for the performance of an action of the thinking of a thought and then setting up a disposition towards that action or thought: Habit maintains passions which allow the self to 'survey objects with greater tranquillity'[167] and in so doing act in a manner which best preserves its being. Two caveats are important here. First, that habit depends on situations that have sufficient stability to allow for habituation, hence Hume's emphasis on security. Second, as Hume makes clear, habit can work in the opposite direction too, to increase passions and to convert pleasure into pain. Here Hume seems to have in mind a process of banalization leading to boredom, whereby what was once a matter of pleasure – his examples are 'the fair sex, or music, or good cheer' – become indifferent. But in such cases indifference leads to displeasure. It is indicative here that he opposes these to more aesthetic experiences ('viewing clouds, and heavens, and trees, and stones'), which are by tendency calm.

The second aspect of the self, which strength of mind requires, is the being with others in community. This brings us to a key concept in Hume's account of the passions, namely, sympathy. Sympathy is that capacity of the self to feel sentiments with another,[168] and this works on the human passions in a double manner: A self can recognize what another is feeling through observing their behaviour and share those feelings and he can feel certain ways because he senses another's sentiments towards him. While the capacity to sense another's feelings and through that to take up an 'objective point of view' becomes crucial for Hume's account of moral judgement, he first introduces the notion of sympathy to explain the sentiment of pride.[169] This capacity to sympathize Hume understands as a receptivity to communication of inclinations and sentiments from others. Indeed, Hume goes so far as to suggest that the self can feel passions more from communication of others than from its own temperament. In this sense sympathy intertwines the self affectively with others. Such intertwining occurs according to the same categories of association as those between impressions and ideas: resemblance, contiguity and causation. Sympathy renders the sentiments of others 'intimately present to us'.[170] This makes possible such passions as pride and humility for which the sentiments of others are constitutive. But the relations here are varied, such that the self seeks praise from those she admires and finds blame from them much more displeasing than from those whose sentiments she does not value.[171] What this means is that relations are necessary for sympathy. The nature of that relation is a matter for which Hume gives varying accounts through his writings, but for our purposes the crucial fact here is that relations are essential to the self as a sympathizing being. A self already finds itself in relation with others, such that its passions are in part constituted, through sympathy, by such relations. In sympathy the self senses itself as someone who is liable to praise or blame not with respect merely to its present actions but in terms of its character as reflected in those actions. What Hume calls the 'two principles of authority [of the one's judging us] and sympathy ... must have a peculiar influence when we judge our own worth and character'.[172] That character as strength of mind is reflected back to us through those sentiments which we sense from others who judge our behaviour.

The self which emerges here seeks stability above all because stability is for Hume a necessary condition of happiness, that pleasure which is more than ephemeral. A being that can achieve such a state achieves tranquillity. This is a tranquillity not of indifference but of calm passions. It is not always possible to achieve, as violent passions will continue to emerge, but a self aware of itself as a being of temporal continuity and sympathetic affectivity can strive to maintain moderation as much as possible. Spinoza seeks to achieve the same goal of tranquillity, but in his case through reason which gives the self freedom from passions and freedom to love God. In that sense, power and freedom are closely aligned for Spinoza, that is, that thing is free 'which exists from the necessity of its nature alone, and is determined to act by itself alone'.[173]

4.5 God and the state

As with Pascal, but with quite different aims and results, both Spinoza and Hume engage in a 'hermeneutics of suspicion' *avant la letter*, seeking to understand what motivates various accounts of God, how these accounts are expressed religiously, and seeking to mould a self in society with others who will be less susceptible to the superstitions and enthusiasms both see as endemic in the religious practice of their day and the wars of religion of relatively recent memory. For both the underlying motives of religion are in the passions in fear and hope, on the one hand, and in love (for Spinoza) and benevolence and sympathy (for Hume) on the other. Neither was in any simple sense an atheist: Spinoza understood theism as a confused account of the philosophically true, namely, that all things were expressions of the divine nature and that the human being finds blessedness in the love of God; Hume, though much more ambivalent than his Dutch predecessor, affirms a divine origin for the order of the universe. In this sense, both Spinoza and Hume oppose degraded religion – superstitious, enthusiastic, ignorant and so forth – to 'true religion'. Spinoza understands the latter positively and develops a full account of true religion, which he defines as 'whatever we desire and do of which we are the cause insofar as we have the idea of God, *or* insofar as we know God'.[174] The philosophical religion for Hume is Sceptical recognition of order without name, one which has beauty, but in which we can find no moral significance except through faith. As he states it (in the voice of Philo),

> the beauty and fitness of final causes strike us with such irresistible force, that all objections appear (what I believe they really are) mere cavils and sophisms; nor can we then imagine how it was ever possible for us to repose any weight on them. But there is no view of human life, or of the condition of mankind, from which, without the greatest violence, we can infer the moral attributes … which we must discover by the eyes of faith alone.[175]

Both Spinoza and Hume intertwine political and moral issues with metaphysical questions. They both see clearly how politics and metaphysics reflect each other because the political and social arrangements of human beings are rooted in their natures, particularly their affective beings, and they both understand the proper political arrangement to reflect human capacity to understand its place in nature. Religious practice and beliefs are subject to critique here because they are rooted in human nature, but in a human nature that suffers from confusion. The total dispelling of such confusion is not possible or can be thought of only as a kind of regulative ideal, one to which we can approximate. For both Spinoza and Hume, the boundary between the philosopher and the common people is a porous one: Both share the same nature and are subject to the same passions; furthermore, both seek the same satisfaction of desire. In political terms this means that both are suspicious of any utopianism.

The existential situation in which religion arises is that of being subject to fortune. The first 'divinity' in Spinoza's 'Theological-Political Treatise' is the fickle Goddess *fortuna*. The powerlessness people feel faced with the vicissitudes of fortune gets expressed in the twin passions of hope and fear. There is a wretchedness here out of which superstition arises.[176] Hume echoes this same thought in the mouth of Philo when he points out that 'when melancholy, and dejected, [the human being] has nothing to do but brood upon the terrors of the invisible world, and to plunge himself still deeper in affliction'.[177] For both thinkers there is a basic ignorance at the heart of this, namely, ignorance of the cause of events. But while for Hume such ignorance is insurmountable such that the most reasonable response is one of Pyrrhonian Scepticism – 'A total suspense of judgement is here our only reasonable recourse'[178] – for Spinoza the task of philosophy is to know the true causes of things, which is the work of reason, but as the minds of ordinary people are 'not able to perceive things clearly and distinctly', the doctrines of true religion need to be communicated by narratives.[179]

Spinoza and Hume both reject the idea of divine providence. Both reject the Stoic understanding of the human place in the cosmos and the Christian understanding of the relation of the human being to God. The self's relation to God cannot be separated from her relation to nature, both her own nature and the universe as a whole. Both Spinoza and Hume reject any argument from design and in so doing reject the 'God of the philosophers' in its Cartesian or (in Hume's case also) Leibnizian guise.[180] For both, the relation to God cannot ground the relation to nature but rather must, if at all, be intrinsic to that relation. For that reason they both reject any account of salvation as a saving *from* nature in the form of an afterlife. This has an immediate political consequence in terms of the religious account of reward and punishment after death. Eternal reward and punishment are incentives to good behaviour and virtue. Implicit in such an account is the view that only through a reference to that which is beyond nature can human beings (or at least the non-philosophers amongst them) be brought to act well. In exploring this topic we need to begin with the state of nature as Spinoza and Hume understood it.

As Hobbes developed the idea of the state of nature, to understand political society it is necessary to suspend it hypothetically. He understood the state of nature without political society as one in which everyone acted out of self-interest and in which there was no moral law and no justice. Only through the sacrifice of power could individuals arise out of such a state, and this sacrifice is made for the sake of security and by means of a contract.[181] While indebted to Hobbes, both Spinoza and Hume contested his account in fundamental ways.

For Spinoza, natural right is equivalent to power. To exercise the power of one's own nature is natural to every being and human beings are not an exception to this. As long as human beings are considered living in the state of nature, there is no law and, as such, no normative difference in the exercise of power. Considered in terms of what attributes nature gives it, the human being is 'born completely ignorant of everything' and is guided only by the 'sole impulse of appetite'. As such, there is no law in nature, hence nothing is prohibited.[182] As in Hobbes, cooperation happens only through a contract and all at once for the sake of security. Spinoza's account here is based on the understanding of the fundamental impulse of entities to preserve and expand their own power. The rights which arise in society can only be justified in terms of such power, but society itself arises out of reflection: 'If we consider that without mutual help, and the cultivation of reason, human beings necessarily live in great misery ... we shall realize very clearly that it was necessary for people to combine together in order to live in security and prosperity.'[183] But such reflection does not lead to a transformation of the natural self but rather simply a change in its strategy: Fundamentally the self does not give up power at all but rather by combining its power with others increases its own power. For this reason Spinoza understands the result of the contract as leading to democracy rather than subjection to the Leviathan.[184]

Hume questions the possibility of such reflection, which in different ways is a common assumption of Hobbes and Spinoza. As he puts it, 'it is impossible, in their wild uncultivated state, that by study and reflection alone, they would be able to attain this knowledge [of the advantage of cooperation]'.[185] Rather, Hume understands society as having arisen out of instinct and habit. The instinct is a sexual one, 'that natural appetite betwixt the sexes, which unites them together, and preserves their union, till a new tie takes place in their concern for their common offspring'. A basic instinct of mutual relation and cooperation lies at the basis of the family for Hume, and within the family, 'custom and habit operating on the tender minds of the children, makes them sensitive of the advantages which they may reap from society'.[186] The family alone, however, does not explain the existence of society. Society needs artifice; it needs a making that arises out of nature but is in excess of nature. Nature gives human beings both obstacles and – in the sentiments inherent in the nature of human beings – the capacity to overcome those obstacles. Hume characteristically begins by comparing human beings to other animals and showing how comparatively ill-equipped the human being is. The human being requires society in order to prosper in nature. Society, in other words, has a clear utility as a means to overcome the natural lacks in the human being.[187] However, this does not explain why society is formed. For Hume, there must be a sentiment in nature which is both natural and yet gives rise to the artificial construction of society.

In assessing Hume's argument here, it is important that he understands actions as morally relevant only as signs of motives: To praise or blame an action is to approve or disapprove of the motive which led to it.[188] It is instructive that in giving examples of basic human motivations, Hume locates them within the family bond: for example, the affection of a father for his child. For Hume, there are primary natural impulses on which morality is based.[189] Morality, however, is an artificial construct based on these natural impulses. Hume pursues this line of thinking with respect to justice: Justice is an artificial virtue, but this does not make it arbitrary. As with the principles arising from the imagination, Hume is here indicating the incompleteness of human nature. A human being needs to artificially complete herself; however, this completion is not possible individually but only through cooperation. Society names this cooperation, which gives to each individual self additional force, ability and security.[190] Society is in the self-interest of each individual, which means paradoxically that an overcoming of partiality for one self and one's family is a matter of self-interest. Again, self-interest for Hume is fundamental to morality and cannot be explained in moral terms. There is a natural impulse, in Spinoza's terms, to self-preservation; this endeavour cannot be countered but can rather be redirected. Such redirection occurs by a kind of sympathy. Although Hume does not speak of sympathy in this regard, instead distinguishing between self-interest as the original motive for justice and sympathy with the public interest as the source of moral approbation,[191] nevertheless the capacity to recognize reciprocal interest in the preservation of property, which Hume compares to two m⟨ pulling the oars of a boat together,[192] requires a sympathy between them. This sympat and reciprocity between people is irreducible for Hume. The self recognizes in anot the same motivations and in so doing allows the violence of his impulses – particu¹ his avarice – to be tempered. The virtue of justice arises from this modification basic sentiment, a modification which, however, is itself basic to human life. In words, the making of convention and society does not come after nature bı constitutive supplement to it.

Artifice is necessary to human nature: Human nature, so to speak, pre-str society through the lack of a natural instinct to public interest, on the one h⟨ the internal limit to his own pursuit of self-interest, on the other. There is n⟨

life without conventions; the human being is through its own natural impulses a *homo faber*, from the beginning habituating herself to reciprocal constraints which enable the pursuit of the self's interests and ultimately the possibility of happiness. The notion of a pre-social state of nature is then an 'idle fiction'[193] in the sense that it is merely speculative. However, it is useful in distinguishing *between* nature, specifically the natural human qualities of selfishness and limited generosity, *and* the conventions necessary to regulate these passions. Nevertheless, when a society is perishing, the virtue of justice becomes useless and the dictates of self-preservation no longer have any place for justice.[194] Similarly, in a situation of overwhelming abundance where there is no need to hold and defend property, there would be no need for justice. The normal state is one of equilibrium between these two extremes. But in this state of equilibrium the feelings of sympathy can extend to the whole of humanity. Indeed increasingly, particularly in the *Inquiry concerning Morals*, Hume speaks of the happiness of humankind as the ultimate aim of generous benevolence and one which can guide human sentiments. Such sentiments are rooted nonetheless in a degree of equality amongst its members, and Hume makes the experiment of imagining a species among human beings which though rational were of such inferior strength both in body and mind that they could never challenge others. We could not expect justice towards such a species, according to Hume. In other words, the artifice of society extends only so far as a reciprocity of power is evident. Beyond that, Hume seems to suggest, slavery of one sort or another is immune to moral sanction.[195] Nevertheless, Hume does suggest a history of progress where society develops from family to wider and wider groups limited only by the 'largeness of men's views and the force of their mutual connection'.[196]

we see here, Hume like Spinoza understands natural right as power. There is no God-appointed or otherwise – which can supersede the claim of any being's justice implies the sympathetic recognition of reciprocal relations of power society. Hume rejects the idea of the original social contract by arguing that not natural and are not intelligible outside of social conventions. Certain are necessary before it is possible to enter into promises. A promise the willing of an obligation into the future, but as morality is based this would mean that the self was willing a new sentiment, which is is rejecting here the implicit Voluntarism behind the social contract its willing individuals entering into contracts outside of social, contexts. He is also denying the pertinence of the account. He reality that most government is based in an usurpation of power internal revolt) and the gradual acceptance of that new reality. that there is no memory of an original contract in the minds ions. In one sense, this may seem an unfair criticism: The tract does not envisage an actual event in history which Hume is pointing to something deeper, namely, that wernment the manner in which such consent is arrived te: If government begins in usurpation, the usurper ituate people to his rule. Furthermore, politics does ubject to fortune and accident. Methodologically, understanding politics requires a sensitivity for the specificity of situations, while recognizing the manner in which different political societies are responding to human nature, particularly in terms of moral duties.[198] Spinoza, too, seeks to understand politics based on actual practice and is suspicious of those who 'conceive of men, not as they are, but as they themselves would like them to be.'[199] He understands political society as rooted in a contract, one which gives over power to the state, but while he thinks this is a rational course, he understands politics as guided as much by passion as by reason.

Spinoza understands the passions of hope and fear as indicating lack of knowledge and weakness of mind. Both are rooted in pain, in the diminution of power, because both are based in doubt and inconstancy.[200] Both these emotions are in opposition to reason such that the more we live by reason, the less we live by hope and fear. These very emotions are for Hume the source of superstition.[201] While for Spinoza these emotions can be conquered by reason through the cultivation of a love of God, this is true because hope and fear are themselves rooted in love: For both Spinoza and Hume these emotions can be countered through the redirection of the affects away from their addiction to temporal events and towards tranquillity for Hume and the eternal for Spinoza. But it is unclear whether anyone can live in the eternal for very long for Spinoza, particularly as an embodied being's existence is always going to be related to time and circumstance. These circumstances are political and also, as we have seen, passionate. If this is the case, then for any self that exists as an individual, the political imperative is to act in union with others to increase power. Spinoza states, 'What is most useful to man is what most agrees with his nature, that is (as is known through itself), man. ... Therefore among singular things there is nothing more useful to man than a man.'[202] This means that the interests of each individual is increased by cooperation and becoming a greater self, that of the (democratic) state. There is here, for Spinoza, a rational progression from love of self, to love of other (human beings) to love of God (and in that of all singular things). But this rational progression is carried out only slowly and faced with the twin realities that the thinking self can never fully live under the species of eternity and lives with others who similarly do not practice, and in many cases are not capable (for whatever reason) of approximating, rational understanding. In that context a twin approach is necessary, combining reason and imagination.

The journey to wisdom is a journey not simply of reason but also of imagination. Indeed, Spinoza states in a letter to Pietr Balling that 'there is almost nothing we can understand without the imagination instantly forming an image'.[203] As images are affections of the human body and the mind is not really different from the body, but rather they name two attributes of the same substance, Spinoza's thought places the imagination in an ambivalent position. On the one hand, it is identified with the first kind of knowledge and is as such vague and confused, on the other hand, throughout the whole journey from the confusion to illumination, the imagination remains essential to the knowing self in its relation to the world. There is here a tension but not any inconsistency: The contemplation and love of God by the eternal mind and the engagement with the world of fellow human beings and other entities in the temporal affective movement of life are two aspects of the one life the relation between which needs to be negotiated but is irreducible. For Hume, too, we find such a tension, with a different emphasis as reason is much weaker than imagination. But at the core of their respective accounts is the view that in relation to God and the state, any purely rational account is incapable of producing the conditions necessary for human happiness. Spinoza's response to fear could just as easily been written by Hume: 'To put aside fear, we must think tenacity in the same way [as other virtues]: that is we must recount and frequently imagine the common dangers of life, and how they can be best avoided and overcome by present of mind and strength of character.'[204]

The twin aspects of the self are reflected in the twin accounts of God that we find in Spinoza, God as nature and the God of revelation, which is one and the same God where the difference is one of the form of human relation to that God. At the beginning of the first chapter of his 'Theological-Political Treatise', Spinoza distinguishes between natural knowledge and prophetic knowledge. The distinction is not – as 'the common people' would claim – a distinction between divine knowledge and human knowledge; both are 'the nature of God, so far as we share in it'.[205] The initial difference between natural knowledge and prophetic knowledge has to do with the recipient: Natural knowledge while taught by its 'practitioners' is such that others may discern for themselves and come to certainty in that manner. The practitioner points others to that which they can then learn themselves. Prophetic knowledge, on the other hand, is such that the prophet as God's interpreter is in a privileged position of disclosing what has been revealed to him to others who have not the benefit of that revelation. They can only accept this on faith.[206] The prophet stands in a relation of authority to his audience in a way in which the philosopher does not, as the philosopher's teaching is not accepted on authority but through reason. The accounts of Scripture say of all the prophets that they received their revelation either through visions or voices and this means through the imagination. Spinoza's point here is that divine revelation is through the body, either through seeing or hearing. Hearing and seeing occurs through modifications of the body which form images. In Hume's terms we could say that these are impressions which are copied in ideas. Such ideas take the forms of words or visions. In any case, they are signs of specific objects of perception which as he states may be real or imaginary.[207]

The distinction of real and imaginary occurs within the imagination itself: The images are of the affections of the body; however, the presence of such affections does not of itself indicate the present existence of an external object. As such the distinction here is not in the first instance between truth and falsity but rather between different actions of the mind, and these Spinoza sees as in tension with one another: Those with the more vivid powers of imagination have less ability in understanding, and those who 'have trained and powerful intellects' have lesser powers of imagination and have it 'under better control'.[208] The distinction here is not between natural abilities but rather between the cultivation of the two sides of the human self: Those who cultivate their imaginations are drawn to words and visions, are less concerned with 'mere understanding', that is, understanding through concepts, but nonetheless use their imagination to come to a figurative account. The person trained in conceptual thought is less concerned with that which comes through the body whether in the form of words or visions and thinks conceptually, for which Spinoza is suggesting language is inessential. But in both cases these are orientations on a continuum, and while intellect is always accompanied by imagination, the imagination seeks confirmation through reason. This need of confirmation shows prophecy is inferior to natural knowledge, which through clear and distinct ideas can attain mathematical certainty, while prophecy can only have 'moral' certainty.[209] The signs themselves are uncertain. Crucially prophetic certainty depended on the individuality of the prophets. Prophetic certainty was dependent on circumstance: on the beliefs of the prophet which would guide his or her understanding of the validity of the signs; on his or her bodily disposition in the form of temperament and crucially on the virtue of the prophet, whether he or she was directed exclusively on the right and the good. On the one hand, this meant that prophecy did not bring new learning: God could only be revealed in line with how the prophet imagined God to be. On the other hand, such revelations disclosed God to people insofar as their imaginations could grasp it. This distinction between imagination and reason becomes in political terms a difference between obedience and freedom. Again this distinction cuts across each individual self: As embodied beings everyone, from the most uneducated to the philosopher, lives in relation to God as both commander and being, because nobody can live without political society, and, outside of utopian dreams, no political society exists without laws and obedience to them.

The prophet, then, is not a philosopher; he or she does not challenge their own preconceived ideas. In the case of Moses, he believed that God was subject to emotions such as mercy, jealousy and kindness, and therefore 'God was revealed to him in conformity with this opinion'.[210] Furthermore, Moses taught the Hebrews a way of life not as a philosopher would by appeal to reason but as a legislator obliging them to live by the rule of law.[211] God adapts his revelation to the understanding and opinions of the prophets and for this reason we need not accept that which is peculiar to their own beliefs. This, according to Spinoza, explains the contradictions in the Scriptures. The divine teaching in the Bible is not that which contradicts philosophical reasoning such as that God is subject to emotions or to change but rather 'alone that it establishes true moral doctrines'.[212] The latter is shown through the attunement of the minds of the prophets on what is right and good.

Spinoza lists three components of the good life: understanding the primary causes of things; acquiring the habit of virtue and hence controlling the passions; and living securely and in good health.[213] This is in line with what he states in the 'Ethics', but here what he makes clear is that divine revelation in the Hebrew Scriptures is significant only with regard to the third, the external goods. With respect to the latter, philosophy is on much less secure ground, but we cannot like the Stoics simply claim these external goods to be insignificant. On the contrary, they are essential to happiness. The prophets are directed towards the securing of this goal and it is for this reason the 'election and vocation [of the Hebrews] lay only in the success and prosperity at that time of their commonwealth'.[214] The revelations are situated, directed not at the eternal but to the temporal. Human decisions should aim to be in line with reason and to be for the good of the collective, while most people who 'hardly live by reason at all' obey the law only out of fear of punishment.[215] The divine law, though, as it prescribes the love of God, cannot be observed out of fear or hope. This is the law inscribed on people's hearts. Spinoza speaks of this with Augustinian terminology, but taken from the latter's own source in Paul, speaking of 'carnal man' and the 'flesh'. This takes up the same thought as in the 'Ethics' where he speaks of the man who is governed by the affects being a slave. So the one who follows the law simply out of fear of punishment is enslaved to the law; the one who follows it from reason is free. It is in relation to this distinction that we can situate Spinoza's understanding of faith as obedience, which falls between slavery and freedom and does so in two ways. First, the one who follows the law without understanding it does not necessarily do so out of fear or hope but can do so out of devotion. Moses 'with his virtue and by divine command' managed to ensure that the Hebrews followed the law out of devotion, not fear, and he did this by introducing religion into the commonwealth.[216] Second, it is the case that in any legal system there will be laws, which do not make rational sense to those who are expected to abide by them. The very specificity of the laws leaves them open to the type of Sceptical critique, which we find in Montaigne. But Spinoza comes to the same conclusion as Montaigne, Descartes and Pascal that for the most part it is better to obey such laws. Reason demands only that thought and expression of thought be free. A government is oppressive 'when it tries to tell them [its subjects] what they must accept as true and reject as false and what beliefs should inspire their devotion to God'.[217] In terms of external action, however, philosophers too must obey the law.

Spinoza and Hume situate the self within a political context and pave the way for understanding the self as living within a state, governed by laws, enforced by authorities, but also free to be itself as a being with desires ends and the means to fulfil those ends. The self, for Hume, seeks through sympathetic relation to others to form a collectivity of mutual benefit through the calming of the passion, particularly those passions which lead to competitiveness. For Spinoza, the self seeks through cooperation with others, reciprocally amalgamating each other's powers, to form a stronger and greater self in the state. The specificity and partiality of the self is provisional, as each individual can combine with others to form a new individual, indeed ultimately forming with all things that individual, which is nature itself. For such a self, the state is not an overcoming of nature, as it the greatest expression of nature. For Hume, too, the state is a movement of nature, rooted in sympathy and affection, where guided by its impressions the self allows nature to direct it.

Spinoza and Hume move away from the transcendent impulses of Descartes and Pascal. The self, operative and thematic in their work, understands itself in terms of the world, directing its passions in seeking the greatest happiness in conjunction with others. Sharing a common naturalism, they transform again the faces of the self: as a communal Stoic, expressing its freedom as the necessary manifestation of divine nature in an immanetized Augustinianism with Spinoza, and as a ironical Sceptic, comfortable in reliance on its own capacity for achieving worldly happiness, a Pelagianism in a world of divine absence, in the case of Hume. Inversions of each other, they left a legacy that a synthesizing thinker could neither ignore nor affirm. It is to that thinker, Kant, to whom we now turn.

5

Desire, *aporia* and reason in Kant

The history of the formation of the Modern self which we have begun charting with Montaigne ends with Kant. This is not to say that after Kant there are no further developments in understanding the self but rather that Kant effects a synthesis, not to say a reconciliation, of the four faces of the Modern self, which forms the backdrop of all subsequent accounts of the self. In Kant we find a self – thematically and operatively – in which Augustinian longing and Pelagian confidence are given critical correction through Pyrrhonian techniques, all guided by a Stoic ascetical discipline.

There has been a strong tendency in reading the history of Modern philosophy to uncouple the epistemological and the metaphysical from the operative and thematic accounts of the self animating these apparently disengaged philosophical doctrines. With respect to Kant, privilege tends to be given to one or other of the Critiques, particularly the *Critique of Pure Reason* and the *Critique of Practical Reason*. If it is taken seriously at all as more than an inchoate collection of ideas, *Critique of Judgement* is employed either with respect to the sublime (Jean-François Lyotard) or political reasoning (Arendt). *Religion within the Boundaries of Mere Reason* and *Opus Postumum* are sometimes even 'understood' as symptomatic of Kant's mental decline. In line with the strategy of this book as a whole, the interpretive position taken up here understands Kant's philosophical work as a totality. Again, in line with the approach to this point, in Kant's case too I will read his philosophical corpus both backwards and forwards, to read, for example, the Critiques in the light of the *Religion within the Limits of Mere Reason* and to read the political and historical writings in the light of his earliest philosophical beginnings. The aim is to show the manner in which the seemingly divergent elements of Kant's philosophical corpus can be seen in their inner unity. For all the transformations in Kant's philosophical journey, certain fundamental elements remain constant, one might even say obsessively constant. Above all we find the question, which emerges in different forms through Montaigne, Descartes, Pascal, Spinoza and Hume, as to how to live in relation to an absconded God. In short, in the course of this and the next chapter it will be shown that the inner unity of Kant's thought is an existential and God-centric one: the human self as God-seeking.

Kant remains as much as Montaigne, Descartes, Pascal, Spinoza and perhaps Hume within the logic of fallenness, but he transforms this logic in fundamental ways, while never overcoming its inherent paradoxes. In doing so, he projects an idea of the self, a transcendental subject, which is disciplined, autonomous and striving for perfection.

This is a desiring self, a self struggling with its bodily and spiritual drives, which ultimately is led and misled by the desires of its rational and its sensual nature. This Kantian self is both capable and incapable, possessed of a good will and yet radically evil, truth-seeking and yet confined to appearance, trusting in the order of nature and in God and yet failing to demonstrate either. The sheer technical complexity of Kant's corpus can often hide the profound existential situation which lies at the core of his philosophical vision. Living in a world stripped of human meaning, the mechanical world of Newtonian science, where no signs of the divine, no beauty, no goodness, nothing which gives human life succour or sense can be found, the self through that rational nature that discloses all this to it, is characterized by a desire for correspondence between inner and outer, between its own rational sense of truth, goodness and beauty, and the nature of things. The lack or failure of such correspondence deeply desired from the nature of that which makes us human is tragic,[1] Kant's philosophical vocation is to show a way to live that tragic condition without succumbing to despair.

This tragic condition concerns not just the individual but society as a whole. While from Descartes onwards the sense of a break with the past and the building up of a new world shaped the way in which the thinkers we have been considering approached ethical and political themes, only with Kant do we see an explicit sense of a historical project. In this he takes up an Augustinian theme but in a Pelagian key: History as a journey to salvation, a journey in which the agency of autonomous selves is crucial.

Critical philosophy is, as Nietzsche claimed, an exercise in philosophical ascetics, the disciplining of philosophical reason in the service of truth and goodness.[2] Ascetics responds to desire; only a desiring being needs to discipline itself. The fundamental desire of human existence which animates Kant's philosophical project is the desire for the supersensible. The sense of the beauty, harmony and order of nature which at the same time functions in a mechanical manner; the origins of this beauty and order in divine will and understanding; the moral sense of rational imperatives; and the desire of reason to unite and harmonize these different senses animate Kant's thought from the earliest writing to *Opus Postumum*. But this desire is increasingly subject to the critical ascetics, which limit reason not to the exclusion of this beauty and divinity but in the face of them. This disciplining ascetics responds to the *aporias*, which Kant articulates in a series of antinomies, *aporias* that disclose an abyss at the heart of philosophy, an abyss where philosophy attempts to articulate the supersensible but finds itself confined to the sensible. Yet the Sceptical is not of itself ascetic; Kant's ascetics are rooted in Stoicism. The playfulness of the antinomic is surpassed by the earnest sense of the law; the aporetic is bridged through an affirmation of the unity of reason and the oneness of self and world, of faith and reason.

Like Augustine, Kant sees the human self to be in danger of being rent apart by fundamental conflicts and sees that this situation can and does give rise to both dogmatism and despair. Only through a Sceptical, but non-fideist, faith can the human self both live with the conflicts that beset him and nonetheless remain true to his real situation. But unlike Augustine, Kant seeks to reach this balance in a Pelagian manner, through a philosophical and practical ascetics. Yet, beginning as he does in the fundamental incapacity of reason, such Pelagianism and the ascetics it supports remain unstable.

Kant's philosophical corpus for all its apparent sobriety and rationalism is beset by fundamental existential questions and anxieties: Kant speaks of reason's 'unremitting' 'cognitive drive [*Erkenntnistrieb*]'.[3] In denying and limiting knowledge to make room for faith, he is attempting to develop a philosophical system that will both acknowledge the power of those questions and anxieties and at the same time secure reason against them. The irony is – and Kant's philosophical project is marked from beginning to end with the recognition of this irony – that reason's own desires and needs intensify such anxieties. In this sense, his project is Pyrrhonian: By limiting the claims to knowledge he is seeking to find tranquillity for the self. The totality of the Kantian system in its theoretical and practical sides, but also in the politico-religious aim towards a kingdom of ends, is guided by the attempt to realize a degree of tranquillity. However, Kant's Augustinian recognition of human depravity and of the limits of knowledge, even self-knowledge, meant that this tranquillity would never be complete. Therein lies the basic conflict at the heart of his system: To aim at tranquillity the self must *act as* a Pelagian, but through its inherent weaknesses can only ever achieve an Augustinian seeking without guarantees.

While Kant's critical project is central to his significance within the history of philosophy, his philosophical ambition well outstripped this project. The Critiques were propaedeutic towards a final metaphysical system. In writing a simplified version of the argument of the First Critique, Kant chose the title of a 'Prolegomena to any Future Metaphysics': critique set the scene for a metaphysics to come. And when Kant speaks of his age as the 'age of critique',[4] this suggests a very particular understanding of the relation of philosophy to history: His Critiques gave expression to his times, but expression to an age which would be superseded. The work of critique was called upon by the age, an age of transition from the obscurity of self-imposed tutelage towards an enlightened age. The age of Enlightenment for Kant was not yet reached; rather, he lives and writes in a time when 'the field has now been opened' to clear away the obstacles to Enlightenment.[5] This age is mirrored in his own work, where the critique of reason, understanding and power of judgement must come *before* the undertaking of a system.[6] To understand Kant, to understand the self operative and thematic in his work, we need to understand his world as a world of transition, even revolution.[7] While seeking to limit reason, Kant was at the same time most alive to its inner dynamism. Of the three questions of philosophy – what do I know?, what ought I to do? and what can I hope for? – the final one is the least developed and indeed the least clearly motivated.[8] While the first two questions concern theoretical and practical reason, respectively, the final question does not refer to an *exercise* of reason. Hope is directed rather at what can unify the domains of reason's concerns; as hope it is directed at something other than the self and its faculties. Crucial to understanding the place of hope in Kant is how the relation of practical and theoretical reason is understood. Against any claim to an absolute primacy of practical reason, I will show that Kant's project is to articulate the hope of a union of the practical and the theoretical. Hope is not only future directed: The self hopes that it is the case that her practical reasoning is happening now in a world which is morally charged, framed by a moral author. It remains hope because such a self can never know this to be the case (even for herself) and – in relation to the future directedness – strives to realize this moral constitution in human society and lives in faith that her moral striving will be granted perfectibility.

This chapter is divided into three sections. It begins with the place of desire, in particular the desire of reason in Kant's project (5.1). Then it continues with a discussion of the antimonic structure of reason and *Schwärmerei* (5.2). The third section deals with freedom and nature (5.3).

5.1 The desire of reason

Kant's critical project is an ascetics of reason. Like any ascetics it implies desire and the subjection to a higher law. The desire in question is a metaphysical desire, one which Kant addresses throughout the trajectory of his philosophical journey. In 'Dreams of a Spirit Seer' he speaks of having 'fallen in love' with metaphysics;[9] in *Opus Postumum* he states,

> In the investigation of nature, human reason is not content to pass from metaphysics to physics; there lies within it an instinct ... to transcend even the latter, to fantasize in a hyperphysics ... in a world of ideas, according to outlines directed towards moral ends – as if God and the immortality of the soul alone (the former as *natura naturans*, the latter as *natura naturata*) could entirely encompass our desire for knowledge in regard to nature in general.[10]

Kant returns, in effect, to the platonic motif of the erotics of reason. Reason is an instinct driven by desire, a desire for harmony and completeness. This desire is transcendent; it cannot be satisfied within the immanence of nature. This is so because reason seeks in nature that which – due to the finitude of embodied reason – remains beyond what can be known: the moral purpose of things. The desire of reason is constitutively unfulfilled; the possibility of despair remains a constant one in his work.[11] One possible response to such desire, and a possible shortcut in avoiding despair, is that of *Schwärmerei* (meaning enthusiasm, fanaticism, superstition, with the etymological sense of swarming, unthinking commitment without good reason). From at least 'Dreams of a Spirit Seer' to *Religion within the Boundaries of Mere Reason*, Kant is haunted by this spectre and continually aims to ward it off. But he is haunted by it precisely because it speaks so directly to metaphysical desire: the desire for access to an intelligible, supersensible world. By declaring his age the age of criticism, Kant places the taming and training of such metaphysical desire at the centre of the intellectual life of his world. The critical project was not simply a solution to a metaphysical or epistemological question, but was one which through disciplining the metaphysical desires of reason could both save humanity from irrationalism and subject human history to its proper destiny, namely, obedience to the law of reason, an obedience expressed in the act of self-giving of the law, auto-nomy.

If the *Critique of Pure Reason* is concerned with 'investigating the foundations of metaphysics',[12] the critical stance towards reason is at once a Sceptical limiting of, and a faith in, reason. At both a theoretical and a practical level Kant displays a fundamental ambivalence concerning human capacity, more specifically human rational capacity: Incapable of knowledge of the thing in itself, human reason can still posit its existence; capable of acting according to duty, human reason can never guarantee the actuality of any such act. Incapable of proving the existence of God, the soul or freedom, human reason nonetheless is capable of giving grounds for acting on their basis. Kant affirms a metaphysical trust in the moral rationality of things, but this trust can only be manifest as hope.[13] Philosophical ascetics is called upon in order to respond to this ambiguous situation. Such an exercise seeks to clearly delimit the boundaries of human capacity while keeping in view the goal of acting in terms of a higher law, which, however, can be fully attained only by a holy being, capable of intellectual intuition, living in a wholly intelligible world. The inherent tension of critical philosophy and its philosophical necessity lies in the postulation of an intelligible world, in which nature and freedom are identical, a world that makes human desire rational, but which critique demonstrates to be incapable of actualization in the world of sensible experience.[14]

As rational beings, humans have desires and needs that exceed their animal natures and their bodily capacities, limited as they are to the sensible. Reason desires and needs that which would fulfil it.[15] To fulfil reason is to find a resting place for reason, a place where reason's quest comes to an end. In this respect, Kant, like Descartes, begins from an account of reason diametrically opposed to that of the Pyrrhonians: Reason does not find tranquillity in its own self-limiting but only in the stilling of its questioning quest. Such a stilling is from the beginning ruled out by Kant, however, and his philosophical project has from the opening words of the Preface of the first edition of the First Critique a tragic quality: 'Human reason has the peculiar fate in one species of its cognitions that it is disturbed [belästigt] by questions which as prescribed by the very nature of reason itself, it is not able to ignore, but which, as transcending all its powers, it is also not able to answer.'[16] Such disturbance characterizes metaphysics in both its theoretical and practical domains. It is a disturbance rooted in desire both natural to reason and yet pointing beyond its capacity. We are here in a classically Augustinian position.

Kant's account of this position in which the self finds itself in its theoretical and practical life, revolves around human finitude, embodiment and desire. While the distinction of theoretical and practical philosophy is central in doctrinal terms, existentially they both have a common source in the constitution of the self. It is in this very constitution that we find the source of the transcendental illusion, which the *Critique of Pure Reason* reveals to us. He speaks of a 'natural and unavoidable dialectic of pure reason',[17] natural (and hence unavoidable) in the sense of being constitutive of pure reason. The nature of reason is in the first place that it is not immediately related to sense experience. Reason in its capacity of unifying rather gives a priori unity to the understanding and the manifold of cognitions that are found there.[18] Furthermore, it is in the nature of reason to pursue a movement from conditioned to unconditional, leading reason to the idea of the highest being. In this sense natural theology is quite within the nature of pure reason: The metaphysical is also the theological.[19] I will return to this question below, but at this stage what is crucial to see is that this nature of pure reason, aiming towards a natural theology and a final unity of all things in God, manifests itself as desire aiming beyond all experience. Kant's use of language here is revealing: 'Reason is driven [*wird getrieben*] through a natural propensity [*Hang*] to transcend the region of experience ... in order to reach the outermost boundaries of all knowledge'.[20] There is here a certain passivity in reason, a passivity not with respect to what is other than it but rather with respect to itself. Reason finds itself driven from within to escape the realm of experience.

This drive of reason, this inner desire, both affirms the nobility of reason and its vulnerability to illusion. In effect, this is a desire for the supersensible. Such desire not only seeks to go beyond sense experience but also tends to mistake the source and scope of its own ideas. For example, in the Introduction to the second edition of the *Critique of Pure Reason*, Kant speaks of reason's 'drive to extension [*Trieb zur Erweiterung*]'.[21] This drive is so powerful that it deceived Plato that he could on the wings of ideas fly in the empty space of pure understanding, like a dove in airless space. The illusion here is facilitated by a lack of resistance. Reason does not encounter resistance from outside itself, hence it requires a *self*-resistance, a *self*-discipline. The desires and needs of reason find neither satisfaction nor resistance. The objects of reason are ideas, which already in Plato are understood as being beyond experience. In returning to Plato in explicating the nature of ideas, Kant seeks to both show the nobility of the desire of reason in its object and prepare the ground for showing the ultimate limits of reason. Plato saw clearly the 'need [*Bedürfnis*]' that reason felt for an object, which both transcends experience and which was no simple phantom of the brain.[22]

Reason's fundamental desire for unity and symmetry is not misplaced; Kant acknowledges and affirms its inner integrity and legitimacy. If this is not affirmed, then the human becomes a peculiarly bereft being, whose very desires lead a self to betray himself, the fundamental instinct of whose reason would be illusory. Kant recognizes this tragic possibility, namely, of being directed and indeed driven towards goals which, while reflecting the nature of reason, are without warrant. The Kantian project is indeed haunted from his awakening from dogmatic slumber to the end by the despair that would follow from such a realization, which would have profound consequences on both a theoretical and practical level. It is in this context that *both* the necessity for reason to be humiliated[23] *and* the limits of that humiliation can be understood. Humiliation is necessary in the face of hubris, in this case the classical hubris of mistaking the human for the divine, of mistaking finite human reason for divine reason. The power of the Sceptical is to humiliate reason and in so doing curb its desire. This desire first and foremost is a desire of unity, harmony, order and beauty, and as such a desire for God as the unifier of theory and practice, of nature and freedom, of is and ought. Kant points continually to infinite reason and holy will as that which is not an illusion in itself but rather which human desire both aims towards and is constitutively incapable of reaching. The humiliation of reason then points to a fundamental incapacity, which only the desire of reason discloses, but points also towards the ideals of reason and will, which finite human beings both glimpse within themselves and yet are of an order of *being* remaining inaccessible to human cognition.[24]

In the light of this we can say that God, far from being at the periphery of Kant's concerns, stands at its very centre. At the centre of Kant's project is the traditional idea of the human being as seeking God, a being guided by the good will, pursuing happiness; the question then becomes how to reach that goal. The metaphysical response is through pure reason, through the proofs of the existence of God. While Kant does affirm such a possibility in his *The One Possible Basis for the Determination of the Existence of God* (1763)[25] and while in his lectures on religion he is less definitive on the question, it is clear that for critical philosophy, God is the *end* of metaphysics both in the sense of its ultimate goal *and* in the sense of showing the failure of metaphysics to realize itself in a theoretical sense. Consistent through all these discussions, from 1763 until *Religion* and the *Conflict of the Faculties*[26] three decades later, is the rejection of the ontological argument, and in this rejection we see a fundamental tenet of Kantian philosophy both in its pre-critical and critical manifestations. Existence is not a real predicate; existence adds nothing to what a thing is. As such, it is impossible to show merely from the nature of anything that such a thing exists. This is significant because it shows that a basic premise of rationalist metaphysics, namely, the identity of thought and being, is rejected by Kant already in his pre-critical period. In this Kant is true, even prior to his Sceptical 'awakening', to Montaigne's dictum of the lack of communication between thought and being. Kant's rejection of the proofs for the existence of God is not simply one consequence among others of his limiting of reason but is the core and fundamental result of that limiting. The ideal of pure reason is God and as such this ideal becomes the object of transcendental theology.[27] But it is here that the fundamental metaphysical questions emerge for Kant. The ideas of reason are further removed from objective reality than the categories of the understanding, because the latter can be concretely shown in appearances, while the ideas of reason 'contain a certain perfection [*Vollständigkeit*] to which no possible empirical cognition can reach'.[28]

If reason cannot show the existence of God, for Kant it nonetheless calls for such a demonstration and does so most insistently in its practical rather than theoretical exercise. This is premised on reason's primarily practical interest, which means the subordination of reason's theoretical to its practical exercise. Reason's practical interest is not rooted in any pathological determination but rather is directed towards its own a priori constitution. The moral law speaks without pathology – without any motivation from the passions – and is directed towards the highest good, which as unconditioned cannot be subject to the irreducible conditioned situation of sensible existence. The interest of reason in the intelligible world is practical in the sense that practical reason is purified of all conditionality, and directs itself to that which, however, can never appear in and of itself to an embodied rational being. The intelligible world appears, then, to reason, but not in such a way that it can be epistemologically validated as an apparent entity. The intelligible world cannot appear to a being that has only sensible access to the world. However, inscribed in reason is the intelligible world, appearing not to perception but to a directedness towards the inapparent manifest in the apparent: through hope. The desire of reason in its practical exercise discloses an ultimate unity of is and ought, of nature and morality, which, however, due to its own constitution, it can neither achieve nor even directly aim towards. Rather, in reflecting upon itself, reason realizes that its practical exercise is ultimately meaningful, only if that intelligible world disclosed in hope is realizable. It can be realizable, however, only in a being in which will and knowledge are one, who knows things only as being conscious of himself as their cause.[29]

It is this notion of God as cause, author and ruler of the world with which Kant closes *Critique of Judgement*. Here he distinguishes clearly between nature in itself and nature for embodied rational beings: For such entities, the mechanical explanation of nature does not lead to an understanding of nature's purposefulness; but this does not mean that such a coming together of mechanism and purpose is *in itself* impossible.[30] A being with only sensible intuition cannot find purpose in the world; at most she can see signs of such purpose, for example, in living entities. But without the human being, 'the whole of creation would be a mere desert, existing in vain and without a final end [*Endzweck*]'.[31] Purpose does not arise from the self simply as a cognizing entity, nor from the self as an entity with sensual desires binding her to nature, but it arises rather from the capacity to desire as a free being, that is, as a being that wills the good, wills what ought to be.[32] A being that wills what ought to be is willing that which nothing existing can justify; ultimately it is willing that which can justify all that is. Such free desire intends an end that is not simply the end of this or that action but an end giving a purpose to all that is. Such purposefulness is felt affectively as gratitude, obedience and humility, which are directed towards duty and which open up the space for the mind to think of an object not of the world, a moral lawgiver to the world.[33] Such a thought does not conflict with knowledge of nature but cannot come from it either; rather, arising out of mood it completes nature on the basis of a purely moral principle. Perceived purpose in things in the world leads only to demonology,[34] while a moral sense of purpose *read back* into the world allows the human being to understand the world as a work of art, while scientifically explaining it in mechanical terms.

Fundamental to critical philosophy, then, is the tension between the desire of reason to find its moral purpose reflected back to it in nature and the ascetic self-limiting of reason's claims. Reason is divided against itself is antinomic.

5.2 Antinomic reason and *Schwärmerei*

Kant's awaking from dogmatic slumber has, according to his own account, two separate sources: Hume and Pyrrhonism. While Hume poses a challenge for Kant, which he responds to by denying the reducibility of knowledge to sense impressions, Pyrrhonism guides his account of metaphysics leading him to define the latter as, in effect, a Pyrrhonian science: a science which curbs dogmatism, does not so much 'extend knowledge, but rather … prevents errors'.[35] In short, 'metaphysics is a science of the limits of human reason'.[36] While the *Critique of Pure Reason* responds to Hume in attempting to overcome him, the antinomies of reason show the irreducibility of Pyrrhonian Scepticism.[37] While for Kant Hume's reduction of causality to habit undermines the very notion of cause and hence of science, the Pyrrhonian Sceptic has correctly understood that human reason is irreducibly aporetic. Indeed, similar to Sextus Empiricus and Socrates, to whom Kant acknowledges his debt in this methodological respect,[38] philosophy in the First Critique is parasitic upon dogmatism: The First Critique at each turn shows the conditionality of any dogmatic claim to know. Kant positions the Critique between the 'two cliffs of scepticism and dogmatism';[39] just as Sextus, Kant sees philosophy as an inquiry and as denying both the dogmatic claims to know and the Sceptical denial of knowledge, which denies 'our duty of always serving reason'.[40]

The problem of dogmatism is not, however, simply an epistemological one; it is fundamentally theological in its reach. This is so because the dogmatist fails to account for the conditionality of human knowledge and in making dogmatic claims seeks to transcend such conditionality either by uncritical reasoning or by appeal to experiences which are exceptions to those conditions. As such, dogmatism blends into *Schwärmerei*, which in its widest sense means for Kant the claim of intuitive immediacy to the supersensible. Such a claim binds together Plato, in whom Kant traces the origins of philosophical *Schwärmerei*, and Kant's contemporary mystic, Emanuel Swedenborg. Kant's reclaiming of platonic erotics is matched by the appeal Swedenborg had for him. The dangers of *Schwärmerei* are not fundamentally different from those of dogmatic metaphysics.[41] In both cases a crucial transgressing of the limit of human experience are at play, one structured in terms of the difference between the sensible and the supersensible. Metaphysics indeed is defined by Kant in terms of that very difference: 'the science which progresses from cognition of the sensible to the supersensible by means of reason.'[42] *Schwärmerei*, on the other hand, Kant understood as the claim to have privileged, intuitive, access to the supersensible. There was for him an inner complicity of metaphysics and *Schwärmerei*, against which only a critical limiting of reason could guard. As such, the task of critique is to think the difference of sensible and supersensible in a manner remaining within the confines of human experience. This attempt has an ultimately Sceptical motivation in the sense of seeing philosophy as concerned with revealing and hence dissolving dogmatism. In their different ways, according to Kant, Locke and Leibniz gave free rein to such dogmatism in metaphysics and by consequence 'opened door and gate' to *Schwärmerei*.[43] For Kant (as he makes clear in the Preface to the second edition of the *Critique of Pure Reason*[44]), critique would undercut *Schwärmerei*.

Kant's sensitivity to the dangers of *Schwärmerei* is rooted in his understanding of the desires of reason. 'Dreams of a Spirit Seer' is perhaps his most personal work allowing us to see, through its irony and playfulness, his own personal temptation – it seems to be an appropriate word here – by the claims of reason and of the spirit seer. Indeed, he begins that work with a very personal confession, that he was 'naïve enough to investigate the truth of some of [this] kind'.[45] He confesses this 'with a certain humiliation', not only because he found nothing in this pursuit but also because the very attempt itself suggests gullibility. He was seeking this truth, and even if in retrospect it seems foolish to have done so, nonetheless, Kant's confesses to sharing in that enthusiasm at the beginning. This is rooted in a common source of metaphysics and religion: a desire for the supersensible. The religious claims to direct access to the supersensible – to God, to angels, to spirits of the dead – paralleled for Kant the metaphysical claim to access to the intelligible world of reason.[46] He states, again in confessional tone, that he 'is very inclined to assert the existence of immaterial natures in the world, and to place [his] own soul in the class of these beings'.[47] His reasons for this, which he describes as very obscure (*sehr dunkel*), relate to animated self-movement, which appears to be irreducible to the outer manifestations of matter. In this way an 'immaterial world', indeed a 'spirit world', is opened up, which appears to exist with only an accidental relation to the material world. Appeals to such immaterial principles are a sign of philosophical laziness, and yet, while philosophically inferior to mechanical explanations of animal movements, they seem often closer to the truth.[48]

For Kant the question is not of truth, but of reason, of distinguishing clearly between the realms of the material and the immaterial. Crucial here is the question of the symbolic: how the material can indicate the immaterial. Kant makes clear that the concepts of reason, which are close to the spiritual, nevertheless generally take on a corporeal clothing.[49] This mixing of the conceptual and the imaginative concerns the inner state of the soul, but in certain 'strange people [*seltsame Personen*]' and only at certain moments, these fanciful pictures of spiritual concepts take on the 'semblance of sensations' and seem to appear to consciousness as external spiritual bodies.[50] These 'silhouettes of sensible things'[51] are experienced as real, even though they have the same status as dreams: products of the mind which are experienced as if real. Swedenborg's experiences are nothing more than waking dreams. What is crucial here is not whether this can be shown or not: It may be that Swedenborg in fact has access to the spirit world, and in his lecture courses Kant leaves this possibility open. Crucial is rather that any such experience cannot be classed as knowledge or belief or opinion, because the subjective conviction cannot be shared.[52] Implicit in Kant's critique of Swedenborg is the recognition that Swedenborg's texts have no *intersubjective* validity: Kant's constant disclaimers concerning the very attempt to discuss Swedenborg indicate that there is something ineffable here. The core of this ineffability is the claim that 'corporeal beings have no substance of their own; they only persist in being by means of the spirit-world' and that hence all material things have a twofold significance: 'an external sense which consists in the relation of matter to itself; and … an internal sense, in so far as material things … designate the forces of the spirit-world'.[53] All the objects of experience have a profound meaning, which, however, is not present in their exterior forms but can be viewed – if at all – only through a privileged access.

It is the claim of privileged access to the interior reality through a faculty of perception, which is not commonly shared, that lies at the heart of *Schwärmerei* for Kant.[54] Critical philosophy seeks to find a touchstone that requires no such appeal to esoteric knowledge. Seen in that way critical philosophy is rooted in a religious disillusionment, a disillusionment with the religious claim to a capacity to discern the supersensible from the sensible and concurrently in a directedness towards equality in relation to knowledge and the communication of knowledge. If such claims to privileged access are to be rejected, it is not because their content can be demonstrated to be false, but because they escape the very possibility of distinguishing between truth and falsity in that domain. The religious disillusionment here does not concern religion *tout court* but rather a Gnostic form of religiosity, which seeks secret knowledge.[55]

It is well to pause here and to acknowledge that in the context of Kant's own publications on religion, political considerations loomed large. Indeed, in 1794 Kant made a promise to the Prussian king, Frederick William II, that he would not publish on religion. In contrast to his predecessor Frederick II, Frederick William was deeply conservative with respect to religion. Even after his death in 1797, the religious conservatives remained powerful in Prussia.[56] In this context it may appear, as many commentators have suggested, that Kant's writings on religion were a veiled attack on religion. However, as I will show, there is nothing in *Religion within the Boundaries of Mere Reason*, which contradicts what is written in other works. Indeed, we can find many parallels between this book and *Opus Postumum*, particularly with respect to the relation of morals and religion.[57] While Kant is certainly guarded in his discussions of religion, there is nothing to suggest insincerity in his accounts.

What Kant does deny is any religiosity based on a claim to privileged access to the supersensible, beyond the limits of human reason. This denial, indeed, lies at the very basis of Kant's approach to religion and (as we will see) to politics. The works and acts of reason must be accessible to the intersubjective world; 'I' must be redeemable in the 'we'. This intersubjective world is that world of which every self is part due to their place at the intersection of the sensible and the supersensible. The claims to supersensible knowledge can only be validated if communicable and only that which can be made sensible can be communicated. It is here that Kant appeals to the Pyrrhonian method in showing the manner in which human reason misunderstands itself due to the mixed nature of human cognition and human existence. It is instructive in this respect to note the places where Kant speaks of angels. Angels, as traditionally understood, are rational but not embodied beings. For Kant, the human destiny outstrips that of angels because the human has access both to the supersensible and to the world of sense; humans experience the sensible world and in encountering that world experience themselves as volitional beings, as opposed to 'will-less angels'.[58] The price for this, however, is that the human is subject, like no other being, to the twin snares of error and evil. The Sceptical method serves to disclose the *aporia* of sensible and supersensible and in so doing to set out the parameters of rational selfhood: how to exist as a human self, as that being in which sensible and intelligible intersect. This is not simply an anthropological question; it is fundamentally a question about the possibility of embodied freedom and embodied knowledge. The antinomies are at the heart of Kant's response to such questions.

Kant claims that Sceptical method and Scepticism – understood as dogmatic empiricism – are different.[59] The Sceptical method breaks with all dogmatism and takes the place of an impartial referee[60] in the face of the unavoidable conflicts of reason. These conflicts arise when reason goes beyond the limits of experience. Reason does not cease to function beyond the limit of experience but rather uncovers necessary connections. However, it is then faced with contradictory position for which there are equally necessary reasons. Faced with these antinomies of reason, this 'dialectical battleground',[61] Kant asks us to refrain from taking sides. We should refrain from doing so because any victory for one side or the other in this tournament is an arbitrary one. In other words, reason reflecting upon itself recognizes both the strengths and weaknesses of each side of the antinomies and that the rational course is to suspend judgement or, as he puts it later, 'to allow the arguments of reason in their great freedom to step out against each other'.[62] This allowing of the play of reason is Sceptical in the Pyrrhonian sense of detachment: Like the referee (or the judge, whose figure he also evokes), in employing this method we detach ourselves from any binding commitment to either side. This movement of detachment makes both the Sceptical method transcendental and transcendental philosophy inseparable from the Sceptical. As he puts it,

> transcendental propositions, which lay claim to insight beyond the region of possible experience, cannot, on the one hand, exhibit their abstract synthesis in any a priori intuition, nor, on the other, expose a lurking error by the help of experience. Transcendental reason, therefore, presents us with no other criterion than that of an attempt to reconcile such assertions, and for this purpose to permit a free and unrestrained conflict between them.[63]

The Sceptical method is not a method of doubt, is not one that works on the 'principle of a technical and scientific ignorance, undermining the foundations of all knowledge, in order, if possible, to destroy our belief and confidence therein', as Kant sees Scepticism as doing.[64] It is, rather, a method which works in acceptance of an irreducible *aporia*, irreducible because in principle no criterion in experience can be found to judge between them.

Yet, the figures which Kant places in relation to this free play, this unrestrained conflict, are those concerned with decision and judgement – the referee and the judge. In effect what is at issue here is the capacity of reason to judge itself, a capacity that requires reason *both* to recognize the sublimity and dignity of its highest aspirations[65] *and yet* accept its own incapacity to either attain those aspirations or withdraw to a place of indifference. Hence, the Sceptical method of letting the two sides play out does not end in an acceptance of disunity but rather requires a further step. What motivates this step Kant refers to in terms of honour, security and interest.[66] We have here no touchstone of truth. The Sceptical method cannot, without contradiction, appeal to such a touchstone: The antinomies show that both thesis and antithesis can be consistently supported. As such, the conflict, while a conflict concerning truth, cannot be decided on the basis of truth. In mediating the conflict then, reason is not motivated by the seeking for truth but rather by a seeking after self-knowledge. The honour and security of reason is in question because the disunity of reason threatens the fundamental desire of reason, namely, the desire for unity. Furthermore, the very goal of the Sceptical method remains elusive: The play of claim and counterclaim does not bring peace to reason but rather disquiet. Only through exploring the origins of this disunity can a 'permanently quiet regime of reason over understanding and sense begin'.[67]

Failing to find that unity with respect to truth, reason is forced to reflect on the interests motivating both sides of the dialectic. These two sides Kant understands as dogmatism and empiricism (which itself tends towards its own dogmatism in a Scepticism that denies the possibility of knowledge). But both sides of this dialectic have their roots in the speculative interests of reason.[68] The interests of reason are divided between a practical interest in the purposeful interconnectedness of human action, the order of the world and the common origin of action and world in proto-entity (*Urwesen*)[69] and an interest in demonstrating the validity of its concepts in intuition-rooted experience.[70] The latter interest is outweighed, however, by reason's overarching architectonic interest, which the empiricist can never satisfy, making, as he does, the completion of the building of knowledge impossible.[71] Yet reason speaks in excess of its own interests, such that if one were to divest oneself of all interests in reason, the claims of reason can still be heard, and these claims to system and to verification would play off each other, leaving such a person in a pure *aporia* of interminable hesitation. Kant again invokes dreams here – 'the shadowy pictures of a dream'.[72]

This situation has similarities with that of Swedenborg, who fails to distinguish between reality and fantasy: the aporiatic state brought about by the Sceptical method places the self in a situation in which the twin dogmatisms of rationalism and empiricism are equally possible. It is when such a self must act that she does so according to principles rooted in practical interests, hence principles rooted in morality and religion. However, the speculative interests of reason remain and need to be secured above all because of their practical implications.

The speculative interests of reason cannot find a peaceful accommodation, because the claims for dogmatism extend beyond all possible experience and hence cannot be shown to be true or false, while the claims of empiricism, although claiming to be true to experience, have the consequence of denying the reality of freedom and hence of morality and religion and furthermore of disappointing the fundamental speculative interest of reason. Kant diagnoses the root cause here to be one of an illusion: a systematic failure to understand the content of one's own claims. The dogmatic and empiricist claims contradict each other only if human reason fails to understand itself. Hence, at the core of the First Critique is an exercise of self-understanding, which every rational self must undergo if reason's own interests are to be fulfilled its desires satisfied.

In a 1783–4 note Kant says that 'the objects of experience can never satisfy reason'.[73] Reason seeking satisfaction beyond the objects of appearance fails to justify itself and is caught in the difference between appearance and the thing in itself. The ascetic limiting of reason amounts to an acceptance that the desires of reason can never be satisfied. The finitude of human life is understood tragically as the ever failing movement of desire; self-understanding is acceptance of this situation. But the acceptance of this situation is predicated on an understanding of the parameters defining it and those parameters are set by human reason itself. In effect, reason comes to acceptance of its situation, through a turning in on itself, such that reason has the task of answering its own questions. In the same way as the objects of experience fail to satisfy reason, so also 'reason cannot be determined, i.e., affected, for otherwise it would be sensibility not reason'.[74] If reason cannot be affected, then it is purely self-determining: There is nothing in reason that reason has not placed there itself. As such, reason can fully answer its own questions and have complete responsibility for itself: 'The idea is the mere creation of reason, which thus cannot itself deny responsibility or shunt it onto an unknown object'.[75] The antinomies of reason do not refer reason to an origin more fundamental than itself, for in that case we must admit reason to be itself affected and determined. Rather, reason finds the origin of its ideas in itself alone. As such the critical approach is premised on the *apathetic nature* of reason considered with respect to *heterogeneous passions* and the consequent complete clarity of reason to itself. But such clarity is possible only in abstraction from every concrete experience, both in terms of its content and in terms of the constitution of the experience itself. Understood as regulative, reason is without object, functioning only to give the law to objects, and once this is understood the 'conflict of reason with itself is fully brought to an end'.[76] The Pyrrhonian Sceptic is not so much defeated as sublated: The conflict of reason with itself is important in showing the limitations of reason, its regulative rather than constitutive place. The latter in turn is shown only once the lines between reason and sensibility are clearly set out in terms of a difference of pathological and non-pathological.

It is with the difference of pathological and non-pathological that the questions of the theoretical and practical employment of reason intersect. The third antinomy pushes the question of being conditioned further to the issue of existence itself: The existence of a conditioned object of experience understood in terms of nature is related to a causal condition, understood in terms of *freedom*. It is related to that which arises of itself. This question of transcendental freedom excites the interests of reason not only, or indeed not primarily, as speculative, but also and in the first instance as practical. 'The practical concept of freedom is grounded on the transcendental idea of freedom.'[77] Here again the question is one of the difference between pathological and non-pathological, as the practical idea of freedom is one of 'the independence of the will from coercion by sensible impulses'. Only on the basis of this latter premise can we make sense of 'ought [*Sollen*]'.[78] Precisely this leads us to the antinomy of practical reason.

The desire of reason is most evident in the practical sphere because here Sceptical doubts are overwhelmed from the beginning. The rational being must think of itself as free. Kant begins the *Critique of Practical Reason* with the affirmation of the concept of freedom as the key stone of the entire building (*Gebäude*) of pure reason (speculative and practical). He does so because freedom, which was shown to be possible but problematic in the theoretical domain, is itself the condition of possibility of the moral law.[79] The argument begins with the moral law as that which the self knows and finds as an essential condition for this law that there are beings, moral beings, who are free. In other words, the argument seeks the capacity in the moral being for the law that her reason shows her to be binding. Yet, the antinomy of reason is not thereby set aside. On the contrary, the manner in which the antinomies are resolved through the transcendental difference of thing in itself and appearance is repeated here, this time with respect to the human being herself – as appearing she is subject to the laws of nature, as thing in itself, she is free.[80]

The freedom of the self is manifest in the mode of its relation to the moral law, which Kant describes as one of 'immediate determination'.[81] Free choice is that which is determined by the moral law, rather than by feeling. But Kant is clear that for the created – as opposed to the divine or angelic – will there needs to be a motivating force. The question then is one of understanding what the motivating force of the law must be. For an action to conform to the law is not to make it moral: The motivating force of that action has to be law itself. Kant's question then is how the moral law alone can have motivating force. As the motivating force against which this is set is one of sensibility and hence of feeling, the motivating force of the moral law must, in denying the inclinations of sensual feeling, have in negative terms an affective consequence. In curbing the feelings rooted in self-love the moral law has as its determinate consequence feelings of pain.[82] The moral law affects the self with a feeling of humiliation: a feeling of disdain (*Verachtung*) interrupting her sense of self-conceit (*Eigendünkel*). This negative feeling is not pathological; it does not arise from being affected by an other but rather is the direct affect of the law on a self as a sensible being. Such negative feeling points to a positive feeling: the feeling of respect (*Achtung*) for the moral law. The question for Kant here is not one of reason against feeling but rather of understanding how reason itself gives rise to feeling.[83] The finite human will does not act simply from reason alone. It does not do so because the self is more (or less) than a rational being: She is also a sensible, affective being, and as such her motivation to act has an affective element. The feeling of respect is that motivating power and it is appropriate to moral action because it is an auto-affective feeling: The feeling of respect comes not from anything other than the self, anything which can be an object of its experience, but rather from that which the self finds within itself, namely, the moral law. Here we see the affects of the law on sensibility and the positive place of moral feeling with respect to moral action.[84] We find here an Augustinian movement: away from the inclinations of self-love, towards the inner self and finally a movement upwards to the law. That upward movement is motivated by a feeling in which the self recognizes in itself the worth of the moral law as superseding all feelings relating to objects of enjoyment and sensual delight. But, if this is an Augustinian movement, it is performed in a Stoic key: The feeling of respect draws on the same insight as the Stoic account of joy as an auto-affective emotion, a feeling of contentment and calm tranquillity, which arises from guiding one's life through reason.

Such tranquillity is, however, always threatened due to the precariousness of the human condition, which, on a practical level, as much as a speculative one, finds itself between the conditioned and the unconditioned. As is the case in the speculative sphere, reason finds itself here related to the contents of experience, specifically the desires and needs of a sensible/rational being, and yet seeks the unconditioned totality of the objects of pure practical reason, namely the highest good.[85] It is here that the antinomy of reason is opened up again, this time in a practical sense: *either* the desire for happiness (*Glückseligkeit*) motivates virtuous maxims *or* virtuous maxims bring about happiness.

5.3 Nature and freedom

In response to the antinomy of practical reason, the Pyrrhonian method again brings Kant to the core of the question of reason. In the practical sphere, however, the question is not one of limiting reason or of reason as regulative, but rather how it is that reason can be constitutive in a world of experience where all objects are by definition conditioned. In such a world, the antithesis is impossible, while the thesis undermines morality itself. Again, the resolution of the antinomy is to distinguish between the intelligible and the sensible worlds, the world of natural causation and the world of pure reason. However, in the case of practical reason the intelligible world is not simply postulated, but access to this world is assumed both in terms of the moral law and in terms of a relation to the author of the world. While theoretical reason poses no questions which it cannot resolve, practical reason opens the human agent towards her incapacity to reconcile virtue and happiness, her incapacity to actualize the highest good.[86]

The question of the highest good has caused and continues to cause not a little embarrassment and confusion among readers of Kant. If happiness must not be a motivation of moral action, how can moral action nonetheless be said to aim towards the highest good? The highest good seems to be neither a motivation nor an obligation (although there is an indirect obligation to aim towards the highest good), making it appear as a residue of pre-critical thought.[87] But if we ask the question of how the Kantian self understands itself, then the issues become clearer. The unity of that self is fundamental for Kant: It must understand itself as a whole, and to do so it is driven to understand the world as a whole. If the motivation of happiness undermines moral judgement, this cannot mean that happiness is somehow irrelevant to the self acting morally, but rather that happiness is fundamentally beyond its capacity to achieve. It is here that the Stoic, Sceptic and Pelagian fail for Kant. If virtue is the worthiness to be happy, then the question is whether virtue and happiness are intrinsically linked such that the striving for virtue is one and the same as the striving for happiness or whether happiness follows virtue as effect to cause.[88] Against the Stoics and the Epicureans, Kant in the 'Analytic of Practical Reason' shows that the maxims of virtue and happiness are not on the same level, such that the relation between them cannot be an analytic one. However, the relation also cannot be derived from experience, so it is both synthetic and a priori. In the discussion which follows, Kant again holds for a strong separation of the intelligible and the sensible, arguing that the causal relation of virtue and happiness can only be 'by chance [*zufällig*]' in the sensible world.[89]

Virtue is not its own reward; rather, the concepts of virtue and happiness are 'totally different elements' of the highest good. The self is capable of virtue but not of happiness for Kant. The Stoic withdrawal of engagement with the world is not possible, because the self is already a being in the world, it is itself constituted by its engagements. It can engage virtuously by following the moral law (although as we will see its capacity is limited in this respect also for other reasons), but this does not lead to happiness.[90] Sceptical *aporia* does not lead to happiness either. The aporetic state recognizes the limitations of the self, but in consequence also its lack of happiness. The self finds itself radically fallen for Kant and cannot, contrary to the Pelagian view, be made worthy of its own happiness. The self is orientated towards the highest good but cannot directly act to achieve that end. In its moral actions it recognizes its incapacity at the heart of its capability. It looks beyond itself, in hope, for the happiness to come. But this hope is not a motivation for action but rather characterizes the self in viewing itself in its relation with the world. Here Kant comes closest to an Augustinian self: desiring that which it knows its own desire can undermine. This conundrum can only be overcome, if, like Augustine, the self trusts in divine providence while striving to be true to what is morally binding for it. As with Augustine (and later Kierkegaard), Kant's concern is (as Frederick Beiser argues) existential: the danger of despair when viewing moral striving as ultimately vain.[91] Such despair is not simply psychological but is rather metaphysical: the effect of the belief that moral reasoning and action take place in a morally indifferent universe. The self in her moral thinking and acting can only aim towards the highest good of a morally realized universe through first acknowledging her constitutive incapacity for bringing it about.

This question of the reconciliation of capacity and incapacity is a recurring theme in *Religion within the Boundaries of mere Reason*.[92] While the goal of an action does not determine its moral worth, every willed action aims at a goal, and moral action aims not only at a good goal but also at the good as a goal. As such, moral action as action aims towards the good, which is not simply the joining of virtue and happiness, but rather the harmonizing of freedom and nature. Such harmony goes beyond the possibility of morality and indeed of any individual, autonomous life. It relates directly to a giver of the moral law in whom the final goal (*Endzweck*) of the world and of the human being is united. It is for this reason that Kant says that 'morality … leads inevitably to religion'.[93]

The mechanistic understanding of nature (specifically Newtonian science) leads to a moral desert, nature which does not conform to human freedom. That realization lay at the core of German philosophical consciousness in the second half of the eighteenth century, in particular the controversy over Spinozism.[94] Kant's critical project in limiting knowledge for the sake of faith leads to the question of how to reconcile faith and knowledge, how in short to live as moral beings in a world seemingly indifferent to the principles, feelings and reasons of morality. While the First and Second Critiques set up the difference of freedom and nature, the *Critique of Judgement* and *Religion within the Boundaries of Mere Reason* attempt to mediate that difference. They do so in two main ways, through analogy and through an ethical dynamic. In both cases the goal is the same: showing in a critical sense how to think the conforming of freedom and nature.

With respect to analogy, Kant makes clear in the Introduction to the first edition of the *Critique of the Power of Judgement* that understanding nature in analogy with art has a subjective, but not objective, validity. Such analogy is demanded by something specific to our capacity for cognition, not by the objects themselves.[95] In so doing, our cognition represents nature no longer simply mechanically, but also technically, as that which is made for a purpose. This adds nothing to philosophy either as a system of knowledge of nature or as freedom – nature as art, Kant tells us, is a 'mere idea'.[96] But this mere idea not only finds a source in the experience of nature itself (in the organization of living beings) but also indicates the possibility of mediation between faith and reason beyond Scepticism and fideism. The reflective power of judgement brings nature into the unity of a system. This is a transcendental principle forming the systematic framework in which the self can live ethically. In other words, this principle can be understood in the context of a quest for home, a quest to understand nature as home. The quest for home is a quest to be in nature – in the sensible realm – while in conformity with 'supernature', the supersensible. While intellect and reason leave the human between these two worlds, the capacity for judgement finds in the sensible the possibility of system and in the intelligible that which gives order to the sensible. It is this relation which allows the move from simple recognition of lawfulness to the postulation of ends, goals, the basis of which lie in the supersensible. Such teleological judgements are not scientific; their significance is existential: Neither science nor morality makes them necessary; only living in nature as a moral being does. As such, the hints which living organisms give as to teleological structures have an existential (and theological) significance: Nature understood teleologically has a purpose, and that purpose is to be found in its author.[97]

The concept of freedom is distinct from natural concepts because of its supersensible nature. Freedom cannot be understood on the basis of sensible intuition. A free act cannot be sensibly perceived, but rather only happenings in the sensible world are accessible to sense experience. These happenings can be understood and explained in mechanical terms. But we cannot be satisfied with simply noting this gulf between these two worlds; we need to think the transition (*Übergang*) from one to the other. While such a transition has little theoretical motivation, it *is* practically motivated. Kant makes clear (although first only in the second edition of the First Critique) that this passage needs to be thought arising from an imperative, an ought: the concept of freedom 'should [*soll*] make the end that is imposed by its laws real in the sensible world'.[98] This requires that nature be so thought that at least the possibility of goals effected by freedom be conceivable. The imperative here is a meta-imperative: All moral imperatives depend on this possibility of actualization of freedom in the sensible world. But this means that the intelligible must have an influence on the sensible. Moral imperatives (whether categorical or hypothetical) demand action: I ought to do this or that. However, such an imperative implies, first, that it is possible to act freely – that freedom can have efficacy in the world – and, second, that nature is such that moral action has sense.

A free act is not motivated by sensual incentives. In the First Critique, freedom is understood as spontaneity; Kant comes to see it as autonomy: not simply acting from itself but acting independently of any motivations deriving from the sensuous being of the self and in accordance with a law which the self gives itself.[99] In any case, freedom requires a space beyond nature and sensibility, even the sensible nature of the free being. Freedom can only be thought as at once other than nature and yet complementary to nature.

It is here that the analogical account becomes one that is dynamic and theological. At the end of the *Critique of Judgement* Kant poses the question as to the final end or goal of nature. He concludes that such a goal cannot be anything natural as things of nature by definition have only mechanical significance: They bring about further effects. Yet if nature is to be thought in conformity with freedom, to be thought as if it has a purpose, then there must be that *in* nature which is not simply *of* nature. Yet, that which is *in* nature but not *of* nature becomes the very purpose of nature itself. This is the paradoxical situation: nature as the realm of heteronomy, where nothing can be scientifically explained except in terms of that which is outside of itself (mechanical causality) not only has within it living organisms that suggest a teleological explanation but furthermore allows arise within itself an autonomous being, which gives itself its own laws and goals.

But the goals of the autonomous being are not unambiguously its own, or rather they are its own as a rational, free being. In setting its own goals, such a being does not simply strive to increase its own pleasure, which would mean to increase its own power as a natural being, but rather seeks that which reason dictates, namely, the good.

The strange nature of human autonomy is manifest in the good will which in willing duty for its own sake does not will it for the sake of a good to be achieved. As such, the end purpose of nature is nothing that the self can set for herself as her own goal, but it is that which she nonetheless wills as occurring through some agency other than her own will.

In the Preface to the first edition of *Religion,* Kant states that 'morality … through religion extends itself to the idea of a mighty moral lawgiver outside the human being, in whose will the ultimate end (of the creation of the world) is what can and at the same time ought to be the ultimate human end'.[100] Moral actions are immanently moral: Their moral rightness can be understood without any reference to the ends which they achieve. Yet, all actions aim for an end, and the achievement of such an end is something to which the moral self cannot be morally indifferent. As such, there is a moral significance in actions which transcend them, even though that transcendent significance neither motivates nor justifies the action itself. The issues here are metaphysical: giving an 'objective practical reality … to the combination, which we simply cannot do without, of the purposiveness [deriving] from freedom and the purposiveness of nature'.[101] There are here for Kant two teleological systems, that of divine providence and that of nature, neither of which we can know, both of which are believed in on the basis of a moral faith. In this, Kant is both close to and decisively at odds with his contemporary and neighbour in Königsberg, Johann Hamann:[102] While for the latter the teleological system of providence can only be accepted on faith and that of nature can be known by reason, for Kant neither can be known; both can be accepted only on faith. However, such faith is not (as for Hamann and indeed Jacobi) a *salto mortale* but rather a rational faith.[103]

The 'objective practical reality' which is in question here is that of a moral universe authored by God, in which human freedom is actualized in the acceptance of the moral law and in which nature finds its proper end in the fulfilment of that law. This 'reality' is manifest in the individual self and in history. In the *Critique of Practical Reason* Kant is still thinking in terms of the individual and is not yet concerned about the historical actualization of freedom collectively in nature. This is clear when we look at the postulations of the immortality of the soul and the existence of God. Kant is at pains to stress the limiting of knowledge to the products of sensible intuition and warns against what he terms the 'mysticism of practical reason', whereby the 'invisible kingdom of God' is understood schematically rather than symbolically, as if it were the object of supersensible intuition.[104] But this separation of sensible and supersensible cannot be absolute given their intersection in the moral being of humanity itself.

The very sensible nature of the human being involves a conflict which makes the complete commensurability (*Angemessenheit*) of the will with the moral law impossible.[105] While, nevertheless, progress is possible towards this ideal, such progress is unending. This unending progress, which can be seen as a whole by an infinite being freed from temporal conditions, is such that the human self can hope for a life after death. But this alone does not ensure the unity of virtue and happiness. The mistake of the Stoics was that by identifying happiness so closely with virtue they effectively set aside the human striving for happiness as such.[106] The concept of the 'Kingdom of God' in Christianity overcomes this deficiency by postulating a world in which nature and morality are brought into a 'harmony, foreign to each as such'.[107] Christian religion offers the hope that morality understood as worthiness for happiness will be fulfilled in another world, one ruled by divine law. Orientation towards this kingdom, in effect the reconciliation of freedom and nature, is a guiding motif of Kant's later work. This 'other world' for humanity as a collective is the kingdom of God on earth, which is a historical task to achieve. This is a task that begins in the heart of each self. The next chapter will take up this theme of Kant's turn to the Pascalian theme of the heart by way of Rousseau.

6

Kant on the heart, evil and grace (starting from Rousseau)

The Kantian project is critical in a propaedeutic sense: Critique prepares the ground for a future metaphysics. The emphasis on future here is not accidental: Before Hegel, Kant understood human knowledge and human destiny in historical terms. The self which thinks through the Critiques is a self of its time, directed towards a future that cannot be reached without a long sojourn in the critical desert. The Kantian self strives to be at home in nature, while always in its essence transcending it. That which is most clear to it, namely, the principles of the understanding, remove it from its innermost self. While the understanding allows it to cognitively apprehend nature and indeed to master it, in Descartes's sense, it does not allow it to know itself, nor indeed the purpose of that nature of which it is a part. The fundamental issue here is the relation between inner and outer: the self as an embodied being in society, subject to both natural causation and the passions of competition and the inner self of feeling and conscience. In tackling these issues we need to pay special attention to that eighteenth-century philosopher, whose portrait looked down from the wall of Kant's study: Jean-Jacques Rousseau.

This chapter is divided into two sections. The first discusses the will and the heart (6.1). The second deals with radical evil, grace and the Kingdom of God (6.2).

6.1 The will and the heart

Respect for the law motivates moral action. Such motivation is a matter of the will, a matter of moral choice. Such moral choice, however, also concerns feeling: It is as much of the heart as of reason. The heart only features in *Religion* as an explicit theme for Kant,[1] yet when read in historical context, that discussion and its relation to his accounts of the will can be understood in a trajectory from Pascal to Rousseau.[2] Rousseau gives a Pelagian reading of Pascal's 'reasons of the heart', and Kant goes a long way in accepting Rousseau's account; yet in one fundamental respect Kant remains closer to Pascal, namely, in his acceptance of original sin. Kant denies the Augustinian account of *inherited* sin and in so doing rejects the sacramental account that Augustine gives. Yet, in his rejection of the claim to a fundamental goodness in the human being beneath the subversions and perversions of civilization, Kant implicitly problematizes the Rousseauian account of the heart. When he comes, in *Religion*, to speak of the heart he does so with respect to the inner sentiment of the moral person, but it is a heart which is necessarily open to that which goes beyond all reason, namely, grace.

While Hume awoke Kant from his dogmatic slumber, Rousseau taught him a fundamental lesson in morality: that all rational beings are equal with respect to moral understanding.[3] The importance of Rousseau's account for Kant is nowhere clearer as in *Religion within the Boundaries of Mere Reason*. The title, indeed, is taken almost verbatim (whether consciously or not) from *Émile*, where Rousseau, in the course of the 'Profession of the Vicar of Savoyard', states, 'The greatest ideas of divinity come to us by reason alone (*par la raison seule*)'.[4] The defence of a religion of reason, the critique of the diversity of cults, the opposition of reason to enthusiasm – *Schwärmerie, l'inspiré* – the moral argument for religion, the critique of revelation – in all these respects Kant echoes and develops themes which we find in the 'Profession'. Yet, Kant's appropriation of Rousseau is not uncritical and the distance from Rousseau can be gleaned in the first pages of *Religion*. Kant places the Rousseauean account of natural human goodness in opposition to the priestly religion's account of a basic fallenness in human nature:[5] the cultic accounts of the Fall against a natural religious account of human goodness. In concluding that the human being is by nature evil, Kant places his account within the ambit of the priestly religion (albeit expressed in conceptual rather than figurative terms). What made his position so difficult and perplexing for his contemporaries (and only somewhat less so for us) is that Kant gives an account that is very close to Rousseau, while denying Rousseau's fundamental starting point, namely, the natural goodness of the human being. In so doing he returns to a type of Pascalian equilibrium between Sceptical Augustinianism and Stoic Pelagianism. But he does so not in the name of a faith which is above reason, nor in the name of a heart which has reasons of which reason cannot know, but rather in the name of a rational faith and a heart which (as with Rousseau) is in harmony with reason. Nevertheless, in the postulates of practical reason, Kant reinscribes Pascal's wager within critical philosophy.[6]

Despite the disposition for good (to which I will return below), the human being has a propensity for evil. Kant's concern in *Religion* is to account for this propensity and its overcoming. His concern is not so much with the metaphysics of morals, which is assumed in this book, but rather with accounting for evil as a modus of illusion: Just as in its theoretical use reason can lead to illusion, the practical use of reason while aiming at the good often fails to reach it. The cause of illusion in this case, however, is the reverse of theoretical reason: While in the latter reason oversteps the limits of human finitude, in the former human finitude blocks the full working through of rational consistency. The question, then, for Kant has to be one of accounting for this conflict in the human self between reason and that which opposes it. The locus of this inner conflict is the heart.

The conflict of the heart lies in the essence of reason, namely, its claim to universality. Practical reason does not privilege the situation of the self, nor of its own self-interest within that situation. As a sensible being the human self is placed in a situation of conflict between the universal claims of reason and the particularity of its own being. That conflict, which can be understood as a conflict of love, between self-love and the love of the moral law, concerns the human self in the totality of its being. The traditional terms, going back to the Hebrew Scriptures, to express that totality, the unity but also strife of reason and sensibility, is 'heart'. In a discussion on Schiller's 'On Grace and Dignity', Kant inquires as to the 'aesthetic constitution' or the 'temperament' of virtue and responds that 'a heart joyous in the *compliance* with its duty (not just complacency in the *recognition* of it) is the sign of genuineness in virtuous disposition' and goes on to speak of 'a joyous frame of mind, without which one is never certain of having *gained* also *a love* for the good, i.e. of having incorporated the good into one's maxim'.[7] Such joy and love are not incidental to morality but lie at its core: To follow the moral law in fear and dejection displays a 'hidden hatred' of the moral law that is incompatible with the genuine incentive of following that law for its own sake, that is, for love of it.[8] While Kant denies that love can be commanded, he does so in respect to 'pathological' love only: As a sensible being I cannot be commanded to have the feeling of love as a preference for a sensible thing. But love for the law is a matter of the heart, a heart which is directed towards the law as nothing alien from itself. Kant refers to this as 'rational self-love',[9] and although he finds the term self-love superfluous here – because it adds nothing to the respect for the law, which is operative – this term does help in making sense of the place of the heart in Kant's account.

The propensity to evil lies in the turning of the heart away from love of the moral law. In its frailty, impurity and depravity the heart is turned away from love of the law through self-love. But what is at issue here is not a choice for Kant between love of the law and self-love, but rather the harmonizing of self-love and love of law: The good heart is a healthy heart in the sense of a heart which has found peace and tranquillity in following the moral law.[10] At play here is a distinction which we find in Rousseau between *amour de soi* and *amour propre*.[11] This distinction is a complex one in Rousseau, but fundamentally the *amour de soi* means self-love in the natural sense of self interest. *Amour propre* is a reflective passion, much in the sense that Hume understood pride and humility, and one which arises when a self finds itself in competition with others. Despite some of Rousseau's statements on this distinction, the *amour propre* is not necessarily negative: A love of self in the reflective comparative sense can be applied within society in a cooperative striving for a higher good. In any case, Kant seems to have the negative sense of *amour propre* in mind when he speaks of a 'radical perversity of the human heart'[12] as the locus of radical evil, in which the self lives its own self-love as other than the love of the moral law. This is a heart in which the moral law remains alienated from the self. The autonomy of the self is gauged in the heart, that is, in the feeling of identity of the self-love and love of the moral law.

While Kant discusses the heart in the context of his practical philosophy, for Rousseau, following Pascal, the heart is that which holds together theory and practice. Sincerity lies at the roots of theory and practice for Rousseau. In both our theoretical claims about the cosmos and our practical claims about what we ought to do, the ultimate test for Rousseau is whether those claims can be made sincerely.[13] This is, however, a negative test: If I cannot claim them with sincerity I cannot claim them to be true, but this does not guarantee their truth. What we are left with in theory and in practice are articles of faith, dogmas which are accepted as compelling not because they have been proven by pure reason but because they are affirmed by the heart. The human being has two main elements, sensibility and reason, one passive and the other active. Between reason and sensibility the heart shares receptivity with sensibility and with reason an active movement towards the truth. But unlike reason, the heart does not mislead (although it can be misled). It is the inner relation of the self to itself. We find the truth by turning within, because that which falsifies is passion that comes from without. From the external world to the inner self the path leads into the depth of the self, its inner nature, where the voice of his Creator can be discerned. The human heart is the gateway to creation, to the created goodness of the human being.[14]

In looking within, what we are seeking is a domain free from the influence of the passions. For Rousseau this inner domain is a domain of the voice. He uses many terms for this: the 'inner voice', the 'voice of nature', the 'voice of conscience', the 'voice of the soul', the 'immortal and celestial voice', the 'cry of remorse', the 'light of reason' and the domain of 'interior light'.[15] This voice is without falsehood and this light is without shadow. Fundamental here is the claim that in this voice, nature speaks in a manner that is not subject to the vagaries of diverse customs. Rousseau's answer to Montaigne's and Pascal's observation that what is allowed on this side of the river is punishable on the far side is to say that the inner voice of nature remains constant because nature is the same on both sides of the river.[16] The nature which remains constant is the created nature, the product of a good God. Indeed, the voice of nature can for Rousseau be taken as the voice of God. It is the voice of a God which does not deceive, which is good and seeks the good for his creatures and which manifests love.[17] It is to the heart of the human being that this voice appeals.

The heart for Rousseau here is certainly an organ of feeling, but as in Pascal this organ is fundamental to both knowledge and conduct. Rousseau distinguishes quite fundamentally between sensation and intelligence, between the passive reception of impressions and the active making of judgements. Sensation is the passive reception of impressions from things in the world. Reversing Descartes, Rousseau argues that truth is not a property of judgements but is the appearing of things as they are. As such, if relations could be sensed, the self would never be wrong. But sensation, he claims, following Locke, is discreet. In sensation, objects offer themselves to me in isolated fashion, unrelated temporally, spatially or in kind. Fundamental to all relations is a sense of being: The relation of the thing sensed to itself in its own identity and to the world around it. But 'the distinctive faculty of the active being or intelligence is the power of giving sense to that word *is*'.[18] For Descartes, as we have seen, error arose from will overreaching the understanding; for Rousseau, on the contrary, I am deceived because I mix the errors of understanding, the errors, that is, of judgement, with the truths of sensation. Rousseau states directly that the 'truth is in the things and not in the mind (*esprit*) which judges them'.[19] Judgement then takes the human being away from truth, because it imposes on nature an act of the spirit. But if that spirit is also part of nature, what can explain such distortion? It is important to see that Rousseau gives an account of intelligence not only as arising out of nature but also a naturalistic account of that arising: Intelligence has no other goal than the preservation of the human (or, indeed, animal) being. Such preservation is good; indeed, the nature of the human being is, like all else in nature, good. If the self is prone to error and, indeed, self-deception, then the source of this cannot be found in nature itself but in something in the human being that goes against nature. Such a going against nature, such a perverting of nature, is a resistance to the good. As such, the source of error is in evil; to find the origin of evil is to find the origin of error.[20]

In short, the question Rousseau poses concerns the origins of evil and concurrently that in the human being that speaks against evil. In Kant's terms, he is exploring the predisposition (*Anlage*) to good and the propensity (*Hang*) to evil.[21] Both centre around the heart. Kant speaks of a threefold predisposition to good, that of animality, humanity and personality. The predisposition of animality is directed to the good in the sense of 'physical or merely mechanical self-love'. Such self-love is directed towards the good of the self and is, in Rousseau's terms, a natural self-love, *amour de soi*, from which no evil emerges. Yet for Kant, this natural self-love is one on which all sorts of vices can be 'grafted'; these vices are 'vices of the savagery of nature ... bestial vices of gluttony, lust and wild lawlessness!'[22] In case of the predisposition of humanity, the vices which are associated with the competitiveness of human culture do not come from nature: Competitiveness itself has a natural and good source but again are 'grafted' onto this nature. Alone, the predisposition to personality allows for nothing evil to be grafted onto it. It is a predisposition to incorporating the moral law into our incentives. The problem, then, is familiar to a reader of Rousseau: Nature aims towards the good, but evil somehow is grafted upon that nature. The question then is how such a grafting takes place.

It is in responding to this question that Kant departs decisively from Rousseau. For the latter, the grafting of evil on good occurs through history, not through nature. In his 'Discourse on the Origins of Inequality', Rousseau charts the manner in which this occurs and does so in relation to the institution of private property which involves an unnatural claim of an individual against his fellows.[23] While Kant does acknowledge the role of society in the origins and overcoming of evil, he nonetheless traces evil to the very nature of the human being. The human being is *by nature* evil, for Kant. But this nature of the human is precisely that which separates the human being from nature *tout court*, that which gives rise to a fundamental rupture with nature in the form of the will, which acts on the basis of freedom.

For Rousseau, the will is not primarily conceived in moral terms. Beginning as he does with the fundamental dichotomy of activity and passivity, Rousseau (speaking through the Vicar of Savoyard) argues that there is nothing in matter except passivity and that movement can only be explained through the intervention of an active force. Echoing Pascal and Descartes, Rousseau argues that prior to all reasoning the self feels the spontaneity of its own movements and in feeling this it recognizes the efficacy of the will.[24] Such a recognition has a cosmological relevance for Rousseau, as what is true of a self's own body must also be true of material nature generally, namely, that only an immaterial will could set it in motion. Questions of conduct – questions of how the self should employ its will – are questions that can be addressed through a seamless argument from the theoretical claims of the existence of a deity whose will animates the material substance of the world and does so in an intelligent manner. The 'article of faith' that the human being is free in its actions comes after those articles of faith concerning God.[25] The will, then, is first cosmological; freedom is first and foremost divine. Human freedom, is part of nature, even if it can be employed against nature. The origin of evil is neither in freedom nor in nature but rather in a historically contingent development of human freedom within society.

Kant refuses this fundamental claim as to the contingent origins of evil, insisting rather on the 'innate guilt' of the human being and indeed on the reality of original sin.[26] Evil cannot have a simply contingent origin because the basis of morality in nature cannot be secured. No morally relevant claim to human goodness can be philosophically secured in this sense. Rather, the freedom which forms the basis of morality can only be understood through a distinct mode of reasoning. Evil in such a context cannot be the historical perversion of nature because nature cannot be understood as the basis of moral goodness or evil. This requires then that human nature be understood neither historically nor in naturalistic terms but rather in a distinct manner, as a distinct form of life which is both part of nature and yet which does not fully conform to the laws which nature in its appearance manifests. Human nature then is the nature of a moral being, which must be understood on the basis of freedom, which cannot be derived from natural kind. It is in such freedom, at the roots of the will which acts on its basis, that evil emerges.

6.2 Radical evil, grace and the Kingdom of God

What can I hope for? This question which guides *Religion* is already to the forefront when Kant discusses the highest good in the First, Second and Third Critiques. Already in the First Critique he speaks of that question as being at once practical and theoretical, in a sense synthesizing the two previous questions concerning knowledge and morality.[27] This hoped-for world is one in which worthiness for happiness is rewarded.[28] The assumption here is straightforwardly Pelagian: The human being is capable of living a virtuous life, and that life will be awarded by God on the basis of such worthiness. The hope, then, is a hope in God and in the moral constitution of creation. The account of hope in the Second Critique not only (as previously noted) introduces a temporal aspect, whereby hope is in unending progress towards the good, but also places the object of hope as much in the worthiness for happiness as in the fulfilment of that worthiness.[29] What is hinted at here becomes a central theme of *Religion*: The temporality of human life is not simply accidental to morality but is rather essential to it because of the incorrigibility of evil. The endless striving to be worthy of happiness points to an inner tension in the human which we saw expressed already by Pascal as that between the Pyrrhonian and the Stoic. In other words, implicit at the end of the Second Critique, but only explicitly acknowledged in *Religion*, is the fundamental and inescapable condition of fallenness and the human need for grace.

In responding to the question of what I can hope for, Kant sets out in more detail than anywhere else in his writings the condition which requires hope. What I hope for is not in my own hands; hope implies both incapacity and heterogeneity. From the outset, then, Kant is outlining conditions which are in contrast with the fundamental principles of his ethical philosophy, namely, 'ought implies can' and autonomy. These conditions are in contrast rather than contradicting, because the issue precisely is that of how an autonomous, capable ethical subject can act in a context of incapacity and heterogeneity. In this sense *Religion* outlines the other side of the problematic of freedom and nature: If a free being is not living in a moral desert, if nature and freedom share the same moral author, how can the free being be reconciled to that author? In short, the question is one of salvation – individual and communal. As no other creature, the human being experiences in his own being the conflict of freedom and nature and it is this conflict which is experienced as fallenness and which Kant describes as radical evil.

The radicality of evil for Kant lies in the ancient conundrum: The human being – even the worst – knows what is right[30] but does not always do what is right. Kant rejects the Stoic understanding of passions as the cause of this, because that would be to undermine human freedom: To act wrongly is to make a free decision to go against the moral law.[31] But that free decision is a decision for nature over freedom, a free decision to follow the incentive of his sensual nature rather than the moral law. Evil is radical because it effects the roots of moral agency, roots which are themselves beyond conceptual understanding. These roots are in the very basis of the human self, which has a bifurcated nature, such that the word 'nature' is used ambiguously when referring to the human being. Hence, when Kant says that the human being is by nature evil, he is not referring to the human as a natural species, because evil (in a moral sense) cannot be found in nature as a realm of mechanical causality. But the human has a free relation to his own sensual nature, and this sets the human apart. The moral law is both rational and without direct relation to his sensual nature. Human nature is to be placed in this tension – which a purely rational being would not experience – and in this tension the human is inescapably a temporal and finite being.[32]

Evil is radical because it 'corrupts the basis [*Grund*] of all maxims'.[33] What this means is that such evil cannot be overcome by human effort alone, because such effort would require the presence of a good maxim as the subjective basis of all maxims, which is not possible due to the corruption brought about by the tendency to evil (*Hang zum Böse*). On the other hand, it must be possible to overcome this tendency because the human being as a free being must be capable of choosing a good maxim. It is important to see that evil, though radical, can never, for Kant, destroy the basic core of goodness in the human being. To say otherwise for Kant would mean that the human being could refuse his own rational nature. The human for Kant is between angels and devils – to do evil out of the incentive of evil is diabolical;[34] to do good without any counter incentive would be to be an angel (and without a body). As we have seen, for Kant, to act is to act out of love – love for the sensual self or love for the rational self. The question then concerns the origin of the transformation from good to evil and from evil to good. Although Kant distinguishes in this discussion between rational and temporal origin, the question of origins can only be understood temporally. Indeed, the underlying question of hope brings Kant inexorably to the question of time and the dynamic of moral change and the question of grace.

Kant defines 'origin' in causal terms: It is the 'descent (*Abstammung*) of an effect from its first cause'.[35] *Abstammung* means 'descent', in the sense of lineage, so what is being looked for here is, so to speak, the birth certificate of evil. This first cause can be understood either in terms of time or in terms of reason. To understand it in temporal terms is to conceive it as a contingent happening in the world. This cannot be the case with evil, however, because if it were, the basis of evil in freedom would be undermined. As such, evil can only have a rational not a temporal origin. This is to assume, however, that time has no other reality than as a form of sensible intuition, where in combining a multiplicity in inner sense it allows for an empirical representation of multiplicity,[36] which in turn is causally ordered. But once we speak of origins and first causes, then we are necessarily speaking not only of time but also of time within a theological context. In short, to speak of a rational origin of evil is to speak of it as descending from freedom; the question, then, is how to understand the temporality of freedom.

Kant explicitly accepts the distinction between original sin and derivative sin,[37] which he understands in terms of a distinction between noumenal and phenomenal. Derivative sin is that evil which appears to us, first and foremost in ourselves, but original sin is the propensity towards evil, which has no temporal ground (and is not inherited). We must qualify this: It has no phenomenal, that is, sensible, temporal ground. The temporality in question here is not a relative temporal change, governed by mechanical laws which operate gradually in a piecemeal fashion, but rather the temporality of immediate qualitative change. This change must be considered in the mode of 'as if'. We cannot perceive the change, even in ourselves; we must, so to speak, rationally reconstruct how it must be, 'as if the human being had fallen into (*greaten*) it without any mediation from the state of innocence'.[38] The verb Kant uses here, *geraten*, is significant: This verb is often associated with strong passions or disturbances, such as to lose composure – *ausser sich geraten* – or to panic – *in Panik geraten* – and also to blunder into something – *in etwas geraten*. Though rooted in freedom, evil happens to the self; the self loses its firm ground, blunders into evil and finds himself all of a sudden outside of the state of innocence. This is the occurrence of a moment; it is similar to what Plato described as '*exaiphnes*'.[39] Between the state before original sin and the sin itself, there can be no mediation, because nothing in the prior state explains it and there is no middle ground between good and evil, no matter of degrees between them. Freedom works in the moment, in 'a moment of action (*Augenblicke der Handlung*)',[40] and this moment is never once and for all: Every evil act originates from a decision, which arises out of innocence in the sense of the propensity to good, which is incorruptible. The philosophical question is how to think this origin and Kant's response is that it remains inconceivable and inscrutable for us. What is inscrutable is precisely the temporality of freedom, which is one of sudden and unmediated change. No reason, no motivation, can explain freedom, because freedom chooses its motivations and its reasons. In that sense in the moment of action the motivations and reasons arise with the action itself, which is the decision to put the individual and the love of the individual above the love of the law. This decision, however, does not lie at the core of the human being but rather responds to temptation: The human being falls into evil through the seduction of an evil spirit (the devilish evil, which is a choice for evil itself, not one led by temptations of the flesh).[41] Where our concepts fail us, we are thrown back on figurative representations, specifically, in this case, that of the serpent in the garden. The serpent represents for Kant the decision for evil for its own sake.

The moral law cannot inspire its own transgression, nor can sensual nature, which in itself is good. Free choice does not explain the origins of evil: Evil comes from the outside; that is why the serpent represents it so well. The human being cannot conceive evil in its own self but needs, so to speak, to be instructed in evil. Such instruction comes from beyond nature, from a 'spirit of an originally more sublime destiny',[42] which chooses evil not (as with human beings) for the sake of its sensual nature but rather for its own sake. Kant here comes very close to a strangely anti-gnostic Manichaeism: He supposes (following his reading of Genesis) a principle of evil in conflict with good, but this principle is not matter but spirit turned against good. This is not so much an explanation of the origins of evil as a rendering them inconceivable: 'from whence the evil in that spirit?', he asks rhetorically.[43] But clearly such spirit knows the moral law and in knowing it turns itself against its imperatives. As such, this is a freedom that chooses to disobey the moral law for no other reason than to assert its own freedom to do so. This ultimate freedom is an angelic freedom, which allows for no revocation. This is so because the choice for evil is a choice to become evil, one which loses all basis for good. The seductive power of such an evil spirit is to lead the human being to reject the moral law, but to do so because of another aspect of its being, namely, its sensual nature. Evil works in the human to disrupt the relation between the two goods out of which it exists: those of reason and those of sense.

Free choice is a response. This does not allay responsibility, but it does complicate the temporal picture: The rational origin of evil points before itself to a past, which it can never make present to itself except in figurative, mythical, terms: the myth of the Fallen Angel. Such a past remains past, but it is a past of every present, because in every present the temptation of that evil is repeated. In this sense, Kant remains Pelagian in rejecting the inheritance of evil, and yet retains the essentials of the Augustinian account: evil as a free act which, however, is beyond human capacity to recapitulate. The origins of evil remains hidden to human reason and action.

Conversely, the change from evil to good is immediate; it cannot be gradually attained through reform of character but rather happens as a revolution in the self. Again there we encounter the temporality of *exaiphnes*, the sudden change from evil to good. This change, however, is not the bringing of something new into human existence but the 'restoration of the original predisposition to good in us'.[44] This restoration, however, is itself inconceivable (or rather 'exceeds all our concepts'). This is so because only the change itself can bring with it its own reasons: The revolutionary change of heart brings with it the acknowledgement that only the moral law can act as an incentive to action once duty is recognized. The temporality of this change is sudden, immediate and irrevocable, but it is precisely a temporality allowing for no passing. While the time of sensible intuition is continuously passing, the revolution of the heart is continually repeated. It is not one moment amongst others because in it the self changes radically, the moment is one of a 're-birth' (as Kant quotes John's Gospel).[45] The revolution of the heart can be only seen by God, that is, by that being who has intellectual intuition. For a being with sensible intuition, this temporality is hidden; all such a being can see is unending becoming. We have here two temporalities, which intersect in hope: The self hopes in the revolution of her heart, while engaged in the unending task of going from bad to better.

The human being is radically hidden from herself; she cannot with any confidence claim to a good conscience. She can only hope that she acts out of a purity of heart, whereby she acts on the incentive of the moral law alone. Kant states,

> Assurance of this [the irrevocable revolution of his heart] cannot of course be attained by the human being naturally, neither via immediate consciousness nor via the evidence of the life he has hitherto led, for the depths of his own heart (the subjective first ground of his maxims) are to him inscrutable. Yet he must be able to *hope* that, by the exertion of *his own* power, he will attain to the road that leads in that direction, as indicated to him by a fundamentally improved disposition.[46]

The result of this revolution, the doing of duty for the sake of duty, is not a cause of wonder: The human being which does her duty is simply doing what reason tells her. Wonder is, however, not only justified but uplifting as well, when she contemplates the original moral predisposition in her. The inconceivability of this predisposition and of human freedom, that is, its hiddenness in the face of the conceptual thought, proclaims its divine origin. Kant sees this sense of divine origin of the moral predisposition as manifest in feeling: in exaltation (*Begeisterung*) and a feeling of sublimity, which accompanies the respect for the law.[47] Such exaltation and feeling of sublimity are not – like the respect for the law – auto-affective but rather are rooted in wonder at that which is incomparably greater than the self, namely, the divine author of her moral nature, a nature which in its depths is hidden from the self.

But such feelings of wonder and sublimity, if they are to have practical worth, must reignite our moral dispositions and as such be brought to bear on the self's temporally contingent actions. This relation of a response to the invisible source and the concrete action as one of continual approximation gives the context for Kant's understanding of divine grace. The process of 'becoming' is one in which within the temporality of sensible intuition the order of the world as it is, seen from the eternal perspective, becomes increasingly manifest. The human self becomes the fulcrum of this development, first as individual, then as community.

The cause of evil is 'an invisible enemy, one who hides behind reason',[48] an enemy working in secret, while the prototype of the good principle 'has come down to us from heaven'.[49] These two invisible realms Christianity represents figuratively (*bildlich*)[50] in terms of heaven and hell, and Kant affirms this account to be philosophically correct in the sense of placing the relation of good and evil as divided by an 'immeasurable gap'. Yet, the self finds itself precisely within that 'immeasurable gap', not finding within itself the means to measure it, but only the capacity to choose to subject itself to one or other but not both of these realms. But this choice does not simply concern the morality of specific actions but rather has cosmological implications: The self in its moral perfection is that which makes the world the object of divine decree and the goal of creation. The personification of this goal is found in the figure of the 'son of God'. But while it is the human duty to elevate to the ideal of moral perfection which we find in the figure of Christ, human beings are not the authors (*Urheber*) of this ideal.[51] It is rather the case that we have to think of human nature as receptive (*empfänglich*) to this ideal. The self is a receptive being – receptive of the temptation to evil but also receptive of the ideal of moral perfection, which is not simply the moral law, but the idea of a highest good which the self experiences as written into her by that being which is both the author of her moral nature and the Creator of this physical existence.

Within the apparent self is the trace of that noumenal source that is the divine origin of the law and the ideal of moral perfection. Yet, inherent in that source and origin is an appeal to human capacity, expressed in Matthew's Gospel, rendered by Kant as 'Be ye holy (in the conduct of your lives) as your Father in Heaven is holy'.[52] The divine command to be holy implies for Kant that the self is capable of holiness, while at the same time it opens up the 'immeasurable gulf' in which the human being finds herself. This immeasurable gulf between the evil out of which she comes and the good to which she aims cannot be overcome in time, understood as the temporal horizon of mechanical causality. This is so because that which appears in such time is overdetermined: It is not simply the making manifest of the moral law, the act done out of duty alone, but also an act in the world, an act with worldly, sensible, contingent conditions. Considered, however, in relation to the disposition towards the good that transcends the senses, this immeasurable gap can be overcome. This can only be seen through the eyes of God who 'as one who knows intimately the heart [*Herzenskündiger*] through his pure intellectual intuition as being a perfected whole even with respect to the deed (the life conduct)'. He goes on in a footnote to clarify that 'the disposition, which takes the place of the totality of the series of approximations carried on *in infinitum*, makes up only for the deficiency which is in principle inseparable from the existence of a temporal being, [namely] never to be able to become quite fully what he has in mind [*im Begriffe*]'.[53] Two temporal perspectives are operative here, the time of mechanical cause and effect and the time of moral life, which lives each moment as the expression and manifestation of the final end and goal of creation.

The problem is that this relation of mechanical time and moral time is obscure to us. In *Religion*, Kant attempts to find ways of overcoming that obscurity and he does so in two ways: through an account of divine grace and through an account of historical (communal) progress. While on an empirical level we can negatively see lack of progress in moral improvement, positively all we have is conjecture, and Kant warns that 'there is ... something awkward about ... feelings of a presumed supernatural origin: One is never more easily deceived than in what promotes a good opinion of oneself'.[54] As such, the self finds itself between despair, on the one hand, and illusory self-confidence, on the other. The Kantian response to such a situation is one of hope and trust without any certainty. This trust cannot be 'grounded on an immediate consciousness of the immutability of our dispositions'[55] but rather is based on the uncertain inference from the consequences of this disposition in the conduct of life. In the face of death, where the very possibility of further affirmation of such an immutable disposition is absent, any rational judgement of the self's moral life will lead only to hopelessness, if not wild despair. In the face of death, the self hopes for another life in which it can come to certainty as to its inner moral disposition. The realization of freedom while occurring in the present life can only be fully known if the self can have an intellectual intuition into himself, which can only occur in another life. However, that other life is not the realization of freedom, but rather the possibility to recognize what has already occurred, namely, the revolution of the heart and moral actions in the present life. What is can only be fully recognized in the future and takes its meaning from that future, which, however, for God is already present.

The temporality of moral life is not simply that of sensible intuition. If it were, the third difficulty Kant raises, namely, how to make good the guilt of past transgressions, would not arise. The past in question here is a past that does not simply pass but is the past continually present in the life of the moral agent. Past transgressions, while actions in the past, continue to have moral significance because they (not the empirical acts themselves but the moral acts of deciding on the basis of incentives which contradict those of the moral law) constitute the moral self[56] and constitute the meaning of her change of heart. In that sense the problem is not simply that the past cannot be undone (physically speaking) but rather that the past transgressions have present significance in the form of moral guilt, which cannot be transferred to another, and which cannot be simply set aside as justice demands such transgressions be punished.

Assuming a revolution of the heart, the birth of a new self, neither the old self nor the new self can expiate its sins: The old self is still living under the evil disposition, while the new self in living under the good disposition does no more than what duty demands and cannot, so to speak, produce a surplus of good to pay back for past transgressions. The answer can only be found in the moment of revolution itself. In that *exaiphnes* there must be a wiping away of guilt. Kant points out that the rejection of the evil disposition and the taking on of the good disposition are not two events but two sides of the one event: This event turns both to the past and to the future and can be understood – using Biblical metaphors – in terms of death and (re-)birth. Such death of the old person involves suffering, the suffering of sorrow for past sins, most fully revealed in the light of the change in disposition. This suffering, however, is not once and for all (as it is figuratively depicted in the suffering of Christ),[57] but rather the moment of conversion is a continual repeating of the departure from the old and the taking on of the new. In that moment is a seeking for forgiveness, which is not addressed to a stern lawgiver – nor to the merciful King, of Jansen and Pascal, but precisely to a God who intimately knows and understands the heart of the convert. It is here, in that knower of the human heart, that the necessary surplus is to be found. In short, the revolution of the heart is fully morally efficacious, that is, it brings about a being pleasing to God, only through an act of divine grace, while its precondition, the turning of the heart to God, is a matter of the self's will alone. This change in disposition is the condition of faith in God's forgiveness.[58] This conversion, if true, is irreversible, because the being which turns back to goodness has taken up that goodness as the supreme maxim of its life, but as the fact of this conversion remains hidden to the self, the eternity of its goodness can only be experienced in the temporality of continual striving.[59]

The temporality of mere becoming which is the human fate as earthbound beings means that the self can never fully earn such forgiveness; all it can do is receive it. This moral receptivity is a mark of subordination to the lawgiver: '*Receptivity* is all that we, on our part, can attribute to ourselves, whereas a superior's decision to grant a good for which the subordinate has no more than (moral) receptivity is called *grace*.'[60] As such, the self's good disposition is the condition for its receptivity of divine grace. But nothing justifies the giving of this grace; in other words, it is not done for the sake of justice: In now doing his duty the moral agent is doing no more than what he ought, which cannot undo past transgressions. Hence, Kant is speaking of divine grace, not divine judgment. In that fundamental sense, Kant cannot be a consistent Pelagian because the forgiveness necessary for salvation is by definition unmerited, the grace medicinal.[61]

Kant is here elaborating a position between the Augustinian and Pelagian: Grace is in response to a change of the human heart and consists in the forgiveness of past transgressions, an undoing of the past that the human being is incapable of achieving. The human being is in her own eyes not worthy of such forgiveness, but this is due to the fact that she can only see herself in her appearance to herself. God can see her in the totality of her being, that being which is manifest now in the conversion of her heart, that self which lives in the moral temporality of that moment in which the turn to good is at once the turning away from evil. The emphasis on the sacramental, on, for example, the sacrament of baptism, which animates Augustine on this question, is absent from Kant's account. Kant's polemic against *Schwärmerei* may have influenced this absence, as Ronald Green suggests,[62] but there appears to be little room in Kant for rituals of worship and devotion derived from a sense of awe in the face of the incomprehensible. In this respect, Kant remains Pelagian in his deep-seated rationalism.

Kant's question – what can I hope for? – is in contrast to the other two questions, expressible equally in the first person plural as it is in the first person singular. I can know and I can act as I ought in isolation from others, I do not need others to for truth or goodness, but hope leads me to the communal, the social. It does so both because of the source of evil and the nature of the highest good. Although radical evil involves a corruption of the individual human will, and although it does not originate in human sensuality, the most destructive vices are rooted in the passions, which occur through 'mutual corruption' within society. As Kant states, 'it is not the instigation of nature that arouses what should properly be called the *passions*, which wreak such great devastation in his originally good predisposition. ... Envy, addiction to power, avarice, and the malignant inclinations associated with these, assail his nature, which on its own is undemanding, *as soon as he is among human beings*.'[63] It is striking that this is the only thematization of the passions per se in *Religion* and occurs when Kant is turning to the communal. The heart, which he has thematized to this point, is the inner working of the human disposition, but as we have seen, evil is traced in the individual to temptation. Here the mythological account of temptation is supplemented by a social genesis of evil: the communal incitement of passions through competition. Here we see again the influence of Rousseau, and despite his rejection of natural goodness in Part 1 of *Religion*, Kant traces the origins of evil in those passions that arise through anxiety with respect to how another sees a self. Such anxiety at being disrespected by another means that the self sees itself as if from another's point of view. The passions are not natural but rather artificial modes of perception whereby the self no longer sees things as they are or as they ought to be but rather sees itself locked into a competitive conflict with another. In the case of each of the vices Kant lists, the natural limits of the self are transcended in an unnatural possessiveness. In this sense, in the fallen state, selves are pitched against each other; the only moral response to this is one of cooperation, where the intersection of the visible and the invisible in the individual is extended to society at large. Only if the members of society strive to develop a society under the flag of virtue for all those who love the good, can the logic of mutual corruption be overcome.

Again, Kant speaks in terms of the relation of invisible and visible, the political relations of positive law and the ethical relations of the laws of virtue. The latter are not enforceable but rather are freely followed. Such laws are those which only God as the intimate knower of the heart can bestow, and an ethical community is a people under such divine commands. In considering this, Kant points to a 'remarkable antinomy of reason with itself',[64] an antinomy rooted in the conflict between two conditions of hope in blessedness, between that which the moral agent cannot achieve, the undoing of its his moral transgressions, and that which he can achieve, reform of his life. The two sides of this conflict are reflected, on the one side, in belief in satisfaction through the sacrifice of Christ, and, on the other side, in the capacity to become worthy of divine pleasure: These sides are in turn reflected in the difference between historical specific faiths and rational religion, between the conditioned and the unconditioned. In the case of Christianity, though, the conflictual relation is given a more concrete, indeed, historical, sense. The belief in the sacrifice of Christ is a belief in a historical contingent event (the life and death of Jesus of Nazareth), which in the Christian understanding had a profound moral impact in wiping out sins:

> The living faith in the prototype of a humanity well-pleasing to God (the Son of God) refers, *in itself*, to a moral idea of reason, insofar as the latter serves for us not only as guideline but as incentive as well; it is, therefore, all the same whether I start out from it (as *rational* faith) or from the principle of a good life conduct.[65]

Even if Jesus of Nazareth were the son of God, there would be no way we could know this, because such a revelation – as an empirical event – would stand outside the conditions of space and time. As such, in moral terms, the historical conditioned event can only act as an exemplar of rational faith, and it can do that only through a projection of reason. In both cases, then, the same practical idea is manifest, namely, that of the moral law. Here again Kant is closer to Pelagius than to Augustine, for whom faith in grace is inseparable from faith in Jesus as the incarnate Christ. Kant states,

> However, if one wished to make the historical faith in the actuality of an appearance, such as has only once occurred in the world, the condition of the one saving faith, then there would indeed be two entirely different principles (the one empirical, and the other rational), and there would arise over them a true conflict of maxims, whether to proceed from the one or the other as starting point, which no reason would ever be able to settle.[66]

Kant is hinting at something incorrigible in such a faith, a belief which lies at the roots of historical religion and which reason cannot dispel. Like empiricism with respect to theoretical knowledge in the First Critique, this side of the antinomy is destructive of morality and religion (though precisely not of historical faith). It does, however, by the same token depart from the antinomy of reason by leaving reason itself behind, viewing faith as if it had such a peculiar force and such a mystical (or magical) influence that, however much we ought to regard it, from what we know, merely as historical, it would nonetheless be in a position of improving the whole human being radically (of making a new man out of him) if he just holds on to it and to all the feelings bound with it, then such a faith would have to be regarded as itself imparted and inspired directly by heaven (with and within the historical faith), and everything, the moral constitution of humankind included, would then be reduced to an unconditional decree of God: 'He hath mercy on whom he will, and whom he will he *hardeneth*', and this, taken according to the letter, is the *salto mortale* of human reason.[67]

These two conditions of faith belong together, but the necessity of that connection can only be seen once 'we assume that one faith can be derived from the other'.[68] But posed in these terms the antinomy cannot be resolved, because the relation of dependence changes depending on where we begin, either with revelation or with reason. But this question is immediately posed in a temporal, historical sense: Either historical, ecclesiastical faith supervenes over pure religious faith or it is a mere vehicle for the latter and will fade away in the distant future. The resolution of this antinomy of reason can be achieved only through historical reflection, that is, through reflection on questions of temporal change. Such reflection, however, reveals the antinomy to be only apparent:[69] The fundamental question at issue in both is the transformation of life conduct. The model of such conduct, the model guiding the revolution of the heart, can be considered either as coming from God or as already contained within the human being. However, in both cases the model of life is not empirically discoverable but is already contained in reason.

The time of the senses cannot allow for a true revelation, because here there is no access to anything which is not caused by something other than itself; nothing appears of itself. 'The basis for the transition to the new order of things must lie in the principle of the pure religion of reason, as a revelation (though not an empirical one) constantly happening [*beständig geschehene*] within all human beings.'[70] The use of the word 'revelation' here is significant: Historical religions recognize the need for revelation, the 'will of the world ruler as revealed to him through reason'.[71] Such revelation is not, as that proclaimed in the historical religions, one which occurs once and for all but rather happens constantly and consistently (*beständig*). This invisible source of revelation discloses itself to reason, and that disclosure is an event, which is responded to differently at different times. Reform occurs through the reflective response to that revelation, which trusts more in divine providence than in the plans for 'outward' revolution, which tend to harm freedom. Yet this constant happening does not invalidate historically specific revelations, those which are proclaimed as founding events for historical faiths. This is so because the relation to religion takes place at the intersection of the visible and the invisible, and it is precisely here that the problem of history is encountered. To enter an ethical community is to undergo a change of heart, which occurs invisibly, yet this invisible happening needs to be validated in the visible realm of human community. This twin need of inner conversion and outer cooperation requires a common commitment to the good, which can only occur through a rational decision which itself is communicable. What is thus communicated, however, are not the laws of a juridico-civil state but rather those of the author of the moral natures of the members of that community. Such laws are not to be obeyed through the limitation of freedom but rather are the expression of freedom. But such an ethical community, as a community of moral beings brought into communal relationship through their obedience to their divine author, remains an ideal in the present. Kant describes this as follows:

> An ethical community under divine moral legislation is a *church* which, inasmuch as it is not the object of a possible experience, is called the *church invisible* (the mere idea of the union of all upright human beings under direct yet moral divine world-governance, as serves for the archetype of any such governance to be founded by human beings). The *church visible* is the actual union of human beings into a whole that accords with this ideal. ... The true (visible) church is one that displays the (moral) kingdom of God on earth inasmuch as the latter can be realized through human beings.'[72]

Later he goes on to speak of the relation of the visible and invisible church in the following manner:

> Now, since a pure religion of reason, as a public religious faith, admits only the mere idea of a church (that is, an invisible church), and since only the visible one, founded on laws, is in need of and susceptible to an organization by human beings, it follows that service under the dominion of the good principle in the invisible church cannot be considered as ecclesiastical service. ... But, since with respect to our duties (which, taken collectively, we must at the same time look upon as divine commands) we nevertheless are at all times at the service of God, the *pure religion of reason* will have all right-thinking human beings as its *servants*. ... However, since every church erected on statutory laws can be the true church only to the extent that it contains within itself a principle of constantly coming closer to the pure faith of religion ... we shall nonetheless be able to posit in these laws, and among the officials of the church founded on them, a *service* of the church (*cultus*), provided that these officials direct their teaching and order to that final end (a public religious faith).[73]

The visible displays or enacts (*darstellt*) the invisible; in its laws and among its servants is posited (*setzen*) a service of the invisible. In this sense the visible contains within it the invisible, and the visible constantly aims towards manifesting more perfectly the invisible. The visible course of history does not of itself give us a sense of a final end towards which historical development is aiming, yet, Kant is able to affirm 'without hesitation', that his own time is the best in the history of the church. What convinces him of this is the potential for the future:

> One need only allow the seed of the true religious faith now being sown in Christianity – by only a few, to be sure, yet in the open – to grow unhindered, to expect from it a continuous approaching [*Annäherung*] to that church, ever

uniting all human beings, which constitutes the visible representation [*sichtbare Vorstellung*] (the schema) of an invisible Kingdom of God on earth.[74]

Between visible and invisible is an inner dynamic, which, unlike in the relation of categories and sensibility alluded to here, involves a continual approaching to a final and perfect representation in visible form of the invisible. This would mark the end of church history, as the historical churches rooted in historically specific revelations would fade into the one rational religion. The self finds herself between the historical cities and churches, which are of human creation and the city of God, the divine Kingdom, which it would be contradictory to suppose human beings should establish.[75] But the human desire for this Kingdom is manifest in religion, in both its rational and non-rational aspects. While the coming of the Kingdom is dependent on divine providence, such providence, it can be rationally hoped, will respond to the human effort to be worthy of it. But that effort is itself bolstered by those displays and enactments of the divine kingdom, which are made visible through human efforts at communication.

Against Gnostic esotericism Kant insists that the visible signs of the invisible are public and rationally redeemable. While not ruling out the possibility of private revelation, only that which is public can be of practical benefit because moral reason concerns each individual in their humanity: The goal of morality is the goal of humanity both in the individual and in the human race as a whole. As such, the communicability of the religious message has to be independent of the specificity of language or learning. The dynamic relation here is between the universal communicability of moral reason and the historically specific and contingent experiential conditions of communication. As the human is both a sensible and a rational being, the modes of communication will inevitably be both sensible and rational. This guides the hermeneutical principles of Kant's reading of Scripture, namely, that the rational is cloaked in the sensible. The task, then, is to read the rational in the sensible; in other words, to read the Scriptures symbolically. Such symbolic reading implies that the rational needs sensible expression to allow itself to be communicated, even though such sensible expression can lead to misunderstanding and misinterpretation.[76] The goal of scriptural interpretation is not simply to disclose this rational core but to in turn transform the sensible through the rational. Historical change occurs in this way, through a transformation of empirical revelation in a striving for rational progress.

The striving after the Kingdom of God is a striving for a state on earth which would symbolically approach the invisible church based on the divine will. Such displaying of the invisible, understood as a making sensible (*Versinnlichung*), can only be understood schematically or symbolically.[77] In this case, as we are no longer in the realm of concepts formed through the understanding, it is only through the making accessible symbolically the invisible that the Kingdom of God has any intersubjective meaning. The intuitive is essential to the proper – that is for Kant theistic – account of God, such that without it we are left with nothing to cognize.[78]

The Sceptical aporetic state in which Kant brings us is not where he leaves us. The Sceptical/Stoical ascetic of the critique of reason leads us to the place where we can confront both fallenness and the potential for salvation, which Kant sees as inherent in the human condition. His philosophical project opens up the possibility of overcoming not so much the division of empiricism and rationalism but the deeper division of grace and nature, in a form of Pelagianism that recognizes the validity of the Augustinian insight into human moral weakness. In doing so he did not, as Derrida claims, develop his moral and political thought under the implicit sign of the death of God[79] but rather opened up the possibility of a thought of God that finally came to terms with the explosive divinity of absolute power, which emerged out of late Medieval Christianity.

Conclusion

There is no self outside of the situational relations in which it is, which it interprets and attempts to mould. The meaning of self is inseparably connected with the sense of world. The formation of the Modern self is a transformation of Ancient and Medieval paradigms responding the situation of disintegration of world. While from this distance we can speak of a breakdown of the *Medieval* world, with the implication of the birth of a new Modern world, lived as a crisis such a breakdown can only appear as a breakdown of the world as such. The turn to the self, beginning with Montaigne, is not then simply a recovery of some former concern – in Stoicism or Augustine, for example – but rather an attempt to rebuild a world in which the claim to a rational order and faith in the Church as mediator of saving grace could no longer be presupposed. The disintegration of the Medieval world allowed a new understanding of the self as it became a central philosophical concern. What this meant was that questions of God and Nature came to be understood in their relation to a transformed sense of self.

The task of the present book has been to chart this transformation in the works of some of the most prominent philosophers of early modernity. Their work responded to, and formed in turn, fundamental changes in the way of being in the world of Europeans at this time, reflected not only in philosophy and science but also in art and literature. Within the realm of music, it can be supposed that 'could a medieval composer hear the high-pitched, anguished cries of Verdi's Otello ... he would be horrified at humanity making so much of itself'.[1] The shift in music from the medieval doxological enactment of praising God to the emphasis on self-expression in nineteenth-century Romantic composers reflects the inward turn to the self, initiated by Montaigne. While this inward movement draws on St. Augustine (most consciously in Pascal, but also in Montaigne and Descartes), the music that expresses the temporal being of that self for Augustine raises it to the eternal and to its own being in the divine order.[2] For the Moderns this sense of the reality of an eternal order expressed in nature as divine creation, which for Augustine is a common inheritance of Platonism, Stoicism and the Scriptures, is far distant, leaving hardly a trace, inspiring both anguished seeking and eventually resigned disbelief.

The formation of the Modern self is manifest in the transformations of the understanding of reason, happiness and the passions in Modernity. These we have understood in terms of the way of being of the self with respect to the world as the relational order – human, natural and divine.

With regard to reason, we have charted these transformations back to the Condemnations of Paris (1277) and the consequent destabilization of the activity of reason in later Medieval and early Modern thought. If what is believed on the basis of religious faith could be either undecidable or unwarranted on rational grounds, then the relation of faith to reason could no longer be characterized as 'faith seeking understanding', but rather as faith and reason in continual conflict. The demands of faith and of reason needed to be reconciled within the self's own sense of itself. The Pelagian sense of reason as manifest in its self-assertion becomes increasingly plausible, while continually troubled by Sceptical recognition of the limits of reason (Hume). Those Sceptical concerns make a thoroughgoing Pelagianism impossible, while at the same time the Augustinian/Thomistic understanding of grace as perfecting nature becomes incomprehensible in the Modern understanding of nature. Therein opens up a dualism of natural and supernatural at the heart of the self's understanding of its self and its ultimate destiny.

The centrality of the goal of happiness is by no means forgotten in Modern philosophy, but it is transformed from the theoretical contemplation of the eternal or salvation through grace into that which human agency can produce or, if incapable of such production, must remain an object of hope. Happiness is no longer a *return* to the divine or to the eternal, but is that which is *to come* in a new world, a world of human making, moulded from an indifferent nature. In short, happiness becomes the object of a historical project for each self working together in community not only with its contemporaries, but also intergenerationally. Reason and faith become historicized for a self understanding itself within the trajectory of a greater destiny.

Despite the importance of the Stoics in the formation of the Modern self, the ideal of *apatheia* was not widely embraced. For all the philosophers we have dealt with, the passions were of crucial philosophical importance and the goal was not to suppress them but rather to bring them into harmony with reason, while recognizing (as Spinoza and Kant both did) that reason is itself passionate, driven by desire and love. The self which is formed here is a passionate self, desiring salvation and mastery.

The self formed in Modernity needs to build anew relations to God, nature and itself. This process went hand in hand with the formation of the Modern world. Such a rebuilding was made necessary by the collapse of the medieval world but was also made possible by the inheritance of Ancient Scepticism and Stoicism, and Medieval Augustinianism and Pelagianism, which each philosopher we have considered adopted and adapted in different ways. The result was a self delving deeper and deeper into its own self and through that self coming to think again as to what it means to reason, how it is possible to be happy and what the sense and purpose of its deepest passions are.

The poet Friedrich Hölderlin called Kant 'the Moses of our [German] nation',[3] who led through the critical desert but never fully entered the promised land of post-critical metaphysics. Those who came after Kant did not – unlike the Israelites – cross the Jordon into the 'promised land'. Since Kant, many deaths have been declared in the critical desert: the death of God (Nietzsche), the death of Nature (Merchant), the death of Man (Derrida) and the death of the Author (Barthes).[4] Concurrently, the four faces of the self in Modernity have each faded as the glory of the new age they proclaimed has given way to ever new captivities, renewed feelings of exile. The self along with

God and Nature have all become more philosophically elusive, where the very project of metaphysics has been proclaimed an idol to be shunned.

As we look back, it seems evident that we have descended from the heights of Modernity. The self which the Moderns formed is constitutive of us, yet the concerns, questions and hopes that motivated them are not ours. The project of mastery of nature out of mastery of self has left us in a new morass, where the plaintive declaration that 'only a god can save us'[5] in the Anthropocene age echoes the anxieties at the origins of Modernity in a tone that is, however, apocalyptic.

If we are living in the afterlife of Modernity, amongst the dispersed testimonies of its former aspirations, the self, Nature and God remain questionable and contested, both within and without the Academy. As we live through new wars of religion and bear witness to Nature as an agent of historical change, we need again to think, more urgently perhaps than ever before, what it means to be a self with others, dwelling in Nature and uncertainly facing a still absconded God, whose hiddenness may not yet be the last word.

Notes

Introduction

1. William Shakespeare, 'As You Like It', in *The Complete Works*, ed. Stanley Wells (Oxford: Clarendon, 1988), 2, 7, 139.
2. In 1690 a history of women philosophers was published in Latin under the title *Historia mulierum philosopharum*, written by Giles Menage. A translation is available under the title *The History of Women Philosophers*, trans. Beatrice H. Zedler (Lanham, MD: University Press of America, 1984). Thanks to Ulrike Hillerkuß for reference to this work. However, it is only in the present day that this acknowledgement of a female philosophical voice has been forcefully articulated, most recently in Rebecca Buxton and Lisa Whiting: *The Philosopher Queens* (London: Unbound, 2020)
3. Reinhart Koselleck, *Futures Past*, trans. Keith Tribe (Cambridge, MA: MIT Press, 1985), 267–88.
4. Ibid., 275.
5. Ibid., 276.
6. The guiding example for this is Martin Heidegger in his account of St. Paul. Heidegger understands Paul's *Letters* from the 'situation' in which he finds himself. With respect to the concerns of this book, I am aiming to interpret the philosophers examined here with respect to how they addressed their situations in their works. See Martin Heidegger, *The Phenomenology of Religious Life*, trans. Matthias Fritsch and Jennifer Gosetti-Ferencei (Bloomington: Indiana University Press, 2010), 61–5.
7. Eugen Fink, 'Operative Concepts in Husserl's Phenomenology', in *Apriori and World*, ed. William McKenna, Robert Harlan and Laurence Winters (Dordrecht: Martinus Nijhoff, 1981), 56–70.
8. Michel de Montaigne, *The Complete Essays of Montaigne*, trans. Donald Frame (Stanford: Stanford University Press, 1965); *Les essais de Michel de Montaigne*, ed. Pierre Villey (Paris: Alcan, 1922); 2, 17, 491 (book, essay and page number): 'We must not always say everything for that would be folly; but what we say must be what we think; otherwise it is wickedness.' Immanuel Kant, 'Letter to Mendelsohn 8th April 1766', in *Philosophical Correspondence*, ed. and trans. Arnulf Zweig (Cambridge: Cambridge University Press), 90; *Briefwechsel: Kant's Gesammelte Schriften 'Akademieausgabe'*, Königlich Preußische Akademie der Wissenschaften, Volume 10 (Berlin: Reimer, 1900) [henceforth AA], 69: 'Although I am absolutely convinced of many things that I will never have the courage to say, I shall never say anything I do not believe.'
9. Naturally, the theses of this book draw inspiration and ideas from others. The principal sources of that inspiration will become clear in the course of the book, but the main debts owed are to the following books: Charles Taylor, *Sources of the Self* (Cambridge, MA: Harvard University Press, 1989); Michael Gillespie, *The Theological*

Origins of Modernity (Chicago: Chicago University Press, 2009); Louis Dupré, *Passage to Modernity* (New Haven: Yale University Press, 1993); Stephen Toulmin, *Cosmopolis* (Chicago: University of Chicago Press, 1992); and Charles Taylor, *A Secular Age* (Cambridge, MA: Harvard University Press, 2007).

1 Four faces of the self in the emergence of modernity

1. Ezek. 1.10.
2. On the significance of the sea metaphor in Modernity, see Hans Blumenberg, *Shipwreck with Spectator*, trans. Steven Rendell (Cambridge, MA: MIT Press, 1997).
3. Ezekiel was a Hebrew prophet whose visions of the four-faced being or beings is understood by many biblical scholars to signify the coming of the Glory of God (*kabod Yahweh*) to Babylon, leaving the temple of Jerusalem and venturing into foreign and 'impure' lands. The four faces of the self in Modernity are a similar migration from their originating contexts to a new, uncertain reality.
4. The templates which we find being employed in this time are not confined to the four we will discuss here – Epicurean, Neoplatonic, Thomistic accounts could also be included, not to mention the more hermetic traditions. However, none of those had the dominance within the main currents of Modern thought as Augustinianism, Pelagianism, Stoicism and Scepticism did. The Epicurean remains a significant, if less explicit, presence, particularly in Montaigne, Spinoza and Hume. On this topic, see Catherine Wilson, *Epicureanism at the Origins of Modernity* (Oxford: Clarendon Press, 2008).
5. The reference is of course to Taylor's *Sources of the Self*.
6. Hans Blumenberg, *The Legitimacy of the Modern Age*, trans. Robert Wallace (Cambridge, MA: MIT Press, 1983).
7. Karl Löwith, *Meaning in History* (Chicago: University of Chicago Press, 2006).
8. Taylor, *A Secular Age*.
9. John Milbank, *Beyond Secular Reason* (London: Wiley Blackwell, 2013).
10. Gillespie, *The Theological Origins of Modernity*.
11. 'God is a debtor to no one since he confers everything gratuitously': Augustine of Hippo, 'The Free Choice of the Will', in *On the Free Choice of the Will, On Grace and Free Choice, and Other Writings*, ed. and trans. Peter King (Cambridge: Cambridge University Press, 2010), 3.16.
12. Cf. Augustine of Hippo, *Confessions*, trans. Henry Chadwick (Oxford: Oxford University Press, 2008), 7.20.
13. This gives metaphysical grounds for the virtue of humility in Augustine. See ibid., 7.9.
14. Reward in this context obeys the logic of debt, whereas faith is possible only in the dynamic of grace. Cf. Augustine of Hippo, 'On the Proceedings of Pelagius', in *Nicene and Post-Nicene Fathers of the Christian Church. Vol. 5*, ed. Philip Schaff, trans. Peter Holmes, Robert Wallis and Benjamin Warfield (Edinburgh: T&T Clark, 1997), 33: 'Whoever, therefore, is worthy to him it is due; and if it is thus due to him, it ceases to be grace; for grace is given, but a debt is paid.' Pelagius, on the other hand, sees reward unproblematically related to merit. See Pelagius, 'On Virginity', in *The Letters of Pelagius and His Followers*, ed. and trans. Brinley Rees (London: Boydell Press, 1991), 74.

15. Cf. Jean-Luc Marion, *In the Self's Place*, trans. Jeffrey Kosky (Stanford: Stanford University Press, 2012), 185–90, 197–201; Jacques Derrida, 'Differance', in *Speech and Phenomena and other Essays*, trans. David Allison (Evanston: Northwestern University Press, 1973), 129–60.
16. The test is itself revealing of grace. As Augustine states it, 'God bids us to do what we cannot, that we may know what we ought to seek from him' ('On Grace and Free Will', in *Nicene and Post-Nicene Fathers*, 32). Cf. John Hare, *The Moral Gap* (Oxford: Clarendon 2002), 25–6.
17. On the figure of doubting Thomas, cf. Glenn Most, *Doubting Thomas* (Cambridge, MA: Harvard University Press, 2005).
18. Augustine of Hippo, *City of God*, trans. Henry Bettenson (London: Penguin 1984), 13.4. As we will see, Kant makes a remarkably similar argument for the necessity of moral faith.
19. See Dietrich Bonhoeffer, *Creation and Fall*, trans. Douglas Bax (Minneapolis: Fortress Press, 2004), 111–2.
20. Friedrich Nietzsche, *Twilight of the Idols*, trans. Reginald Holingdale (London: Penguin, 1968), 38: 'I am afraid we cannot get rid of God because we still have faith in grammar.'
21. Cf. Philipp Cary, *Augustine's Invention of the Inner Self* (Oxford: Oxford University Press, 2006), 29–30.
22. Augustine of Hippo, *Confessions*, 7.10.
23. See Augustine, 'Of the Spirit and the Letter', in *Nicene and Post-Nicene Fathers*, 47.
24. Cf. Cary, *Augustine's Invention of the Inner Self*, 73–4.
25. See Augustine of Hippo, *Confessions*, 4.12.
26. Cf. Augustine of Hippo, *The Trinity*, trans. Stephen McKenna (Washington, DC: Catholic University of America Press, 2002), 6.10.12; on beauty in Augustine, see Jean-Michel Fontanier, *La Beauté selon Saint Augustin* (Rennes: Presses Universitaire de Rennes 2008).
27. Augustine of Hippo, *The Trinity*, 6.10.
28. Cf. John Milbank, *Theology and Social Theory* (London: Wiley Blackwell, 2006), 434.
29. Cf. Marion, *In the Self's Place*, 43–5; and John Manoussakis, *The Ethics of Time* (London: Bloomsbury, 2017), 38.
30. Augustine of Hippo, *Confessions*, 7.7: 'You knew what I endured but no man knew.'
31. For example, John Chrysostom, *Homilies on Genesis: The Fathers of the Church vol. 87*, trans. Robert Hull (Washington, DC: Catholic University of America Press, 2006); Basil of Caesarea, 'Hexaemeron', in *Saint Basil Collection* (London: Aeterna Press, 2016), 187–258; Augustine, *On Genesis*, trans. Ronald Teske (Washington, DC: Catholic University of America, 1991).
32. See Augustine of Hippo, *Confessions*, 11.12.
33. Cf. Henri de Lubac, *The Mystery of the Supernatural*, trans. Rosemary Sheed (London: Geoffrey Chapman, 1967), 77–8.
34. See Augustine of Hippo, *The Trinity*, 15.17.
35. As Hannah Arendt puts it, Augustine's 'quest … is for the God of the human heart' (*Love and Saint Augustine* (Chicago: University of Chicago Press, 2014), 25).
36. See Augustine of Hippo, *City of God*, 9.4–5.
37. Blumenberg, *Legitimacy of the Modern Age*, 53–61.
38. Quoted by Arendt, *Love and Augustine*, 9–10.
39. Cf. Augustine of Hippo, *Confessions*, 11.
40. Pelagius, 'On the Divine Law', in *Letters of Pelagius*, 91–2.

41. Pelagius, 'On Chastity', in ibid., 173–4.
42. See Augustine of Hippo, 'On Grace and Free Will', 9: 'And yet the determination of the human will is insufficient, unless the Lord grant it victory in answer to prayer that it enter not into temptation.'
43. Augustine of Hippo, 'On Nature and Grace', in *Nicene and Post-Nicene Fathers*, 20.
44. Augustine of Hippo, *Confessions*, 10.2.
45. See Augustine of Hippo, *The Trinity*, 10.5: 'For it [the mind] is not sufficient to itself, nor is anything at all sufficient to him who departs from Him who is alone sufficient.'
46. Augustine of Hippo, *Confessions*, 8.9.
47. Ibid.
48. Cf. Augustine of Hippo, *City of God*, 14.26.
49. See Pelagius, 'To Demetrias', in *Letters of Pelagius*, 38; 'On the Possibility of not Sinning', in ibid., 168.
50. Augustine, 'Free Choice of the Will', 2.13.
51. Ibid., 2.19.
52. Cf. Augustine of Hippo, *City of God*, 14.11.
53. Pelagius, 'On Virginity', 77.
54. Ibid.
55. Ibid., 82: 'No Christian is permitted to sin.'
56. Cf. Augustine of Hippo, 'On Nature and Grace', 22.
57. See *Letters of Pelagius*, 44. See also Sebastian Thier, *Die Kirche bei Pelagius* (Berlin: de Gruyter 1999), 74–5, 78–9.
58. As Brinley Rees makes clear, in contrast to Augustine, for Pelagius, God's acts of grace come from without rather than within. See *Pelagius: A Reluctant Heretic* (London: Boydell Press, 1988), 36.
59. Augustine, 'Of the Spirit and the Letter', 13. The passage in the book of Romans ends as follows: 'The real Jew is one who is inwardly a Jew, and real circumcision is in the heart, a thing not of the letter but of the spirit' (2.29).
60. Augustine, 'Of the Spirit and the Letter', 6. This echoes the famous account of raiding an orchard as a boy: 'Our real pleasure consisted in doing something that was forbidden' (*Confessions*, 2.4).
61. See Pelagius, 'On the Possibility of not Sinning', in *Letters of Pelagius*, 167: 'If even human nature thinks it unfair to order anyone to do something impossible, how perverse it is to believe God to be capable of something which not even the nature of mortals would respect!' This text was probably written by a follower of Pelagius rather than Pelagius himself, but it reflects what we know of his teaching. See also 'To Demetrias', 53–4.
62. 'To Demetrias', 37.
63. Augustine of Hippo, *Confessions* 5.10–11.
64. Pelagius, 'To Demetrias', 38. Cf. Thier, *Kirche bei Pelagius*, 53.
65. See *Confessions*, 7.13–14.
66. On this theme, see Thier, *Kirche bei Pelagius*, 79–80.
67. Pelagius, *Letters of Pelagius*, 113.
68. Augustine of Hippo, 'On Nature and Grace', 39.
69. Pelagius, 'To Demetrias', 39. Cf. Pelagius, *Commentary on St. Paul's Letter to the Romans*, trans. Theodore De Bruyn (Oxford: Clarendon Press, 1993), 65.
70. Pelagius, *Letter and Confession of Faith to Innocent I*, confession 25; see also Their, *Kirche bei Pelagius*, 81–9.
71. Augustine of Hippo, 'On Nature and Grace', 59.

72. See Henri de Lubac, *Augustinianism and Modern Theology*, trans. Lancelot Sheppard (New York: Crossroad Publishing, 2000), 145–83.
73. For this reason Pelagius emphasizes the example of Christ as one to imitate. See, for example, Pelagius, 'On the Christian Life', in *Letters of Pelagius*, 112–3: 'He is a Christian who is one not only in name but in deed, who imitates and follows Christ in everything.'
74. Augustine, 'Of the Spirit and the Letter', 7.
75. Pelagius, *Letters of Pelagius*, 82.
76. Augustine, 'On Forgiveness of Sins and Baptism', in *Nicene and Post-Nicene Fathers*, 2.4.
77. Augustine, 'Of the Spirit and the Letter', ch. 20.
78. For this reason Augustine recognizes the need for a Sceptical moment in faith, but one which does not rest with doubt. See Augustine of Hippo, 'Against the Academicians', in *Against the Academicians and The Teacher*, trans. Peter King (London: Hackett, 1995), 1–93; and *Confessions*, 5.10.
79. Pelagianism was condemned at the Church councils of Carthage (418) and Ephesus (431).
80. This term is a problematic one, but the basic issue here is that Augustine's account of grace for many who followed him in rejecting Pelagianism did not give enough account to human agency. As we will see, this becomes a particularly contentious issue in the wake of the Reformation and the revival of Augustinianism in early modernity more generally.
81. Despite these differences, it seems to me to overstate the case to say, as William Bouswama does, that Stoicism and Augustinianism are 'antithetical versions of human existence' ('The Two Faces of Humanism: Stoicism and Augustinianism in Renaissance Thought', in *A Usable Past* (Berkeley: University of California Press, 1990), 20).
82. To speak here of 'autonomy' is certainly anachronistic. Nevertheless, the basis of an account of the autonomous self is already contained in Pelagius's work, which directly and (mostly) indirectly influences the development of the idea of autonomy, as we will see.
83. Epictetus, 'Discourses', in *Discourses and Selected Writings*, ed. and trans. Robert Dobbin (London: Penguin 2008), 4.1.175.
84. Epictetus, 'Fragments', in *Discourses and Selected Writings*, 4.
85. Epictetus, 'Discourses', 1.6.
86. Epictetus, 'Enchiridion', in *Discourses and Selected Writings*, 17.
87. Ibid., 11: 'Did a child of yours die? No, it was returned … Why concern yourself with the means by which the original giver effects its return?'
88. Seneca, 'On Anger', in *Moral and Political Essays*, ed. and trans. John Cooper and J. F. Procopé (Cambridge: Cambridge University Press, 1995), 2.2.
89. Epictetus, 'Fragments', 9.
90. Epictetus, 'Enchiridion', 20: 'If someone succeeds in provoking you, realize that your mind is complicit in the provocation.'
91. Epictetus, 'Discourses', 2.8.11.
92. See ibid., 1.22.
93. Ibid., 1.1.
94. Ibid., 1.12.34.
95. Hannah Arendt, 'Willing', in *The Life of the Mind* (London: Harcourt and Brace, 1978), 74.

96. Ibid., 74–5.
97. Epictetus, 'Discourses', 4.1.99.
98. An issue which was much debated in Antiquity and is still a matter of scholarly debate is the relation of Pyrrhonian to Academic Scepticism. The distinction is often ignored by the philosophers of Modernity. It is the rediscovery of Pyrrhonian Scepticism which was decisive in reigniting Scepticism in Modernity, and for this reason I am concentrating almost exclusively on it here. I will, however, have occasion below (particularly with respect to Hume) to return to the distinction of Academic and Pyrrhonian Scepticism. On this question, see Luciano Floridi, *Sextus Empiricus* (Cambridge: Cambridge University Press, 2002).
99. Sextus, at the beginning of his *The Skeptic Way: Outlines of Pyrrhonism*, trans. Benson Bates (Oxford: Oxford University Press, 1996), divides philosophers into three groups: dogmatists, who think they have found the truth; academics, who doubt everything; and Sceptics, who continue to seek the truth. Significantly, and we will return to this in the next section, Pico della Mirandola, who we know possessed Greek manuscripts of Sextus, writing in the fifteenth century, divides all thinkers into dogmatists, who affirm; academics, who deny; and Pyrrhonists, who doubt. See Don Allen, *Doubt's Boundless Sea* (Baltimore: John Hopkins University Press, 1969), 75–7.
100. Sextus, *Outlines*, 1.7.
101. Ibid., 1.4: 'The Skeptic way is the disposition (*dunamis*) to oppose phenomena and noumena to one another ... with the result that, owing to the equipollence among things and statements thus approved, we are brought first to *epoché* and then to *ataraxia*.'
102. Ibid., 1.10.
103. Ibid., 1.12.
104. Ibid., 1.20–22.
105. Ibid., 1.7.
106. Sextus Empiricus, *Against the Logicians*, trans. Richard Bett (Cambridge: Cambridge University Press, 2006), 2.20.
107. Ibid., 1.63.
108. Ibid., 1.344.
109. Ibid., 1. 383.
110. Blumenberg, *The Legitimacy of the Modern Age*, 8.
111. Cf. Dupré, *Passage to Modernity*, 79–90.
112. Blumenberg, *The Legitimacy of the Modern Age*, 37–51.
113. See Hans Jonas, *The Gnostic Religion* (Boston: Beacon Press, 2001), 48–100. On the influence of Gnosticism in Modernity, cf. Cyril O'Regan, *Gnostic Return in Modernity* (Albany: SUNY Press, 2001).
114. Blumenberg, *The Legitimacy of the Modern Age*, 47–50, 129–36.
115. For an account which emphasizes the importance of monotheism for the development of a concept of world, see Klaus Held, *Der biblische Glaube* (Frankfurt a. M.: Klostermann, 2018).
116. See Paul, 'Letter to the Ephesians', 1.10.
117. Cf. Koselleck, *Futures Past*, 62. On the history of the early modernity as one of 'Christianization', see Taylor, *A Secular Age*, 66–7.
118. Cf. Kurt Flasch, *Einführung in die Philosophie des Mittelatlers* (Berlin: Wissenschaftliche Buchgesellschaft, 1994), 2.
119. David Piché, *La Condemnation Parisienne de 1277* (Paris: Vrin, 1999), 58.
120. Alain de Libera, *Raison et Foi* (Paris: Seuil, 2003), 182.

121. Piché, *La Condemnation,* 106–7 (my translation).
122. On the theme of the supernatural in Aquinas and later, see Dupré, *Passage to Modernity,* 171–2. Dupré places the emergence of the supernatural as a separate domain in the sixteenth century, downplaying the development of this distinction much earlier, in fact, contemporaneous with Aquinas, as witnessed particularly in Boethius of Dacia, Siger of Brabant and to some extent also in Albert the Great. On these developments, see Libera, *Raison et Foi,* 100–18.
123. Thomas Aquinas, *Summa Theologia,* trans. Fathers of the English Dominican Province (Allen, TX: Thomas More, 1981), 1, q.1, a. 8, ad. 2.
124. Boethius of Dacia, *De Aeternitate mundi* (Berlin: Gruyter, 1964), 59.
125. See Simo Knuuttila, *Emotion in Ancient and Medieval Philosophy* (Oxford: Oxford University Press, 2004), 205.
126. See Gillespie, *The Theological Origins of Modernity,* 21–3, on the emphasis on divine omnipotence and how this was taken up by William of Okham.
127. See Thomas Aquinas, *Summa Contra Gentiles: Book Three,* trans. Vernon Bourke (Notre Dame, IN: University of Notre Dame Press, 1975), ch. 67.
128. Piché, *La Condemnation,* 98–9 (my translation into English).
129. See Libera, *Raison et Foi,* 221–30 and 268–70 on the ambiguous place of Aquinas and Albertus Magnus with respect to these condemnations.
130. Cf. Luciano Bianchi, 'Students, Masters, and 'Heterodox' Doctrines at the Parisian Faculty of Arts in the 1270s,' *Recherches de Théologie et Philosophie Médiévales,* 76 (2009): 75–109; Alain de Libera, *Penser au Moyen Âge* (Paris: Seuil, 1991); and John Wippel, 'The Condemnations of 1270 and 1277 at Paris,' *Journal of Medieval and Renaissance Studies,* 7 (1977): 169–201.
131. Pierre Duhem, *Medieval Cosmology,* trans. Rojer Ariew (Chicago: Chicago University Press, 1985), 4, claims that the 1277 Condemnations is the 'birth certificate' of Modernity. Cf. Piché, *La Condemnation,* 287.
132. William of Ockham, 'Quodlibeta' 6 Q. 6, in *Philosophical Writings,* trans. Philotheus Boehner and Stephen Brown (Indianapolis: Hackett, 1990), 25.
133. This consequence was anticipated by the 1277 Condemnations of Aristotelian doctrines on the basis of a claim to the omnipotence of God. On this theme, see Milbank, *Beyond Secular Reason,* 34–49. Cf. Dupré, *Passage to Modernity,* 15–41.
134. On possible worlds in Medieval thought, see Rémi Brague, *La Sagesse du Monde* (Paris: Fayard, 1999), 265–7. The quotation is from page 267.
135. Dupré, *Passage to Modernity,* 40. Following Duns Scotus, Ockham affirms the relata to be prior to the relation; see Marilyn Adams, 'Ockham on Will, Nature and Morality', in *The Cambridge Companion to Ockham,* ed. Paul Spade (Cambridge: Cambridge University Press, 1999), 247–9.
136. Martin Heidegger, *Introduction to Metaphysics,* trans. Gregory Fried and Richard Polt (New Haven: Yale University Press 2000), 7–8.
137. See Aquinas, *Summa Contra Gentiles,* 3.112.
138. Ockham, 'Quodlibeta' 1 Q. 13, in *Philosophical Writings,* 28.
139. Ibid., 138.
140. Implicit here is the fruitful analysis of Stephen Toulmin's two beginnings of Modernity, one humanistic and literate, the other rationalist and scientific. See Toulmin, *Cosmopolis,* 23–44.
141. Cf. Gillespie, *The Theological Origins of Modernity,* 23.
142. See Gen. 1.24: 'Let us make man in our own image, in the likeness of ourselves.'
143. Aquinas, *Summa Theologia,* 1, Q. 93, a. 4.

144. Augustine of Hippo, *City of God*, 11.26.
145. Cf. Gillespie, *The Theological Origins of Modernity*, 20–1.
146. Arendt, 'Willing', 117. Cf. Taylor, *Sources of the Self*, 135–8.
147. *The Trinity*, 14.8.
148. See Arendt, 'Willing', 120.
149. Epictetus, 'Fragments', 9.
150. See Adams, 'Ockham on Will', 255–7.
151. See Brague, *Le Sagesse du Monde*, 238.
152. The question here is whether revelation is compatible with reason or is not compatible. For a classic account of this question, see Stephen Evans, *Faith beyond Reason* (Grand Rapids, MI: Eerdmann, 1998)
153. Ockham, 'Quodlibeta' 5, Q. 1, in *Philosophical Writings*, 97–100.
154. Franz Rosenzweig, *Star of Redemption*, trans. William Hallo (Notre Dame, IN: Notre Dame Press 1985), 106–7.
155. Augustine of Hippo, *City of God*, 21.8.
156. Pascal was one of the earliest to view with horror this infinite universe and its indifference to human life. See Brague, *La Sagesse du Monde*, 279–80. On the relation of this sense of meaninglessness in Pascal to Gnosticism, see Jonas, *The Gnostic Religion*, 320–30.
157. Alluding here to the title of Don Allen's book.
158. On the history of the passions and the emergence of 'emotions' in Modernity, see Thomas Dixon, *From Passions to Emotions* (Cambridge: Cambridge University Press, 2003).
159. See Günther Abel, *Stoizismus und frühe Neuzeit* (Berlin: de Gruyter 1978), 36–9.
160. Justus Lipsius, *On Constancy*, trans. John Stradling (Liverpool: Liverpool University Press, 2006), 1.1.
161. Ibid., 1.3.
162. See Abel, *Stoizismus und frühe* Neuzeit, 25–6.
163. Lipsius, *On Constancy*, 1.4.
164. See Taylor on the hyper-Augustinianism of early modernity, *Sources of the Self*, 246–7.
165. The classic debate of the period between Erasmus and Luther exemplifies this, with Luther playing the role of Augustine and Erasmus that of Pelagius. This example also brings out the complexities of this debates as Erasmus saw himself writing within an Augustinian framework. Erasmus/Luther, *Free Will and Salvation*, trans. Gordon Rupp (London: SCM Press, 1969).
166. Pelagius, 'To Demetrias', 45.
167. *The Trinity*, 14.8.
168. Dupré, *Passage to Modernity*, 124.
169. Luther/Eramus, *Free Will and Salvation*, 189: Carnal reason 'thinks man is mocked by an impossible precept, whereas we say that he is warned and aroused by it to see his own impotence'.
170. William of Ockham, *Predestination, God's Foreknowledge and Future Contingents*, translated by Marilyn Adams and Norman Kretzmann (Indianapolis: Hackett, 1983), 77–9.
171. De Lubac, *The Mystery of the Supernatural*, 89–9.
172. See ibid., 89.
173. A nature without any supernatural end.
174. Fransesco Petrarch, *The Secret*, trans. Carrol Quillen (Boston: Bedford St. Martins, 2003), 55–6.

175. Augustine *Confessions*, 8.12.
176. Ibid.
177. Augustine of Hippo, *City of God*, 5.8.
178. Petrarch, *The Secret*, 83.
179. Ibid., 59.
180. Ibid., 148.
181. Pico della Mirandola, *Oration on the Dignity of Man*, trans. Franseco Borghesi (Cambridge: Cambridge University Press, 2012), 117.
182. Ibid., 135.
183. Ibid., 145.
184. Ibid., 135.
185. Ibid., 149.
186. Ibid., 153.
187. Ibid., 163–9. These mysteries are to be found in Christianity and Judaism, but also among the Ancient Greeks, and it is significant that he ends the 'Oration' with reference to the Eleuusinian mysteries.
188. See *City of God*, 14.9: 'Their feeling of pride increases in exact proportion as their feeling of pain decreases.'
189. Augustine of Hippo, *Confessions*, 11.29.
190. Cf. José Neto, *The Christianization of Pyrrhonism* (Dordrecht: Kluwer 1995).
191. The Scepticism which arose in early modernity is, however, relatively discontinuous with forms of Medieval Scepticism. On this theme, see Charles Schmitt, 'The Rediscovery of Greek Scepticism in Modern Times', in *The Skeptical Tradition*, ed. Myles Burnyeat (Berkeley: University of California Press, 1983), 226–8.
192. Quoted in Stephen Menn, *Descartes and Augustine* (Cambridge: Cambridge University Press, 2002), 191.
193. Augustine of Hippo, 'Against the Academicians', 2.12.24.
194. Sextus, *Outlines*, 1.14.135–140.
195. It is in the light of this that we can appreciate Terence Penelham's claim that 'the theme of the hiddenness of God is the most important legacy of Sceptical fideism' ('Skepticism and Fideism', in *The Skeptical Tradition*, 307).
196. In this respect I agree with Löwith when he claims that Scepticism and faith have the same results with respect to the outcome of history, namely, a resignation in the face of the unpredictability of historical issues (*Meaning in History*, 199). Faith and Scepticism merge in Modernity as a rejection of the presumption of confidence in history and in meaning generally. For a critical discussion of Blumenberg's account of Augustine, see Joseph Rivera, 'Blumenberg's Problematic Secularization Thesis: Augustine, Curiositas and the Emergence of Late Modernity', *Religions*, 12, no. 5 (2021): 297.
197. On this question, see Jerome Schneewind, *The Invention of Autonomy* (Cambridge: Cambridge University Press, 1998).
198. In this sense, Blumenberg's analysis is correct, that what we find both with the rise of Christianity and Modernity are new answers ill-suited to respond to the questions which motivated the systems that they replace. This he terms a process of 're-occupation of answer positions' (*Legitimacy of the Modern Age*, 69). However, the substitution is not as 'clean' as I think Blumenberg assumes. In any case, what is 're-occupied' is a particular mode of Christianity – theology in the sense of the synthesis of Aristotle and Scripture – and that which does the reoccupying are rethought and reimagined Ancient Greek and Christian modes of being a self.

199. This understanding as Scepticism as doubt, which in effect conflates Pyrrhonianism and Academic Scepticism, can already be found in the sixth-century scholar St. Bede's philosophical lexicon. Cf. Floridi, *Sextus Empiricus*, 17-18.
200. *Sexti Empirici Opera graece et latine: Pyrrhonias institutiones continens* (Lipsiae: Kuehnianae, 1840), ch. 16.
201. Ibid., ch. 11.
202. Cf. Myles Burnyeat, 'The Sceptic in His Time And Place', in *Scepticism from the Renaissance to the Enlightenment*, ed. Richard Popkin (Ann Arbor: University of Michigan Press, 1997), 29-32.
203. Julia Annas and Jonathan Barnes put it well: 'The Pyrrhonists are not assuming that when we attend to the "appearances" we are attending to a peculiar sort of entity, a mental image or sense datum ... to attend to appearances is simply to attend to the way in which things appear.' (*The Modes of Scepticism* (Cambridge: Cambridge University Press, 1985), 23).
204. Cf. Floridi, *Sextus Empiricus*, 74-6; and Allen, *Doubt's Boundless Sea*, 77.
205. Cf. Richard Popkin, *The History of Scepticism* (Chicago: University of Chicago Press, 1979), 5-16.
206. Montaigne, *Essays*, 1, 12, 375.

2 Montaigne: Sceptical alterity

1. 'An exercise in approaching a horizon of possibilities' in Lawrence Kritzman's words (*The Fabulous Imagination* (New York: Columbia University Press, 2009), 4).
2. Montaigne, *Essays*, 1, 26, 108-9.
3. Ibid., 3, 2, 611.
4. Furthermore, the Augustinian movement within goes hand in hand with a movement above towards God. See Philipp Carey, *Augustine's Invention of the Inner Self* (Oxford: Oxford University Press, 2000). Jean Starobinski, *Montaigne in Motion*, trans. Arthur Goldhammer (Chicago: University of Chicago Press, 1985), 12, emphasizes this difference. For an analysis of this question of autobiography in Montaigne and Augustine, see Nicholas Paige, *Being Interior* (Philadelphia: University of Pennsylvania Press, 2001), 21-64. On the rhetorical devices Montaigne employs in portraying himself, see Steven Rendall, 'The Rhetoric of Montaigne' s Self-Portrait: Speaker and Subject', *Studies in Philology*, 73, no. 3 (1976): 285-301. This question becomes problematized by Rousseau in his *Confessions*, which can be seen as a reply, in places a parody, of Augustine's *Confessions*. Cf. Ann Hartle, *The Modern Self in Rousseau's Confessions* (Notre Dame, IN: University of Notre Dame Press, 1983).
5. He uses this term twice in the *Essays*. Although he does not cite Nicholas of Cusa, Cusa's works were in his library and he does seem to have been influenced by him. On this theme, see Raymond Esclapez, 'Montaigne et Nicolas de Cuse. Le thème de la "docte ignorance" dans les Essais', *Littératures*, 18 (1988): 25-40.
6. Montaigne, *Essays*, 3, 1, 601: 'head high, face and heart open.' Cf. Pierre Manent, *Montaigne*, trans. Paul Seaton (Notre Dame, IN: University of Notre Dame Press, 2020), 49.
7. See Montaigne, *Essays*, 3, 2, 613.
8. On the history of the concept of 'crisis', see Reinhart Koselleck and Michaela W. Richter, 'Crisis', *Journal of the History of Ideas*, 67, no. 2 (2006): 357-400. Thanks to Blake Ewing for alerting me to this article.

9. *Essays*, 2, 12, 409.
10. Cf. Donald Frame, 'Did Montaigne betray Sebond', *Romantic Review*, 38, no. 4 (1947): 297–326.
11. Lucien Lefebvre, *The Problem of Unbelief in the Sixteenth Century* (Cambridge, MA: Harvard University Press, 1982, 353): 'To speak of rationalism and free thought when we are dealing with an age when the most intelligent of men ... [w]ere truly incapable of finding any support in philosophy or science against a religion whose dominance was universal, is to speak of an illusion.'
12. Cf. Ann Hartle, *Accidental Philosopher* (Cambridge: Cambridge University Press, 2003), 135–44.
13. For the classic account of Montaigne as a Sceptical fideist, see Frédéric Brahami, *Le scepticisme de Montaigne* (Paris: Presses Universitaire de Paris, 1997).
14. Montaigne, *Essays*, 1, 37, 169.
15. Ibid., 2, 10, 298.
16. Cf. Steven Rendall, 'Dialectical Structure and Tactics in Montaigne's 'Of Cannibals', *Pacific Coast Philology*, 12 (1977): 56–63.
17. Montaigne, *Essays*, 1, 27, 132.
18. The 'wisest school of philosophers' as he says (ibid., 2.15, 463).
19. Ibid., 2, 12, 374.
20. Cf. ibid., 1, 51, 220.
21. On this, see Manent, *Montaigne*, 24.
22. Montaigne, *Essays*, 2, 12, 422.
23. Ibid., 1, 14, 33.
24. Ibid., 1, 51, 220.
25. For the discussion of illusion, see ibid., 3, 11, 789; on dreams, apart from scattered references the only sustained discussion is with respect to divination through dreams, see ibid., 3, 13, 843.
26. Ibid., 2, 16, 474; see also ibid., 3, 2, F. 613: 'Others ... see not so much your nature as your art.'
27. Ibid., 2, 1, 244.
28. Ibid., 2, 1, 242.
29. Ibid., 3, 13, 824: 'My own life mirrored in that of others.'
30. Ibid., 2, 6, 243.
31. Ibid., 2, 16, 474.
32. Ibid., 3, 2, 611.
33. See Edmund Husserl, *Ideas Pertaining to a Pure Phenomenology, Book 1*, trans. Fred Kersten (The Hague: Kluwer, 1983), 56–7.
34. Montaigne, *Essays*, 2, 17, 499.
35. Ibid., 2, 3, 251.
36. Hartle (*Accidental Philosopher*, 23) puts it very well when she says that his 'credulity *is* his scepticism'.
37. Montaigne, *Essays*, 2, 3, 134.
38. Ibid., 2, 12, 328.
39. Ibid., 3, 8, 704.
40. Ibid., 2, 17, 480.
41. Ibid., 1, 23, 79.
42. Ibid., 1, 23, 80.
43. Ibid.
44. 'Custom' and 'habit' are rendered by the same word '*coutume*' in Montaigne's French.

45. Montaigne, *Essays*, 2, 30, 539.
46. Ibid., 1, 49, 216.
47. Ibid., 1, 23, 83.
48. Ibid.
49. Gen. 18.14.
50. See Hartle, *Accidental Philosopher*, 161–2. In this Montaigne draws on the Voluntarist notion of possibility. On the latter, see Milbank, *Beyond Secular Reason*, 34–49.
51. Montaigne, *Essays*, 3, 10, 773.
52. See ibid., 2, 37, 598.
53. On this topic, see Kritzman, *The Fabulous Imagination*, 161; and Ann Hartle, *Montaigne and the Origins of Modern Philosophy* (Evanston, IL: Northwestern University Press, 2013), 7–10.
54. Montaigne, *Essays*, 3, 11, 785.
55. Ibid.
56. Cf. Maurice Merleau-Ponty, 'Reading Montaigne', in *Signs*, trans. Richard McCleary (Evanston, IL: Northwestern University Press, 1964), 203: 'As there is an invocation of an unknown god in Montaigne, there is the invocation of an impossible reason.'
57. Montaigne, *Essays*, 1, 23, 80.
58. See ibid., 1, 27, 132: 'If we call prodigies or miracles whatever our reason cannot reach, how many of these appear continually before our eyes.'
59. Augustine appears to make the same point, but while for Montaigne the monstrous shows us the wonders of nature, for Augustine they show us that God 'is to do what he prophesied', namely, to raise the dead in the next life. See *City of God*, 21.9, 983. The monstrous as deformed does not exist for Augustine, but for Montaigne everything is monstrous as he rejects (taking Ockham to his logical conclusion) the idea of fixed form. See Brahami, *Le scepticisme de Montaigne*, 81–2.
60. Montaigne, *Essays*, 3, 11, 787.
61. See Edmund Husserl, *Experience and Judgement*, trans. James Churchill (Evanston, IL: Northwestern University Press, 1973), 340–8.
62. Montaigne, Essays, 2, 1, 242: '*Distinguo* is the most universal member of my logic.'
63. Ibid., 2, 14, 463.
64. Ibid.
65. Ibid., 1, 23, 80.
66. Ibid., 1, 49, 216.
67. Ibid., 3, 2, 611.
68. Cf. Hartle, *Accidental Philosopher*, 23, 103.
69. Cf. Montaigne, *Essays*, 2, 10, 297.
70. Ibid., 3, 19, 780.
71. See Paul Ricoeur, *Freud and Philosophy*, trans. Dennis Savage (New Haven: Yale University Press, 1977), 495–6.
72. On the return to the pre-philosophical see Hartle, *Accidental Philosopher*, 106.
73. Montaigne, *Essays*, 1, 54, 227.
74. Ibid., 1, 23, 86.
75. Ibid., 3, 13, 815; the famous line in the *Metaphysics* reads, 'By nature all men [sic] long to know', Aristotle, *Metaphysics*, trans. Hugh Lawson-Tancred (London: Penguin, 1998), 980a1.
76. Montaigne, *Essays*, 2, 17, 497.
77. Ibid., 2, 15, 463.
78. Ibid., 3, 13, 815.

79. Ibid.
80. Ibid., 3, 13, 816.
81. Ibid., 3, 13, 821.
82. Ibid., 3, 1, 604: 'Justice in itself, natural and universal, is regulated otherwise and more nobly than that other, special, national justice, constrained to the need of our governments ... *we use only the shadow and reflection of it* [justice] (Cicero).'
83. Ibid., 3, 13, 822.
84. Ibid.
85. Ibid., 3, 13, 818.
86. Ibid., 3, 13, 830.
87. Ibid., 3, 13, 855–6.
88. Ibid., 3. 13, 855.
89. Ibid., 2, 17, 485.
90. Ibid., 3, 13, 856.
91. Ibid.
92. Ibid., 3, 13, 857.
93. Ibid., 3, 13, 835.
94. Hartle, *Montaigne and the Origins of Modern Philosophy*, 41–3.
95. Montaigne, *Essays*, 2, 12, 324. I will return to this quotation in the final section.
96. Ibid., 2, 12, 325.
97. Cf. ibid., 1, 26, 128.
98. Ibid., 3, 2, 615.
99. Ibid., 2, 18, 504.
100. Ibid., 2, 6, 273.
101. Augustine, *City of God*, 11.26.
102. Montaigne, *Essays*, 'To the Reader', 2.
103. Ibid., 1, 14, 38.
104. Ibid., 1, 20, 61.
105. Ibid., 1, 20, 60: 'He who has learned to die has unlearned how to be a slave.' On the Stoic basis for Montaigne's account, see Kritzman, *The Fabulous Imagination*, 10–13. On the comparison to Pascal on this issue, see Manent, *Montaigne*, 29–30.
106. Montaigne, *Essays*, 2, 6, 270.
107. Ibid., 'To the Reader', 2.
108. Ibid., 3, 17, 834.
109. Ibid., 2, 16, 468.
110. Ibid., 2, 12, 423.
111. Ibid., 2, 12, 326.
112. Ibid., 2, 12, 455.
113. Plutarch, 'Que signifioit ce mot E'i, qui estoit engravé sur les portes du temple d'Apollo en la ville de Delphes', in *Les oeuvres morales & meslees de Plutarque*, volume 12, trans. Jacques Amyot (into French) (Paris: Imprimerie de Vascosan, 1572), 356–357A–E.
114. Montaigne, *Essays*, 1, 56, 234.
115. Ibid., 1, 56, 229–30.
116. Ibid., 1, 56, 232.
117. Ibid., 2, 12, 403.
118. Ibid., 1, 56, 229.
119. Ibid., 1, 20, 56.
120. Ibid., 2, 16, 471.

121. Ibid., 2, 16, 478.
122. Ibid., 2, 16, 471.
123. In this context Montaigne speaks of the self's doubleness. See ibid., 2, 16, 469: 'We are, I know not how, double within ourselves, with the result that we do not believe what we believe and cannot rid ourselves of what we condemn.'
124. Ibid., 2, 16, 470.
125. Ibid., 2, 16, 474.
126. Ibid.
127. Ibid., 2, 17, 491.
128. Ibid.
129. See the essay 'Of Friendship', in ibid., 1, 28, 135–44.
130. Ibid., 2, 17, 491.
131. Ibid., 3, 9, 747.
132. Ibid., 2, 11, 306.
133. Ibid., 1, 1. 240.
134. Ibid., 3, 2, 611.
135. Ibid., 2, 1, 239.
136. Ibid., 3, 2, 610.
137. See ibid., 2, 37, 574: 'trace the course of my mutations'.
138. Ibid., 3, 2, 610.
139. Ibid., 2, 11, 312.
140. Cf. ibid., 2, 11, 309 and 3, 5, 682.
141. Ibid., 1, 20, 56.
142. Ibid., 1, 20, 57.
143. Ibid., 1, 30, 148.
144. Ibid., 1, 14, 462–3.
145. Ibid., 2, 15, 463.
146. Augustine, *Confessions*, 10, 1.
147. Ibid., 1, 1.
148. Ibid., 3, 2, 610
149. Ibid., 3, 2, 612.
150. On this topic, see Hartle, *Accidental Philosopher*, 109–10.
151. Montaigne, *Essays*, 1, 9, 23.
152. Ibid., 3, 2, 612.
153. Ibid.
154. Ibid.
155. Ibid., 3, 2, 613.
156. Ibid.
157. Ibid., 3, 2, 615.
158. Ibid., 3, 2, 617.
159. Ibid., 3, 2, 619.
160. Ibid., 3, 2, 614.
161. Ibid., 3, 2, 620.
162. Ibid.
163. Ibid., 2, 12, 457.
164. Ibid., 2, 12, 321. As Brahami argues, Montaigne is here rejecting the Pelagianism of Sebond and denying that reason can reach beyond the natural to the supernatural. See Brahami, *Le scepticisme de Montaigne*, 24, 59.
165. Montaigne, *Essays*, 2, 12, 324.

166. Sextus, *Outlines*, 1, 14, 79.
167. Montaigne, *Essays*, 2, 12, 326, my emphasis.
168. Ibid.
169. Ibid., 2, 12, 325.
170. For an account of Montaigne as a 'conformist fideist', see Terence Penelham, *God and Skepticism* (Dordrecht: Springer, 2012), 23–6.
171. Montaigne, *Essays*, 2, 12, 326.
172. Ibid., 2, 39, 539. Cf. Kritzman, *The Fabulous Imagination*, 57–65.
173. Montaigne, *Essays*, 2, 12, 329.
174. Sextus, *Outlines*, 1, 14, 36–78.
175. Montaigne, *Essays*, 2, 12, 331.
176. Ibid., 2, 12, 333.
177. Ibid., 2, 12, 343.
178. Ibid., 2, 12, 337.
179. Ibid., 2, 12, 369.
180. Ibid., 2, 12, 370.
181. Ibid., 2, 12, 369–70: 'Let us bring to it [supernatural and heavenly knowledge] nothing of our own except obedience and submission.'
182. Ibid., 2, 12, 371–2.
183. Ibid., 2, 12, 372.
184. Ibid., 1, 21, 68.
185. Ibid., 2, 12, 374.
186. Ibid., 2, 12, 375.
187. Ibid. Cf. Starobinski, *Montaigne in Motion*, 80–1.
188. Montaigne, *Essays*, 2, 12, 329.

3 Descartes, Pascal and the ambiguity of the self

1. On this theme of rupture between these two eras, see Toulmin, *Cosmopolis*, 45–56.
2. On happiness in Descartes, see Adriaan Peperzak, 'Life, Science, and Wisdom According to Descartes', *History of Philosophy Quarterly*, 12, no. 2 (1995): 133–53. On the relation of practical and speculative knowledge in Descartes, see Rémi Brague, *The Kingdom of Man*, trans. Paul Seaton (Notre Dame, IN: Notre Dame University Press, 2018), 70–2.
3. On the history of Jansenism, see William Doyle, *Jansenism* (London: Macmillan, 1999).
4. For an account of Molina's theology of grace, see Matthias Kaufmann and Alexander Aichele, *A Companion to Luis de Molina* (Leiden: Brill, 2014).
5. Cf. Leszek Kolakowski, *God Owes Us Nothing* (Chicago: University of Chicago Press, 1995), 86–102.
6. On the relation of Cartesianism to Jansenism, cf. Tad Schmaltz, 'What Has Cartesianism to Do with Jansenism?' *Journal of the History of Ideas*, 60, no. 1 (1999): 37–56.
7. Cf. Michel Le Guern, *Pascal et Descartes* (Paris: Nizet, 1971), 10–11.
8. 'The eternal silence of these infinite spaces terrifies me,' Blaise Pascal, *Pensées*, trans. Alban Krailsheimer (London: Penguin Books, 1966), 201. This edition is based on the edition edited by Louis Lafuma, *Pensées* (Paris: Seuil, 1962).

9. Rene Descartes, 'Meditations', in *The Philosophical Writings of Descartes, Vol. 2*, trans. John Cottingham, Robert Stoothoff and Dugald Murdoch (Cambridge: Cambridge University Press 1984), 12; *Oeuvres de Descartes. Tome 7*, ed. Charles Adam et Paul Tannery (Paris: Vrin, 1966) [henceforth AT 7], 35, 51; Pascal, *Pensées*, 503: 'nature is the image of grace'.
10. On the autobiographical nature of the 'Discourse', see Jonathan Rée, 'Descartes' Comedy', *Philosophy and Literature*, 8, no. 2 (1984): 153.
11. René Descartes, 'Discourse on Method', in *The Philosophical Writings of Descartes, Vol. 1*, trans. John Cottingham, Robert Stoothoff and Dugald Murdoch (Cambridge: Cambridge University Press, 1984), 117; *Oeuvres de Descartes. Tome 6*, ed. Charles Adam et Paul Tannery (Paris: Vrin, 1967) [henceforth AT 6], 13: 'We are all children before being men and had to be governed for some time by our appetites and our teachers'.
12. Ibid., 113; 4 (my emphasis).
13. I use the term 'Sceptical' here to refer to the state of being Sceptical, because it is prior to any systematic, directed Sceptical doubt which could be properly termed Scepti*cism*.
14. Richard Davies refers to this rightly as a 'polemic' and as a case of Descartes's 'circumscribed by intransigent Pyrrhonism' (*Descartes, Belief, Virtue and Scepticism* (London: Routledge, 2001), 160–5). The figure of Eudoxos in René Descartes, 'The Search for Truth', in *Philosophical Writings of Descartes, Vol. 2*, 400–20; *Oeuvres de Descartes. Tome 10*, ed. Charles Adam et Paul Tannery (Paris: Vrin, 1970) [henceforth AT 10], 495–527, embodies the benefits of being spared such book learning.
15. Descartes, 'Discourse', 113; AT 6, 6.
16. René Descartes, 'Rules for the Direction of the Mind', in *Philosophical Writings of Descartes, Vol. 1*, 21–4; *Oeuvres de Descartes. Tome 10*, ed. Charles Adam et Paul Tannery (Paris: Vrin, 1974) [henceforth AT 10], 381–7.
17. Descartes, 'Discourse', 115; AT 6, 9.
18. Descartes, 'Rules', 16; AT 10, 372.
19. René Descartes, *Conversation with Burman*, trans. John Cottingham, Robert Stoothoff and Dugald Murdoch (Oxford: Clarendon Press, 1976), 32; *Oeuvres de Descartes. Tome 5*, ed. Charles Adam et Paul Tannery (Paris: Vrin, 1968) [henceforth AT 5], 159.
20. René Descartes, 'Letter to Hector-Pierre Chanut, 1st February 1647', in *The Philosophical Writings of Descartes, Vol. 3: The Correspondence*, trans. John Cottingham, Robert Stoothoff and Dugald Murdoch (Cambridge: Cambridge University Press, 1991), 309; *Oeuvres de Descartes. Tome 4*, ed. Charles Adam et Paul Tannery (Paris: Vrin, 1967) [henceforth AT 4], 608.
21. Geneviève Rodis-Lewis, *La Morale de Descartes* (Paris: PUF, 1998), 37–8, n. 1.
22. Descartes, 'Meditations', 53–4; AT 7, 76–7.
23. René Descartes, 'Passions of the Soul', in *Philosophical Writings of Descartes, Vol. 1*, 345; *Oeuvres de Descartes. Tome 11*, ed. Charles Adam et Paul Tannery (Paris: Vrin, 1967) [henceforth AT 11], 362–3.
24. Cf. Descartes, 'Discourse', 117; AT 6, 13.
25. René Descartes, 'Letter to Marin Mersenne, March 1636', in *Philosophical Writings of Descartes, Vol. 3*, 339; *Oeuvres de Descartes. Tome 1*, ed. Charles Adam et Paul Tannery (Paris: Vrin, 1965) [henceforth AT 1], 51: 'The Plan of a Universal Science which is capable of raising our Nature to its Highest Degree of Perfection.'
26. Descartes, 'Discourse', 117; AT 6, 13: 'We are all children before being men and had to be governed for some time by our appetites and our teachers.'

27. On Descartes's ambiguous relationship with Scepticism, see Richard Popkin, *The History of Scepticism* (Oxford: Oxford University Press, 2003), 158–73.
28. This cannot be dismissed as an angelic view of the human but rather is a breaking from the body as fallen in order to retrieve it following its methodological 'cleansing'. Against the 'angelic' interpretation, see John Cottingham, *Philosophy and the Good Life* (Cambridge: Cambridge University Press, 1994), 83.
29. Cf. Descartes, 'Meditations', 40; AT 7, 57.
30. Descartes, 'Passions', 349; AT 11, 372.
31. Cf. Deborah Brown, *Descartes and the Passionate Mind* (Cambridge: Cambridge University Press, 2006), 149.
32. Descartes, 'Meditations', 15; AT 7, 23.
33. René Descartes, 'Principles of Philosophy', in *Philosophical Writings of Descartes, Vol. 1*, 205–6; *Oeuvres de Descartes. Tome 8*, ed. Charles Adam et Paul Tannery (Paris: Vrin, 1974) [henceforth AT 8], 19–20.
34. Cf. Descartes, 'Meditations', 40–1; AT 7, 58.
35. Descartes, 'Passions', 347; AT 11, 366–7.
36. Ibid., 345; 364.
37. Ibid., 347; 367.
38. Pascal, *Pensées*, 119.
39. Ibid., 121.
40. Ibid., 130.
41. Ibid., 131.
42. See ibid., 933.
43. Ibid., 133.
44. Descartes, 'Passions', 361; AT 11, 397–8.
45. Cf. Tamás Pavlotis, *Le rationalisme de Pascal* (Paris: Editions de Sorbonne, 2007), 92–5. As we will see, Descartes also critiques curiosity in a manner which is very similar to Pascal and seems to share – directly or indirectly – a common lineage to Augustine. However, for Descartes, curiosity is a vice because it is an admission of ignorance, where there should be none (with regard to nature) and a lack of awe and reverence where that is appropriate (with respect to God). See Brown, *Descartes and the Passionate Mind*, 142–3.
46. Pascal, *Pensées*, 45.
47. Ibid., 410.
48. Cf., Pavlotis, *Le rationalisme de Pascal*, 15–20.
49. *Pensées*, 539.
50. On the difference between will and heart, see Jean Laporte, *La Coeur et le raison selon Pascal* (Paris: Elzevir, 1950), 85–101.
51. James Peters, *The Logic of the Heart* (Ada, MI: Baker Academic, 2009), 172.
52. Descartes, 'Passions', 387; AT 11, 451–2.
53. See Pascal, *Pensées*, 199: 'They [human beings] cannot understand what the body is, far less the spirit and least of all how the body can be combined with the spirit.'
54. See ibid., 110. Cf. Pavlovits, *Le rationalisme de Pascal*, 45–6.
55. Pascal, *Pensées*, 110.
56. Cf. Peters, *Logic of the Heart*, 168–72.
57. See Descartes, 'Discourse', 16–7; AT 6, 11–13.
58. Cf. Sextus, *Outlines*, 1.15, 164–74.
59. Descartes, 'Discourse', 113; AT 6, 5.
60. Ibid., 142; 61.

61. Ibid., 118; 15.
62. See Descartes, 'Principles', 186–7, 289; AT 8, 14–16, 327.
63. Ibid., 186; 14.
64. Descartes, 'Meditations', 12; AT 7, 17.
65. Ibid., 17; 18; ibid., 13; 19 (translation modified); ibid., 14; 21 (translation modified) and ibid., 15; 22, respectively.
66. Ibid., 15; 23.
67. Ibid., 16; 24.
68. Cf. ibid.: 'I myself may perhaps be the author of my own thoughts.'
69. See ibid., 36; 52.
70. Cf. 'Meditations', 27; AT 7, 38–9: 'There cannot be another faculty both as trustworthy as natural light [*cui aeque fidam ac lumini isti*], and also as capable of showing me that such things are not true. But as for my natural impulses … I do not see which I should place greater trust in them [*in ulla alia re magis fidam*].' In the Sixth Meditation he states, 'I reckoned that a great deal of confident should not be placed in what I was taught by nature [*non multùm fidendum esse putabam iis quae a naturâ docentur*]' (ibid., 53; AT 7, 96).
71. Ibid., 19; 28.
72. Ibid., 40–1; 58.
73. Twice Descartes speaks of receiving the will from God: ibid., 39; 41 and 56; 60.
74. See ibid., 58; 40.
75. Cf. Le Guern, *Pascal et Descartes*, 125–7.
76. Blaise Pascal, 'Conversation with Monsieur de Sacy', in *Pensées and Other Writings*, trans. Honor Levi (London: Penguin, 2008), 189; 'Entretien de M. Pascal avec M. de Sacy sur Épictète et Montaigne', in *Oeuvres Complètes, Tome 2*, edi. Michel Le Guern (Paris: Gallimard, 2000), 96. Cf. Neto, *The Christianization of Pyrrhonism*, 37–47. On Pascal's use of Scepticism more generally, see Robert Miner, 'Pascal on the Uses of Scepticism' *Logos*, 11, no. 4 (2008): 111–22.
77. Vincent Carraud, *Pascal et la Philosophie* (Paris: PUF, 1992), 87 (translation mine).
78. Pascal, 'Conversation', 190; 95.
79. *Pensées*, 83.
80. Ibid., 131.
81. Ibid., 54.
82. Ibid., 558.
83. Ibid., 126.
84. Ibid., 128.
85. Ibid., 60. The source of this idea is in Montaigne as we have already seen.
86. Ibid., 33.
87. See Popkin, *The History of Scepticism*, 158–73.
88. *Pensées*, 114.
89. Ibid., 400.
90. Ibid., 199.
91. Cf. ibid., 109, 76.
92. Ibid., 418.
93. Ibid.
94. Ibid. Pascal may be directly responding to Montaigne here: 'What am I to choose? What you like, provide you choose. There is a stupid answer … by which we are not allowed to know that we do not know' (*Essays*, 2, 12, 373). On this parallel, see Manent, *Montaigne*, 228, n. 10.

95. *Pensées*, 418.
96. Descartes, 'Principles', 179; AT 8, 2.
97. Descartes, 'Meditations', 61; AT 7, 89 (translation modified).
98. Descartes, 'Rules', 9; AT 10, 359.
99. Ibid., 14; 368.
100. Ibid., 15; 369.
101. Ibid., 15; 370.
102. I say 'adurational' instead of atemporal, because it is not so much out of time as being a moment which does not endure, a purely punctual moment. This same structure is repeated in Descartes's understanding of the cogito, as we will see later.
103. Descartes, 'Rules', 25; AT 10, 388 (my emphasis).
104. Descartes, *Conversation with Burman*, 3; AT 5, 144.
105. Descartes, 'Meditations', 12; AT 7, 7.
106. Cf. on the strategy of the 'First Meditation', Harry Frankfurt, *Demons, Dreamers and Madmen* (Princeton: Princeton University Press, 2007), 60–75.
107. Descartes, 'Meditations', 16; AT 7, 24. The English translation follows the French referring to 'something else [*quelque chose autre*]'; in the original Latin the word used is *diversum*, meaning 'facing in a different direction', 'opposed', 'contrasting'.
108. Cf., René Descartes, 'Letter to Mersenne, 6 May 1630', in *Philosophical Writings of Descartes, Vol. 3*, 24–5; AT 1, 149.
109. Descartes, 'Meditations', 33; AT 7, 49.
110. Ibid., 24; 34.
111. Cf. ibid., 31; 45–6.
112. This is not to suggest that deception is a possibility for the true God, as has been argued by Émile Bréhier, *La Philosophie et son passé* (Paris: Vrin, 1940), 113–16. For a critique of this position, see Martial Gueroult, *Descartes selon l'orde des raisons I* (Paris: Aubier, 1953), 42–9. What is common to both the God of the First and the Third Meditations is the attribute of all-powerfulness, and this amounts for Descartes to the claim that God is a Creator of essences.
113. Descartes, 'Principles', 200; AT 8, 13.
114. Descartes, 'Meditations', 43; AT 7, 62.
115. Cf. 'Fourth Set of Objections', 150; AT 7, 214.
116. 'Fourth Set of Replies', 171; AT 7, 246–7.
117. *Pensées*, 110.
118. Ibid.
119. Ibid.
120. Ibid., 513.
121. Descartes, 'Discourse', 116; AT 6, 11.
122. *Pensées*, 154.
123. Ibid., 196: 'It affects our whole of life to know whether the soul is mortal or immortal.'
124. The original subtitle of the 'Meditations' read '*in qua Dei existentia et animæ immortalitas demonstrator* [in which the existence of God and the immortality of the soul is demonstrated]'. Arnauld pointed out that the most Descartes had demonstrated was the distinction of body and soul ('Fourth Set of Objections', 143–4; AT 7, 204). In response, Descartes accepted this objection ('Fourth Set of Replies', 161; AT 7, 229) and then silently modified the subtitle in the French translation and subsequent Latin edition to '*dans lesquelles l'existence de dieu et la distinction réelle entre l'âme et le corps de l'homme sont démonstrées*' and '*in quibus Dei existentia*

et animae humanae a corpore distincto demonstrantur, respectively: 'in which the existence of God and the real distinction between body and soul in humans is demonstrated.'
125. Cf. René Descartes, 'Letter to Constantin Huygens, 25 January 1638', AT 1, 507. On the importance of medicine in Descartes's understanding of his own project, cf. Steven Shapin, 'Descartes the Doctor: Rationalism and Its Therapies', *British Journal for the History of Science*, 33, no.2 (2000): 131–54; and Vincent Aucante, *La philosophie médicale de Descartes* (Paris: PUF, 2015).
126. On the important shift in the meaning of capacity from receptivity to 'naturally self-satisfied power' and the relevance of this to questions of grace and nature, see Jean-Luc Marion, *Cartesian Questions* (Chicago: Chicago University Press, 1999), 94.
127. Descartes is non-committal on this question, understanding it as a problem for theology not for philosophy. See Descartes, *Conversation with Burman*, 50; AT 5, 178.
128. *Pensées*, 134.
129. Ibid., 132.
130. Ibid., 427.
131. Ibid., 136.
132. Ibid.
133. Ibid., 143.
134. Ibid., 3.
135. Pascal understands thinking of the infinite in the submission of reason as contemplation. See Pavlotis, *Le rationalisme de Pascal*, 96. Kant uses the term 'contemplation' is a strikingly similar manner in the *Critique of Judgement* as we will later.
136. For such an interpretation, see Penelham, 'Skepticism and Fideism', 302–5. For a critique of this interpretation, see Peters, *The Logic of the Heart*, 87–8, n. 78.
137. Ibid., 172.
138. Ibid., 193: 'It is pitiful to see so many Turks, heretics, unbelievers follow in their fathers' footsteps, solely because they have been brought up to believe that this is the best course.' Pascal probably has Montaigne's statement, discussed above, about being a Christian as one is a German, that is, by the accident of birth.
139. Descartes, 'Meditations', 3; AT 7, 2.
140. Pascal, *Pensées* 110; cf. 449.
141. Cf. Descartes, 'Letter to Mersenne, 6 May 1630', in *Philosophical Writings of Descartes, Vol. 3*, 24; AT 1, 149.
142. Ibid., 24; 150.
143. Descartes, 'Letter to Mersenne, 27 May 1630', in *Philosophical Writings of Descartes, Vol. 3*, 25; AT 1, 152.
144. Cf. ibid., 25–6; 153.
145. Descartes, 'Meditations', 36; AT 7, 52.
146. Ibid., 46–7; 67–8.
147. Ibid., 37; 53.
148. Ibid., 39; 55 (word within diamond brackets a later addition in French translation).
149. Pascal, *Pensées*, 131.
150. Ibid., 431.
151. *Pensees* 234: 'God wishes to move the will rather than the mind.'
152. Ibid., 418.

153. Ibid., 149. In another fragment he states, 'If we claim that that man is too slight to deserve communion with God, we must indeed be great to be able to judge' (ibid., 231).
154. Ibid., 449.
155. Ibid., 444.
156. As Schneewind (*The Invention of Autonomy*, 4–11) makes clear, the idea of autonomous reason develops slowly in Modernity. It is an indication of Pascal's prescience that he say it as if already formed in Descartes and reacted against it.
157. Descartes, 'Discourse', 122–5; AT 6, 23–8.
158. Ibid., 122; 23.
159. Ibid., 123; 24–5.
160. Ibid., 124; 26.
161. Ibid., 124; 27.
162. Ibid., 123; 24.
163. See René Descartes, 'Letter to Elisabeth, 6th October 1645', in *Philosophical Writings of Descartes, Vol. 3*, 269; AT 4, 307–8.
164. Descartes, 'Passions', 396–7; AT 11, 472–3.
165. Ibid., 390; 460.
166. On the contribution of Princess Elisabeth of Bohemia to the development of the early modern understanding of the passions, cf. Renée Jeffrey, 'The Origins of the Modern Emotions: Princess Elisabeth of Bohemia and the Embodied Mind', *History of European Ideas*, 43, no. 6 (2016): 547–59; and Delphine Kolesnik-Antoine and Marie-Frédérique Pellegrin (eds.), *Élisabeth de Bohême face à Descartes: deux philosophes?* (Paris: Vrin, 2014).
167. Elisabeth of Bohemia, 'Letter to Descartes 13 September, 1654', in *The Correspondence between Princess Elisabeth of Bohemia and René Descartes*, trans. Lisa Shapiro (Chicago: University of Chicago Press, 2007), 110; AT 4, 289.
168. Descartes, 'Passions', 391; AT 11, 460.
169. René Descartes, 'Letter to Elisabeth, 18th August 1645', in *Philosophical Writings of Descartes, Vol. 3*, 262; AT 4, 277: 'Happiness consists solely in contentment of the mind ... in order to achieve contentment which his solid, we need to pursue virtue.'
170. Lipsius, *On Constancy*, 1.4.
171. Ibid.
172. Descartes, 'Discourse', 142–3; AT 6, 62.
173. Descartes, 'Meditations', 19; AT 7, 28.
174. Ibid., 40; 58.
175. Descartes, 'Letter to Elisabeth, 6th October 1645', in *Philosophical Writings of Descartes, Vol. 3*, 273; AT 4, 314; cf. Brown, *Descartes and the Passionate Mind*, 175.
176. René Descartes, 'Letter to Elisabeth, 3rd November 1645', in *Philosophical Writings of Descartes, Vol. 3*, 277; AT 4, 334; cf., Rodis-Lewis, *La morale de Descartes*, 34.
177. Descartes, 'Passions', 339; AT 11, 351.
178. Ibid., 339; 350.
179. Ibid., 353; 381.
180. Ibid., 355–6; 386.
181. Ibid., 350; 374–5. On this topic, see Amelie Rorty, 'Cartesian Passion and the Union of Mind and Body', in *Essays on Descartes Meditations*, ed. Amelie Rorty (Berkeley: University of California Press, 1986), 318: 'The passions show ... that, taken together, mind and body form a whole with interlocked functions, directed to the well-being of that whole.'

182. Brown (*Descartes and the Passionate Mind*, 209) calls for such a reading backwards from the 'Passions' to the 'Meditations', with a different, but compatible, aim.
183. See Lisa Shapiro, 'Je ne regrette rien: Elisabeth et Descartes und la psychologie morale de regret', in *Elisabeth de Bóheme face à Descartes*, ed. Delphine Kolesnik-Antoine and Marie-Frédérique Pellegrin (Paris: Vrin, 2014), 155–70.
184. Amélie Rorty, 'The Structure of Descartes' Meditations', in *Essays on Descartes Meditations*, ed. Amélie Rorty (Berkeley: University of California Press, 1986), 41.
185. Descartes, 'Replies to Fourth Set of Objections', 159; 226.
186. Despair and Hope:

> I feel as if I have fallen unexpectedly into a deep whirlpool which tumbles me around so that I can neither stand at the bottom nor swim to the top. Nevertheless I will make an effort and once more attempt the same path. ... [Like Archimedes] I too can hope for great things if I manage to find just one thing. (Descartes, 'Meditations', 16; AT 7, 24)

187. Descartes, 'Passions', 377; AT 11, 432.
188. Ibid., 379; 436.
189. Descartes, 'Second Set of Replies', 103; AT 7, 145.
190. Rorty rightly sees generosity as the ancestor of Kant's respect for the moral law (Rorty, 'Cartesian Passion', 527).
191. Descartes, 'Passions', 385; AT 11, 447.
192. Pascal, *Pensées*, 597.
193. Ibid., 60.
194. Ibid., 65.
195. Cf. ibid., 60: 'Such is the caprice of man that there is not a single [universal law].'
196. Ibid., 113.
197. Ibid., 200.
198. Ibid., 418.
199. Descartes, *Conversation with Burman*, 30–1; AT 5, 165.
200. *Pensées*, 418.
201. Ibid., 418.
202. Ibid., 131.
203. Ibid., 821.
204. Ibid., 824.
205. Descartes, 'Passions', 356; AT 11, 387.
206. Ibid., 357; 389.
207. Ibid., 357–8; 390–1.
208. Pascal, *Pensées*, 97.
209. Ibid., 118.
210. Ricoeur, *Freud and Philosophy*, 33–5.
211. *Pensées*, 148.
212. Kolakowski, *God Owes Us Nothing*, 93: 'By condemning by proxy the teaching of Augustine [through its condemnation of Jansenism], [the Church] demolished the main theological barrier between itself and modernity.'
213. Ibid., 197.
214. Kolakowski speaks of actors here, but he means the characters.
215. Ibid., 196.
216. See the classic statement of this argument in George Steiner, *The Death of Tragedy* (London: Faber and Faber, 1961), 332–3.

217. Jeremy Worthen, 'Christianity and the Limits of Tragedy', *New Blackfriars*, 70, no. 825 (1989): 111.
218. René Descartes, 'Letter to Elisabeth, January, 1646', in *Philosophical Writings of Descartes, Vol. 3*, 283; AT 4, 355.
219. René Descartes, 'Letter to Elisabeth, May/June, 1645', in *Philosophical Writings of Descartes, Vol. 3*, 251–2; AT 4, 219–20.

4 Spinoza and Hume on the good life

1. On Spinoza's Stoicism, see Firmin de Brabander, *Spinoza and the Stoics* (London: Continuum, 2007); and Jon Miller, *Spinoza and the Stoics* (Cambridge: Cambridge University Press, 2015).
2. On Hume's Scepticism, see Peter Fosl, *Hume's Scepticism* (Edinburgh: Edinburgh University Press, 2020); Zuzana Parusniková, *David Hume: Sceptic* (Dordrecht: Springer 2016); and Robert Fogelin, 'Hume's Scepticism', in *Cambridge Companion to Hume*, ed. David Norton (Cambridge: Cambridge University Press, 1993), 90–116.
3. Cf. Gilles Deleuze, *Expressionism in Philosophy*, trans. Martin Joughin (New York: Zone Books, 2009).
4. Benedict de Spinoza, 'The Ethics', in *Collected Works Volume 1*, ed. and trans. Edwin Curley (Princeton: Princeton University Press, 1985), 1D6: 'a substance consisting of an infinity of attributes, of which each one expresses an eternal and infinite essence'. David Hume, *Treatise of Human Nature* (London: Thoemes Press, 1996), 1.1.1; 15 (reference given as book, part and section; page number).
5. While our historiography for the most part considers these two figures in separate historical trajectories, this is both a historical anachronism and fails to recognize the points of dialogue between them. There are, nevertheless, useful comparative studies, including Annette Baier, 'David Hume, Spinozist', *Hume Studies*, 19, no. 2 (1993): 237–52; Wim Klever, 'Hume Contra Spinoza?', *Hume Studies*, 16, no. 2 (1990), 89–105; Douglas den Uyl and Lee Rice: 'Spinoza and Hume on Individuals', *Reason Papers*, no. 15 (Summer 1990): 91–117; and Richard Popkin, 'Hume and Spinoza', *Hume Studies*, 5, no. 2 (1979): 65–93.
6. Kever, 'Hume Contra Spinoza?', 92, points out this structural parallel.
7. Hume, *Treatise*; 7.
8. Spinoza, 'Ethics', 2 Preface.
9. Donald Rutherford, 'Salvation as a State of Mind: The Place of *Acquiescentia* in Spinoza's *Ethics*', *British Journal for the History of Philosophy*, 7, no. 3 (1999): 447–73.
10. Spinoza, 'Ethics', 5P42 Schol. (translation modified).
11. Hume, *Treatise*; 550.
12. Benedict de Spinoza, 'The Emendation of the Intellect', in *Collected Works Volume 1*, ed. and trans. Edwin Curley (Princeton: Princeton University Press, 1985), 9; 9 (reference as paragraph; page number).
13. Spinoza, 'Ethics', 4 Appendix 5.
14. Ibid., 4 Appendix 8.
15. Augustine of Hippo, *On Christian Teaching*, trans. Roger Greene (Oxford University Press, 1999), 2, 8.
16. The question of 'calm emotions' in Hume will be discussed in section 4.4.
17. See David Hume, 'Dialogues concerning Natural Religion', in *Principal Writings on Religion*, ed. John Addison (Oxford: Oxford University Press, 2008), 1; 37–8: 'The

mind must remain in suspense between them [competing arguments]; and it is that very suspense or balance, which is the triumph of scepticism.' Hume drew on Academic and Pyrrhonian Scepticism in its Ancient sources and in their Modern appropriations, as Fosl (*Hume's Scepticism*) shows.
18. Spinoza, 'Ethics', 1P8, Schol.
19. Benedict de Spinoza, 'Political Treatise', in *Collected Works 2*, ed. Edwin Curley (Princeton: Princeton University Press, 2016), 8, 27 (reference given as paragraph, page number).
20. Spinoza, 'Ethics', 1, Appendix.
21. Spinoza, 'Emendation of the Intellect', 16; 11.
22. Ibid., 17; 12.
23. Demea puts in in the 'Dialogues, Part 11', in *Principal Writings*, 114: 'I joined alliance with you [Philo] to prove the incomprehensible nature of the divine Being.'
24. Spinoza, 'Emendation of the Intellect', 18; 12.
25. Ibid., 31; 17.
26. Ibid., 23; 14–15.
27. Cf. Spinoza's letters to Oldenburg regarding Boyle's experiments where he clearly privileges a priori reasoning, 'Letter 6, Spinoza to Oldenburg, 1662', *The Letters*, trans. Samuel Shirley (Indianapolis: Hackett, 1995), 71–84. Cf. Johnathan Israel, *Radical Enlightenment* (Oxford: Oxford University Press, 2001), 71–2.
28. Hume, *Treatise*; 8.
29. We have seen this already with Montaigne, see p. 48 above, and indeed it is more probable that Hume developed his method from him rather than Newton and Boyle. Hume would have had access to Montaigne's *Essays* while at La Fléche composing his *Treatise*. See Dario Perinetti, 'Hume at La Flèche: Skepticism and the French Connection', *Journal of the History of Philosophy*, 56, no. 1 (2018): 59.
30. Sextus, *Outlines*, 1, 3, 7: 'The Skeptical Way is called Zetetic from its activity of questioning.'
31. Hume, *Treatise*, 1.4.7; 331.
32. Ibid., 1.4.7; 334.
33. Hume, 'Dialogues, Part 1', in *Principal Writings*, 35–6.
34. Spinoza, 'Letter 21, to van Blyenbergh, 28th January 1665', in *Letters*, 150.
35. See Spinoza, 'Ethics', 5P35 Schol.: 'Our salvation (*salvus*) or blessedness or freedom, consists … in a constant and eternal love of God.' While Brague (*The Kingdom of Man*, 88) interprets 'salvation' in Spinoza simply as a metaphor, this implies reference to primary, literal sense, presumably an orthodox Christian one. However, Spinoza is aiming to understand salvation in the absence of an afterlife. For a more positive account cf. Brabander, *Spinoza and the Stoics*, 22–4.
36. Benedict de Spinoza, 'Theological-Political Treatise', in *Collected Works Volume 2*, ed. and trans. Edwin Curley (Princeton: Princeton University Press, 2016), 66; 135 (Gebhardt numbering followed by page number in Curley edition).
37. Spinoza, 'Ethics', 5P26 (translation modified).
38. *Natura sive Deus* – nature or God – is a phrase which occurs throughout the 'Ethics'. We will thematise the question of God in section 4.5.
39. Spinioza, 'Ethics', 5P23 Schol.
40. See 'Ethics', 5P24.
41. Brabander, *Spinoza and the Stoics*, 56.
42. Hume, *Treatise*, 1.3.16; 224.
43. Ibid., 1.3.16; 227.

44. Spinoza, 'Ethics', 3P39 Schol.
45. Ibid., 2D3.
46. Cf. Heidi Ravven, 'Spinoza's Path from Imaginative Transindividuality to Intuitive Relational Autonomy', in *Spinoza and Relational Autonomy*, ed. Aurelia Armstrong, Keith Green and Andrea Sangiacomo (Edinburgh: Edinburgh University Press, 2019), 100–1.
47. Hume, *Treatise*, 1.1.1; 15–6.
48. See Spinoza, 'Ethics', 2P44 Schol.
49. See ibid.
50. Ibid., 2P49 Schol.2.
51. Ibid., 2P5D.
52. Ibid., 2P5.
53. Ibid., 2D4.
54. Ibid., 3P1D.
55. There are exceptions particularly with respect to colour, cf. Hume, *Treatise*, 1.1.1; 20–1.
56. Ibid., 1.1.3; 25.
57. See ibid., 1.1.4; 23–9.
58. Gilles Deleuze, *Empiricism and Subjectivity*, trans. Constantin Boundas (New York: Columbia University Press, 1991), 24.
59. Hume, *Treatise*, 1.3.4; 11–2.
60. Ibid., 1.4.6; 323.
61. Ibid., 1.4.6; 322.
62. Ibid., 1.4.6; 323.
63. Ibid., 1.4.2; 270.
64. Ibid. 1.4.6; 312.
65. Ibid., 1.4.6; 311.
66. Ibid., 1.4.6; 315.
67. Ibid., 1.4.2; 264.
68. Ibid., 1.4.2; 249.
69. Ibid., 1.2.3; 56.
70. Ibid.; 1.4.2; 254.
71. Ibid., 1.4.2; 259–60. See also p. 268 where Hume speaks of 'a kind of instinct or natural impulse'.
72. Spinoza, 'Ethics', 2P30D.
73. Ibid., 2D5.
74. Ibid., 2P18 Schol.
75. Spinoza, 'Emendation of the Intellect', 81; 35–6.
76. Ibid., 82; 36.
77. Spinoza, 'Ethics', 2P18.
78. Ibid., 2P40 Schol.2.
79. Ibid., 2P17 Schol.
80. See ibid., 2Post2.
81. Ibid., 2Post5.
82. It is not totally clear what Spinoza has in mind here. Marin Lin, 'Memory and Personal Identity in Spinoza', *Canadian Journal of Philosophy*, 35, no. 2 (2005): 255, suggests that he means the brain, which seems plausible. However, the account could equally be applied to the muscles.
83. See Spinoza, 'Ethics', 2P17.

84. See ibid., 2P16.
85. See ibid., 2P17 Cor.
86. Ibid., 2P18 Schol.
87. Ibid.
88. See ibid., 2P17.
89. See Hume, *Treatise*, 1.1.1; 17.
90. Ibid., 1.2.6; 92. As Kant later puts it 'being is not a real predicate'. See section 5.1.
91. Ibid., 1.1.7; 39.
92. Ibid., 1.1.7; 36.
93. Ibid., 1.2.4; 63
94. Cf. Spinoza, 'Ethics', 2P28.
95. Cf. Michael della Rocca, 'Playing with Fire: Hume', in *The Oxford Handbook of Spinoza*, ed. Michael della Rocca (Oxford: Oxford University Press, 2018), 476–9.
96. See Hume, *Treatise*, 1.3.3; 79–80.
97. Ibid., *Treatise*, 1.3.3; 81.
98. Spinoza, 'Ethics', 1D1.
99. See Spinoza, 'Letter to Lodwewijk Meyer, 20th April 1663', in *Letters*, 102: 'It is to the existence of modes that we apply the term duration; the corresponding term for the existence of Substance is Eternity'; and David Hume, *Inquiry concerning Human Understanding: Philosophical Works Volume 4* (London: Thoemmes Press, 1996), 4.2; 41: 'that the course of nature may change, and that an object, seemingly like those which we have experienced, may be attended with different or contrary effects'.
100. Hume, *Inquiry concerning Human Understanding*, 1; 6; ibid., 4; 39; *Treatise* 1.3.16; 228; ibid., 1.4.1; 233.
101. Hume, *Inquiry concerning Human Understanding*, 10.2; 148.
102. See Hume, *Treatise* 2.3.1; 50: 'Whether we consider mankind according to differences of sexes, ages, governments, conditions or methods of education; the same uniformity and regular operations of natural principles are discernible. Like causes still produce like effects; in the same manner as in the natural action of the elements and the powers of nature.'
103. See Ibid., 1.2.5; 77–8.
104. 'On the Immortality of the Soul', in *Philosophical Works Volume 4*; 547.
105. Hume, *Treatise*, 1.3.14; 206.
106. Hume, 'Dialogues, Part 12', in *Principal Writings*, 48.
107. Hume, *Inquiry concerning Human Understanding*, 5.2; 62.
108. Hume, 'Dialogues, Part 6', in *Principal Writings*, 72–3.
109. Hume, *Treatise*, 1.3.6; 116.
110. Ibid., 1.3.12; 172.
111. Ibid., 1.3.12, 173–4.
112. Ibid., 1.3.7; 129.
113. Ibid., 1.3.8; 136.
114. Ibid., 1.3.5; 116.
115. On this background, see John Wright, 'Ideas of Habit and Custom in Early Modern Philosophy', *Journal of the British Society for Phenomenology*, 42, no. 1 (2011): 23–7.
116. On the different ways of rendering 'ratio' in translating 'Ethics', see Lin, 'Memory and Personal Identity in Spinoza', 248–54.
117. Spinoza, 'Ethics', 2L3D. On this theme, see Matthew Kisner, 'Spinoza on Natures: Aristotelian and Mechanistic Routes to Relational Autonomy', in *Spinoza and*

Relational Autonomy, ed. Aurelia Armstrong, Keith Green and Andrea Sangiacomo (Edinburgh: Edinburgh University Press, 2019), 74–97.
118. Spinoza, 'Ethics', 2L7 Schol.
119. Hume, *Treatise*, 1.4.6; 312.
120. Ibid., 1.4.2; 260.
121. Spinoza, 'Ethics', 2L2.
122. Ibid., 2P44.
123. See Hume. *Treatise*, 1.4.2; 241–2.
124. Spinoza, 'Ethics', 4, Pref.
125. Hume, *Treatise*, 1.3.14; 207.
126. Ibid., 1.3.14; 218.
127. Ibid., 2.1.2; 6.
128. Ibid.
129. Ibid., 1.1.2; 22 (my emphasis).
130. Ibid. (my emphasis).
131. On the move between the self in Book One and Two of the *Treatise*, see Elizabeth Radcliffe, *Hume, Passion and Action* (Oxford: Oxford University Press, 2018), 183–6.
132. Hume, *Treatise*, 2.1.1; 4. Hume is not terminologically consistent in his use of emotions and passions; his use of the term 'emotion' is one of the earliest in English, probably following Descartes's use of the term in the 'Passions'. Cf. Dixon, *From Passions to Emotions*, 104–5.
133. Spinoza, 'Ethics', 3Pref.
134. Ibid., 3D2.
135. See ibid., 5Pref.
136. Hume, *Treatise*, 2.1.2; 6.
137. See 'Ethics', 3P3 Schol.
138. Hume, *Treatise*, 2.3.3; 166.
139. Spinoza, 'Ethics', 3P7.
140. See David Hume, 'The Sceptic', in *Essays: Moral; Political; and Literary*, ed. Eugene Millar (Indianapolis: Liberty Classics 1987), 156–7.
141. Ibid., 180.
142. Spinoza, 'Ethics', 2P49.
143. See Hume, *Treatise*, 2.1.7; 28.
144. Cf. ibid., 2.1.10; 47.
145. Ibid., 2.1.2; 7–8.
146. Ibid., 2.2.2; 79.
147. Spinoza, 'Ethics', 3P13 Schol.
148. Spinoza is not totally consistent here; at 'Ethics', 4P18 Schol., he speaks of self-love using the verb *amare*: '*unusquisque seipsum amet* [everyone love himself]'.
149. Hume, *Treatise*, 2.3.3; 168. On the 'inertness of reason', cf. Radcliffe, *Hume, Passion and Action*, 29–64.
150. Spinoza, 'Ethics', 4P7.
151. See ibid., 5D1, 5D2 and 4Pref.
152. Ibid., 4P8.
153. See ibid., 3P3.
154. Ibid., 3Def. Affects 1.
155. See James Fieser, 'Hume's Classifications of the Passions', *Hume Studies*, 18, no. 1 (1992): 1–17.

156. Cf. Katharina Paxman, 'Imperceptible Impressions and Disorder in the Soul', *Journal of Scottish Philosophy* 13 no. 3 (2015), 265–78; and John Immerwahr, 'Hume on Tranquillizing the Passions', *Hume Studies*, 18, no. 2 (1992): 293–314.
157. Hume, *Treatise*, 2.1.1; 4.
158. Ibid., 2.3.3; 169.
159. Ibid., 2.3.4; 172.
160. Ibid., 2.3.3; 170. For a discussion of strength of mind, particularly its roots in Hume's account of sympathy, see Jane McIntyre, 'Strength of Mind: Prospects and Problems for a Humean Account', *Synthese*, 152, no. 3 (2006): 393–401.
161. See David Hume, *Inquiry Concerning the Principle of Morals: Philosophical Works Volume 4* (London: Thoemmes Press, 1996), 6, 303–4; cf. Radcliffe, *Hume, Passion and Action*, 160–7.
162. Immerwahr distinguishes usefully in this regard between kinds of passions and how they are experienced. See 'Hume on Tranquillizing the Passions', 295.
163. Hume, *Treatise*, 2.3.4; 171.
164. Ibid.
165. Ibid., 2.3.5; 175.
166. Ibid., Hume is clearly thinking here in terms of Descartes's animal spirits and his account of wonder.
167. Ibid., 2.3.5; 176.
168. Seventeenth-century usage was closer to the original Greek; *syn-* 'together' and *pathos* 'feeling'.
169. Hume, *Treatise*, 2.1.11; 56–61.
170. Ibid., 2.1.11; 56.
171. Ibid., 2.1.11; 58: 'We are ... better pleased with the approbation of a wise man than a fool.'
172. Ibid., 2.1.11; 57.
173. Spinoza, 'Ethics', 1D7.
174. Ibid., 4P37 Schol. 1.
175. Hume, 'Dialogues, Part 10', in *Principal Writings*, 104.
176. Spinoza, 'Theological-Political Treatise', 5; 66.
177. Hume, 'Dialogues, Part 12', in *Principal Writings*, 127–8.
178. Ibid., 9; 118.
179. Spinoza, 'Theological-Political Treatise', 76–8; 149. As Charlie Huenemann (*Spinoza's Radical Theology* (London: Routledge, 2014), xv) makes clear, Spinoza should be seen as a religious reformer rather than presenting a complete rejection of religion.
180. See Hume, *Inquiry concerning Human Understanding*, 11; 157: 'You find certain phenomena in nature. You seek a cause or author. You imagine that you have found him. You afterwards become so enamoured of this offspring of your brain, that you imagine it impossible but he must produce something greater and more perfect that the present scene of things.'
181. Cf. Thomas Hobbes, *Leviathan* (Oxford: Clarendon Press 2012), 1, 13–15.
182. Spinoza, 'Theological-Political Treatise', 21; 383.
183. Ibid., 16; 284.
184. On Spinoza's defence of democratic government, see de Brabander, *Spinoza and the Stoics*, 91–5. Spinoza does (as de Brabander notes) show some ambiguity towards democracy, but this seems in contradiction to the thrust of his thought.
185. Hume, *Treatise*, 3.2.2; 250.
186. Ibid., 3.2.2; 251.

187. Ibid., 3.2.2; 250: 'It is by society alone he is able to supply his defects, and raise himself up to an equality with his fellow-creatures, and even acquire a superiority above them.'
188. Ibid., 3.2.1; 240–8.
189. Ibid., 3.2.1; 241–2.
190. Ibid., 3.2.2; 249–50.
191. Ibid., 3.2.2; 266.
192. Ibid., 3.2.2, 255.
193. Ibid., 3.2.2; 260.
194. See Hume, *Inquiry Concerning the Principle of Morals*, 3; 249.
195. See ibid., 3; 253. This passage may be read in the light of the infamous footnote to 'On Natural Characters'. On the latter issue, see John Immerwahr, 'Hume's Revised Racism', *Journal of the History of Ideas*, 53, no. 3 (1992): 481–6.
196. Hume, *Inquiry Concerning the Principle of Morals*, 3; 254.
197. Hume, 'On the Original Contract', in *Selected Essays*, ed. Stephen Copley and Andrew Edgar (Oxford: Oxford University Press, 1993), 278.
198. This emphasis can be traced to the influence of Machiavelli. On this theme cf. Frederick Whelan, *Hume and Machiavelli* (London: Lexington, 2006).
199. Spinoza, 'Political Treatise', 1; 503.
200. See Spinoza, 'Ethics', 4P47 Schol.
201. See Hume, 'Of Superstition and Enthusiasm', in *Selected Essays*, 39–40.
202. Spinoza, 'Ethics', 4P35 Cor.1.
203. Spinoza, *Letters*, 17; 126.
204. Spinoza, 'Ethics', 5P10 Schol.
205. Spinoza, 'Theological-Political Treatise', 15; 73.
206. Ibid., 16; 74.
207. Ibid., 28; 92.
208. Ibid., 29; 94.
209. Ibid., 30; 95.
210. Ibid., 39–40; 105.
211. Ibid., 41; 106.
212. Ibid., 99; 172.
213. See ibid., 46; 114 and 70; 139–40.
214. Ibid., 48; 114. As de Brabander puts it, 'there is simply no salvation apart from civic harmony, in contrast to the Stoic sage who can be happy even on the rack' (*Spinoza and the Stoics*, 124).
215. See Spinoza, 'Theological-Political Treatise', 59; 129. On the centrality of the concept of obedience in Spinoza's reading of the Scriptures, see Carlos Fraenkel, 'Spinoza's Philosophy of Religion', in *The Oxford Handbook of Spinoza*, 288–91, 393.
216. Spinoza, 'Theological-Political Treatise', 75–6; 149–50.
217. Ibid., 239; 337.

5 Desire, *aporia* and reason in Kant

1. Nietzsche in his early writings recognized Kant as a tragic thinker: Alluding to Kant he states, 'The philosopher of tragic cognition. He subdues the unleashed drive to knowledge [*Wissenstrieb*]' (Friedrich Nietzsche, *Philosophy and Truth*, ed. Daniel

Breazeale (New York: Humanities Press, 1979), 11). Even more directly he states, 'The human longing to be completely truthful in the midst of mendacious nature is noble and heroic! But only possible in a very relative way. That is tragic. That is Kant's tragic problem' (ibid., 29). Cf. Keith Ansell-Pearson, 'Nietzsche's Overcoming of Kant and Metaphysics: From Tragedy to Nihilism', *Nietzsche Studien*, 16, no. 1 (1987): 318.

2. Friedrich Nietzsche, *Genealogy of Morals*, trans. Douglas Smith (Oxford: Oxford University Press, 2008), 3, 12, 97–9.
3. Immanuel Kant, *Critique of Pure Reason*, trans. Norman Kemp-Smith (New York: St. Martin's Press, 1929), B716; A708. Kemp-Smith translates this as 'our unceasing endeavour to extend our knowledge [*unseres unablässig zur Erweiterung strebenden Erkenntnistriebes*]'.
4. Ibid., A XI.
5. Immanuel Kant, 'What is Enlightenment?', in *On History*, ed. Lewis White Beck (New York: Bobbs-Merril, 1963), 9.
6. See Immanuel Kant, *Critique of Judgement*, trans. Paul Guyer (Cambridge: Cambridge University Press, 2000), 66; AA 5, 178–9.
7. The question of Kant's response to political revolution is a complex one. On that theme, see Lewis Beck, 'Kant and the Right of Revolution', *Journal of the History of Ideas*, 32, no. 3 (1971): 411–22; and Ferenc Féher, 'Practical Reason in the Revolution', *Social Research*, 56, no. 1 (1989): 161–85.
8. In a letter to Carl Friedrich Stäudiln dated 4 May 1793, Kant adds a fourth question, What is man?, noting that he has lectured on that subject over twenty years; see Kant, *Correspondence*, 458; AA 11, 429. This letter accompanies a copy of *Religion within the Boundaries of Mere Reason* and states that he had tried to complete his response to the question, What can I hope for? Michael Despland (*Kant on History and Religion* (Montreal: McGill University Press, 1973), 159) argues that Kant sees *Religion*, not the Third Critique, as putting a finishing touch to this tripartite system. In a similar vein, Chris Firestone (*Kant and Theology at the Boundaries of Reason* (Farnham: Ashgate, 2009), 145–63) understands *Religion* as transforming moral faith into religious faith. In contrast, for Arina Davidovich (*Religion as a Province of Meaning* (Minneapolis, MNI: Fortress Press, 1993), 51–66), *Religion* is a retrograde step from the Third Critique, which is the true culmination of his Critical project. I will show below that *Religion* and the Third Critique can most profitably be read in relation to each other as both aiming towards a unification of reason.
9. Immanuel Kant, 'Dreams of a Spirit Seer', in *Theoretical Philosophy 1755–1770*, trans. and ed. David Walford (Cambridge: Cambridge University Press. 1992), 354; AA 2, 368.
10. Kant, *Opus Optimum*, trans. Esker Forster (Cambridge: Cambridge University Press, 1993), 17; AA 21, 405.
11. On the theme of despair in Kant, cf. Allen Wood, *Kant's Moral Religion* (Ithaca, NY: Cornell University Press, 2009), 155–60; and Ronald Green, 'Kant and Kierkegaard', in *Kant and the New Philosophy of Religion*, ed. Chris Firestone and Stephen Palmquist (Bloomington: Indiana University Press, 2006), 171–3.
12. Immanuel Kant, 'Letter to Moses Mendelssohn, 16th August 1783', in *Correspondence*, 202; AA10, 344.
13. See Gordon Michalson, *Fallen Freedom* (Cambridge: Cambridge University Press, 1990), 18: 'a deep metaphysical trust in Kant that the universe makes moral sense'.
14. Immanuel Kant, *Notes and Fragments*, trans. Paul Guyer (Cambridge: Cambridge University Press, 2002), 257: 'If we had complete insight into the nature of things

then nature and freedom, the determination of nature and the determination of ends, would be entirely identical. So it is with God; hence all ends in the world follow simultaneously from the essence of things and in an original being would be identical with his nature' (from 1778 to 1780).
15. As Davidovich (*Religion*, 4), puts it, Kant likens reason to a 'dynamic agent driven by interests and needs, [which] cannot rest until it reaches ultimate answers'.
16. Kant, *Critique of Pure Reason*, A VII (translation modified). The word *belästigt* is quite properly translated as 'burdened'. I translate here as 'disturbed' to bring out the sense of this burden disturbing the self, indeed, bringing psychological cares on the self, which connotations are on surface in German.
17. Ibid., B354; A298.
18. Cf. ibid., B359; A302.
19. Cf. ibid., B614-5; A586-7 and Kant, *Notes and Fragments*, 263: 'The end of all metaphysics is God' (from 1780 to 1781).
20. Kant, *Critique of Pure Reason*, B825; A797 (translation modified).
21. Ibid., B8 (translation modified).
22. Ibid., B371; A314.
23. Cf. ibid., B823; A795.
24. On hubris and the good will, see Inga Römer, *Das Begehren der reinen praktischen Vernunft* (Hamburg: Meiner, 2018), 40-4.
25. Immanuel Kant, *The One Possible Basis for the Determination of the Existence of God*, trans. Gordon Treash (Lincoln: University of Nebraska Press, 1994).
26. Immanuel Kant, 'The Conflict of the Faculties', in *Religion and Rational Theology*, trans. and ed. Allen W. Wood and George di Giovanni (Cambridge: Cambridge University Press, 2012), 237-327.
27. Cf. Kant, *Critique of Pure Reason*, B608; A580.
28. Cf. ibid., B596; A568.
29. Kant, *Critique of Practical Reason*, trans. Lewis Beck (London: Macmillan, 1993), 131-2; AA 5, 125-6.
30. Immanuel Kant, *Critique of the Power of Judgement*, trans. Paul Guyer (Cambridge: Cambridge University Press, 2000), 286-7; AA 5, 418-9.
31. Ibid., 308-9; 442.
32. Ibid., 309; 442-3.
33. See ibid., 311-2; 445-7.
34. See ibid., 310-1; 444.
35. Kant, *Notes and Fragments*, 83.
36. Ibid., 24.
37. Kant's dialectic is indebted to Hume, and the Sceptical method of the antinomies are meant to overcome Hume, not in the sense of rejecting him, but as an extension of Humean insights. It is significant in discussing Kant's account of moral and religious faith (see section 6.3) that Kant was introduced to Hume by Johann Hamann, who (along with Jacobi) understood Hume's Sceptical stance as setting faith above reason: 'Hume needs faith if he is to eat an egg … Reason is not given to you to make you wise, but to make you aware of your folly and ignorance.' Hamann, 'Letter to Kant 27th July, 1759', in Kant, *Philosophical Correspondence*, 42. Cf. Manfred Kühn, 'The Reception of Hume in Germany', in *The Reception of Hume in Europe*, ed. Peter Jones (London: Continuum, 2005), 122-3.
38. Kant, *Notes and Fragments*, 83.
39. Ibid., 271.

40. Ibid., 276.
41. See Robert Butts, *Kant and the Double Government Methodology* (Dordrecht: Reidel, 1984); Gregory Johnson, 'The Sea of Melancholia: Kant on Philosophy and Enthusiasm', in *Kant and the New Philosophy of Religion*, ed. Chris Firestone, 43–61 (Bloomington: Indiana University Press, 2006); and Gottlieb Florschütz, *Swedenborgs verborgene Wirkung auf Kant* (Würzburg: Königshausen & Neumann, 1992). In 'Dreams', Kant asks, 'Why should it be more respectable to allow oneself to be misled by credulous trust in the sophistries of reason than to allow oneself to be deceived by an incautious belief in delusory stories?' Kant, 'Dreams', 343; AA 2, 356.
42. Immanuel Kant, 'What Real Progress has Metaphysics made in Germany since Leibniz and Wolff', in *Theoretical Philosophy after 1781*, trans. and ed. Henry Allison, Peter Heath and Gary Hatfield (Cambridge: Cambridge University Press, 2002), 353; AA 20, 260.
43. Kant, *Critique of Pure Reason*, B128.
44. See ibid., BXXXIV.
45. Kant, 'Dreams', 306; 318. Florschütz (*Swedenborgs*, 25) speaks of the 'Dreams' as Kant's attempt to liberate himself from this attachment.
46. Florschütz speaks of a split (*zweispalt*) between the critique of reason and moral hope. *Swedenborgs*, 54.
47. Kant, 'Dreams', 314–15; 327.
48. Ibid., 318–19; 331. Palmquist is correct in stating Kant only rejects fanatical, superstitious mysticism. Reason, Palmquist goes on, is for Kant the ultimately unknowable mystery out of which arises all our human capacities for knowledge and goodness. See Stephen Palmquist, *Kant's Critical Religion* (London: Routledge, 2019), 310–53.
49. Kant, 'Dreams', 326; 339.
50. Ibid., 327; 340 (translation modified). This echoes some of what Spinoza said about prophets. See above, pp. 148–9.
51. Ibid. (translation modified).
52. As Wood (*Kant's Moral Religion*, 14–15) points out, for Kant both faith and knowledge are characterized as ways of holding judgements which are valid for everybody, while opinion's insufficiency is based on lacking that capacity.
53. Kant, 'Dreams', 350; 364.
54. Cf. Johnson, 'The Sea of Melancholia', 55.
55. Also rejected here is the Thomistic and indeed Augustinian understanding of the supernatural as the perfecting of the natural.
56. For a detailed account of this context, see Immanuel Kant, *Religion and Rational Theology*, trans. and ed. Allen Wood and George di Giovanni (Cambridge: Cambridge University Press, 1996), xvi–xxii.
57. See *Opus Postumum*, 198; AA 22, 104: 'Categorical imperative which our reason expresses through the divine. Freedom under laws, duties *as* divine commands. There is a God.'
58. Kant, *Lectures on Philosophical Theology*, trans. by Allen Wood and Gertrude Clarke (Ithica, NY: Cornell University Press, 1978), 116.
59. Cf. Kant, *Critique of Pure Reason*, B421; A424.
60. Ibid., B451; A423.
61. Ibid., B450; A422.
62. Ibid., B535; A507.
63. Ibid., B454; A426.

64. Ibid., B452; A424.
65. Ibid., B491; A463.
66. Ibid., B 492: A464.
67. Ibid., B493; A465.
68. On the questions of the interests of reason, see Ronald Green, *Religious Reason* (Oxford: Oxford University Press, 1978), 69-72.
69. Kant, *Critique of Pure Reason*, B494; A466.
70. Ibid., B497; A469.
71. Ibid., B502; A475.
72. Ibid., B503; A475.
73. Kant, *Notes and Fragments*, 271.
74. Ibid., 127.
75. Kant, *Critique of Pure Reason*, B507; A479.
76. Ibid., B544; A516.
77. Ibid., B561; A533.
78. Ibid., B562; A534.
79. Kant, *Critique of Practical Reason*, 3-4; 3-4.
80. Ibid., 6; 6.
81. Ibid., 75; 72 (translation modified).
82. Ibid., 76; 73.
83. See Philip Rossi, 'The Final End of All Things', in *Kant's Philosophy of Religion Reconsidered*, ed. Philip Rossi and Michael Wreen (Bloomington: Indiana University Press, 1991), 147: 'The feeling of respect marks out the one sensible effect that Kant is willing to affirm as having its origin in the intelligible causality that we represent as autonomy.'
84. Kant, *Critique of Practical Reason*, 77-8; 74-5.
85. Ibid., 114; 108.
86. Ibid., 126; 119.
87. Cf. Christopher Insole, 'The Irreducible Importance of Religious Hope in Kant's Conception of the Highest Good', *Philosophy*, 83, no. 325 (2008): 333-51; and Frederick Beiser, 'Moral Faith and the Highest Good', in *The Cambridge Companion to Kant and Modern Philosophy*, ed. Paul Guyer, 597-8 (Cambridge: Cambridge University Press, 2006), showing how Kant identifies the 'highest good' with the 'kingdom of grace' in Augustine and Leibniz.
88. Kant, *Critique of Practical Reason*, 116-7; 110-11.
89. Ibid., 121; 114 (translation modified).
90. As Jerome Schneewind (*Invention of Autonomy*, 544) makes clear, Kant believed that Epicureanism had to be added to Stoicism; happiness required the satisfaction of non-moral as well as moral desires.
91. See Beiser, 'Moral Faith', 616, where he compares Kant to Camus. See also Davidovich, *Religion*, 20.
92. This work is the only major work completed after the three Critiques. It is a work which, as Despland has shown, introduces a key new element into Kant's thought, namely, the problem of 'the existence of a temporal being as such' (*Kant on History and Religion*, 160). The problem of being time-bound introduces for Kant new problems with the question of freedom, which leads him to the issue of evil and puts the question of the relation of the intelligible and the sensible into a new and historical context.
93. Immanuel Kant, *Religion within the Boundaries of Mere Reason*, ed. Allen Wood and George di Giovani (Cambridge: Cambridge University Press, 1998), 35; AA 6, 6.

94. Cf. Frederick Beiser, *The Fate of Reason* (Cambridge, MA: Harvard University Press, 1987), 48–94.
95. Kant, *Critique of the Power of Judgement*, 7; AA 20, 201.
96. Ibid., 10; 205.
97. Cf. Bernard Reardon, *Kant as Philosophical Theologian* (London: Rowman & Littlefield, 1988), 69–75.
98. Kant, *Critique of Judgement*, 63; AA 5, 176.
99. On this distinction, see Henry Allison, 'Kant on Freedom of the Will', in *The Cambridge Companion to Kant and Modern Philosophy*, ed. Paul Guyer (Cambridge: Cambridge University Press, 2006), 387–99. See also Rossi, 'The Final End of all Things', 137–8.
100. Kant, *Religion*, 35–6; 6–7.
101. Ibid., 35; 5.
102. Cf. John Betz, *After Enlightenment* (London: Wiley-Blackwell, 2012), 238–40.
103. Belief functions both theoretically and practically, but the distinction between these are not in content but, as Firestone (*Kant and Theology*, 85) puts it, in style.
104. Kant, *Critique of Practical Reason*, 74; 70–1.
105. Ibid., 128–9; 122 (translation modified).
106. Ibid., 133–4; 126–7.
107. Ibid., 135; 128.

6 Kant on the heart, evil and grace (starting from Rousseau)

1. The heart is, however, essential to the understanding of religion for Kant. As he states, religion is 'the heart's disposition to fulfil all human duties as divine commands' (*Religion within the Boundaries of Mere Reason*, 98; 84).
2. On this trajectory, see Manent, *Montaigne*, 42–8. See also Mark Hulliung, 'Rousseau, Voltaire and the Revenge of Pascal', in *The Cambridge Companion to Rousseau*, ed. Patrick Riley (Cambridge: Cambridge University Press, 2001), 57–78; and Harvey Mitchell, 'Reclaiming the Self: The Pascal-Rousseau Connection', *Journal of the History of Ideas*, 54, no. 4 (1993): 637–58.
3. On this point and on the role of the 'heart' in Rousseau, see James Lawler, *Matter and Spirit* (Rochester, NY: University of Rochester Press, 2006), 454–6 and 467–512.
4. *Émile or On Education*, trans. Christopher Kelly and Allan Bloom (Lebanon, NH: United Press of New England, 2010), 459.
5. Kant, *Religion*, 45–6; 19–20.
6. For Kant's explicit use of the figure of the wager in respect of belief, see Kant, *Critique of Pure Reason*, B853; A825. On this theme in Kant, see Onora O'Neill, 'Kant on Reason and Religion', *Tanner Lectures*. Available online: https://tannerlectures.utah.edu/_documents/a-to-z/o/oneill97.pdf (accessed 2 November 2020), 280–1.
7. Kant, *Religion*, 49; 24.
8. Ibid., 49; 25.
9. Ibid., 66–7; 46. On the positive sense of self-love in Rousseau, see Lawler: *Matter and Spirit*, 454.
10. Kant, *Religion*, 66; 46: 'The inner principle of a contentment only possible for us on condition that our maxims are subordinated to the moral law.'

11. Cf. Rousseau, 'Discourse on the Origins of Inequality' 2.1, note 15, in *The Discourses and Other Early Political Writings*, ed. and trans. Victor Gourevitch (Cambridge: Cambridge University Press, 2019), 218. On this distinction, cf. Frederick Neuhouser, *Rousseau's Theodicy of Self-Love* (Oxford: Oxford University Press, 2008).
12. Kant, *Religion*, 60; 37.
13. Rousseau, *Émile*, 279.
14. Ibid., 293.
15. Ibid., 449, 451, 454.
16. Ibid., 452.
17. Ibid., 439.
18. Ibid., 430.
19. Ibid., 431–2.
20. Ibid., 454.
21. Kant, *Religion*, 50–2; 26–8 and 52–5; 29–32.
22. Ibid., 51; 26.
23. Rousseau, *Discourse* 2.2; 164–85.
24. Rousseau, *Émile*, 432–3.
25. Ibid., 439.
26. Cf. Kant, *Religion*, 60; 38 and 55; 31, respectively.
27. Kant, *Critique of Pure Reason*, B833–4; A805–6.
28. Ibid., B841; A813.
29. Ibid., A223.
30. Kant, *Religion*, 58; 36.
31. Ibid., 77; 57.
32. Michalson puts it pithily, 'Being evil by nature is a 'nature' we freely elect' (*Fallen Freedom*, 63).
33. Kant, *Religion*, 59; 37.
34. Ibid., 58; 35.
35. Ibid., 61; 39.
36. Kant, *Critique of Pure Reason*, B177–8; A138–9.
37. Kant, *Religion*, 55; 31.
38. Ibid., 62; 41.
39. Plato, *Parmenides*, trans. Mary Louise Gill (Oxford: Oxford University Press, 2008), 156d1–e5.
40. Kant, *Religion*, 63; 41.
41. Ibid., 65; 44.
42. Ibid.
43. Ibid.
44. Ibid., 67; 46.
45. Ibid., 66; 47.
46. Ibid., 71; 51.
47. Ibid., 70; 50.
48. Ibid. 77; 57.
49. Ibid., 80; 61.
50. Ibid., 79; 60.
51. Ibid., 80; 61.
52. Ibid., 84; 66.
53. Ibid., 85; 68.

54. Ibid.
55. Ibid., 88; 71.
56. Kant refers to them as 'the *most personal* of all liabilities' (ibid., 89; 72).
57. Ibid., 91; 74-5.
58. See Jacqueline Marina, 'Kant on Grace: A Reply to His Critics', *Religious Studies*, 33, no. 4 (1997): 392: 'Change in disposition will bring with it the faith in such absolution, and not the other way around.'
59. On the irreversibility of conversion and its similarity to Luther, see Reardon, *Kant as Philosophical Theologian*, 103-5.
60. Kant, *Religion*, 91; 75.
61. On this point, see Marina, 'Kant on Grace', 381-2.
62. Cf. Ronald Green, 'Religious Ritual: A Kantian Perspective', *Journal of Religious Ethics*, 7, no. 2 (Fall 1979): 233.
63. Kant, *Religion*, 105; 94.
64. Ibid., 103; 116.
65. Ibid., 125; 119.
66. Ibid., 126; 119-20.
67. Ibid., 127; 120-1.
68. Ibid., 123; 116.
69. Ibid., 126; 119.
70. Ibid., 128; 122.
71. Ibid., 127; 122.
72. Ibid., 111; 101.
73. Ibid., 153; 152.
74. Ibid., 135; 131-2.
75. Ibid., 151-2; 152: 'God must himself be the author of his Kingdom.'
76. This is in line with the Augustinian principle of taking figuratively what cannot be understood in terms of good morals and true faith. See Augustine of Hippo, *On Christian Teaching*, 3.33.
77. Immanuel Kant, *Critique of the Power of Judgement*, trans. Paul Guyer (Cambridge: Cambridge University Press, 2000), 225; 348.
78. Ibid.
79. Jacques Derrida, 'Faith and Knowledge', in *Acts of Religion*, trans. Samuel Weber, ed. Gil Anidjar (London: Routledge, 2013), 50-1.

Conclusion

1. Deryck Cooke, *The Language of Music* (Oxford, Oxford University Press, 1962), 109.
2. 'That supreme and eternal origin of rhythms and similarity and equality and order,' Augustine of Hippo, *De Musica liber VI*, transl. Martin Jacobsson (Stockholm: Almqvist och Wiksell, 2002), VI, XVII, 57. Augustine's account of time is motivated by a hope directed not towards a future that passes away but to an outstretching (*non distentus, sed extentus*), which attains the simple, atemporal unity of a saved self. Cf. Augustine of Hippo, *Confessions*, 11.29.
3. Friedrich Hölderlin, *Sämtliche Werke. Volume 4, Part 1*, ed. Friedrich Beisener and Adolf Beck (Stuttgart: Kohlhammer, 1943), 304.

4. See, respectively, Friedrich Nietzsche, *The Gay Science*, trans. Josefine Nauchkhoff (Cambridge: Cambridge University Press, 2001), 3, 108, 109; and 3, 125, 119–20; Carolyn Merchant, *The Death of Nature* (New York: Harper Collins, 1980); Jacques Derrida, 'The Ends of Man', in *Margins of Philosophy*, trans. Alan Bass (Chicago: University of Chicago Press, 1982), 121; Ronald Barthes, 'The Death of the Author', in *Image, Music, Text*, trans. Stephen Heath (London: Fontana, 1977), 142–9.
5. Martin Heidegger, '"Only a God Can Save Us": Der Spiegel's Interview with Heidegger', *Philosophy Today*, 20 (1976), 267–84.

Bibliography

Abel, Günther. *Stoizismus und frühe Neuzeit: Eine Enstehungsgeschichte*. Berlin: de Gruyter 1978.
Adams, Marilyn. 'Ockham on Will, Nature and Morality'. In *The Cambridge Companion to Ockham*, edited by Paul Spade, 245–72. Cambridge: Cambridge University Press, 1999.
Allen, Don. *Doubt's Boundless Sea: Skepticism and Faith in the Renaissance*. Baltimore: John Hopkins University Press, 1969.
Allison, Henry. 'Kant on Freedom of the Will'. In *The Cambridge Companion to Kant and Modern Philosophy*, edited by Paul Guyer, 381–515. Cambridge: Cambridge University Press, 2006.
Annas, Julia, and Barmes, Jonathan. *The Modes of Scepticism*. Cambridge: Cambridge University Press, 1985.
Ansell-Pearson, Keith. 'Nietzsche's Overcoming of Kant and Metaphysics: From Tragedy to Nihilism'. *Nietzsche Studien*, 16, no. 1 (1987): 310–39.
Aquinas, Thomas. *Summa Contra Gentiles: Book Three*, translated by Vernon Bourke. Notre Dame, IN: University of Notre Dame Press, 1975.
Aquinas, Thomas. *Summa Theologica*, translated by Fathers of the English Dominican Province. Allen, TX: Thomas More, 1981.
Aucante, Vincent. *La philosophie médicale de Descartes*. Paris: PUF, 2015.
Arendt Hannah. *Love and Saint Augustine*. Chicago: University of Chicago Press, 1996.
Arendt, Hannah. 'Willing'. In *The Life of the Mind, 1–239*. London: Harcourt and Brace, 1978.
Aristotle. *Metaphysics*, translated by Hugh Lawson-Tancred. London: Penguin, 1998.
Augustine of Hippo. *Against the Academicians and The Teacher*, translated by Peter King. London: Hacket, 1995.
Augustine of Hippo. *City of God*, translated by Henry Bettenson. London: Penguin 1984.
Augustine of Hippo. *Confessions*, translated by Henry Chadwick. Oxford: Oxford University Press, 2008.
Augustine of Hippo. *De Musica liber VI*, translated by Martin Jacobsson. Stockholm: Almqvist och Wiksell, 2002.
Augustine of Hippo. 'Of the Spirit and the Letter'. In *Nicene and Post-Nicene Fathers of the Christian Church. Vol. 5: Saint Augustine: Anti-Pelagian Writings*, edited by Philip Schaff, translated by Peter Holmes, Robert Wallis and Benjamin Warfield, 80–115. Edinburgh: T&T Clark, 1997
Augustine of Hippo. *On Christian Teaching*, translated by Roger Greene. Oxford: Oxford University Press, 1999.
Augustine. *On Genesis*, translated by Ronald Teske. Washington, DC: Catholic University of America, 1991.
Augustine of Hippo. 'On Grace and Free Will'. In *Nicene and Post-Nicene Fathers of the Christian Church. Vol. 5: Saint Augustine: Anti-Pelagian Writings*, edited by Philip Schaff, translated by Peter Holmes, Robert Wallis and Benjamin Warfield, 436–65. Edinburgh: T&T Clark, 1997.

Augustine of Hippo. 'On Nature and Grace'. In *Nicene and Post-Nicene Fathers of the Christian Church. Vol. 5: Saint Augustine: Anti-Pelagian Writings*, edited by Philip Schaff, translated by Peter Holmes, Robert Wallis and Benjamin Warfield, 116–51. Edinburgh: T&T Clark, 1997.

Augustine of Hippo. *On the Free Choice of the Will, On Grace and Free Choice, and Other Writings*, edited and translated by Peter King. Cambridge: Cambridge University Press, 2010.

Augustine of Hippo. 'On the Merits and Remission of Sins, and on the Baptism of Infants'. In *Nicene and Post-Nicene Fathers of the Christian Church. Vol. 5: Saint Augustine: Anti-Pelagian Writings*, edited by Philip Schaff, translated by Peter Holmes, Robert Wallis and Benjamin Warfield, 12–78. Edinburgh: T&T Clark, 1997.

Augustine of Hippo. 'On the Proceedings of Pelagius'. In *Nicene and Post-Nicene Fathers of the Christian Church. Vol. 5: Saint Augustine: Anti-Pelagian Writings*, edited by Philip Schaff, translated by Peter Holmes, Robert Wallis and Benjamin Warfield, 178–212. Edinburgh: T&T Clark, 1997.

Augustine of Hippo. *The Trinity*, translated by Stephen McKenna. Washington, DC: Catholic University of America Press, 2002.

Barthes, Ronald. 'The Death of the Author'. In *Image, Music, Text*, translated by Stephen Heath, 142–9. London: Fontana, 1977.

Basil of Caesarea. 'Hexaemeron'. In *Saint Basil Collection, 4 Books, 187–258*. London: Aeterna Press, 2016.

Baier, Annette. 'David Hume, Spinozist'. *Hume Studies*, 19, no. 2 (1993): 237–52.

Beck, Lewis. 'Kant and the Right of Revolution'. *Journal of the History of Ideas*, 32, no. 3 (1971): 411–22.

Beiser, Frederick. 'Moral Faith and the Highest Good'. In *The Cambridge Companion to Kant and Modern Philosophy*, edited by Paul Guyer, 588–629. Cambridge: Cambridge University Press, 2006.

Beiser, Frederick. *The Fate of Reason: German Philosophy from Kant to Fichte*. Cambridge, MA: Harvard University Press, 1987.

Bermúdez, Jose. 'The Originality of Cartesian Skepticism: Did It Have Ancient or Mediaeval Antecedents?' *History of Philosophy Quarterly*, 17, no. 4 (2000): 333–60.

Betz, John. *After Enlightenment: The Post-Secular Vision of J. G. Hamann*. London: Wiley-Blackwell, 2012.

Bianchi, Luciano. 'Students, Masters, and 'Heterodox' Doctrines at the Parisian Faculty of Arts in the 1270s'. *Recherches de Théologie et Philosophie Médiévales*, 76 (2009): 75–109.

Blumenberg, Hans. *The Legitimacy of the Modern Age*, translated by Robert Wallace. Cambridge, MA: MIT Press, 1983.

Blumenberg, Hans. *Shipwreck with Spectator: Paradigm of a Metaphor for Existence*, translated by Steven Rendell. Cambridge, MA: MIT Press, 1997.

Boethius of Dacia. *De Aeternitate mundi*. Berlin: Gruyter, 1964.

Bonhoeffer, Dietrich. *Creation and Fall*, translated by Douglas Bax. Minneapolis, MN: Fortress Press, 2004.

Bouswama, William. 'The Two Faces of Humanism: Stoicism and Augustinianism in Renaissance Thought'. In *A Usuable Past: Essays in European Cultural History*, 19–73. Berkeley: University of California Press, 1990.

Brahami, Frédéric. *Le scepticisme de Montaigne*. Paris: PUF, 1997.

Brague, Rémi. *La Sagesse du Monde: Histoire de l'expérience humaine de l'univers*. Paris: Fayard, 1999.

Brague, Rémi. *The Kingdom of Man: The Genesis and Failure of the Modern Project*, translated by Paul Seaton. Notre Dame, IN: University of Notre Dame Press, 2018.
Bréhier, Émile. *La Philosophie et son passé*. Paris: Vrin, 1940.
Brown, Deborah. *Descartes and the Passionate Mind*. Cambridge: Cambridge University Press, 2006.
Burnyeat, Myles. 'The Sceptic in His Time and Place'. In *Scepticism from the Renaissance to the Enlightenment*, edited by Richard Popkin, 13–43. Ann Arbor: University of Michigan Press, 1997.
Butts, Robert, *Kant and the Double Government Methodology*. Dordrecht: Reidel, 1984.
Buxton, Rebecca, and Whiting, Lisa. *The Philosopher Queens*. London: Unbound, 2020.
Carraud Vincent. *Pascal et la Philosophie*. Paris: PUF, 1992.
Cary, Phillip. *Augustine's Invention of the Inner Self: The Legacy of a Christian Platonist*. Oxford: Oxford University Press, 2006.
Chrysostom, John. *Homilies on Genesis: The Fathers of the Church: A New Translation vol. 87*, translated by Robert Hull. Washington, DC: Catholic University of America Press, 2006.
Compagnon, Antoine. 'Montaigne: de la Traduction des Autres à la Traduction de Soi'. *Littérature*, no. 55 (1984): 37–44.
Conche, Marcel. *Montaigne et la philosophie*. Paris: PUF, 1996.
Cooke, Deryck. *The Language of Music*. Oxford: Oxford University Press, 1962.
Cottingham, John. *Philosophy and the Good Life: Reason and the Passions in Greek, Cartesian and Psychoanalytic Ethics*. Cambridge: Cambridge University Press, 1994.
Cottingham, John. 'The Cartesian Legacy'. *Proceedings of the Aristotelian Society, Supplementary Volumes*, 66 (1992): 1–21.
Davidovich, Adina. *Religion as a Province of Meaning: The Kantian Foundation of Modern Theology*. Minneapolis, MN: Fortress Press, 1993.
Davies, Richard. *Descartes: Belief, Virtue and Scepticism*. London: Routledge, 2001.
De Brabander, Firmin. *Spinoza and the Stoics: Power, Politics and the Passions*. London: Continuum, 2007.
Deleuze, Gilles. *Empiricism and Subjectivity: An Essay on Hume's Theory of Human Nature*, translated by Constantin Boundas. New York: Columbia University Press, 1991.
Deleuze, Gilles. *Expressionism in Philosophy: Spinoza*, translated by Martin Joughin. New York: Zone Books, 2009.
Della Mirandola, Pico. *Oration on the Dignity of Man*, translated by Franseco Borghesi. Cambridge: Cambridge University Press, 2012.
Della Rocca, Michael. 'Playing with Fire: Hume, Rationalism and a Little Bit of Spinoza'. In *The Oxford Handbook of Spinoza*, edited by Michael della Rocca, 464–81. Oxford: Oxford University Press, 2018.
Derrida, Jacques. 'Differance'. In *Speech and Phenomena and other Essays*, translated by David Allison, 129–60. Evanston, IL: Northwestern University Press, 1973.
Derrida, Jacques. 'The Ends of Man'. In *Margins of Philosophy*, translated by Alan Bass, 109–36. Chicago: University of Chicago Press, 1982.
Derrida, Jacques. 'Faith and Knowledge'. In *Acts of Religion*, translated by Samuel Weber, edited by Gil Anidjar, 42–101. London: Routledge, 2013.
Descartes, René. *Conversation with Burman*, translated by John Cottingham. Oxford: Clarendon Press, 1976. French edition: *Oeuvres de Descartes. Tome 5*, edited by Charles Adam et Paul Tannery. Paris: Vrin, 1968.
Descartes, René. 'Discourse on Method'. In *The Philosophical Writings of Descartes, Vol. 1*, translated by John Cottingham, Robert Stoothoff and Dugald Murdoch, 109–175.

Cambridge: Cambridge University Press, 1984. French original: *Oeuvres de Descartes. Tome 6*, edited by Charles Adam et Paul Tannery, 1–78. Paris: Vrin, 1967.

Descartes, René. 'Meditations on First Philosophy including the Objections and Replies'. In *The Philosophical Writings of Descartes, Vol. 2*, translated by John Cottingham, Robert Stoothoff and Dugald Murdoch, 1–397. Cambridge: Cambridge University Press, 1984. French original: *Oeuvres de Descartes. Tome 7*, edited by Charles Adam et Paul Tannery. Paris: Vrin, 1966.

Descartes, René. 'Passions of the Soul'. In *The Philosophical Writings of Descartes, Vol. 1*, translated by John Cottingham, Robert Stoothoff and Dugald Murdoch, 325–404. Cambridge: Cambridge University Press, 1984. French original: *Oeuvres de Descartes. Tome 11*, edited by Charles Adam et Paul Tannery. Paris: Vrin, 1967.

Descartes, René. 'Principles of Philosophy'. In *The Philosophical Writings of Descartes, Vol. 1*, translated by John Cottingham, Robert Stoothoff and Dugald Murdoch, 117–291. Cambridge: Cambridge University Press, 1984. French original: *Oeuvres de Descartes. Tome 8*, edited by Charles Adam et Paul Tannery. Paris: Vrin, 1974.

Descartes, René. 'Rules for the Direction of the Mind'. In *The Philosophical Writings of Descartes, Vol. 1*, translated by John Cottingham, Robert Stoothoff and Dugald Murdoch, 7–78. Cambridge: Cambridge University Press, 1984. French original: *Oeuvres de Descartes. Tome 10*, edited by Charles Adam et Paul Tannery. Paris: Vrin, 1974.

Descartes, René. *The Philosophical Writings of Descartes, Vol. 3: The Correspondence*, translated by John Cottingham, Robert Stoothoff and Dugald Murdoch. Cambridge: Cambridge University Press, 1991. French originals: *Oeuvres de Descartes. Tome 1, 4 and 5*, edited by Charles Adam et Paul Tannery. Paris: Vrin, 1965, 1967, 1968.

Descartes, René. 'The Search for Truth'. In *The Philosophical Writings of Descartes, Vol. 2*, translated by John Cottingham, Dugald Mrdoch and Robert Stoothoff, 400–20. Cambridge: Cambridge University Press. 1984. French Original: *Oeuvres de Descartes. Tome 10*, edited by Charles Adam et Paul Tannery. Paris: Vrin, 1970.

Despland, Michael. *Kant on History and Religion*. Montreal: McGill University Press, 1973.

Dixon, Thomas. *From Passions to Emotions: The Creation of a Secular Psychological Category*. Cambridge: Cambridge University Press, 2003.

Doyle, William. *Jansenism: Catholic Resistance to Authority from the Reformation to the French Revolution*. London: Macmillan, 1999.

Duhem, Pierre. *Medieval Cosmology: Theories of Infinity, Place, Time, Void, and the Plurality of Worlds*, translated by Rojer Ariew. Chicago: University of Chicago Press, 1985.

Dupré, Louis. *Passage to Modernity: An Essay in the Hermeneutics of Nature and Culture*. New Haven: Yale University Press, 1993.

Elisabeth, Princess of Bohemia. *The Correspondence between Princess Elisabeth of Bohemia and René Descartes*, translated by Lisa Shapiro. Chicago: University of Chicago Press, 2007.

Epictetus. 'Discourses'. In *Discourses and Selected Writings*, edited and translated by Robert Dobbin, 1–206. London: Penguin 2008.

Epictetus. 'Echiridion'. In *Discourses and Selected Writings*, edited and translated by Robert Dobbin, 219–45. London: Penguin 2008.

Epictetus. 'Fragments'. In *Discourses and Selected Writings*, edited and translated by Robert Dobbin, 207–18. London: Penguin 2008.

Erasmus/Luther. *Free Will and Salvation*, translated by Gordon Rupp. London: SCM Press, 1969.
Esclapez, Raymond. 'Montaigne et Nicolas de Cuse. Le thème de la "docte ignorance" dans les Essais'. *Littératures*, 18 (1988): 25–40.
Evans, Stephen. *Faith beyond Reason*. Grand Rapids, MI: Eerdmann, 1998.
Féher, Ferenc. 'Practical Reason in the Revolution: Kant's Dialogue with the French Revolution', *Social Research*, 56, no. 1 (1989): 161–85.
Fieser, James. 'Hume's Classifications of the Passions and its Precursors'. *Hume Studies*, 18, no. 1 (1992): 1–17.
Fink, Eugen. 'Operative Concepts in Husserl's Phenomenology'. In *Apriori and World*, edited by William McKenna, Robert Harlan and Laurence Winters, 56–70. Dordrecht: Martinus Nijhoff, 1981.
Firestone, Chris. *Kant and Theology at the Boundaries of Reason*. Farnham: Ashgate, 2009.
Flasch, Kurt. *Einführung in die Philosophie des Mittelatlers*. Berlin: Wissenschaftliche Buchgesellschaft, 1994.
Floridi, Luciano. *Sextus Empiricus: The Transmission and Recovery of Pyrrhonism*. Cambridge: Cambridge University Press, 2002.
Florschütz, Gottlieb. *Swedenborgs verborgene Wirkung auf Kant*. Würzburg: Königshausen & Neumann, 1992.
Fogelin, Robert. 'Hume's Scepticism'. In *Cambridge Companion to Hume*, edited by David Norton, 90–116. Cambridge: Cambridge University Press, 1993.
Fontanier, Jean-Michel. *La Beauté selon Saint Augustin*. Rennes: Presses Universitaire de Rennes 2008.
Fosl, Peter. *Hume's Scepticism: Pyrrhonian and Academic*. Edinburgh: Edinburgh University Press, 2020.
Fraenkel, Carlos. 'Spinoza's Philosophy of Religion'. In *The Oxford Handbook of Spinoza*, edited by Michael della Rocca, 277–407. Oxford: Oxford University Press, 2018.
Frame, Donald. 'Did Montaigne betray Sebond?' *Romantic Review*, 38, no. 4 (1947): 297–326.
Frankfurt, Harry. *Demons, Dreamers and Madmen*. Princeton: Princeton University Press, 2007.
Gillespie, Michael. *The Theological Origins of Modernity*. Chicago: Chicago University Press, 2009.
Green, Ronald. 'Kant and Kierkegaard on the Need for Historical Truth: An Imaginary Dialogue'. In *Kant and the New Philosophy of Religion*, edited by Chris Firestone and Stephen Palmquist, 157–78. Bloomington: Indiana University Press, 2006.
Green, Ronald. *Religious Reason: The Rational and Moral Basis of Religious Belief*. Oxford: Oxford University Press, 1978.
Green, Ronald. 'Religious Ritual: A Kantian Perspective'. *Journal of Religious Ethics*, 7, no. 2 (Fall 1979): 229–38.
Gueroult, Martial. *Descartes selon l'orde des raisons I*. Paris: Aubier, 1953.
Hare, John. *The Moral Gap: Kantian Ethics, Human Limits, and God's Assistance*. Oxford: Clarendon, 2002.
Hartle, Ann. *Michel de Montaigne: Accidental Philosopher*. Cambridge: Cambridge University Press, 2003.
Hartle, Ann. *Montaigne and the Origins of Modern Philosophy*. Evanston, IL: Northwestern University Press, 2013.
Hartle, Ann. *The Modern Self in Rousseau's Confessions. A Reply to St. Augustine*. Notre Dame, IN: University of Notre Dame Press, 1983.

Hartle, Ann. 'Montaigne and Skepticism'. In *The Cambridge Companion to Montaigne*, edited by Ullrich Langer, 193–206. Cambridge: Cambridge University Press, 2005.
Harris, James. 'The Government of the Passions'. In *The Oxford Handbook of British Philosophy in the Eighteenth Century*, edited by James Harris, 270–88. Oxford University Press, 2013.
Heidegger, Martin. *Introduction to Metaphysics*, translated by Gregory Fried and Richard Polt. New Haven: Yale University Press 2000.
Heidegger, Martin. '"Only a God Can Save Us": Der Spiegel's Interview with Heidegger'. *Philosophy Today*, 20 (1976): 267–84.
Heidegger, Martin. *The Phenomenology of Religious Life*, translated by Matthias Fritsch and Jennifer Gosetti-Ferencei. Bloomington: Indiana University Press, 2010.
Held, Klaus. *Der biblische Glaube*. Frankfurt a. M.: Klostermann, 2018.
Hadot. *Philosophy as a Way of Life*. London: Wiley-Blackwell, 1995.
Hobbes, Thomas. *Leviathan*. Oxford: Clarendon Press, 2012.
Hölderlin, Friedrich. *Sämtliche Werke. Grosser Stuttgarter Ausgabe, Volume 4, Part 1*, edited by Friedrich Beisener and Adolf Beck. Stuttgart: Kohlhammer, 1943.
Huenemann, Charlie. *Spinoza's Radical Theology*. London: Routledge, 2014.
Hulliung, Mark. 'Rousseau, Voltaire and the Revenge of Pascal'. In *The Cambridge Companion to Rousseau*, edited by Patrick Riley, 57–77. Cambridge: Cambridge University Press, 2001.
Hume, David. *Essays: Moral; Political; and Literary*, edited by Eugene Millar. Indianapolis: Liberty Classics, 1987.
Hume, David. *Inquiry concerning Human Understanding: Philosophical Works Volume 4*. London: Thoemmes Press, 1996.
Hume, David. *Inquiry concerning the Principle of Morals: Philosophical Works Volume 4*. London: Thoemmes Press, 1996.
Hume, David. *Principal Writings on Religion, Including Dialogues concerning Natural Religion and the Natural History of Religion*, edited by John Addison. Oxford: Oxford University Press, 2008.
Hume, David. *Treatise concerning Human Nature: The Philosophical Works Volume 1 and 2*. London: Thoemmes Press, 1996.
Hume, David. *Selected Essays*, edited by Stephen Copley and Andrew Edgar. Oxford: Oxford University Press, 1993.
Husserl, Edmund. *Experience and Judgement*, translated by James Churchill. Evanston, IL: Northwestern University Press, 1973.
Husserl, Edmund. *Ideas Pertaining to a Pure Phenomenology and to a Phenomenological Philosophy, Book 1*, translated by Fred Kersten. The Hague: Kluwer, 1983.
Immerwahr, John. 'Hume on Tranquillizing the Passions'. *Hume Studies*, 18, no. 2 (1992): 293–314.
Immerwahr, John. 'Hume's Revised Racism'. *Journal of the History of Ideas*, 53, no. 3 (1992): 481–6.
Insole, Christopher. 'The Irreducible Importance of Religious Hope in Kant's Conception of the Highest Good'. *Philosophy*, 83, no. 325 (2008): 333–51.
Israel, Johnathan. *Radical Enlightenment: Philosophy and the Making of Modernity 1650–1750*. Oxford: Oxford University Press, 2001.
Jeffrey, Renée. 'The Origins of the Modern Emotions: Princess Elisabeth of Bohemia and the Embodied Mind'. *History of European Ideas*, 43, no. 6 (2016): 547–59.
Jonas, Hans. *The Gnostic Religion: The Message of the Alien God and the Beginnings of Christianity*. Boston: Beacon Press, 2001.

Johnson, Gregory. 'The Sea of Melancholia: Kant on Philosophy and Enthusiasm'. In *Kant and the New Philosophy of Religion*, edited by Chris Firestone, 43–61. Bloomington: Indiana University Press, 2006.

Kant, Immanuel. *Critique of the Power of Judgement*, translated by Paul Guyer. Cambridge: Cambridge University Press, 2000. German Original edition: *Kritik der Urteilskraft. Kants Gesammelte Schriften 'Akademieausgabe', Königlich Preußische Akademie der Wissenschaften, Volume 5*. Berlin: Reimer, 1912.

Kant, Immanuel. *Critique of Practical Reason*, translated by Lewis Beck. London: Macmillan, 1993. Original German edition: *Kritik der praktischen Vernunft. Kants Gesammelte Schriften 'Akademieausgabe', Königlich Preußische Akademie der Wissenschaften, Volume 5*. Berlin: Reimer, 1900.

Kant, Immanuel. *Critique of Pure Reason*, translated by Norman Kemp-Smith. New York: St. Martin's Press, 1929. Original German edition: *Kritik der reienen Vernunft. Kants Gesammelte Schriften 'Akademieausgabe', Königlich Preußische Akademie der Wissenschaften, Volumes 3 and 4*. Berlin: Reimer, 1900.

Kant, Immanuel. *Lectures on Philosophical Theology*, translated by Allen Wood and Gertrude Clarke. Ithaca, NY: Cornell University Press, 1978. Original German edition: *Vorlesungen über die philosophische Religionslehre. Kants Gesammelte Schriften 'Akademieausgabe', Königlich Preußische Akademie der Wissenschaften, Volume 28*. Berlin: Reimer, 1972.

Kant, Immanuel. *Notes and Fragments*, translated by Paul Guyer. Cambridge: Cambridge University Press, 2002.

Kant, Immanuel. *Philosophical Correspondence*, edited and translated by Arnulf Zweig. Cambridge: Cambridge University Press, 1999. Original German edition: *Briefwechsel. Kants Gesammelte Schriften 'Akademieausgabe', Königlich Preußische Akademie der Wissenschaften, Volume 10*. Berlin: Reimer, 1900.

Kant, Immanuel, 'The Conflict of the Faculties'. In *Religion and Rational Theology*, translated and edited by Allen W. Wood and George di Giovanni, 237–327. Cambridge: Cambridge University Press, 2012. Original German edition: 'Der Streit der Fakultäten'. In *Kants Gesammelte Schriften 'Akademieausgabe', Königlich Preußische Akademie der Wissenschaften, Volume 5*, 5–116. Berlin: Reimer, 1907.

Kant, Immanuel. *Religion within the Boundaries of Mere Reason*, edited by Allen Wood and George di Giovani. Cambridge: Cambridge University Press, 1998. Original German edition: *Religion innerhalb der Grenze von blossen Vernunft. Briefwechsel. Kants Gesammelte Schriften 'Akademieausgabe', Königlich Preußische Akademie der Wissenschaften, Volume 6*. Berlin: Reimer, 1914.

Kant, Immanuel. *The One Possible Basis for the Determination of the Existence of God*, translated by Gordon Treash. Lincoln: University of Nebraska Press, 1994. Original German edition: 'Der einzig mögliche Beweisgrund zu einer Demonstration des Daseins Gottes', *Kants Gesammelte Schriften 'Akademieausgabe', Königlich Preußische Akademie der Wissenschaften, Volume 2*, 65–163. Berlin: Reimer, 1905.

Kant, Immanuel. 'What Real Progress has Metaphysics made in Germany since Leibniz and Wolff'. In *Theoretical Philosophy after 1781*, translated and edited by Henry Allison, Peter Heath and Gary Hatfield, 337–424. Cambridge: Cambridge University Press, 2002. Original German edition: 'Welches wirklichen Fortschritte, did the Metaphysik seit Leibnizens und Wolffs Zeiten in Deutschland gemacht hat?' *Kants Gesammelte Schriften 'Akademieausgabe', Königlich Preußische Akademie der Wissenschaften, Volume 20*. Berlin: Reimer, 1942.

Kaufmann, Matthias, and Alexander Aichele. *A Companion to Luis de Molina*. Leiden: Brill, 2014.

Kisner, Matthew. 'Spinoza on Natures: Aristotelian and Mechanistic Routes to Relational Autonomy'. In *Spinoza and Relational Autonomy: Being with Others*, edited by Aurelia Armstrong, Keith Green and Andrea Sangiacomo, 74–97. Edinburgh: Edinburgh University Press, 2019.

Klever, Wim. 'Hume Contra Spinoza?' *Hume Studies*, 16, no. 2 (1990): 89–105.

Knuuttila, Simo. *Emotion in Ancient and Medieval Philosophy*. Oxford: Oxford University Press, 2004.

Kolakowski, Lezsek. *God Owes Us Nothing: A Brief Remark on Pascal's Religion and on the Spirit of Jansenism*. Chicago: University of Chicago Press, 1995.

Koselleck, Reinhart. *Futures Past*, translated by Keith Tribe. Cambridge, MA: MIT Press, 1985.

Koselleck, Reinhart, and Michaela W. Richter. 'Crisis'. *Journal of the History of Ideas*, 67 no. 2 (2006): 357–400.

Kritzman, Lawrence. *The Fabulous Imagination: On Montaigne's Essays*. New York: Columbia University Press, 2009.

Kühn, Manfred. 'The Reception of Hume in Germany'. In *The Reception of Hume in Europe*, edited by Peter Jones, 98–138. London: Continuum, 2005.

Laporte, Jean. *La Coeur et le raison selon Pascal*. Paris: Elzevir, 1950.

Lawler, James. *Matter and Spirit: The Battle of Metaphysics in Modern Wester Philosophy before Kant*. Rochester, NY: University of Rochester Press, 2006.

Lefebvre, Lucien. *The Problem of Unbelief in the Sixteenth Century: The Religion of Rabelais*, translated by B. Gottlieb. Cambridge, MA: Harvard University Press, 1982.

Le Guern, Michel. *Pascal et Descartes*. Paris: Nizet, 1971.

Libera, Alain de. *Penser au Moyen Âge*. Paris: Seuil, 1991.

Libera, Alain de. *Raison et Foi. Archéologie d'une crise d'Albert le Grand à Jean-Paul II*. Paris: Seuil, 2003.

Lin, Martin. 'Memory and Personal Identity in Spinoza'. *Canadian Journal of Philosophy*, 35, no. 2 (2005): 243–68.

Lipsius, Justus. *On Constancy*, translated by John Stradling. Liverpool: Liverpool University Press, 2006.

Löwith, Karl. *Meaning in History: The Theological Implications of the Philosophy of History*. Chicago: University of Chicago Press, 2006.

Lubac, Henri de. *Augustinianism and Modern Theology*, translated by Lancelot Sheppard. New York: Herder and Herder, 2000.

Lubac, Henri de. *The Mystery of the Supernatural*, translated by Rosemary Sheed. London: Geoffrey Chapman, 1967.

Manent, Pierre. *Montaigne: Life without Law*, translated by Paul Seaton. Notre Dame, IN: University of Notre Dame Press, 2020.

Manoussakis, John. *The Ethics of Time: A Phenomenology and Hermeneutics of Change*. London: Bloomsbury, 2017.

Marion, Jean-Luc. *In the Self's Place: The Approaches of Saint Augustine*, translated by Jeffrey Kosky. Stanford: Stanford University Press, 2012.

Marion, Jean-Luc. *Cartesian Questions: Methods and Metaphysics*. Chicago: Chicago University Press, 1999.

Marina, Jacqueline. 'Kant on Grace: A Reply to His Critics'. *Religious Studies*, 33, no. 4 (1997): 379–400.

McFarlane, Ian. 'The Concept of Virtue in Montaigne'. In *Montaigne: Essays in Memory of Richard Sayce*, edited by Ian MacFarlane and Ian Maclean, 77–100. Oxford: Oxford University Press, 1982.
McIntyre, Jane. 'Strength of Mind: Prospects and Problems for a Humean Account'. *Synthese*, 152, no. 3 (2006): 393–401.
Menage, Giles. *The History of Women Philosophers*, translated by Beatrice H Zedler. Lanham, MD: University Press of America, 1984.
Menn, Stephen. *Descartes and Augustine*. Cambridge: Cambridge University Press, 2002.
Merchant, Carolyn. *The Death of Nature: Women, Ecology and the Scientific Revolution*. New York: Harper Collins, 1980.
Merleau-Ponty, Maurice. 'Reading Montaigne'. In *Signs*, translated by Richard McCleary. Evanston, IL: Northwestern University Press, 1964.
Michalson, Gordon. *Fallen Freedom: Kant on Radical Evil and Moral Regeneration*. Cambridge: Cambridge University Press, 1990.
Michalson, Gordon. 'The Problem of Salvation in Kant's Religion within the Limits of Reason Alone'. *International Philosophical Quarterly*, 37, no.3 (1997): 319–28.
Milbank, John. *Beyond Secular Reason: The Representation of Being and the Representation of the People*. London: Wiley Blackwell, 2013.
Milbank, John. *Theology and Social Theory: Beyond Secular Reason*. London: Wiley Blackwell, 2006.
Miller, Jon. *Spinoza and the Stoics*. Cambridge: Cambridge University Press, 2015.
Miner, Robert. 'Pascal on the Uses of Scepticism'. *Logos*, 11 no. 4 (2008): 111–22.
Mitchell, Harvey. 'Reclaiming the Self: The Pascal-Rousseau Connection'. *Journal of the History of Ideas*, 54, no. 4 (1993): 637–58.
Montaigne, Michel de. *The Complete Essays of Montaigne*, translated by Donald Frame. Stanford: Stanford University Press, 1965. French Original: *Les essais de Michel de Montaigne*, edited by Pierre Villey. Paris: Alcan, 1922.
Most, Glenn. *Doubting Thomas*. Cambridge, MA: Harvard University Press, 2005.
Neto, José. *The Christianization of Pyrrhonism: Scepticism and Faith in Pascal, Kierkegaard, and Shestov*. Dordrecht: Kluwer 1995.
Neuhouser, Frederick. *Rousseau's Theodicy of Self-Love*. Oxford: Oxford University Press, 2008.
The New Jerusalem Bible: Study Edition. London: Darton, Longman and Todd, 1994.
Nietzsche, Friedrich. *The Gay Science*, translated by Josefine Nauchkhoff. Cambridge: Cambridge University Press, 2001.
Nietzsche, Friedrich. *Philosophy and Truth: Selections from Nietzsche's Notebooks of the Early 1870's*, edited by Daniel Breazeale. New York: Humanities Press, 1979.
Nietzsche, Friedrich. *Twilight of the Idols and the Anti-Christ*, translated by Reginald Holingdale. London: Penguin, 1968.
Ockham, William of. *Ockham: Philosophical Writings*, translated by Philotheus Boehner and Stephen Brown. Indianapolis: Hackett, 1990.
Ockham, William of. *Predestination, God's Foreknowledge, and Future Contingents*, translated by Marilyn McCord Adams and Norman Kretzmann. Indianapolis: Hackett, 1983.
O'Neill, Onora. 'Kant on Reason and Religion', Tanner Lectures. Available online: https://tannerlectures.utah.edu/_documents/a-to-z/o/oneill97.pdf (accessed 2 November 2020).
O'Regan, Cyril. *Gnostic Return in Modernity*. Albany: SUNY Press, 2001.

Paige, Nicholas. *Being Interior: Autobiography and the Contradictions of Modernity in Seventeenth Century France*. Philadelphia: University of Pennsylvania Press, 2001.
Paganini, Gianni. *Skepsis: Le Débat des Modernes sur le Scepticisme*. Paris: Vrin, 2008.
Palmquist, Stephen. *Kant's Critical Religion: Volume Two of Kant's System of Perspectives*. London: Routledge, 2019.
Parusniková, Zuzana. *David Hume: Sceptic*. Dordrecht: Springer, 2016.
Pascal, Blaise. 'Discussion with Monsieur de Sacy'. In *Pensées and Other Writings*, translated by Honor Levi, 182–92. Oxford: Oxford University Press, 1995. French original: 'Entretien de M. Pascal avec M. de Sacy sur Épictète et Montaigne'. In *Oeuvres Complètes, Tome 2*, edited by Michel Le Guern, 82–98. Paris: Gallimard, 2000.
Pascal, Blaise. *Pensées*, translated by A. J. Krailsheimer. London: Penguin, 1966. French original: *Pensées*, edited by Louis Lafuma. Paris: Seuil, 1962.
Pavlotis, Tamás. *Le rationalisme de Pascal*. Paris: Editions de Sorbonne, 2007.
Paxman, Katharina. 'Imperceptible Impressions and Disorder in the Soul: A Characterization of the Distinction between Calm and Violent Passions in Hume'. *Journal of Scottish Philosophy*, 13, no. 3 (2015): 265–78.
Pelagius. *Commentary on St. Paul's Letter to the Romans*, translated by Theodore De Bruyn. Oxford: Clarendon Press, 1993.
Pelagius. 'Letter and Confession of Faith to Innocent I'. Early Church Texts. Available online: https://earlychurchtexts.com/public/pelagius_letter_and_confession_to_innocent.htm (accessed 8 January 2021).
Pelagius. *The Letters of Pelagius and His Followers*, edited and translated by Brinley Rees. London: Boydell Press, 1991.
Penelham, Terence. *God and Skepticism: A Study in Skepticism and Fideism*. Dordrecht: Springer, 2012.
Penelham, Terence. 'Skepticism and Fideism'. In *The Skeptical Tradition*, edited by Myles Burnyeat, 287–318. Berkeley: University of California Press, 1983.
Peperzak, Adriaan. 'Life, Science, and Wisdom According to Descartes'. *History of Philosophy Quarterly*, 12, no. 2 (1995): 133–53.
Perinetti, Dario. 'Hume at La Flèche: Skepticism and the French Connection'. *Journal of the History of Philosophy*, 56, no. 1 (2018): 45–74.
Peters, James. *The Logic of the Heart*. Ada, MI: Baker Academic, 2009.
Petrarch, Franscesco. *The Secret*, translated by Carrol Quillen. Boston: Bedford St. Martins, 2003.
Piché, David. *La Condemnation Parisienne de 1277*. Paris: Vrin, 1999.
Popkin, Richard. 'Hume and Spinoza'. *Hume Studies*, 5, no. 2 (1979): 65–93.
Popkin, Richard. *The History of Scepticism: from Savonarola to Bayle*. Oxford: Oxford University Press, 2003.
Radcliffe, Elizabeth. *Hume, Passion and Action*. Oxford: Oxford University Press, 2018.
Ravven, Heidi. 'Spinoza's Path from Imaginative Transindividuality to Intuitive Relational Autonomy: From Fusion, Confusion and Fragmentation to Moral Integrity'. In *Spinoza and Relational Autonomy: Being with Others*, edited by Aurelia Armstrong, Keith Green and Andrea Sangiacomo, 98–114. Edinburgh: Edinburgh University Press, 2019.
Reardon, Bernard. *Kant as Philosophical Theologian*. London: Rowman & Littlefield, 1988.
Rée, Jonathan. 'Descartes's Comedy'. *Philosophy and Literature*, 8, no. 2 (1984): 151–66.
Rees, Brinley. *Pelagius: A Reluctant Heretic*. London: Boydell Press, 1988.
Rendall, Steven. 'The Rhetoric of Montaigne's Self-Portrait: Speaker and Subject'. *Studies in Philology*, 73, no. 3 (1976): 285–301.

Rendall, Steven. 'Dialectical Structure and Tactics in Montaigne's 'Of Cannibals'. *Pacific Coast Philology*, 12 (1977): 56–63.
Ricoeur, Paul. *Freud and Philosophy*, translated by Dennis Savage. New Haven: Yale University Press, 1977.
Rivera, Joseph. 'Blumenberg's Problematic Secularization Thesis: Augustine, Curiositas and the Emergence of Late Modernity'. *Religions*, 12, no. 5 (2021): 297–313.
Rodis-Lewis, Geneviève. *La Morale de Descartes*. Paris: PUF, 1998.
Römer, Inga. *Das Begehren der reinen praktischen Vernunft: Kants Ethik in phänomenologishcen Sicht*. Hamburg: Meiner, 2018.
Rorty, Amélie. 'Cartesian Passion and the Union of Mind and Body'. In *Essays on Descartes Meditations*, edited by Amelie Rorty, 513–34. Berkeley: University of California Press, 1986.
Rorty, Amélie. 'The Structure of Descartes' Meditations'. In *Essays on Descartes Meditations*, edited by Amelie Rorty, 1–20. Berkeley: University of California Press, 1986.
Rosenzweig, Franz. *The Star of Redemption*, translated by William Hallo. Notre Dame, IN: University of Notre Dame Press, 1985.
Rossi, Philip. 'The Final End of All Things'. In *Kant's Philosophy of Religion Reconsidered*, edited by Philip Rossi and Michael Wreen, 132–64. Bloomington: Indiana University Press, 1991.
Rousseau, Jean Jacques. *Émile or On Education*, translated by Christopher Kelly and Allan Bloom. Lebanon, NH: United Press of New England, 2010.
Rousseau, Jean Jacques. *The Discourses and Other Early Political Writings*, edited and translated by Victor Gourevitch. Cambridge: Cambridge University Press, 2019.
Rutherford, Donald. 'Salvation as a State of Mind: The Place of *Acquiescentia* in Spinoza's Ethics'. *British Journal for the History of Philosophy*, 7, no. 3 (1999): 447–73.
Schmaltz, Tad. 'What Has Cartesianism to do with Jansenism?' *Journal of the History of Ideas*, 60, no. 1 (1999): 37–56.
Schmitt, Charles. 'The Rediscovery of Greek Scepticism in Modern Times'. In *The Skeptical Tradition*, edited by Myles Burnyeat, 225–52. Berkeley: University of California Press, 1983.
Schneewind, Jerome. *The Invention of Autonomy: A History of Modern Moral Philosophy*. Cambridge: Cambridge University Press, 1998.
Seneca. 'On Anger'. In *Moral and Political Essays*, edited and translated by John Cooper and J. F. Procopé. Cambridge: Cambridge University Press, 1995.
Sexti Empirici Opera graece et latine: Pyrrhonias institutiones continens. Lipsiae: Kuehnianae, 1840.
Sextus Empiricus. *The Skeptic Way: Outlines of Pyrrhonism*, translated by Benson Bates. Oxford: Oxford University Press, 1996.
Sextus Empiricus. *Against the Logicians*, translated by Richard Bett. Cambridge: Cambridge University Press, 2006.
Shakespeare, William. *The Complete Works*, edited by Stanley Wells. Oxford: Clarendon, 1988.
Shapin, Steven. 'Descartes the Doctor: Rationalism and Its Therapies'. *British Journal for the History of Science*, 33, no. 2 (2000): 131–54.
Shapiro, Lisa. 'Je ne regrette rien. Elisabeth et Descartes und la psychologie morale de regret'. In *Élisabeth de Bohême face à Descartes: deux philosophes?*, edited by Delphine Kolesnik-Antoine and Marie-Frédérique Pellegrin, 155–70. Paris: Vrin, 2014.

Spinoza, Benedict de. 'The Ethics'. In *Collected Works Volume 1*, edited and translated by Edwin Curley, 408–617. Princeton: Princeton University Press, 1985. Origin Latin: https://home.kpn.nl/rudolf.meijer/spinoza/works.htm?lang=E.

Spinoza, Benedict de. 'The Emendation of the Intellect'. In *Collected Works Volume 1*, edited and translated by Edwin Curley, 3–45. Princeton: Princeton University Press, 1985.

Spinoza, Benedict de. *The Letters*, translated by Samuel Shirley. London: Hacket, 1995.

Spinoza, Benedict de. 'Theological-Political Treatise'. In *Collected Works Volume 2*, edited by Edwin Curley, 65–54. Princeton: Princeton University Press, 2016.

Starobinski, Jean. *Montaigne in Motion*, translated by Arthur Goldhammer. Chicago: University of Chicago Press, 1985.

Starobinski, Jean. 'The Body's Moment', translated by John A. Gallucci. *Yale French Studies*, no. 64 (1983): 273–305.

Steiner, George. *The Death of Tragedy*. London: Faber and Faber, 1961.

Taylor, Charles. *Sources of the Self: The Making of the Modern Identity*. Cambridge, MA: Harvard University Press, 1989.

Taylor, Charles. *A Secular Age*. Cambridge, MA: Harvard University Press, 2007.

Thier, Sebastian. *Die Kirche bei Pelagius*. Berlin: de Gruyter 1999.

Toulmin, Stephen. *Cosmopolis: The Hidden Agenda of Modernity*. Chicago: University of Chicago Press, 1992.

Tournon, André. 'Self-Interpretation in Montaigne's Essais'. *Yale French Studies*, no. 64 (1983): 51–72.

Uyl, Douglas Den, and Rice, Lee. 'Spinoza and Hume on Individuals'. *Reason Papers*, no. 15 (1990): 91–117.

Whelan, Frederick. *Hume and Machiavelli: Political Realism and Liberal Thought*. London: Lexington, 2006.

Wilson, Catherine. *Epicureanism at the Origins of Modernity*. Oxford: Clarendon Press, 2008.

Wippel, John. 'The Condemnations of 1270 and 1277 at Paris'. *Journal of Medieval and Renaissance Studies*, 7 (1977): 169–201.

Wood, Allen. *Kant's Moral Religion*. Ithaca, NY: Cornell University Press, 2009.

Worthen, Jeremy. 'Christianity and the Limits of Tragedy'. *New Blackfriars*, 70, no. 825 (1989): 109–17.

Wright, John. 'Ideas of Habit and Custom in Early Modern Philosophy'. *Journal of the British Society for Phenomenology*, 42, no. 1 (2011): 18–32.

Index

Academic Scepticism 198 n.98
   Augustine and 37, 54
   Hume and 216 n.17
   Pyrrhonian Scepticism and 20, 39, 67,
      198 n.99, 202 n.199
Adam 12, 14–15, 17, 27, 99–100, 119
afterlife
   Hume on 113–15
   Kant on 3
   Montaigne on 54
   Pascal on 95
   Spinoza on 120, 144, 216 n.35
Albertus Magnus 25
angels 35
   Descartes and 106
   fallen 179
   Kant and 164, 177, 179
   Montaigne and 62, 63
   Pascal and 76. *See also* Immortality of
      the Soul
anger 18–19, 137
animality 19, 120, 129–30, 175
   death and 54
   humanity and 59, 62, 155
   instinct and 120
animal spirits 79, 120 n.166
anxiety
   death and 54
   despair and 106
   doubt and 7, 22, 30, 38, 68
   grace and 34
   Pascal on 94
apatheia 36, 59, 115, 140, 163, 190
appetite 58–60, 62, 63, 144
aporia 72, 88
   Descartes and 81–2, 84, 106
   Kant and 161–3, 166
   Montaigne and 49–50, 53, 60
   Pascal and 87–8, 94, 108
   Sceptical 20–1, 37
   translation into Latin 38–9

Aquinas, St. Thomas 24, 25, 26, 27–8
Arendt, Hannah 19, 27, 151
Aristotle 24, 25, 47
Arnaud, Antoine 95, 212 n.124
arrogance 85, 99, 100
artifice 145–6
ascetics
   Kant and 152, 154, 155, 163
   Stoical 18, 30, 40, 187–8
atheism 7, 42, 99, 132, 143
Augustine, St. 9–17, 23, 27, 29, 32, 36–7,
      74, 189, 190
   Descartes and 74–5
   Jansenism and 70
   Kant and 152, 153, 155, 165, 166, 171,
      179, 183, 184
   Montaigne and 54–5, 60–1, 204 n.159
   Pascal and 77, 79, 95, 97, 110
   Spinoza and 113–14, 115–16, 135,
      138, 149–50
Augustinianism 31, 34–5, 39, 70–1, 104,
      110, 172, 190
authority church 37
   customary 102
   divine 39, 47, 49, 56, 65, 83
   legal 87
   prophetic 148
   social 72–3, 101, 142
   traditional 139
autobiography 11, 41, 72
autonomy 38, 67, 114, 138, 152, 168–9,
      173, 176–7. *See also* Reason
      (autonomy of)
auto-affectivity
   Hume and 115, 124, 134–5,136, 137
   Kant and 165, 180
Avicenna 25

baptism 16–17, 60–1, 183
beauty
   of creation 28, 66

divine 11
　Descartes and 99
　Grace and 64
　Hume and 136, 140, 143
　Kant and 152, 156
belief
　Hume on 131,
　Kant on 160, 162
　living without 39, 72
　Pascal on 78
　natural 79
benevolence 109, 146
Blumenberg, Hans 8, 12, 22, 23, 38, 201 n.198. See also Self (-assertion)
body 13, 19, 131–2
　affectivity and 125–7, 139, 147–8
　habit and 51, 108–9
　power of 135
　renunciation of 34, 71, 101
body and soul/mind 34, 101
　Descartes and 74–8, 83, 104–8
　Hume and 130
　Montaigne and 51–2, 54, 56, 62
　Pascal and 79, 108–9
　Spinoza and 119, 147. See also Soul
Boethius of Dacia 24
boredom 77, 141
Boyle, Robert 118
Braque, Rémi 26, 216 n.35
building(s) 91, 94, 102, 104, 111, 152, 163, 164

Calvin, John 31, 70
causality 19
　Aquinas on 25
　causa sui 98, 128
　Descartes on 89, 98–9
　efficient 98, 122
　final 47, 133, 143
　Hume on 120, 123, 128, 130, 137, 143, 220 n.180
　Kant on 158, 177–8, 181
　Montaigne on 48
　natural and supernatural 24
　Pascal on 79
　Spinoza on 114, 116, 125–7, 131–2, 135
certainty
　Descartes and 82–3, 89–93, 103, 105–6
　Hume and 140

Kant and 181
Pascal and 87, 88, 94
Scepticism and 21, 39, 43, 67, 68, 87
Spinoza and 148–9
chance 56–7, 95, 123, 130, 166. See also Fortune (*fortuna*)
choice 19, 53, 88, 103, 110
　free 71, 164, 179
　moral 171, 173, 178–80
Christ 11, 97
　Augustine and 15–17, 32, 34
　example of 13, 180, 182, 197 n.73
　incarnated 23, 99, 100, 184
　Pelagius and 16–17, 32
Christianity 2, 12, 23–5, 37, 64, 97, 201–2 n.198
　Kant and 169–70, 180, 184, 186–7
　and other religions 65–6, 97
　Pascal and 70, 97–100
　and tragedy 110
Church
　authority of 39 (*see also* authority)
　Christian 28, 30, 110, 189 (*see also* Christianity)
　historical 187
　visible and invisible 186–7
Cicero 36–7, 39
comedy 1, 44, 49, 87, 111
communication 55–6, 78, 142, 157, 160, 187
community 102, 117, 141, 184, 185–6
competition 171, 173, 183
concupiscence 17, 77, 109
Condemnation of Paris (1277) 24–5, 190
conscience 34–5, 39
　Kant and 180
　Montaigne and 46, 56–7, 59, 61–4
　Rousseau and 174
consent 17, 67, 146
constancy 30–1, 58, 102–3, 116, 124, 132
contingency 12, 25–6, 31, 33
　Descartes and 103
　and evil 175–6, 177–8
　Hume and 133
　Montaigne and 47, 49, 52–3
　Spinoza and 133, 139
conversion 17, 34, 60, 113–14, 182–3, 184
cooperation 117, 144–5, 147, 150, 183–4, 185–6

creation 36
   Augustine and 10, 13–14, 41, 60
   beauty of 28, 66
   Biblical account of 2, 12
   Descartes and 91, 93, 98–9, 104
   Gnostic account of 15–16, 23
   and grace 9, 12, 14–15
   Kant and 158, 169, 176, 180
   'out of Nothing' 12
   Pelagius and 13–14, 16
   and salvation 8, 60
   Voluntarism and 28, 98
crisis 7–8, 22, 31–2, 36, 42, 69, 189
curiosity 77–8, 105, 209 n.45
custom
   Descartes and 75, 81, 86–7, 102
   Hume and 117, 129, 131, 141, 145
   Montaigne and 46–8, 49, 53–4, 62
   Pascal and 107–8
   Rousseau and 174
   Spinoza and 127

death
   Augustine and 9
   Descartes and 95
   and the Fall 15
   Hume and 114–15
   Kant and 181, 182
   Montaigne and 54, 61–2
   Pascal and 77, 94–5, 108
deception 73, 83
deduction 89–90, 93–4. *See also* intuition
della Mirandola, Giovanni Pico 35–6
democracy 144, 147
Derrida, Jacques 9, 188, 190
Deleuze, Giles 123
Descartes, René 2, 7, 29, 31, 45, 69–111, 113, 116, 120, 121, 150, 152, 155, 174, 175
   on the cogito 83, 90–5
   on the evil genius 73, 91
   on natural light 83, 88, 210 n.70
   on the passions 74–6, 78, 92, 101, 103, 104–6, 111
   on a provisional moral code 101–3, 107, 117
desire
   and the ascetic 152
   Augustine and 10, 11, 12, 27, 34–5, 36

   Descartes and 103–7
   Hume and 134
   for knowledge 50, 77, 78–9, 81
   and lack 28,
   Montaigne and 53, 59, 64
   paradox of 16
   Platonic 20
   of reason 152, 154–8, 159, 162–4
   sexual 13, 51, 63, 77
   Spinoza and 113–14, 115, 138, 139, 143
   for the supersensible 152
   Stoic 17
   and will 28, 74 (*see also* Will)
despair 51, 67, 69, 83, 99, 106, 140, 152, 154, 156, 166–7, 181, 214 n.186
devotion 109, 150, 183
dignity 56, 85, 108, 110, 162
diversion/distraction 77, 95
diversity 44, 47, 48, 50–1, 60, 69, 80–1, 86, 107–8
dogma 20, 39, 49, 173
double truth 24–5
doubt
   Academic Scepticism and 37
   and anxiety 30, 68
   and *aporia* 38–9, 72
   Descartes and 73, 75, 81–2, 89–94, 98, 102, 104, 105–6
   and *epoché* 20, 22
   Montaigne and 45, 47, 49–50, 60, 64, 67
   Pyrrhonians and 40
dreams 160, 163
Duns Scotus 25, 84
Dupré, Louis 26, 32, 199 n.122
duty 103, 155, 158, 159, 169, 173, 179–81, 182

Elisabeth, Princess of Bohemia 103, 104, 110
enjoyment 52, 57, 59, 115, 165
Epictetus 17, 18–19, 42, 85
Epicurus 57
Epicureanism 59, 68, 113, 194 n.4
epoché (suspension of judgement) 19, 20, 21, 37, 198 n.101. *See also* Doubt (and *epoché*)
   Descartes and 82–3, 101
   Kant and 161
   Montaigne and 42, 44, 49, 60, 67–8

Pascal and 87, 94
Erasmus, Desiderius 31, 33, 39
eternal truths 71, 91, 93, 98
eternity
  and God 24–5, 36
  love of 115
  under the species of 94, 119–20, 147
  and time 13, 36, 149, 182, 189
  of the World 24, 133
evil
  origins of 14–16, 74 (*see also* Kant (radical evil))
  and the passions 105, 120, 139
  punishment of 119
  repentance of 103
exaiphnes 178, 179, 182
experiment 29, 118, 146
external goods 117, 149

faith
  crisis of 7
  and good works 37
  and grace 9, 38, 97–8, 104, 108, 184
  and the heart 182
  historical 184–5
  and morals 143, 169
  natural and supernatural 96–7, 99
  and prophets 148–9
  rational 169, 172, 184
  and reason 22, 24–5, 28–9, 32, 36, 37, 39–40, 42, 55, 64–8, 72, 99, 101, 104, 152–3, 167–8, 172, 184–5, 190
  and trust 9, 83
  seeking understanding 190. See also Fideism, Obedience
fallenness
  Augustine on 10, 13, 14–17, 27, 29, 60
  Descartes on 70–1, 74–5, 81, 82–4, 104
  and the Fall 2, 8, 9, 13–14, 36
  Hume on 120
  Kant on 166, 172, 176–7, 178–9, 183, 187–8
  logic of 74, 151
  naturalized 63–4
  Pascal on 70–1, 76–9, 85–7, 95–7, 99, 100, 107, 108–9
  Spinoza on 119
  Voluntarism and 33
family 145–6

fear 134, 142–3, 147–8, 150, 173
fictitious, the 124, 131
fideism 42, 96, 97, 152, 167
Fink, Eugen 4
forgiveness 13, 17, 61–2, 182–3
fortune (*fortuna*) 18, 47, 56–8, 61, 63, 102, 137, 140, 143
freedom
  created 11–12
  and evil 10, 14
  Hume on 116
  and grace 16, 32–3, 104
  Kant on 163, 164
  and moral law 177–81
  and nature 155–6, 167–70, 175–6
  and the passions 17, 105
  to philosophize 117
  political 149–50, 185–6
  and sin 17
  Spinoza on 116, 142
  Stoic 36
Freud, Sigmund 109
friendship 42, 54, 57, 109

Galileo, Galilei 29
Gassendi, Pierre 38, 39
generosity 57, 70, 107, 146
Gillespie, Michael 8
glory 9, 11, 55, 56–7, 63, 108, 194 n.3
gnosticism 12, 23, 31, 36. See also Manicheanism
god
  as creator 12, 16, 25, 26, 83–4, 91, 92–3, 98–9, 104, 158
  discourse about 9–10, 33, 56
  divine names 55
  hidden 7, 37–8, 47, 68–9, 88, 96, 99, 151, 191
  image of (*imago dei*) 27
  and inward turn 10–11
  kingdom of 169–70, 186–7
  and law 149–50,
  love of 79, 100, 109–10, 115–16, 119, 127, 135, 138, 143, 147, 149–50
  and morals 169, 180,
  omnipotence of 25, 34, 41, 68, 91, 133
  as redeemer 95, 99–100, 104, 110
  revelation of 16, 28–9, 36, 55, 66, 96–7, 104, 148–9, 172, 184, 185, 187

sovereignty of 28, 70–1, 104, 107
will of 12, 25–9, 31–5, 65, 83–4, 91, 93. *See also* authority, Cause (*causa sui*), Christ, Contingency, Fallenness, Forgiveness, Gnosticism, Grace, Heart, Nominalism, Obedience, Prayer, Providence, Salvation, Trinity, Voluntarism
grace 8–9
  Aquinas and 24, 40
  Augustine and 10–17, 24, 29, 32–3, 34, 37–8, 40
  Descartes and 83, 98, 104
  Kant and 180–4
  Luther and 32–3
  Montaigne and 63–4, 64–7
  Pascal and 70–1, 85, 96, 108–9, 110
  Pelagius and 13–17, 32–3
  William of Ockham and 33
Gregory of Nyssa 28
guilt 17, 110, 176, 182

habit 13, 15
  Descartes and 75, 89, 90, 93, 103, 108
  Hume and 120, 130–1, 141, 145
  Montaigne and 46, 50–1, 58, 61–3, 89
  Pascal and 86, 108–9
  Spinoza and 149
Hamann, Johann 169, 223–4 n.37
happiness
  Augustine on 34,
  Descartes on 69–70, 99, 101–2, 107, 111
  Hume on 120, 140–1, 146
  Kant on 157, 166–7, 169–70, 176
  Montaigne on 68
  Pascal on 69–70, 76–7, 94, 95, 101, 107, 108–9, 110
  Sceptic 22, 88, 106
  Spinoza on 115, 120, 148, 149
  Stoic 19, 108–9
hatred 114–15, 137–8, 140, 173
heart, the
  Augustine and 12, 13, 15, 34
  Kant and 171–3, 175, 179–85
  Montaigne and 42, 57, 59, 64
  Pascal and 70, 78–80, 88, 94, 96–7, 100
  revolution of 179–80, 181–2, 185
  Rousseau and 172, 173–4

health 111, 117, 149
Hegel, G. W. F. 2, 171
Heidegger, Martin 26, 193 n.6, 229 n.5
hermeneutics of suspicion 109, 142
Hobbes, Thomas 81, 138, 144
Hölderlin, Friedrich 190
holiness 13, 15, 28, 155, 156, 181
homo faber 145–6
honour 57, 162
hope
  Descartes on 106, 214 n.186
  and faith 9, 40
  Montaigne on 54, 65
  Pascal on 95
  Spinoza on 142–3, 147, 149–50
  Kant on 153, 155, 157–8, 166, 169, 176–7, 179–80, 181, 183–4, 190
hubris 156
Hume, David 113–25, 127–48, 150, 151, 158, 172, 173
  on the association of ideas 116–17, 121, 123, 124, 133, 142,
  atomism of 123, 130
  on causality 128–31, 132–3
  on calm and violent emotions 118–9, 135–6, 140–1
  on the passions 136–40
  on stability 129, 130, 140–1
  on sympathy 130, 141–2, 145, 146, 150
humility 8, 13, 33
  Montaigne and 46, 51, 52
  Pascal and 79–80, 86
  Hume and 134, 136–7, 140, 142, 173
  Kant and 158
Husserl, Edmund 45, 48, 118

identity 42, 45
  and the cogito 92–3
  Hume and 123–5, 133
  Spinoza and 131–3
ignorance
  Augustine on 14
  Descartes on 72–3, 105
  Hume on 143
  Kant on 162
  learned 41, 67
  Montaigne on 41, 47, 49, 54, 67
  Pascal on 76–7, 85–6, 95
  Spinoza on 119

illusion 44, 63, 155, 156, 163, 172
imagination
   Descartes on 89, 104, 116
   Hume on 122-5, 128, 133, 134, 137
   Montaigne on 63, 67
   Spinoza on 121, 125-7, 136, 139, 147-9
immortality of the soul 54, 95-6, 154, 169, 211-12 n.124
impressions
   Hume and 113, 121-7, 131-2, 134-5, 142
   Stoics and 17, 18-19, 28, 55, 65
indifference of the Will 12, 19, 28
   Descartes on 75-6, 105
   Montaigne on 50, 52-3, 59-60
instinct
   Augustine on 10
   Hume on 120, 139, 144-6
   Kant on 154, 156
   Pascal on 79, 86, 95
intuition
   Descartes and 89-90, 92-4
   Kant and 155, 158, 162, 168, 169, 178, 179-80, 181-2
   Spinoza and 119, 132
irresolution 58, 103, 105

Jacobi, Friedrich Heinrich 169
Jansen, Cornelius 70-1, 182
Jansenism 71, 110
Jesuits 31, 71
Jesus of Nazareth, *see* Christ
joy
   Descartes on 9, 105, 111
   Hume on 120, 140
   Spinoza on 138, 139
   Kant on 165, 173
judgement
   Augustine and 10, 12
   Descartes and 74, 76, 84, 102-3, 106
   Kant and 167
   Montaigne and 43-4, 46, 49, 62, 64, 67
   Pascal and 86
   Rousseau and 174
   Sceptics and 21
   Stoics and 18-20. See also *Epoché* (suspension of judgement)
justice 14-5, 33, 51-2, 64-5, 107, 145-6, 182-3, 205 n.82

Kant, Immanuel 2, 5, 8, 151-70, 171-3, 175-88
   anti-Gnosticism of 160, 179, 187
   on the antinomies of reason 152, 158, 161-2, 163-4, 165-6, 184-5, 223-4 n.37
   on the good will 152, 157, 158, 169
   on the highest good 157, 165-7, 176, 180-1, 183
   on radical evil 173, 177, 183
   on respect (*Achtung*) 165, 171, 173, 180
   on *Schwärmerei* (fanaticism) 154, 159-60, 183
   on the supersensible 152, 154, 156, 159-61, 167-8, 169
Kierkegaard, Søren 166
Kolakowski, Leszek 110
Koselleck, Reinhart 2

language 9-10, 53, 54-6, 148-9, 187. *See also* Prayer
law
   Augustine and 17
   Montaigne and 46, 50-1
   moral 154-5, 157-8, 164-5, 166-70
   and obedience 149-50
   Pascal and 109
   Pelagius and 15-16, 17
   and state of nature 144
Leibniz, Gottfried Wilhelm 5, 129, 144, 159
Lipsius, Justus 31, 103
Locke, John 5, 159, 174
Löwith, Karl 8, 201 n.196
Lucretius 113
Luther, Martin 32-3

Machiavelli, Niccolò 81
Manicheanism 15-16. *See also* Gnosticism
Marcion 16, 23, 32
martyrs 9, 65
measure
   Descartes and 87
   Kant and 180
   Montaigne and 43-4, 46, 47, 50, 52
   Pascal and 94, 109
melancholy (*melancholia*) 69-70, 118, 143
memory
   Augustine on 13, 27-8, 32

Descartes on 89–90, 94
Hume on 119, 122–4, 131, 134
Montaigne on 61–2
Spinoza on 125–6
Metaphysica specialis 7, 22
method
   Descartes on 45, 73–4, 90–1, 96, 102, 104, 105–4
   Hume on 118, 119, 123, 124
   Kant on 158–9, 161–3
   Pascal on 78
   Spinoza on 116, 118, 123, 131
Milbank, John 8
miracles 29, 34, 44, 47–8, 54, 64, 128
Molina, Luis de 71
Molinism 70–1
monster/monstrous 29, 46, 48, 66, 204 n.59
Montaigne, Michel de 5, 7, 8, 39, 41–68, 69, 72, 74, 78, 80–1, 85–6, 89, 100, 102, 103, 108, 117, 150
   'credulity' of 42, 46, 66, 82, 117–8
   on enemies 41–2
   on presumption 41, 46, 49–50, 51, 52, 53–4, 60, 62
   on strangers 45, 48, 57
   writing himself 53–6
Moses 149, 190

naturalistic/naturalized 29, 63, 150, 174
Newton, Issac/Newtonian 118, 152, 167
Nietzsche, Friedrich 9, 109, 152, 190, 222 n.1
nominalism 26, 55, 127
nothingness 32, 75, 87, 91, 103, 109
novelty 23, 51–2, 61, 105, 141

obedience/disobedience
   Augustine and 11, 13, 14–15, 34
   Descartes and 74
   Montaigne and 49, 51, 67
   Pelagius and 14–15
   Spinoza and 119, 149–50, 154, 158
   Kant and 186
operative (vs. thematic) concept 3–4, 57, 73, 75, 115, 141, 150, 151, 153
opinion 56, 62, 102, 103, 149, 160
original Sin
   Augustine on 9, 16–17, 60

Descartes on 74
Kant on 171, 176, 178
Montaigne on 46, 63
Pascal on 77
Pelagius on 14, 17. *See also* Fallenness, Sin

pain
   Hume on 120, 134, 135–6, 137, 141
   Kant on 165
   Montaigne on 63
   Spinoza on 147
Pascal, Blaise 69–72, 76–80, 84–8, 94–101, 107–11, 113, 171–2, 173–4, 176, 182, 200 n.156
   on the wager 88, 108, 172
   on wretchedness (*misère*) 77, 83, 87, 88, 95, 99, 100, 110
Paul, St. 23, 34, 67, 150
Pelagianism 12, 31–3, 34, 36, 38
   Descartes and 60, 70, 84, 85, 93, 104, 110
   Hume and 113–14, 116, 138
   Kant and 151, 152, 153, 166, 176, 179, 183, 190
   Rousseau and 171
Pelagius 13–17, 32, 56, 68, 184
Petrarch, Francesco 34–5
Plato/Platonic 10–11, 20, 25, 27, 32, 36, 154, 156, 159, 178
pleasure
   Augustine on 13
   Hume on 120, 134–8, 141
   Montaigne on 59–60, 64, 68
   Pascal on 77
   Spinoza on 113
Plotinus 10, 16
Plutarch 55
Port-Royal 70, 78, 85
prayer 9, 13, 34, 55, 56. *See also* Language
pre-philosophical, the 4, 49, 91, 92
pride 77, 85, 109, 134, 136–8, 140, 142, 173
progress 71, 146, 169, 176, 181, 187
promise/promising 8, 9, 65, 100, 102, 146
prophets 14, 16, 148–9
providence 9, 18, 23, 28
   Blumenberg on 37–8
   Descartes on 95, 105, 107, 111
   Hume on 144

Kant on 166, 169, 185, 187
Spinoza on 144
Stoic account of 24–5, 103
punishment 9, 14–15, 144, 149–50
purpose
  divine 115
  of life 8, 9, 17–18, 34
  moral 154, 158, 168,
  of things 18, 26, 47, 158
Pyrrhonian Scepticism 17–18, 19, 21, 38–9, 40, 42, 198 n.98
  Descartes and 82, 84, 86–7
  Hume and 129, 143
  Kant and 153, 158–9, 161–2, 164, 165
  Montaigne and 44, 49, 50, 56, 67
  Pascal and 88, 110

reason
  autonomy of 31, 69, 100–1
  and desire 152, 154, 156, 157–8, 162, 164
  humiliation of 78, 96, 156
  and instinct 10, 86, 120, 139, 154, 156
  and the passions 78, 136–7, 139–40. *See also* Faith (reason and)
redemption 95, 97, 99–100, 104, 107–8, 110
reformation, the 7, 42. *See also* Erasmus, Luther
regret 60, 63, 103
regulative ideas 66, 142, 164, 165
relationality 26, 128, 130, 189
religion
  and enthusiasm 115, 154, 172
  and faith 184–7
  Hume on 119, 129–30, 133, 142–3
  Kant on 159–61, 163, 167, 169–70, 172, 184–7
  Montaigne on 52, 65–6
  Pascal on 96–7, 100–1, 110
  Rousseau on 172
  Spinoza on 142–3, 150
  and superstition 115, 118, 143, 147, 154
  wars of 54, 69, 139, 142, 191
remorse 102, 103, 174
repentance 60–3, 103
repetition 90, 130–1, 132, 141
responsibility 32–3, 36, 38, 63, 163
revelation, *see* God (revelation of)

reverence 49, 56, 83, 99
Ricoeur, Paul 49
Rosenzweig, Franz 29
Rousseau, Jean Jacques 171–2, 173–5, 183

sacrifice 109, 125, 144
  of Christ 16, 184
sadness 77, 105, 110–11, 120, 139
salvation 2–3, 8, 30, 34, 40, 53, 71
  Augustine and 16, 17, 34, 37, 54, 60
  Gnosticism and 23
  Kant and 152, 177, 183, 187–8, 190
  Montaigne and 54
  Pascal and 95, 96, 98, 100, 110
  Spinoza and 119, 144. *See also* Fallenness
scepticism
  Academic and Pyrrhonian 20, 36–7, 39, 198 n.98
  Augustine and 37
  Christianization of 36–7, 39–40
  Descartes and 72, 80–3, 84, 88
  and doubt 40
  Hume and 120, 121, 129–30, 143
  Kant and 158–9, 161–2, 167
  Modern revival of 30, 36–40
  Montaigne and 42, 45–6, 65
  Pascal and 107
  'self-contradiction' of 21, 55
  and tranquillity 20–2
  and wisdom 37. *See also* Pyrrhonian Scepticism
secularization 7, 8, 23, 25, 37–8
security 140–1, 144–5, 162
self
  assertion 14, 17, 30, 33, 36, 38, 70, 100, 190
  creation 35
  discipline 21, 30, 35, 68, 103
  exposure 53, 54
  formation 35, 53, 54
  interest 28, 138, 139, 140, 144, 145, 172
  love 57, 77, 138, 165, 172–3, 175
  preservation 31, 145–6
  relation 11, 27, 52–3, 55, 57, 59–60, 93, 134, 138
  responsibility 33, 36, 38, 40, 106–7, 135. *See also* Auto-affectivity, Love, Responsibility

Seneca 18, 58, 64
sentiments 88, 118, 137, 141–2, 146
Sextus Empiricus 19–22, 37, 38–40, 65, 66, 67, 81, 158–9
sin 4, 9, 13–17, 83, 84, 103, 110, 178. *See also* Forgiveness, Original Sin, Prayer
sincerity 57–8, 75, 173
slavery 54, 146, 150
social contract 144–7
society
   Descartes on 74–5, 91, 102–3, 111
   Hume on 128, 136, 144–6
   Kant on 175–6, 183–4
   Rousseau on 173, 175
   Spinoza on 116, 117, 144, 149
Socrates 51, 63, 158
soul, the 24, 113–14
   Augustine on 10, 16, 34
   Descartes on 109, 110–11
   Hume on 120, 130, 134
   Kant on 155, 160
   Montaigne on 44, 45, 63–4, 67–8. *See also* Immortality of the soul
Spinoza, Baruch 113–23, 125–9, 131–3, 135–9, 142–4, 146–51, 190
   on adequate/inadequate ideas 122, 125, 126, 127, 129, 135, 139
   on blessedness 138, 143
   on 'common notions' 133
   on endeavour to be (*conatus essendi*) 125, 131, 132, 145
   on expression 113, 119, 120, 122, 127, 133, 135, 136, 150
   on forms of knowledge 115, 125, 126, 127, 132, 138
   on the passions 135–40
   on prophecy 148–9
state of nature 144, 146
Stephanus, Henricus 38
stoicism
   Ancient 17–20, 22, 23, 24–5
   Descartes and 76, 78, 84, 85, 103, 110
   and fate 34
   Kant and 151, 152, 165, 166, 173, 176, 177
   Modern 30–1, 34, 35–6
   Montaigne and 50, 54, 58–9, 64
   Pascal and 86, 95, 108

Spinoza and 115, 116, 117, 128, 133, 135, 140, 144, 150
   and tranquillity 22, 56, 68
   and virtue 33–4
   and will 28, 34, 36, 50, 58, 76. *See also Apatheia*, Tranquillity, Will
strength of mind 103, 140–2
Suarez, Franz 33
suffering 15, 18, 102, 182
supernatural, the 24, 33, 35, 190, 199 n.122
   Kant on 181
   Montaigne on 64, 65, 67
   Pascal 96–7
superstition, *see* Religion (superstition)
Swedenborg, Emanuel 159–60, 163

Taylor, Charles 8
teleology 26, 167–8, 169
Tempier, Étienne 24
temptation 178, 179, 180–1, 183
Tertullian 28
testimony 29, 44–5, 46, 47, 48, 55–6, 62, 82, 101. *See also* Trust, Witness
theology
   and grace 37
   natural 155–6
   and Nominalism 55
   and Philosophy 24–5, 27, 35, 71
   and Politics 139
   Transcendental 157
   and Voluntarism 29, 32
time
   and *apatheia* 36
   and freedom 178
   of habit 75, 90
   of the heart 94
   historical 2, 184
   inner 18, 125
   of judgement 19
   mechanical 181
   moral 181
   of self 36
   of the world 18–19. *See also* Eternity
Toulmin, Stephen 199 n.140
tragic/tragedy 1, 44
   Descartes and 110–11
   Kant and 152, 155, 156, 222 n.1
   Pascal and 87, 110
   Spinoza and 120

tranquillity (*ataraxia*)
  Augustine and 12–13, 37
  Descartes and 83, 106
  Hume and 113, 116, 140–1, 142, 147
  Kant and 153, 155, 165, 173
  Montaigne and 41, 43, 47, 49–50, 56, 57, 60, 64, 67–8
  Pascal and 87–8
  Sceptics and 17–18, 20–2, 38, 39–40
  Spinoza and 113, 116, 147
  Stoics and 17–18, 19, 22
Trinity, doctrine of 11–12, 27, 32, 53–4
trust
  and faith 9, 83
  and the heart 79–80
  and hope 155
  of judgment 43
  and relationality 26
  and revelation 101
  and Scepticism 20, 21
  in the senses 82–3
  and Stoicism 30

uncertainty 3, 7, 29, 38, 42, 68, 69, 82–3, 86, 94, 130, 140
unhappiness 87, 96, 115, 120
usurpation 12, 87, 107–8, 146
Utopianism 143, 149

Via moderna 24, 25, 29, 37
vice 62, 63, 116, 137
virtue 31
  Descartes on 103, 107
  Hume on 114, 116, 137, 140, 145–6
  Kant on 166–7, 169, 184
  Montaigne on 54, 56–7, 57–8, 59–60, 61, 63–4
  natural 33–4
  Spinoza on 149–50
visible/Invisible 34, 66, 183–4, 185–7
Voluntarism 8, 26–8, 32, 33, 36, 40, 41, 66, 72, 91, 98, 99, 146

will, the
  and choice 19
  and deception 73
  freedom of 13–15, 33–6, 73, 75, 83–4, 106–7, 135, 137, 176
  of God 12, 26, 31–3, 65, 94–5
  and intellect 14, 27–8, 83–4, 93, 103–4, 107–8, 121–2
  and law 15
  and the passions 12–13, 19, 36, 74, 76, 77–8, 107–8
  perversion of 14
  weakness of 15
William of Ockham 25–6, 28–9, 33
wisdom
  Descartes on 72, 88–9, 99, 106–7
  Hume on 118, 119
  Montaigne on 58, 67
  Pascal on 94
  Sceptical 37
  Spinoza on 114, 115, 118, 119, 147
  Stoic 103
witnessing 9 45, 57, 64
wonder 51, 75, 76, 99, 105, 180
world 20, 25, 28, 30, 36, 43, 72, 123
  crisis of 22, 31–2, 36
  and divine 7, 19, 23, 29
  and self 70
  as a stage 1, 8, 18, 42
worldly/unworldly 23, 35, 102
Worthen, Jeremy 110

Printed in the USA
CPSIA information can be obtained
at www.ICGtesting.com
LVHW011647091223
766046LV00004B/110